Dr. David Eifrig Jr.'s
BIG BOOK OF RETIREMENT SECRETS

STANSBERRY
RESEARCH

Published by Stansberry Research

Edited by Fawn Gwynallen, Laura Bente, Amanda Cuocci

About Stansberry Research

Founded in 1999 and based out of Baltimore, Maryland, Stansberry Research is the largest independent source of financial insight in the world. It delivers unbiased investment advice to self-directed investors seeking an edge in a wide variety of sectors and market conditions.

Stansberry Research has nearly two dozen analysts and researchers – including former hedge-fund managers and buy-side financial experts. They produce a steady stream of timely research on value investing, income generation, resources, biotech, financials, short-selling, macroeconomic analysis, options trading, and more.

The company's unrelenting and uncompromised insight has made it one of the most respected and sought-after research organizations in the financial sector. It has nearly one million readers and more than 500,000 paid subscribers in over 100 countries.

About the Author

 Dr. Eifrig is the editor of three Stansberry Research newsletters... His largest monthly publication, *Retirement Millionaire,* shows 100,000-plus readers how to live a millionaire lifestyle on less money than you'd imagine possible. *Retirement Trader* shows readers a safe way to double or triple the gains in their retirement accounts with less risk. *Income Intelligence* shows investors how to analyze the income markets to maximize their income and total returns.

Doc has one of the best track records in the financial-newsletter business. From 2010 to 2014, he closed 136 winning positions in a row for his *Retirement Trader* subscribers.

Before joining Stansberry Research in 2008, Dr. Eifrig worked in arbitrage and trading groups with major Wall Street investment banks, including Goldman Sachs, Chase Manhattan, and Yamaichi in Japan. He has also published peer-reviewed medical research. After retiring from Wall Street, Dr. Eifrig attended medical school to become a board-eligible ophthalmologist. At Stansberry Research, he shares his love for empowering people with his finance and medical knowledge.

Acknowledgements

There are many people in my life to whom I owe thanks. And writing a book is a defining moment whereby it's easy to remember who helped out.

This book started out catalyzed by Mike Palmer. He's a great copywriter, good golfer, and fantastic idea man. He was critical in the brainstorming and launching of my newsletter *Retirement Millionaire*. With this book, he nudged a nerve... "Hey Doc, wanna do a book like those *Bottom Line* books?"

His junior assistant, Ken Millstone, spent his first assignment reading and collecting the outline. My assistant, Laura Bente, spent days and weeks updating, collecting, and compiling even more for the book. It soon went from 300 to 500-plus pages under her guidance.

Of course, thanks go out to Brian Hunt, officially my Editor in Chief and unofficially the little guy on my shoulder – sometimes nagging, more often encouraging. He weighed in with lots of "wows," "I like it," and "good stuff."

This book was then handled by our book czar, Fawn Gwynallen. The most wonderful thing about working with her is that she cares about making something the best it can be. I can hardly wait to see what she does with my next book.

Our cover was designed by Tony Merola, a talented guy with an eye for creative ideas. Without him, my books wouldn't sell half as well.

Of course, there are many others who helped along the way: Michele Atkinson, Lauren Thorsen, Amanda Cuocci, Jill Peterson, and Tyler Seabolt. To these folks, thanks for helping out, as you always do.

Here's to your health...

Dr. David Eifrig, Jr.

Table of Contents

Part IV
The Keys to Investment Success

Part V
Foods to Seek Out, Foods to Avoid

Part VI
You and Your Doctor

Part VII
Health Tips and Secrets

Part VIII
Beat the Health Care System

Part IX
How to Create a Richer Retirement

Part X
Protect Your Privacy:
Essentials of Digital and Everyday Privacy in America

Foreword

By Brian Hunt

If you're reading this book for the first time, I'm jealous.

I'm jealous of what you're about to experience.

One of the greatest joys in life is learning a useful new idea.

It's learning the secret to having lots of energy... It's learning how to attract more freedom and abundance in your life... It's learning how to live a long, healthy life... It's learning about an amazing new place to visit.

The book you hold in your hands is a treasure trove of useful ideas like these.

Many of the ideas concern your health. Many concern your wealth. Many will simply leave you thinking, "I'm really glad I know that."

My friend Dr. David Eifrig has a brilliant, curious, questioning, and scientific mind. He's a tireless student of life. He achieved more by the age of 30 than most people achieve in their entire lives.

"Doc," as his friends call him, got his MBA from one of America's most prestigious business schools. He became a trading specialist at the top Wall Street bank Goldman Sachs. After tiring of the financial world, he went to medical school and became an M.D. Doc has been published in peer-reviewed science and medical journals.

Then he started writing a retirement advisory – *Retirement Millionaire* – which has become one of the most popular publications in America.

Along the way, Doc bottled his own label of wine, acquired dozens of good friends, wrote several books, got his pilot's license, and traveled the world.

This varied list of accomplishments is the product of a curious mind. It's also the reason I say Doc is the closest thing to a "human Google" I've ever found. When I have an important question about business, health, investment, travel, food, or anything else... I (and many other people) go to Doc... who has the answers.

What type of diet leads to the longest, healthiest life?

What is the best way to invest my retirement account?

What are the key questions to ask a doctor before you take any of his advice?

If you have questions like this, the *Big Book of Retirement Secrets* is for you. It's a treasure trove of wisdom and well-researched ideas from one of America's smartest, most highly accomplished people. Inside, you'll find dozens of useful ideas for living a life full of health, freedom, and abundance.

As I mentioned, learning a useful new idea is a great joy. You're about to encounter many.

I hope you enjoy learning from him as much as I have.

Regards,

Brian Hunt
Editor in Chief
Stansberry Research

PART I

The *Retirement Millionaire* Manifesto

— Introduction —

Look at Retirement in a Completely Different Way

Starting today, I want you to look at retirement in a completely different way.

Erase the dangerous information you've been spoon-fed since you were too young to know the difference about your money, your health, and how things work in America.

This dangerous information feeds dangerous beliefs... beliefs like *"Go to a good school and get a job with a big corporation, and it takes care of your retirement"*... *"Buy mutual funds and everything will be fine by the time you retire"*... or *"Wall Street will take care of your money"*...

Can you really believe politicians and their promises that Social Security will take care of you?

Notice the phrase that keeps coming up? It's among the scariest phrase in the English language... especially when Wall Street and Washington D.C. get involved. Here it is again:

"Take care of..."

Starting today, I want you to realize Wall Street and Washington are not here to "take care of" you. Both are in the business of false promises. Both are in the business of selling fear so they can collect huge amounts of money from you and me. They are the world's best at what they do.

Wall Street calls the money it collects from you "fees." Washington calls

1

the money it takes "taxes." And most Americans just pay up. After all, they're being "taken care of."

I want you to end this sort of thinking.

I went to two of America's top schools with the people who run the institutions I just mentioned. I worked many years for the most respected firm on Wall Street. I traveled the world on our clients' dime.

After "retiring" from Wall Street, I went to medical school at the University of North Carolina and became an eye surgeon. I have published research in the top medical journal in my field. I've seen and experienced the worst of the U.S. health care system.

I made a lot of money on Wall Street... enough to pay for a comfortable retirement. Slogging through 10 years of medical school and training was no picnic. But as an eye surgeon, I can easily make $500,000 a year.

And yet in 2007, I retired for a second time... to write *Retirement Millionaire* for my publisher Stansberry Research.

I decided to write this monthly newsletter because I realized too many of my friends and family – and worse, the general population – are being lied to over and over. Every single day.

Whether it involves investing or medicine, we are inundated with lies from the government and the vested interests that control it. Most of what they've told you is pure B.S. Most of it is deceitful marketing from some ad agency. They truly don't care about you. All they want is your money. "We the people," has become "us, the suckers."

In this book, you'll find the best "how to" guide to set yourself up for the richest retirement possible. I'll show you how to invest without worrying about money again. I'll show you how to travel for less than you're used to – in some cases, 50%-100% less. I'll even help you avoid dangerous medical advice.

And I'll show you ways to collect free cash that not one financial advisor will ever show you.

But first, let's explore what's happening in America...

— 1 —

Stop Thinking Like a Serf

Most Americans today think just like a medieval serf...

Tend to your job, keep your mouth shut, fight whomever the king wants you to fight, send him a big chunk of your earnings, and he'll take care of you.

> *66 If you don't act now, people will be telling you what to do with your money, health, and retirement dreams. 99*

This serf mindset has been carried on with our more modern idea of retirement.

When the world went from an agricultural to an industrial/military economy, governments created the concept of pensions. Worse, the government told you at what age you had to stop working and making money.

Then we created a looming nightmare: Social Security – the regulation that requires young workers to pay for the older ones to sit around.

I don't know about you, but I don't want anyone telling me when and where to sit down.

If we don't act now, that's what's coming for us. People will be telling us what to do with our money, health, and retirement dreams.

Unfortunately, America's "streets" are crumbling. Here are the facts...

Social Security is bankrupt. In 2004, the benefits paid out began exceeding the tax revenues brought in. Worse, no actual assets support Social Security. So the government must use current cash flow to fund a future liability. Imagine telling your doctor you want health care today, but you'll pay him in 20 years.

The website for the Congressional Budget Office (essentially the government's accountants) will show you page after page of tables and graphs explaining how this will all work out OK.

But the bottom line is this: As of 2014, the Treasury owed $2.7 trillion to the Social Security "Trust Fund." Yep, you heard that right... $2.7 trillion. I wouldn't count on this for retirement money. It's unlikely the Treasury will ever be able to pay this debt back. I mean, how much debt will the world allow us to create?

Wall Street is ripping you off. Ever heard the last names Mozilo, Fuld, or Thain? These guys were the chief executive officers of Countrywide Financial, Lehman Brothers, and Merrill Lynch. They all drove their companies to extinction (or near extinction), while taking out huge paychecks along the way.

Countrywide's Angelo Mozilo sold hundreds of millions of dollars of stock while driving his company into oblivion. As it lost 85% of its value, he sold stock privately and often ahead of company announcements. The Securities and Exchange Commission (SEC) charged him with insider trading and securities fraud in 2009. But he still got a $110 million severance package. Absurd.

Lehman's Dick Fuld sat in front of a congressional committee in 2008 and blamed "the press" for his company's fall to bankruptcy. But since 2000, he had taken $500 million in compensation, while driving the bus off the cliff.

And don't forget the whiz kid, John Thain of Merrill Lynch. He earned $200 million for working less than a year. And while his company was collapsing, he repeatedly reported everything was fine.

As if that weren't enough... guys like Mozilo and his family will get free health care for life as part of their severance deals. As if they couldn't afford health care.

America's health care system is rated among the lowest in the developed world. In spite of what the government wants you to think... in 2014, the U.S. ranked only No. 26 on international lists for infant mortality rate – a well-recognized measure of health.

Even the Czech Republic and Slovakia ranked as having a lower infant mortality rate than America. And yet, we also run one of the most expensive systems in the world. It's a shame.

As of 2014, we spend $7,960 per person per year on health care in the U.S. Switzerland spends only about $5,344. France spends even less – $3,978 per person per year. *We spend more than 17% of our gross domestic product on mediocre (at best) health care.*

Between Social Security and health care, I get scared thinking about my retirement. But I am genuinely terrified by **the devaluing of my U.S. dollar**...

In 2004, I could spend a lovely week in Europe for $1,000. In 2014, that $1,000 would barely buy me a plane ticket, let alone a couple nights in a modest hotel room in Paris. But don't worry, our government will "take care of it."

The American retiree is facing the most dangerous situation ever. You can't think like folks did in the 1950s... You can't depend on the "nanny corporation" or the "nanny state" to take care of you.

That's why I want you to leave the serf mentality behind and adopt the mentality of a retirement millionaire.

What Is the *Retirement Millionaire* Mindset?

It's a mindset of personal independence, rational thought, and questioning the bankrupt policies of our government.

It's a mindset where you refuse to follow the herd and let Wall Street and Washington pick your pockets every single day.

It's a mindset where you take advantage of incredible wealth-building opportunities no broker or financial planner will ever tell you about. Once you see what I'm talking about, you'll understand most brokers and financial planners are blind as well... or just after another big "fee."

For instance, did you know you can buy stocks for 20% below their commonly quoted market price? I bet you didn't... because this little-known method doesn't make your broker any money.

Did you know you can collect 15% in annual "dividend" payments for owning gold? Did you know several large, safe "utility" stocks can provide you almost 25% income in just six months?

At *Retirement Millionaire*, we question the vested interests that steal from us and tell us lies. I'm talking about big mutual-fund companies like Fidelity Investments and Legg Mason... the Food and Drug Administration (FDA)... the International Revenue Service (IRS)... Wall Street investment banks... the Federal Reserve... and the American Association of Retired Persons (AARP).

Mentioning the names of these organizations isn't going to win me any friends. (Many of you probably carry AARP cards in your wallets. But trust me, that group exists largely to sell you life insurance.)

Heck, I could probably tell you about how great these organizations are and collect a lot of advertising revenue for doing so on my publisher's website. But I won't.

These organizations are probably ripping you off right now.

Sure, many fine people work at Goldman Sachs, the FDA, and Fidelity. But right now, each of these organizations has a vested interest in not giving you the whole story. They want you to be a lemming. They want you to act like a serf.

In 2008, I discovered my own sister was being ripped off. Fidelity had her in a mutual fund that paid 0.02% instead of the 2.45% fund she had asked to be placed in. She was angry when she realized this!

These companies don't worry about your investments or health. They want you to feel stupid so they can "take care of" you.

No matter what, respected firms like Goldman will issue bullish research reports on stocks they need to push onto the public to earn investment-banking fees. Fidelity won't tell you that most of its mutual funds don't even beat savings-account returns. It needs to earn fat management fees from you.

The FDA and the government will tell you it's fine to load a child with Ritalin, but they outlaw marijuana. (I don't smoke the stuff personally. But I can tell you it's 100 times less harmful than many drugs the FDA has approved.)

I've dedicated my life – my search for truth – to digging beneath the mass media headlines... to learning the safest way to invest... the right way to travel... the right things to put into my body... and learning the four tenets of a *Retirement Millionaire* mentality.

We'll cover them in steps...

Step No. 1:

Reject the Misinformation of Wall Street and Washington. Think Independently.

Let's go back to the first sentence of this book...

"I want you to look at retirement in a completely different way."

The first step to looking at retirement in a different way is to reject conventional wisdom at almost every turn. It is to think and act independently.

The U.S. government is inept. Think about the bankruptcies of Fannie Mae and Freddie Mac. Think about the I-35 bridge collapse in Minnesota in 2007. (I drove over that bridge 45 minutes before it fell.) Think about the ridiculous endless wars in the Middle East and sky-high tax rates.

Our presidents are inept, too. There's little difference between the Democrats and the Republicans. Both parties promise "change." But they must have a different notion of change than I do...

I've heard that promise often in my 30-year career, and all I've seen are more taxes, more needless foreign wars, more handouts to the lazy, a declining school system, and a culture that rejects independent thinking.

But believe it or not, I am an optimist. Always will be. And I can tell you that despite the problems facing us, **there's plenty of good news – and a rich retirement ahead – if you'll start thinking independently and stop following crowds**...

For instance, I shook my head when many of my friends put most of their retirement savings into tech stocks in 1999. One doctor I knew from medical school would sneak into his office between patients and surgical cases to trade tech stocks.

He was thrilled to know my Wall Street background... and he immediately brought me into his office to show me how much money he'd made on Qualcomm at $100 per share. He told me how easy it was. He even had a few "hot" tips from his broker. He was so proud that he'd borrowed money in his stock margin account, leveraged his home equity, and even had his wife's money involved.

> 66 *Despite the problems facing us, there's plenty of good news – and a rich retirement ahead – if you'll start thinking independently and stop following crowds...* 99

I was shocked by his lack of common sense. What I told him next got a roaring laugh. I said...

> Take all but 5% of your portfolio out of Qualcomm, and don't have more than 20% of your wealth in any one sector like technology. It's too dangerous to have all your money in one spot... especially when you don't even know the value of these businesses.

He told me I didn't understand the markets and "technology was the future of America."

When I saw him again in 2003... he had lost his house, his life savings, and his wife. He had gained weight. He was unhappy. Why did he listen to his broker and not me? He didn't know.

Do you think Wall Street was worried about him while tech stocks were crashing? No way...

> ### *DO WHAT I DO*
>
> **Make sure you have an exit strategy (like a trailing stop).**

It was worried about its Porsches and Manhattan condos. It was selling billions in stock to investors, while calling those same stocks "pieces of s**t" behind closed doors.

I was also sad to see a friend of mine lose everything in the collapse of Las Vegas real estate in 2008. She left an illustrious singing career in New York to semi-retire in the desert. She started speculating in real estate right at the top... right when the "crowd" was doing it. She was convinced those $350,000 homes were going to $500,000 just by her buying them. She planned to hold them for just a couple years, but she got caught in the hype.

Her lender assured her she could handle the debt no matter what. She assumed they would never give her the money if there was any risk. She got fooled, and so did the banks. Her story ended badly... just like many others'.

It's easy to get caught up in a popular investment mania... like tech stocks in 1999 or real estate in 2006. It's basic human nature to feel good when you're part of the crowd. Primitive man was conditioned to go with the crowd. Hunting and raising children required the efforts of the tribe. He'd die if he were kicked out of the tribe.

In modern day, mindlessly following others into a crowded investment theater will get you trampled. What would happen if someone yelled fire? Instead, do what I do and make sure you have an exit strategy before the fire (like a trailing stop).

And while you're thinking about your own economic safety, don't forget about your health. That's why I first started writing my newsletter. People I knew wanted to hear evidence and science-based health stories. So I wrote them. I learned to question conventional thinking...

Don't ever let doctors and government groups tell you what to do about your health.

Don't end up like 68-year-old William Johnson. He was triaged late one night by his local hospital's ER, where I was serving my "acting internship." (That's when a hospital or clinic gives fourth-year medical students increased responsibility and privileges.)

Mr. Johnson was complaining of weakness. His family said he was slurring his words. The nurse assured him and the family that he was fine and perhaps had a bit of "dementia" coming on. I was only a medical student. But within seconds of my exam, I knew he'd had a stroke. His history was textbook. He was clearly having a "brain attack."

When blood stops flowing to parts of the brain, the stroke can do permanent and costly damage within minutes. I immediately knew what he needed and tried to convince the staff he was high priority. He needed an aspirin and perhaps surgery. But I was just a lowly medical student, how could I know more than them?

Sadly, he was throwing blood clots from his heart into his brain. By the time he received treatment (the next day), it was too late. Once oxygen is blocked from brain tissue, it's almost impossible to repair, especially if you're older.

Don't let this happen to you. Think independently about your health care and prevent this sort of thing from ever happening.

Once you realize how important independent thinking is, you'll easily learn you don't need a ton of money to be wealthy or healthy...

Step No. 2:

Don't Believe You Need a Million Dollars to Live a Rich Retirement

When I saw my friend Hank – a respected liver specialist – "working" on a golf course, I wondered if he was having money troubles.

But it turns out, Hank had found a simple way to get golf for free.

I'll tell you more about Hank's story later, in Part IX Chapter 6.

The point here is, it's easy to get the best things in life at a deep discount... or absolutely free. In this book, I'll show you how to get free vacations, free golf, and even free cash.

Ever wanted to try the RV life? There's a way you can rent a $120-a-day recreational vehicle for less than $25 a day. A simple secret about the RV business lets you travel in style for 80% less than what everyone else is paying.

Do you enjoy dining out? For years, I've used a plan that lets me bring along a friend for dinner and pay nothing. Yep, that's right. I buy my meal and my guest is free. My friends love it when I call them up for dinner. Better yet, it costs me nothing.

Sure, I can't dine at three-star restaurants in Manhattan this way. But I've had some wonderful Indian food, some incredible Mexican dishes, and tossed back many a free beer using my simple plan.

Now that you're thinking out-of-the-box and your food is nearly free, it's time to think about traveling around the world.

Step No. 3:
Start Thinking Internationally – Use Your 'Mental Passport'

People laugh at me when I tell them I'd go to India for heart surgery.

After all, aren't there hundreds of millions of illiterate poor people there? Isn't India a "dirty" country?

Sure... India has its problems. But it's also home to some of the finest... and cheapest... health care services in the world. Take Escorts Heart Institute in Delhi and Faridabad for instance... This hospital performs close to 18,000 heart operations a year with a death rate one-half of the U.S. rate.

Thinking about plastic surgery? South American countries like Brazil and Argentina are well known for their world-class outcomes. The

U.S. accredits many of the hospitals, and most surgeons are U.S. board certified. Their records are superb.

Why is it so inexpensive? Simple. Without insurance companies and middlemen to siphon your hard-earned dollars, the cost of medical care is just that, the cost of care. The lower price doesn't harm quality, and everyone's happy.

As you think about your retirement choices for medical care, place of residence, and vacations, realize the rest of the world is becoming more and more important relative to the U.S. It's becoming richer and more advanced. You couldn't have gotten a first-class hip replacement surgery in Thailand in the 1990s. In 2014, you can.

Thinking internationally works for investments as well.

Markets in China, Brazil, India, the Middle East, and Eastern Europe have enormous populations. (China and India have more than 2.5 billion people between them.) And they're in the early stages of becoming large, modern economies. That means huge opportunities for investors.

But we want to be smart about investing in this growth. Most "emerging markets" are prone to wild booms and busts. Their accounting standards and business laws are often vague and confusing. That's why I like to have experts do the work for me and then send me a payment check in return.

You read that right... I said "check," not "bill." The experts do the work for us, and then they pay us.

The experts I'm talking about are blue-chip, dividend-paying American companies with decades of experience in foreign countries. For example, Intel gets more than 80% of its revenue from overseas. Coca-Cola gets 78% of its revenue in foreign lands.

Who knows better? Some analyst sitting behind a desk in New York? Or the people on the ground in those countries working for those companies?

For my safe retirement money, **this is the ultimate way to invest in emerging markets**... **owning a slice of a world-class, wealth-**

compounding machine like ExxonMobil, Coca-Cola, or Intel. These companies offer both safety and exposure to emerging markets.

There are even more ideas overseas. International real estate is another opportunity...

In 1989, only three countries in the world (the U.S., Australia, and the Netherlands) offered investors real estate investment trusts (REITs). REITs are baskets of real estate assets, like office buildings, apartments, and shopping malls that trade like stocks. At times, they pay huge dividends. In 2014, at least 22 countries had REITs.

Extraordinary opportunities are all around you in health care, permanent residences, vacations, and investments. You just have to use your "mental passport," locate them, and think like a retirement millionaire. And don't worry at all, I'll be your tour guide.

> **66** *This is the ultimate way to invest in emerging markets... owning a slice of a world-class, wealth-compounding machine like ExxonMobil, Coca-Cola, or Intel.* **99**

And now... the fourth essential part of the *Retirement Millionaire* mindset...

Step No. 4:
Don't Ever Retire

Don't ever retire!

Too many people work and save all their lives only to retire and discover they are bored... literally to death. Many succumb to depression and disease (even terminal illnesses) because they are unprepared for the mental shift in retirement.

A shocking study in 2005 showed that people who retire at age 55 die twice as fast as those who keep working. So don't stop working, and don't retire.

Of course, when I say, "don't retire," I don't mean you need to be chained to your desk until they carry you from your cubicle feet first. Let me show you what I mean...

Dick and Meredith started golfing and gardening in their early 50s. They wanted to be active as they approached retirement. She plays golf with the ladies group on Thursday, he with the men's on Friday. Saturday or Sunday, they usually play with another couple and follow that with a casual lunch or dinner with friends in the clubhouse.

Another couple, Tom and Terri, do their own things but are increasing their activities the closer they get to retirement. He plays tennis, and she runs and does yoga. She organizes a book club.

He follows the local college teams by volunteering as a basketball and baseball coach – coaching makes him feel like part of a community, which motivates him and makes him feel younger and more alive. The school then makes him the junior varsity coach and pays him a nominal amount. Talk about fun.

Or take Chris and Brenda of Mutt Lynch Winery... Although in the wine business for 30 years – Brenda had been a winemaker on the side for 10 years – they wanted the business to be their main jobs. They figured it meant less money. But over five years, they slowly left their corporate jobs and turned their love of wine and winemaking into a viable business that they do in "retirement."

They have twins, a dog, and their own life. And they love it. Finally, they have their own winery and spend half the amount of time "working" as they used to. And they're actually making the same amount of money as before.

Step No. 5:
Do Things You Love to Do

It's critical to discover things you like to do and start doing them now. If you find something you love to do, occasionally you can make a little money from it, like Tom. The key is the joy you derive from the activity, but if you net a little income... all the better.

This will also help you plan for expenses and income needs for your hobbies. As you progress into your 70s and 80s, the cash will be there to support you. Most important, finding things to do in retirement gives you time to discover what you want to do as you age.

Perhaps you'll do what I do... grow tomatoes by the pound and trade with neighbors for peppers, apples, and nuts. Or you might find your vegetables are worthy of the local farmer's market. No matter what, an opportunity is waiting for you... maybe even one that supplements your income.

Remember, your government isn't the safest investment to count on for retirement. And your doctor doesn't really care about your health like you and your family do.

> ### *DO WHAT I DO*
>
> **Grow tomatoes by the pound and trade with neighbors for peppers, apples, and nuts. Or you might find your vegetables are worthy of the local farmer's market.**

If you're thinking about retirement or are retired, this book is required reading. I'll share with you simple ideas for improving your health and wealth.

I hope you'll enjoy reading it as much as I enjoyed writing it.

PART II

Retirement Loopholes

— 1 —

A Simple, Ingenious Way to Find Previously-Undiscovered Wealth

Own a house? The Federal Housing Administration will give you money today and never make you pay it back while you're alive.

Depending on where you live, a fortune may be waiting there for you to tap. If you live in an average home, you can easily get $200,000. If you are in a "major" city, $362,790 awaits you.

Do you live in an exotic location like Alaska, Guam, Hawaii, or the Virgin Islands? How does a half-a-million dollars sound? The government will actually give you $544,185.

It's called a reverse mortgage.

Think about this amazing deal for a moment. You and your spouse can live in your current home without a worry in the world. The money you get today can be spent on whatever dreams you have. And because the reverse mortgage is a nonrecourse loan, only the home is mortgaged. All the other assets you have are safe and can't ever be repossessed by the bank.

> **66** *Depending on where you live, a fortune may be waiting there for you to tap. If you live in an average home, you can easily get $200,000. If you are in a 'major' city, $362,790 awaits you.* **99**

The reverse mortgage is a simple, ingenious way to find previously-undiscovered wealth. In a typical mortgage, you obtain a loan for the purchased real estate and then slowly, over the life of the loan, pay it back to the bank.

The reverse mortgage works exactly the opposite of a regular or "forward" mortgage. You get the bank to pay you while your health is good. Then you turn the tables on the bank, and you don't have to pay them back until you die.

Lenders offer three types of reverse mortgages:

1. **Single-Purpose**: This loan is restricted to paying for home repairs or tax bills. It's intended for low-income borrowers, so don't waste any time on them.

2. **Home Equity Conversion Mortgage (HECM)**: This is the most common type of reverse mortgage. It uses the house's value (up to $417,000) to determine the loan. And it's insured by the Department of Housing and Urban Development (HUD).

3. **Proprietary**: The company lending the money backs this loan instead of the government. This loan works for people who have homes worth more than $500,000. But the government doesn't regulate the fees.

Before you apply for these loans, the U.S. government requires everyone to "meet" with an approved independent counselor prior to getting the loan. The counselor explains all the costs, features, and pros and cons of receiving these loans. This law stems from unscrupulous practices back in the late 1970s and early 1980s, when lenders took advantage of the elderly.

I found old news stories where lenders harassed the elderly or sweet-talked old ladies into sharing equity in their property. This caused disasters during the real estate boom. Lenders wanted to take out their money, but the old ladies wanted to stay in their homes.

Today, these practices are outlawed. The lender can't kick you out, nor can it own equity.

Worried about your credit history? Don't be. Credit is not an issue, unless you've defaulted on other federal loans. The loan requirements are simple and easily met.

You must:

- Be at least 62 years old.

- Own the property with little or no balance on your mortgage.

- Live in the home as your primary residence.

Then you'll receive approval from a reverse-mortgage counselor.

The amount you can get from your home is based on your age, the value of your home, current interest rates, and whether you "roll" your closing costs into the loan.

Generally, the older you are, the more valuable your home, and the lower the interest rates... the more money you receive. For example, if your house is worth $400,000 and you're 65 years old, you can get $168,000. If you are 85, you can get $300,000.

Once you're approved, you can receive your loan money in several ways. You can take the money either as a lump sum, a stream of payments, or as a line of credit.

When you create a line of credit, the available credit grows automatically over time. It grows at a rate of 0.5% over the interest rate you're charged.

For example, you can get a reverse mortgage for $200,000, but take out only $100,000 now. Over 10 years, your $100,000 remaining line of credit could grow to $200,000. You can do whatever you want with these funds.

Of course, interest accrues on the first and second $100,000 payments, but you don't have to pay them back while you're living in your home. Isn't this amazing? **So whatever you do, don't tap the full line of credit initially, and watch your credit line grow over time**.

What Things Should You Be Aware of Before Getting a Reverse Mortgage?

- Shop with several lenders and compare their total costs.

- The amount owed can never be more than the value of the home.

- The loan balance grows over time. This should not make you nervous, although your heirs might be.

The real issue is your heirs.

Some of you may think this is a crazy thing to do. You might worry about the dangers of losing your home. You may question if you want to leave your heirs the equity in your home rather than use it yourself.

I can answer the first concern easily: The loans are safe, and they make sense.

I can't answer the other concern for you. But I know if my mother had wanted to buy a new car or take a fancy vacation using the money she had saved over her lifetime, I would have absolutely urged her to do it. Anything else is simply selfish on my part.

If you decide to do a reverse mortgage, your heirs might protest at first. Just explain to them that all you're doing is borrowing against money you've already saved over your lifetime.

It's your money. And you can do anything with it you wish.

— 2 —

How to Get Paid to Eat Potato Chips, Watch TV, and More

Part of my job is to tell you about unique ways to save money and make some extra cash on the side. Consider this next *Retirement Millionaire* tip...

A healthy, fulfilling life has plenty of indulgences. Of course, folks should be moderate in their junk-food intake. But eating a few chips from time to time is no big deal... and it could help you make some money.

Yes, you can get paid to eat potato chips.

Some businesses want nothing more than your opinion as a consumer. These businesses will pay you to simply offer your opinion on things like new food and beverages, product designs, and even TV shows – the kinds of things we use on a daily basis. If you have some free time and are willing to be honest with your opinions, why not get paid?

The folks who do this sort of thing are regular folk like you and me. They get paid – sometimes hundreds or even thousands of dollars a year – to criticize and praise their favorite goods and services.

In short, the money comes from market research firms. You may have heard of a few, like McCormick Consumer Testing. This company will pay you to sample foods with various seasonings.

One of my friends – the guy who first told me about this unique opportunity – participates in a McCormick consumer taste test as often as once a month. He gets paid $30 to try different flavored Doritos. The

> **66** *If collecting hundreds or even thousands of dollars a year by offering up your opinions sounds intriguing to you, here's what to do...* **99**

best part is, these studies usually last no more than 10 minutes. That's like getting paid hundreds of dollars an hour to sit and eat chips!

Sampling chips is just one example. Some of America's biggest companies hire these research firms to conduct studies on other things: new TV shows, business ads, cell phones, and surgeries. You name it, there's a survey for it. These research groups are scattered across the country and are looking for your opinion.

My friend received money to watch a new commercial for Comcast. As he says, "All I did was watch the commercial, offer my opinion on the piece, and then I got paid $100 for my participation."

Even medical groups will pay you. One business that specializes in performing Lasik procedures paid several dozen people to offer their opinion on one of its new ads.

Don't worry, you'll never have to travel, pay money, or do an ounce of work to qualify. Once the research firm has your name, it will contact you depending on the needs of the studies it's conducting. So many studies are going on at once, there's a good chance these firms are looking for someone like you.

So if collecting hundreds or even thousands of dollars a year by offering up your opinions sounds intriguing to you, here's what to do...

Step 1: Open up the yellow pages, and look under "market research." Call up the companies listed and let them know you're interested in participating in focus groups. This is a great way to get on their lists. You can also search online on websites like FindFocusGroups. com or GreenBook.org.

You should also apply for focus groups you see advertising in the newspaper, on Craigslist, or through hospitals and health clinics. I found a 90-minute focus group for "Asthma and COPD Sufferers" on Craigslist in Baltimore. The study paid me $100 just for my time and opinions.

These groups can be anywhere. For example, if you're at the mall and see someone standing in the walkway with a clipboard, <u>don't ignore him</u>. He likely works for a market research group and wants to pay you for your opinion.

Step 2: Once you've registered, keep your phone on at all times. Focus groups will contact you at their convenience, and you'll be asked a series of questions on the spot. Take the time to complete the questionnaire over the phone.

Most of the time, these studies fill up fast. If you try to call back, chances are the study will be filled. Also, be honest when answering questions and try to articulate your answers. Researchers are looking for people who aren't afraid to give their opinions.

Step 3: If you do qualify for a focus group, remember the date, time, and location of the study. If you're late or don't bother showing up, you can bet they'll never contact you again.

Step 4: Speak up! You won't do anybody any good if you say nothing during these focus groups. Businesses are looking for people who know how to speak their minds. You need to contribute to be considered for future studies.

— 3 —

Protect Your Documents, Don't Waste Money on 'Identity Theft Protection' Scams

Don't worry about identity theft. A *New York Times* article pointed out that services claiming to help with identity theft are hype. I agree. You don't need to spend hundreds of dollars a year to protect yourself.

One identify-theft-protection company, LifeLock, agreed to pay the FTC $11 million for deceptive business practices and fraudulent advertising. But the odds of your identity being stolen are low. Less than 4% of people in a year have their identity stolen.

In most cases, they are minor cases... like a stolen credit-card number. That's a nuisance. But if you report the fraud, your credit-card company usually takes care of the lost money – unless you notice it too late (like months later).

Many credit-card companies even notice the fraud before you do. My coworker Fawn had a Chase credit card. Chase called her about a fraudulent charge minutes after the charge was posted to her account. The company froze her account immediately before other damage could be done and sent her a new credit card overnight.

Also, the majority of identity theft happens by stolen paper documents – in other words, old-school theft. Be careful of people, like in-home caretakers, who know their way around your house. Believe it or not, it's actually safer to go electronic by signing up for paperless billing and bank statements when offered.

What do I do? I regularly (at least monthly) look at my accounts online to catch anything early. And I keep my passwords "long and strong." Using the name of your dog, your house number, and an exclamation point makes a weak password (Frankie605!)... These are all things easily figured out by a troublemaker.

A strong password has a combination of numbers, letters, and symbols (the characters above the numbers on your keyboard) that are nearly random.

Your Life Insurance Policy Could Be Worth Thousands (or Millions) to Your Family NOW

Nate Gibson threw away $250,000 in 2004.

He wadded up a quarter-million bucks and chucked it in the trash.

You see, Nate was utterly clueless the "security" he threw out was worth a substantial amount of money to a small group of powerful investors. You need to know his story because you, too, could have a stash of wealth in your sock drawer and not even know it.

The story began in 1911 when the U.S. Supreme Court decided the securities we're talking about were worth something. Justice Oliver Wendell Holmes wrote that this type of security "has become in our days one of the best recognized forms of investment and self-compelled saving."

In the 21st century, few people know about the secret market for these assets – *although millions of everyday folks own them.*

I'm talking about life insurance. The standard life-insurance policy you probably have right now can generate substantial income for you *while you're still alive.*

The Supreme Court's 1911 ruling essentially deemed life insurance a security. So policies can be traded, just like a stock or a bond. There's also a "secondary" market for selling these securities. Nearly $12 billion worth of this stuff was sold in 2008, up from $240 million in 2002.

It's called the "life settlements" market. A life settlement is simply the sale of a life insurance policy. The seller (the original policy holder) gets cash up front. The buyer gets the payoff from the policy when the covered person dies.

Let me explain how selling a life-insurance policy works...

My friend Nate had two life insurance policies that were about to expire. Instead of continuing the coverage, he let them lapse – and that's where he made his big mistake. Those policies seemed worthless to him. But people in the life-settlements business would have paid him big money for them.

He and his wife had kept these policies in his dresser drawer. When I looked at copies of his old policies, I cringed. I estimate he literally threw away about $250,000.

That's when I realized we were on to something special. I started researching it further and discovered this market could bring millions of dollars to the right people. Here's the story...

The ideal candidate for a life settlement is 65-70 years old with less than 15-20 years of life expectancy remaining. The average 70-year-old man, for example, has an expectancy of 13.27 more years. A 70-year-old woman has an expectancy of 15.72 more years.

When you sell your life insurance, the policy is actually more valuable the worse your health is. The life-insurance policy has value depending on several other factors, too...

- The lower the "cash surrender" value, the better. (Some policies "bank" a portion of the premiums you pay. So if you cancel the policy, you get back some of the value you have built up over the years... This is the policy's "cash surrender" value.)

- Loans against the policy reduce the value of the policy.

- Lower premiums are worth more than higher ones.

The amount you receive from selling your policy is a percentage of the death-benefit amount (value of the policy). It varies depending on personal circumstances, but you can receive anywhere from 20% to 65% of the death benefit. This means if you have a million-dollar term policy, you could get as much as $650,000 by selling it.

Some people with less than two years to live, say with a known terminal illness, can get an even larger percentage... But I don't recommend doing this unless your circumstances are very unusual. These policies are known as "viaticals," which comes from the Latin "preparations for a journey."

Emotions run high once someone receives a medical death sentence and the person's estate or family is set to receive the full amount relatively soon. In these cases, cash needs could easily be met with a loan against the policy as opposed to cashing out early with a life settlement. Why settle for less than you'll get relatively soon?

I spoke with two advisors who work with families and individuals to help them determine whether a life settlement makes sense. The stories they shared about sellers brought tears to my eyes.

One guy, R.L., was 68 years old with a $1 million, 10-year term policy that was rolling over into its 11th year with a renewal offer. The offer increased his annual premium to $30,000 a year from the $8,000 a year he paid previously. He couldn't afford the new amount and didn't think insurance was that important to him anymore. Around this same time, his doctor told him he had Stage IIIB lung cancer and three years to live.

He was still relatively active and felt good, so he and his wife decided to spend the money from his life-insurance policy while they could enjoy things together. They converted the policy to permanent coverage – something most term policies allow you to do – and then sold it.

They got $640,000. They tucked a large chunk of that away to support her after R.L's death. But they used the rest over the following year, traveling the world together arm in arm.

Another person, S.G., was 80 when her Alzheimer's worsened. She needed full-time, in-home care. Her husband decided to cash in the $1.5 million, whole-life policy with a cash-surrender value of $72,000. Instead, he sold it for $535,000. So he received a total of $607,000 and used it to pay her $4,000-a-month nursing bill.

When he initiated his life settlement, he told his financial advisor he needed the money now "for health care expenses and if she dies in the next few years I'll still have a large amount of money left over. My kids are doing OK, and they'll eventually get my insurance money, but I need financial help right now."

One question you should ask yourself is: Why should I execute a life settlement? There are many reasons:

- Your premiums have gotten too expensive to keep paying.

- You're divorced or your spouse has died, so the intended beneficiary has changed.

- You need to pay for expensive health care.

- You want to eliminate premiums and purchase a smaller policy.

- You want financial security today.

- You want to salvage a lapsing policy (like Nate should have done).

By the way, be sure to get full disclosure of how much your insurance broker is making. As of late 2014, Arizona, California, Florida, New York, Virginia, and Illinois require complete and full disclosure. The brokers I met said they take the greatest of 6% of the face value or 30% of the amount over the cash-surrender value, but I suspect they might negotiate these prices.

Those rates mean they got $60,000 for helping R.L. and $93,600 for S.G. The broker doesn't take any risk in setting these up. Why should he get so much of your money? If I ever did one of these, I'd negotiate a rate of 3%-4% of face value with a maximum fee of $20,000-$25,000 for any amount greater than $500,000. The paperwork is the same.

Who Makes the Markets in These Securities?

Large financial companies (with insurance experience) like Berkshire Hathaway, General Electric, and many large insurers pool these policies together and resell them to other big investors looking for a reliable rate of return.

> *Before you let an old life-insurance policy lapse, consider a life settlement. Or if your cash-surrender value is low and you want more money, talk with your insurance or financial adviser.*

Many of these pools of securities provide 10%-12% internal rates of returns to their investors, and of course, all the policies eventually pay off.

One other thing you should know is a little creepy. **Once you complete a life settlement, the company will assign you a "tracking agent," who literally keeps tabs on you until you die.**

For obvious reasons, the company wants to know when it can collect on your policy. You've sold the policy and already have your money, so you don't care anymore. But the company does. And that means a periodic phone call or e-mail to make sure you're still kicking. Don't worry, they're highly regulated and can't harass you.

So before you let an old life-insurance policy lapse, consider a life settlement. Or if your cash-surrender value is low and you want more money, talk with your insurance or financial adviser.

If you truly need (or want) the money and your kids raise hell, tell 'em where to stuff it. *You gave them life, love, and a roof over their heads.* As far as I'm concerned, that's all you owe them. This is your money. It's your decision. And you deserve to be happy and do what *you* want.

— 4 —

This Loophole Increases Your Social Security Income 30%

With this strategy, you and your spouse can start receiving Social Security benefits as soon as you are eligible. Then, using something known as the "Spouse Benefits" provision, you can claim a lot MORE MONEY a few years later.

Kiplinger Personal Finance columnist Mary Beth Franklin estimates this loophole can boost your income from Social Security by more than 30%.

Before we show you exactly how it works, you need to understand two things:

1. The longer you wait to collect, the more you will receive every month.

2. Your spouse can collect 50% benefits based on your work record.

Most people assume when they retire, they'll be collecting benefits based on their own work history. However, the government also offers "spouse benefits," which entitle you to collect a monthly check... worth up to 50% of whatever your spouse is collecting.

So here's what you can do...

- First, one member of the

> 66 *Kiplinger Personal Finance columnist Mary Beth Franklin estimates this loophole can boost your income from Social Security by more than 30%.* 99

couple (let's say the wife) files for benefits as soon as she is eligible. Right now, that's at age 62.

- Simultaneously, the husband files for spousal benefits at 50% of hers. The husband does NOT file for his benefits when he is eligible... Instead, he waits to reach full retirement age (say 66). He delays filing for his own 100% benefits. The longer he waits to file, the more his benefits will be worth.

- Once the husband's benefits are maximized, he files for his own benefits. The wife is then able to "step up" her benefits to the higher payout. (She can collect her benefits plus file for the spouse benefits... up to the total amount that her husband collects.)

> ## Making the Most of Your Social Security
>
> There are many factors to consider... and navigating the paths you can take regarding your benefits is difficult and time consuming. A Social Security office might not be the best way to determine how to get the most out of your benefits. Especially if, like me, you don't count on the government to act in your best interest.
>
> Kiplinger's Social Security Solutions tool can help you figure out the best strategy for your money. A do-it-yourself version of the tool costs $49.95 or $124.95 for expert help. Visit kiplinger. socialsecuritysolutions.com/ or call 866-762-7526, ext. 20 to speak with an advisor. (We're not affiliated with Kiplinger's Social Security Solutions, and we receive no compensation.)

Here again: The wife files and the husband gets a spouse benefit. Then a few years down the road, the husband files and the wife gets a spouse benefit.

It sounds a little confusing, but it's definitely worth crunching the numbers.

This is the secret Timothy Westcott and his wife Marilyn, from Minnesota, used. Marilyn wanted to collect Social Security as soon as she was eligible, but Timothy wanted to keep working until he was 70. So Marilyn filed for benefits... When Timothy realized how the system works, he filed to get "spouse benefits," worth 50% of what Marilyn collected.

As Timothy told *Kiplinger's Personal Finance*...

> I never dreamed that I could draw spousal benefits. I submitted my application. And within 10 days, I had received a check for $2,760 retroactive to February 2008.

Timothy and Marilyn added an extra $700 a month to their income... that's $8,400 a year.

When Timothy reaches age 70, he'll file for his own benefits. Marilyn will get Timothy's spouse benefits. And they'll collect an even higher payout.

What's also good is if Timothy dies first, his wife will get a much bigger benefit than she would have received if they'd both started collecting their Social Security as soon as they became eligible.

According to a report from the Boston College Center for Retirement Research, titled "Strange But True: Claim Social Security Now, Claim More Later," typically, the higher wage-earner should collect "spouse benefits" when eligible... and delay his or her own benefits to let the payout build up.

Assuming the wife was the lower wage earner, the way to maximize your total benefits is to have the wife claim benefits at 62, and the husband delay until 69.

Does this loophole work for you?

Well, you must be married. At least one of you must be healthy enough to delay claiming benefits until age 69. And both spouses must have an earnings history. The Boston College study found that the higher and more equal your earnings, the more you have to gain.

One thing to keep in mind: If you start collecting Social Security or spouse benefits before you turn 66, you're locking in a permanently lower percentage for your spouse benefits.

WHAT TO DO: If the numbers make sense, call the Social Security Administration's toll-free number: 800-772-1213. Set up an appointment with a representative at your local Social Security office. Have them work through the possibilities with you, and take advantage of this extra money.

— 5 —

Tax-Exemption Tips That Could Save You Thousands of Dollars

Most people don't believe me when I tell them how much I love doing my taxes. But I do.

I love the complexity and ever-changing rules. It's like one big springtime crossword puzzle. (I once had a graduate school professor tell me if you understand taxes, you'll always have a job. And so for love and a little bit of job security, I continue my studies.)

My favorite strange and random-seeming loophole in the U.S. tax code is what I call "**the Masters exemption**." In fact, I drive home to Augusta, Georgia every year to spruce up my house and take advantage of the tax break.

Visitors flock to Augusta every year for the Masters tournament. Many years ago, the wealthy course owners called their buddies in D.C. and, in exchange for the incredible hospitality of the locals, convinced the federal government to exempt two weeks (technically, 14 days) of rental income from a home every year.

You heard it right. I rent my home for the week of the Masters and recoup nearly four months of mortgage payments, all tax-free. (It's technically not an exemption at all. The IRS classifies the rent as "non-taxable income.")

It's an incredible deal, and it's not just for landowners in Augusta. You can take advantage of the Masters exemption anywhere. So if you have a second home, consider renting it out for two weeks every year. I know people who earn enough money every year to pay for the yearly property taxes and upkeep on their summer homes.

How to Lower Your Tax Bill

I want to share a few tips to lower your tax bill. (I said I like *doing* my taxes, not *paying* them.)

Some of these ideas could easily make your wealth increase. At the very least, you'll see why I love taxes.

An easy way to do them yourself is to do what I do... **File on your own through an online tax service**. I use <u>TurboTax</u>.

If your situation is complex, an accountant might be better. On the other hand, I have found so many errors over the years in friends' tax returns, I just don't understand why people pay $125-$150 an hour to have someone enter numbers into a computer. If you already have the pile of documents and receipts assembled in front of you, it will take less than three hours of your time to enter the stuff in TurboTax.

I recommend you try it for 15 minutes. See how simple it is. One thing about TurboTax: It's conservative and doesn't play fast and loose with the rules. That's how the software keeps you from making mistakes.

Tax credits are the most powerful IRS killer there is. These credits are simply deducted from the total amount you owe to the state. So be sure to look at these next three ideas closely and see if they might work for you. (They all lower the amount of income tax you have to pay to the government.)

First... If your income is low, you must absolutely do this one. **It's a tax credit for contributions to your retirement accounts**. In other words, it reduces your tax bill.

The tax credit is huge – up to 50% of a maximum $2,000 contribution for individuals and

> ### DO WHAT I DO
>
> **File on your own through an online tax service. I use TurboTax.**

a $4,000 contribution for joint filers. However, there is an income limit of $30,500 for singles, $45,750 for heads of households, and $61,000 for joint filers.

You qualify for this tax credit as long as you fall within those income limits, are older than 18, are not a full-time student, and are not claimed as a dependent on another person's tax return.

For example, if you qualify and put $1,000 into a retirement account, the government gives you a tax credit of $500. Put in $2,000, and the government gives you $1,000. That's like getting a 50% return on your money. It's because a tax credit is a dollar-for-dollar credit on your taxes – it's not just a deduction. This is cold, hard cash back.

If your income qualifies, you should take advantage of this free money from the government – no matter your age.

You can also easily do this in a Roth IRA. And you should.

Second... Are you thinking about going to school but your budget is tight? Or do you have kids in school right now? **Don't forget about the American Opportunity credit**. This tax credit essentially makes the first $2,500 of school free. And the credit is 40% refundable. So you still get a tax refund from the government even if you don't owe any taxes. You can only use the credit for qualified purchases, like tuition and enrollment fees.

Another tax credit, equal to 20% of your annual college tuition is called the Lifetime Learning Credit. It's good for $2,000 per year for an unlimited number of years. As with the American Opportunity credit, you must use this credit for purchases like tuition and enrollment fees.

Here are a few deductions for those of you in school or those considering taking some classes to learn another skill or even just for fun. The best part is that you get these deductions whether you itemize or not...

1. If you are a student, you can deduct up to $4,000 for tuition and fees from federal taxes. This and the tax credit almost makes going back to school free.

2. You can once again deduct up to $2,500 for interest on school loans.

Third... If you are over the age of 70 and a half and have extra money that you want to make sure goes to your heirs tax-free, don't forget to fill up your **Roth IRA. You can put in $6,500 a year. And any earnings in the future are not taxed to you or your heirs**.

Fourth... Did you lose a spouse within the past two years? Did you sell or are you considering selling your house? **Surviving spouses get a hefty tax-break**. You get to take the full $500,000 capital-gain exclusion as if you were still married (normally the exclusion is only $250,000 for singles). This rule began December 31, 2007.

I hope this isn't your case, but if it is, you should at least know you can keep the money that you and your spouse worked so hard to amass. Don't let the IRS steal it from you.

You Can Wipe Away Debt – Sometimes

First off, let's get something straight. I believe in civil contracts. Each of us is morally responsible and accountable for the obligations we accept freely.

Personal debt is no different. Once you agree to borrow money and pay it off, those debts are yours unless a bankruptcy court releases you from them.

I understand that sometimes well-meaning people get in over their heads. I've seen my own sister struggle under mortgage and credit-card debt to the point of bankruptcy twice. I didn't like her choices, but they were hers. She suffered the consequences.

If, like her, you find yourself up to your eyeballs in credit-card debt, you can take advantage of some laws and legitimate strategies for easing your burden a bit.

Before I share what I've discovered, you need to understand the purpose of debt.

Debt is simply a way for you to own and control more than you can currently afford from your savings. When you take on debt, you are agreeing to use future earnings to pay for something you want now. In general, **if it's something consumed – like a car or clothes or airplane tickets – all you're doing is stealing from your future to satisfy your present desires or needs**. Eventually, it will not work.

But if you're taking on debt to produce things — say by owning a sandwich shop — you're betting you will make more money than the debt costs. Once you pay it back, you'll have even more money than when you started. And of course, the rate of return on your investment must be more than the rate of interest you pay or you'll end up poorer, too.

So what can you do if you're in too deep? The only way to truly "wipe away debt" is in bankruptcy. However, you can protect yourself from lawsuits and harassing collection agencies. It turns out all 50 states set a legal expiration date on credit-card debt. In other words, your creditors have a limited amount of time to collect what you initially agreed to pay them. After that, you can simply tell them to leave you alone. They must obey.

This time limit is called the **statute of limitations (SOL)**. And in most states, it runs three or four years. Here's how it works: Say you have debt of $15,000 on a credit card you have not used, paid on, or communicated with the company about for a couple years. After three years, the debt is considered expired. And if anyone calls you up about it or tries to collect on the debt, just tell them, "The debt is expired." And hang up. Voilà, for all practical purposes, that debt is gone.

Note, I said you haven't *"communicated about the debt"* with the company. That's the catch. The statute of limitations starts running from the date of last activity. Again, the rules vary from state to state. (You should research the laws where you live.) But essentially, if you have ANY interaction with the company, the clock resets.

If you pay off a little bit, the clock starts over. If you call the company and talk to them about the debt, the clock restarts. So if you happen to be in this predicament and the clock has been running, don't interact in anyway with the creditor. If the company threatens to sue you, ask for "proof of the debt." This is the only response that doesn't reset the clock.

Once the SOL deadline comes, the creditor can no longer sue you for the debt. But as I mentioned, the debt still exists. The creditor simply has no recourse to recover it in the courts. And telling it "the debt is expired" prevents it from contacting you again. All by law.

No matter your ethical or moral view on paying back your debt, the law protects you from a lifetime of harassment. If you're in a debt situation where this makes sense, please check with your state laws to uncover the exact time limits. Look online at your state's website (usually the state's initials followed by .gov, for example www.md.gov for Maryland) under "debt" for specifics.

If you don't feel it's right to renege on your debt, but still face big debt problems, you can do two other things.

First, **negotiate with your creditor**. If your circumstances are truly dire – no job, no assets, or no income – you can document this fact. Create a financial statement, including a balance sheet and income statement. Have it verified by someone reputable who knows your financial circumstances – tax preparer, bank officer, etc.

Share that with your creditor and explain the likely outcome is bankruptcy. If you did have to declare bankruptcy, the creditor would receive nothing or very little. Instead, suggest a 50% or more cut in the amount of debt you owe.

At that point, you might also have fees and penalties tacked on in past statements. Ask for those to be removed, too. Once the company sees you have no income or a negative net worth (your debt is greater than your assets), it will be willing to negotiate a deal.

And one other tip: Be sure to ask the creditor to remove any bad marks on your credit report once you settle, even the one that says you settled for less than what was owed. The creditor is not required to oblige, but it's helpful to ask and see what you can work out.

The second thing to do – and do it right away – is to **get the creditor to lower the interest rate on your card**. Several years ago, I missed a payment on my American Express credit card due to a travel snafu. My next statement showed the interest rate had jumped up to 33%. I quickly called and told them to change it back to 10% or cancel the card. They did. And you can easily do the same thing.

If you have trouble, be polite and call back until you find the right supervisor to help you make things better. If you're like the average American with a balance of $8,000, lowering the interest rate down 4%-5% can easily save you a couple hundred dollars a year. And look out for deals of 0% with a balance transfer. Just be sure to pay those off regularly. The rate pops up again if you're late or miss a payment.

Finally, if you haven't done it already, remember to get your free credit report from a credit-reporting service like Experian, TransUnion, and Equifax. By law, you can get one a year from each service. I rotate through each of them every six months or so since they each have slightly different information in their databases. You can get the report online from www.AnnualCreditReport.com.

Another Amazing Way to Get Cash If You Own a Home, WITHOUT Moving

After a decade on Wall Street and befriending some of the top bankers, lawyers, and investment advisors in America, I can tell you that the world is full of loopholes...

There are many opportunities to take money back from the government or even tap some of the value of your home while you live in it.

Don't worry... you won't be obliged to any Wall Street scam artist or Washington scum by following my advice.

Your only obligations will be to your own financial freedom. By following the herd, most folks miss out on my *Retirement Millionaire* "free money" opportunities.

My team and I have found ways for you to extract free money out of your home... and get extra money from Social Security you didn't know existed. We've also uncovered a loophole that allows you to start withdrawing your money from your IRA without penalty. And how about converting plain old air into cash?

None of these opportunities require the help of a lawyer. But they are true loopholes in a system designed to screw the little guy. Unfortunately, the more folks who find out about these loopholes, the more likely they'll be shut down by Washington. *So please don't tell anyone else.*

Here are the details...

You can use your home to raise a substantial amount of extra cash.

I've discovered a remarkable company in San Diego called EquityKey that can help you live your retirement dream. It offers large sums of cash in exchange for an investment in your real estate. Let me explain...

If you are between 18 and 85 years old and own your home, EquityKey will pay you a lump sum today in exchange for a share of the future appreciation of your property.

In exchange for cash today, you agree to share the future gains in your property's value with EquityKey when you sell or transfer ownership of your house. You can do whatever you want with the cash, and the home remains yours forever.

Whether you live in or have a vacation or second home, these folks can help you.

From an article in *U.S. News and World Report*:

> **❝ You can use your home to raise a substantial amount of extra cash. ❞**

> Gladys Tully, 72, got $106,000, and used the money to pay part of the principal of her mortgage and remodel her bedroom and bathroom, without giving up her passions: painting, the large garden and orchard on her property, and a hiking trip to Europe every year.

I'm not talking about a first or second loan on the property. It's not a loan at all. There are no monthly payments or interest charges. And

EquityKey has zero control over what you do with the house *until you sell or transfer it*. Only at the end of the transaction is EquityKey entitled to its portion of the appreciation... if any.

Again, you're essentially selling a right to share between 30% and 75% of the future appreciation on your home. In exchange for this right, EquityKey pays you a lump sum.

The best part is that you get to keep all the current equity you have in your home. EquityKey takes some of the risk of owning real estate from you. It recoups the money it pays you now through future long-term growth in the property.

The company will pay between 6% and 17% of current property value in exchange for 30%-75% of the future increase in value of the property as measured by the Standard & Poor's/Case-Shiller Index.

EquityKey has partnered with financial-services company Standard & Poor's to use its monthly index for 20 of the largest metropolitan areas across the country to independently measure and report changes in residential home values.

This gives homeowners and investors transparency and confidence in changes in home values until the property is sold and the transaction ends. If your property sells for more than what the index suggests, you keep the entire surplus.

The application and underwriting is quick and easy. If you have at least 35% equity in your home (meaning if you have a $600,000 home, your current loans cannot exceed $422,000) and are current on your payments, you can close the transaction and receive a lump sum payment in as little as two weeks.

Let the Wind Provide Free Money for Your Retirement

My friend Paul has some land in Maine. He is one of the few doctors I know who understands investing well.

For years, Paul has taken his extra cash and bought land in North Carolina and Maine. His plan has always been to harvest trees – beautiful old hardwoods. He sells some of them and makes gorgeous furniture from the others. But there was one venture that intrigued me the most...

I couldn't believe what I was hearing. Paul was putting up a wind turbine on a ridge on his land and was going to sell it back to the utility company. The numbers looked great.

The turbine cost about $1 million to install. But most states offer rebates and incentives to do this sort of green-energy project. Maine offered a state rebate of $100,000 plus a 35% rebate of total project cost. That cut Paul's costs to $550,000.

A small business loan for 15 years at 3% interest means a monthly cost of $3,800. Let's add some other maintenance and insurance, and round it up to $4,000 per month. Now let's look at the income...

A windmill that size generates about 1 million kilowatt-hours (kWh) per year. The utility offered to pay him about $0.06 per kWh. This means about $60,000 a year, or $5,000 per month. But it gets better. The IRS allowed for a tax credit of 1.8 cents per year for wind-powered energy – a tax credit of $18,000, or $1,500 per month.

With the tax benefit of the credit and the positive cash flow from the wind-power, Paul would net about $2,500 per month in cash from the one windmill. If the neighbors don't mind, he could put up several of these. Not bad income for his retirement: $30,000 per year tax-free on land that was basically worthless.

Notice that what makes the math work for Paul is the tax incentives and benefits. It's rare for various government agencies to come together and present great investment opportunities like this one. In *Retirement Millionaire*, we watch for similar opportunities and share our findings so you can improve the quality of your retirement and live a richer life.

How to Tap Your IRA Right Now

Sitting on a pile of IRA money? Want to buy your dream piece of real estate, but don't have a job or enough cash flow? This secret is for you. Some of you may want to retire today, but aren't yet 59.5 years old.

Using this little-known secret in the IRS code, you can get your money right now without paying any IRS penalties or fines.

Your broker probably doesn't want you to know about this. If you start taking your money out of your account, his fees to manage your IRA get smaller. But through an IRS loophole, you can retire today and begin your "Early IRA Distribution" tomorrow.

Our method is perfectly legal and simple to do. Even the rationale behind the loophole makes sense.

You can take money out, pay taxes on it (but no fines or early withdrawal penalties), use whatever you need, *AND* still make regular contributions to a separate IRA if you'd like. Here's how...

IRS rule 72(t)(1) provides for a 10% tax on early distributions taken from an IRA before the age of 59.5. But if you take out your IRA money in what the IRS calls "substantially equal periodic payments" for at least five years or until you reach 59.5 years, you pay no penalty. All you do is pay regular income tax rates on the income (which you would have eventually done anyway).

The IRS allows you to determine the amount using one of three different methods...

1. **Required Minimum Distribution (RMD)**: To determine your RMD, the IRA takes your account balance from the previous December 31 and divides it by the IRS' life-expectancy factor. It's recalculated every year based on your account balance and the current federal interest rate.

2. **Fixed Amortization**: This method takes the starting balance on your account, assumes the interest you'll make, and – using

your life expectancy – determines a fixed payment amount.

3. **Fixed Annuitization**: This is nearly identical to the fixed amortization method. The calculation differences are subtle and don't make much difference in the payments you receive.

The calculations for these three methods are a bit more involved. But this gives you the general idea.

Essentially, the methods look at tables to estimate your life expectancy and apply an interest rate to the IRA balance. The methods provide a dollar amount that you may pull out every year.

A *Forbes* article shows how a chiropractor, Alfonse DeMaria, took $700,000 in his IRA and converted it to a $3,000-a-month income stream. He bought himself a six-bedroom home with 269 acres in rural New York to enjoy with his family.

"My kids and I can start enjoying the house now rather than 25 years from now," he said. "And it will still be here then, too."

The different IRS methods give slightly different amounts, so the best choice may vary depending on your needs. Here's an example straight from the IRS, although I've simplified it a bit. (That IRS code is dense in places.)

Mr. B is 50 years old and has $400,000. In the first year...

1. The RMD method will give him $11,695.91.

2. The Fixed Amortization method would allow $23,134.27.

3. The Fixed Annuitization method allows for $22,906.88.

As you can see, the amounts vary. Carefully consider each method. If you take out more money earlier, you'll have less later and vice versa. The IRS tables and math are not that difficult. Regardless, I urge you to seek more advice from a tax accountant or financial planner before acting.

And don't worry about changing your mind. Say you start with one method, the RMD, and find you need more money later. The IRS allows you to change your method one time. So you could switch to one of the fixed methods in later years and take out more when you're older.

One of the questions I always hear is "How long do I do this?" The answer is five years, or until you turn 59.5, whichever comes *last*. So if you start this at age 48, you must continue for another 11.5 years. If you started at age 57, you would need to continue until 62 years of age. You have to take the payments for the required number of years. You can't change your mind and stop taking payments early.

If you have a large sum of money in your 401(k) and are thinking about an early retirement, this secret really helps provide a source of income. It's simple to do.

Just roll the money over to a self-directed IRA and start taking it out using this method. Perhaps you don't need that much income? Consider rolling your 401(k) into two different IRAs. Keep one growing and start the 72(t)-withdrawal process in the other. Again, this is legal and simple.

Happy retirement!

— 6 —

The Free Silver Loophole:

How to Legally Remove Silver from the U.S. Banking System and the Five Magic Words to Ask Your Banker

A major loophole in the U.S. retail banking system allows you to get real, "hold-in-your-hand" silver from practically any FDIC-insured bank in the U.S... essentially for free.

All you do is walk into a typical branch and ask for it... The teller will simply hand it over as part of a totally free transaction.

You don't even need an account with the bank where you want to collect your silver...

I'm not talking about getting discounted silver or undervalued coins. I'm talking about walking into almost any ordinary bank and asking any teller one, specific question. Then after a short, free transaction... you potentially walk out with a handful of real silver.

You're probably wondering how this is possible... Is there really a loophole in our financial system that enables you to get this

> **❝ A major loophole in the U.S. retail banking system allows you to get real, 'hold-in-your-hand' silver from practically any FDIC-insured bank in the U.S... essentially for free.**
>
> *All you do is walk into a typical branch and ask for it...* **❞**

51

incredibly valuable asset essentially for free?

I had this exact question when I began researching this situation. But it's true... Banks hand out silver – if you know what to ask for.

Before I describe how it works, let me explain why having real silver is so important...

Silver Is the Best Chaos Protection for Your Portfolio

The U.S. Congress established its monetary system in 1792 and agreed to mint coins using both gold and silver. At the time, you needed 15 ounces of silver to buy one ounce of gold. (In other words, what we call the "silver-to-gold ratio" was 15:1.)

That ratio was well established. Fifteen ounces of silver had roughly equaled an ounce of gold for the previous four *centuries* (according to the 1932 edition of the U.S. Geological Survey *Minerals Yearbook*).

But in the early 20th century, governments around the world (notably the U.S.) stopped backing their money with gold. People started hoarding gold, driving up its value, and the ratio went haywire. It cracked 71:1 during the Great Depression.

A variety of political and economic factors calmed the gold market, and the ratio narrowed (though not to pre-Depression levels). It eventually bottomed out at a little more than 20:1 in the 1960s... when the U.S. stopped backing its currency with silver. People then bought up silver coins, driving the price of silver higher relative to the price of gold.

But guess what? In 2009, enthusiasm for gold pushed the ratio back to near its decades-high of 71:1... exactly where it was in the last depression, when people were crazy for gold.

No one can know future price moves. But it's smarter to own the metal near a low rather than near its all-time high.

You have a lot of ways to invest in silver. The best way I've found allows you to take physical possession of silver without paying huge markups to the spot price. It doesn't require any risky leverage or buying mining companies that may or may not be around in a year...

This incredible silver loophole might be my most unusual find yet...

How to Start Getting Your Silver Today

A small group of banks in the U.S. possess a certain type of government-created coin, which does not circulate widely in the general population...

These coins were originally produced during the early part of the 20th century. They were part of government mandate H.R. 2934, which created money that was respected and easy to use. More than 750 million of these coins were minted, all containing varying amounts of silver.

These coins – which contain as much as 90% pure silver – were designed by many of the best sculptors and engravers of the day... people like Augustus Saint-Gaudens, Charles E. Barber, and Gilroy Roberts. One of these coins is even listed by the Professional Coin Grading Service (PCGS) as one of the 20th century's most beautiful silver coins.

The coins were date-stamped and engraved with official U.S. government markings to ensure authenticity.

The government intended to keep these unique "silvers" in circulation. But the feds ceased production in 1971 because people were hoarding them and not circulating them.

The banks still hold large quantities of these coins. The U.S. government minted more than 2 billion silver half-dollars during the 1900s. If you assume that just 1% of them are still out there... that's probably about 20 million 50-cent pieces left in the banking system.

The key to this is... if the bank has half dollars, you can exchange your ordinary paper dollars for a roll of half dollars for the face amount. So $10 will get you 20 half-dollars. Just walk in, and say these five magic words: "**Do you have half dollars?**"

Sometimes, banks have possession of these coins and sometimes they don't. Half dollars aren't popular and don't circulate as much as other denominations of coins – like dimes and nickels. So banks may have very few on hand.

But this is also our opportunity... This so-called "coin-roll hunting" isn't as effective with commonly used denominations. The supplies of pre-1965 coins (the most valuable) have been picked over much more thoroughly.

To increase your odds of finding valuable half-dollars... I recommend you visit rural banks. They likely won't have a lot of customers looking for silver half dollars. If the bank doesn't have silver half-dollar rolls, ask the teller if he can order some for you. Just make sure you won't be charged for the order.

I also recommend looking in March and April. People deposit lots of change in these two months... probably to help pay taxes.

The Inside Tracks

Of course, with a little more effort, you can try getting on "The List," as one gentleman we talked to called it.

"I started bringing the tellers baked goods like cookies and cream-cheese pies. I sent them postcards when I went on vacations... mowed lawns for a few of the older tellers," he said. "In other words, it's a popularity contest with the other guys who are after the hand-rolled halves. Treat the tellers nicely, and they will put you at the top of their 'List.'"

If you're friendly with the tellers, they can hold half dollars for you and alert you when they have new ones in.

One important thing to remember... most banks will let you exchange dollars for rolled coins without an account. But if you're taking coins back to the bank or asking for half dollars to be ordered, the bank may require you to have an account there.

Also, a word of caution, **this opportunity is not infinite**. The government doesn't print silver coins... *As more people catch on to the* *opportunity and squirrel away these coins, the number of coins making their way into rolls will dwindle.* Eventually, silver half dollars will effectively disappear...

When will that happen? It's anyone's guess.

The important thing to remember is that once the word really starts to spread, I expect this free silver will become increasingly difficult to find.

This loophole is closing... and exactly how fast it will close is impossible to predict. Opportunities like this don't stick around forever. Those who act sooner will undoubtedly reap the best results.

So if this idea interests you, I strongly recommend you consider it carefully, but act swiftly... When we first began researching this idea in 2011, we estimated the chances of success were about 25%. But as it becomes popular, that could decrease to 15%, or even 10%.

> **66** *As more people catch on to the opportunity and squirrel away these coins, the number of coins making their way into rolls will dwindle. Eventually, silver half dollars will effectively disappear...* **99**

Let's recap how you can get your silver coins...

- Walk into a bank and ask for half dollars.

- Change your paper money for real silver.

- Rural banks offer the best chance of finding these coins.

- Visit banks in March and April.

- Get on "The List" by becoming friendly with tellers.

- Some banks require an account when returning coins or ordering rolls.

Where to Sell Your U.S. Coins

Selling silver and gold can be risky if you don't know who you're dealing with. Over the years, we at Stansberry Research have formed some reliable contacts in all areas of the financial world. Here are some of those folks... and feel free to tell them we sent you. The names are:

Asset Strategies International
1700 Rockville Pike, Suite 400
Rockville, MD 20852
Phone: 800-831-0007 or 301-881-8600
Fax: 301-881-1936

Camino Coin
1301 Broadway Ave.
Burlingame, CA 94010
Phone: 800-348-8001 or 650-348-3000

PART III

Investment Secrets

— 1 —

The Essentials of Asset Allocation

The single most important factor in your investing success has nothing to do with picking the right stocks. It has nothing to do with paying attention to what the president or Congress say.

It has nothing to do with the state of the economy. It has nothing to do with knowing how to "time the market."

The single most important factor in your investing success is 100 times more important than any of those things.

Ignorance and mismanagement of this factor ruin more retirements than every other factor combined. Yet, most investors never give this idea any thought...

This vitally important idea is called "**Asset Allocation**."

I hope I have your interest... If you understand the ideas in this chapter, you could use them to create a lifetime of safe wealth generation.

We'll start our learning process with a story. It's one of the saddest retirement stories I know. And worse, I hear it repeated over and over...

Please Don't Ever Do This

A good friend of mine worked for decades at a nationwide mortgage lender. (I promised to not use his name or company.)

Throughout his career, he meticulously socked away money in his 401(k) retirement account. By the time he was ready to retire, he had several million dollars saved up. Retirement looked easy.

But there was just one problem... 90% of his savings was invested in the stock and stock options of his company.

When the housing market collapsed in 2007, shares of his company fell. He was worried, but his account balance was still healthy. So he left his retirement with his company's stock...

But the stock market kept going down. Eventually, the bottom fell out. From September 2008 to March 2009, his family's retirement savings went from $3 million to $500,000. *In a span of just six months, his past and his future were wiped out.*

And worst of all, at the exact moment he should have been buying more stock, he panicked. He sold everything near the bottom and sat on the small pile of cash, trembling. As a result, he missed the upswings over the next four years that doubled the stock market's value.

His critical mistake was an error in asset allocation.

Why Financial Institutions Won't Ever Talk About This With You

You'll almost never hear folks in the finance and investing industry mention the words "asset allocation."

You won't hear it from brokers who spend their days pitching stock ideas to their clients. You won't hear it from most of my peers in the publishing industry. And forget about a discussion of the topic on the cable news providers, like CNBC.

The reason is, asset allocation is simply boring. It doesn't sell.

People would much rather buy research about a hot pick than read about asset allocation. Since the customer is paying the bills, that's what he gets.

But if you're not familiar with what asset allocation means, don't be intimidated... it's easy to understand.

Simply put: Asset allocation is how you balance your wealth among stocks, bonds, cash, real estate, commodities, and gold. *This mix is the most important factor in your retirement investing success.*

Keeping your wealth stored in a diversified mix of investable assets is the key to avoiding catastrophic losses.

If you keep too much wealth – like 90% of it – in one or two stocks and the stock market goes south, you'll suffer badly no matter how good the companies are. That was my friend's downfall. He had allocated virtually all his wealth into a single asset – the stock of one company. When a crisis struck that company, he was in deep trouble.

Or if you quit your nursing job to move to Florida and put all your wealth in rental real estate in 2006, you'd have been wiped out in a big real estate crash (like many folks were in 2008).

The same goes for all asset classes... gold, oil, bonds, real estate, blue-chip stocks, etc.

> **66** *Keeping your wealth stored in a diversified mix of investable assets is the key to avoiding catastrophic losses.* **99**

Concentrating your retirement nest egg in just a few stocks or a few different asset classes is way too risky. *Keeping your eggs in one basket is always a fool's game.*

At *Retirement Millionaire*, we won't place all your hard-earned money on one number and spin the roulette wheel. We prefer to play the odds and keep them in our favor... something that produces plenty of safety and upside. Here's how you should think about asset allocation...

The Four Asset Categories You Always Need

The idea of allocating assets across different categories is based on the mathematical phenomenon known as "correlation." Correlation –

specifically *positive* correlation – means that when one asset goes up in price, the other does, too.

Looking back in history, we can measure the correlations (or lack of correlation) among many asset categories. And we know that assets like cash, stocks, bonds, and gold are correlated to different factors. **That means holding some of each at all times will protect you from catastrophe in one of the asset categories**.

No. 1 Essential: Cash Is King

One of the secrets of *Retirement Millionaire* is to avoid thinking like others... like how we think about cash.

Most folks treat cash like a disease... They can't get rid of it fast enough. Invest it all, they think. Get in "the action." Or dumber yet, they spend it all.

But having a large cash balance somewhere makes it a lot easier to sleep at night... and sleeping well is worth millions. Besides, cash is sometimes a great investment, too...

Here's a little-known fact: When looking at one-year holding periods over the past 33 years, cash returned more than both stocks and bonds about 17% of the time. Let me repeat that another way.

In one out of six years, holding cash outperforms stocks and bonds. This is an amazing fact. Few investment advisers or brokers will explain it to you. Ask them. They won't know the answer is one year out of six.

OK, OK, I know during those 33 years, stocks averaged 11% annual returns, bonds averaged 8%, and cash averaged only 6%. But still, cash was frequently king.

The greatest benefit to holding cash is it ensures you always have money ready when great investment opportunities come up. When stocks and real estate become relatively expensive, you'll want to raise cash. When stocks and real estate are getting cheap, you'll want to put that cash to work.

Legendary investors hoard cash all the time. The richest man in the world, Warren Buffett, does this. In 2005, a full year and a half before the 2007 peak in stock prices, he began raising cash. He just couldn't find any deals compelling enough to risk his shareholders' capital. At one point, Buffett held more than $40 billion in cash.

In general, I recommend holding between 10% and 45% of your portfolio in cash. When you find an asset like stocks, commodities, or real estate that is extraordinarily cheap, you can lower your cash position to take advantage of the values.

No. 2 Essential: Always Own Stocks

The stock market is a wonderful place to compound wealth *when you buy great companies at great prices.*

If you want to get wealthy over time, owning stocks is easily the best way to do it. Most people already know this, but most people don't know how it happens. And it doesn't happen slowly, it happens quickly...

Fidelity researchers found that $10,000 invested in the S&P 500 Index in 1980 grew to $300,000 by 2007. But if you missed just the best 30 of those 7,000 days, you would have made only $51,000. Miss the best five days, and you would have only made $90,000. Think about that...

If you missed the five best days over a 27-year period, your return would have dropped from 2,900% to 800%.

I don't know about your ability to time the market, but it's hard to imagine anyone picking exactly which five days to be invested in stocks. This is why you must always be in stocks. No other passive investment vehicle compares with stocks.

One guide to determine what percentage of your portfolio you should dedicate to stocks is the "**100-minus-age**" rule. Just take 100% and subtract your age. So if you're 60, the rule says you should have 40% of your portfolio in the stock market. This is a great place to start when trying to decide how much to have in stocks.

But... if you're 75 years old, 25% may still be a little high for you. Given my cautious outlook on stocks, you may want to hold just 10% of your investable assets in stocks.

No. 3 Essential:
Fixed-Income Investments Are the Foundation

Fixed-income securities – like bonds – are designed to give you your initial investment back after a fixed period of time... in exchange for income along the way.

> *66 Adding safe fixed-income investments into your portfolio is a simple way to stabilize your investment returns and guarantee wealth without worry. 99*

Depending on your age and your taste for risk, they can be good to own. Bonds add a level of certainty with regular interest payments. And the return of principal makes these excellent investments.

Consider corporate bonds: One beauty of bondholding is a concept called "seniority." This means if a company gets into financial trouble, bondholders get their money before others. (For example, stockholders are last in line.)

This makes it easier to own bonds than stocks – especially if you're more than 70 years old. That's the age when most folks need to be overwhelmingly concerned with preserving their retirement money and income... not so much concerned with increasing it.

Bonds are also a simple way to lock up cash at higher rates than checking or money-market accounts. For most people, receiving a stream of interest payments at a fixed rate plus a nearly guaranteed return of capital is what helps them sleep well at night.

Adding safe fixed-income investments into your portfolio is a simple way to stabilize your investment returns and guarantee wealth without worry. Knowing you will get a check from the government or a company before anyone else gets money is a great feeling.

No. 4 Essential:
Occasionally, You Can Hedge Against Chaos

When inflation roars, the things you buy cost more... In other words, your U.S. dollar loses value. So unless you hold something that preserves its value, you can become poorer. You need to devote a portion of your portfolio to assets that protect you from this craziness...

> *66 For pure wealth protection in a financial crisis, there's no substitute for physical gold and silver. 99*

Stocks are great during inflation. But owning gold during turbulent times is critical. Gold has generally held its value for hundreds of years. Its scarcity keeps it valuable. And throughout human history, the wealthy have used it as a hedge against calamity. Similarly, silver has shared much of gold's allure.

You can devote up to 10% of your portfolio to these "chaos hedges"... depending on the political and monetary climate.

When the time is right, one way to get exposure to a "chaos hedge" is to buy shares of an exchange-traded fund like SPDR Gold Shares (NYSE: GLD). It buys, holds, and sells physical gold. The fund's shares reflect the performance of gold bullion.

For pure wealth protection in a financial crisis, there's no substitute for physical gold and silver. Ultimately, funds involve banks and other electronic shuffling. Physical gold and silver do not. They just sit in your safe deposit box or at home.

No. 5 Essential:
Diversification Is the Key to Wealth

Diversification is probably the most misunderstood and misused phrase in finance.

For example, most people don't know how many stocks it takes to be diversified. The host of a well-known TV money show once asked this question of callers: "Are you diversified?" According to him, five stocks in different sectors makes you diversified.

This is simply not true, and it is a dangerous notion.

Economist Harry Markowitz earned a Nobel Prize in 1990 for his efforts combining math, physics, and stock picking. According to his work (and the research of others who have refined it), the ideal diversified portfolio has somewhere between 10 and 20 stocks. Most academicians agree that no more than 20 stocks are needed.

The table below shows risk decreases (measured as the average standard deviation) with more stocks in the portfolio.

You can see that going from just one stock to 20 stocks decreases risk from 49.2% to 21.7%. But going from 20 to 100 stocks only reduces the amount of risk from 21.7% to 19.7%. This is only a decrease of two percentage points. It's hardly worth the time and energy to add another 80 stocks, especially if the gains are miniscule.

Number of Stocks in Portfolio	Average Standard Deviation of Returns
1	49.24%
2	37.36%
6	26.64%
10	23.93%
20	21.68%
100	19.69%
200	19.42%
1,000	19.21%

To quote the legendary Warren Buffett, "wide diversification is only required when investors do not understand what they are doing."

So once you have your money in stocks, bonds, cash, and gold, make sure you remember to diversify. You need about 10-20 stocks at a time. And don't put more than 4%-5% in any one stock position. Don't overdo it.

So in summary, consider a "retirement conservative" asset allocation for a 65 year old that looks like this:

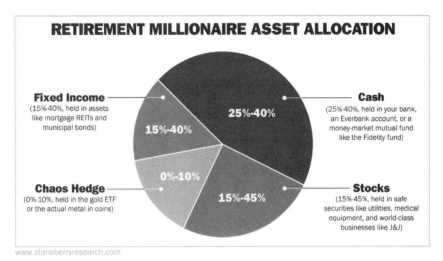

RETIREMENT MILLIONAIRE ASSET ALLOCATION

Fixed Income
(15%-40%, held in assets like mortgage REITs and municipal bonds)

Cash
(25%-40%, held in your bank, an Everbank account, or a money-market mutual fund like the Fidelity fund)

Chaos Hedge
(0%-10%, held in the gold ETF or the actual metal in coins)

Stocks
(15%-45%, held in safe securities like utilities, medical equipment, and world-class businesses like J&J)

25%-40%

15%-40%

0%-10%

15%-45%

www.stansberryresearch.com

Within each category, don't put more than 5% of your money in any one stock.

You'll notice the percentages I've given have a wide range. That's on purpose. Everyone has their own situation... different obligations to family, different passive income, different living standards. I can't give out a "stocking cap" set of guidelines. I'm just presenting a safe set of guidelines you can use to make changes that best fit you and your family.

— 2 —

You Need a 'Retirement Lifeboat' Overseas

In late 2009, I attended a private offshore meeting with 300 or so enemies of the U.S. government.

The meeting took place at a beachside resort on the outskirts of one the world's premier banking havens.

It's believed billions of dollars in laundered drug, arms, and hush money are parked in this country... a country that has been invaded several times by U.S. troops in the last 100 years – the last time in 1989.

Scattered throughout the room were people of all ages and walks of life. I fully expected a few to be sued someday by Uncle Sam. One of the higher-profile members of this group has already been a target. We'll call him Mr. X.

Why are these folks enemies of the U.S. government?

They refuse to surrender their lives and assets to be wasted by the mushrooming U.S. government. To save the wealth they've created over a lifetime of hard work, they are building an international "lifeboat."

You may laugh at my claim that folks interested in international asset protection are "enemies" of the U.S. But I can assure you, this is how our government sees them.

Actually, I hope you're also an "enemy" of the tax-and-spend parasites in Washington, D.C. And I hope you take several simple steps to safeguard some of your wealth immediately.

Mr. X is an excellent source of information on 100% LEGAL asset protection. He's a lawyer who has worked for years dealing with these issues and helping wealthy people protect their assets.

Three Simple Tips from Mr. X

Between bailing out bloated, rotting-from-the-head-down carmakers, forgiving bad mortgages, and giving away health care to more than 45 million people... our government has racked up inconceivable debts. By late 2014, we were sitting on nearly $20 trillion in debt.

> **66** *Anyone contemplating wealth preservation and international diversification must understand two U.S. government concepts: income tax and reportable assets.* **99**

Without belaboring the point, it's unimaginable that the U.S. can pay off its debts in my lifetime. But it's going to try... or rather, pretend to try. The only way to do that is to tax the beejeezus out of anyone with a few assets to his name.

The U.S. government and several states have repeatedly proposed a wealth tax. Yep, people with more than a certain amount of assets could face a tax on their hard-earned stash. (That's above and beyond anything you paid in income tax accumulating that "wealth.")

Look, this is not a problem just for the wealthy. This is for anyone with a lifetime of savings. Under the current path, everyone who has something will be forced to give it up to those who don't have anything. And worse, we'll be forced to give it to those too lazy to work for anything. I don't know about you, but first and foremost, I want to decide to whom my money goes. I don't want some bureaucrat in D.C. telling me how kind I have to be.

Anyone contemplating wealth preservation and international diversification must understand two U.S. government concepts: **income tax** and **reportable assets**.

If you hold assets offshore, some are reportable to the government and some are not. And if you make income while overseas, it's all reportable, although the first $97,600 a year is exempt.

In our tips below, we've listed ways to legally avoid both reporting assets and paying income taxes while your assets are overseas.

Before I jump in, I need to give you one other piece of advice: <u>Keep this to yourself</u>. All my suggestions are legal. I would never advise you to do anything illegal. But that doesn't mean the government *wants* you to do these things...

If too many people start talking about these things and taking the steps below, the government could easily change the rules. Our lifeboat will disappear.

Tip No. 1: Open a Foreign Bank Account – Soon

If you open a foreign financial account with less than $10,000, you do not have to report the assets. This comes under the Foreign Bank and Financial Authority (FBAR) regulations. The IRS states you only have to report if:

- You have financial interest in, signature authority over, or other authority over one or more accounts in a foreign country.

- The aggregate value of all foreign financial accounts exceeds $10,000 at any time during the calendar year.

If you keep more than $10,000 overseas, you must report it or risk fines and jail time. (Up to 50% of your assets and up to five years in prison, if a judge decides the oversight was willful.)

Be careful about interest-earning accounts, too. Let's say you put $9,990 in an account in January and you earn enough interest to take you over $10,000 by year-end. Well, guess what? Now, you must report the assets and the income.

One more secret: Nothing prevents your spouse and other family members from doing the same. A family of six could keep about $59,000 in accounts overseas and not need to report it. Again, this is all legal and a great way to diversify your portfolio around the world.

Tip No. 2: Buy a Little Bit of Land

Real estate is perhaps the best way to keep assets overseas. The reason is simple. It's not reportable. And if it generates no income, you pay no tax on it either. Some of the smartest folks I know invested in foreign real estate and now have millions of dollars in assets offshore and out of the reach of the government.

Also, several countries (Panama and Costa Rica, for example) allow you to invest in real estate and even sustainable timber farms. With enough money invested, you can get a permanent visa and even citizenship after five years with little or no questions asked. In addition, real estate can be made more liquid if you place it in a corporation or trust. This makes it easier to sell or transfer your assets.

The publications *International Living Magazine* and *Live and Invest Overseas* are two great resources for learning more about international real estate opportunities. You can learn more at their websites: www. internationalliving.com and www.liveandinvestoverseas.com.

TIP No. 3: Gold in the Bank

And last, my absolute favorite tip for keeping wealth out of the United States...

Bullion gold and silver (and other metals) are not reportable, nor do they generate taxable income until you sell them. So keeping bullion in a private and secure place outside the U.S. is a simple way to hold (and move) assets out of the country.

One of the simplest ways to do this is opening a safe deposit box in Canada. All you need to open a Canadian safe deposit box are two forms of identification – a passport and a driver's license will do – and an in-person visit to the bank. (This can vary slightly depending on the bank, so call the bank you're interested in first.)

One bank you can open a safe deposit box with is the Royal Bank of Canada (www.rbcroyalbank.com). Some banks do not allow you to store currency or legal tender in a safe deposit box. So call the bank you're interested before making the trip.

You can use your box to store precious metals, cash, and other items you want out of the U.S. government's eyes. And the box fees are similar to the fees you'd pay at an American bank.

Transporting your gold to Canada may seem frightening to some people. I've heard stories of people having their gold confiscated by ignorant customs officials. But taking gold into Canada is 100% legal as long as you declare it to customs. (You have to declare any amount of currency over $10,000.)

Of course, it's also risky to carry large amounts of gold as you travel. So...

If you don't want to handle transporting precious metals or cash to Canada yourself, you can use a professional transport service. Although this can be expensive if you're only moving a small amount of wealth.

A third option is to purchase your gold or silver in Canada. This means you don't have to carry large amounts of cash or precious metals while you travel.

— 3 —

Rare Gold Secrets

Every investor should own some gold.

The reason is, gold is the quintessential "chaos hedge." Gold outperforms many other asset classes during times of great economic and political stress.

If violence broke out in the streets and the paper currency of the U.S. government was worthless, you'd need something to barter for essential goods and services. You'd need something universally recognized for holding value throughout history.

In short, you'd need gold and silver coins.

The same holds true for more mundane forms of "chaos." Through the chaos of the dot-com bubble burst in 2000... the mortgage crisis eruption in 2007... and the global economic contraction... gold rose more than 400% compared with the benchmark S&P 500 stock index, which rose a mere 25%.

And as the U.S. government printed money to cover the payments on its epic debts and pay the salaries and benefits of millions of useless employees... the price went higher.

But instead of buying "regular" gold, there's a rare form of gold that could prove to be much more profitable.

> **❝ Gold is the quintessential 'chaos hedge.' Gold outperforms many other asset classes during times of great economic and political stress. ❞**

Take a look at what this rare gold did during the last gold bull market between 1978 and 1989...

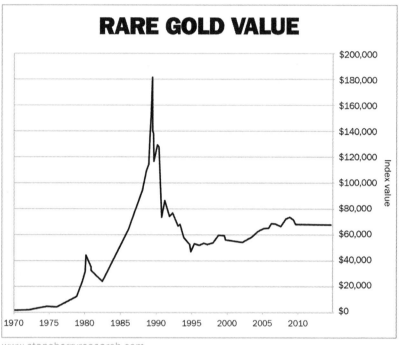

RARE GOLD VALUE

This rare form of gold shot up 2,550%. That's almost 18 times higher than regular gold prices during the same period.

What's more... if you happened to invest $1,000 in this rare gold in 1950, it would have been worth $593,000 30 years later – gaining an average of 28% every single year.

This investment is beyond the reach of any government or corporation. Some of the richest families in the world used this gold investment to preserve their family wealth and grow dynasties.

But you don't have to be the scion of wealth to take part. Anyone can invest in gold this way as a "chaos hedge" for their portfolios.

No one in the investment advisory community has written more extensively about this gold investment than my colleague at Stansberry Research Dr. Steve Sjuggerud. His analysis of this gold investment is among the best I've read on the subject.

Everyone should consider adding this investment to their portfolios. His report is below. At the end, I'll recommend my personal favorite way to take advantage of this investment idea...

———————•———————

The Secret Gold Investment

By Dr. Steve Sjuggerud

The investment is a form of gold.

But it's not your typical gold investment.

It has nothing to do with mining stocks, mutual funds, options, futures, or bullion. Instead, this is a kind of currency used for centuries by the richest families to profit on financial windfalls created by governments around the world.

This secret currency is not old-fashioned or obsolete. Look through the rolls of the richest people in the world, and you'll find dozens of families using this investment to both grow and safeguard their wealth. For example...

- The Rothschild family: At one time, this was the wealthiest family in the world.

- The Onassis family: Greek shipping magnate Aristotle Onassis married Jackie Kennedy after President John F. Kennedy died.

> **66 It has nothing to do with mining stocks, mutual funds, options, futures, or bullion. Instead, this is a kind of currency used for centuries by the richest families to profit on financial windfalls created by governments around the world. 99**

- The Hunt family: H.L. Hunt made his billions as an oil wildcatter in Texas.

- The DuPont family: Their descendants today run the second-biggest chemical company in the United States.

- The Morgan family: Patriarch J.P. Morgan was one of the richest railroad men of the 20th century.

- The Adams family: This family famously produced two presidents – John Adams and John Quincy Adams.

- The Hopkins family: Johns Hopkins gave money to build the university and the world-famous hospital, which both bear his name in Baltimore, Maryland.

- The Green family: American businesswoman and financier Henrietta "Hetty" Green was once the wealthiest person in the world, wealthier than Bill Gates.

- The royal Farouk family: This family produced the last two kings of Egypt.

This investment is like gold, only better – with the potential for much higher returns.

- From 1972 to 1974, this investment rose 348%, according to an index that keeps track of its market as a whole. At the same time, the S&P 500 stock market index dropped 34%.

- From 1976 to 1980, the stock market plummeted 35%, according to the S&P 500. The investment I want to tell you about realized 1,195% profits.

- Then between 1987 and 1989, investors who took advantage of the secret currency saw profits of 665%. Stocks, meanwhile, went on a roller coaster ride – up and down dozens of times during this period.

When Wall Street investment bank Salomon Brothers included this vehicle in its 2001 annual investment survey, it ranked No. 1 over the prior 20-year span, with an annual return of 17.3%. In other words, <u>it was the single most profitable thing you could do with your money over 20 years</u>.

It beat stocks, bonds, gold, silver, artwork, diamonds, U.S. Treasury bills, real estate, and oil, according to an article in the *Chicago Tribune*.

I can understand why you may believe I'm exaggerating the power of this gold secret to safeguard and grow your wealth.

After all, you may have never heard of it before. Most investors haven't. But the truth is, you can use the secret currency to make as much money as you want. The problem is, no one else is likely to tell you about it. Why should they?

But if this investment is good enough for the world's wealthiest families – the Rothschilds, DuPonts, Morgans, Adamses, Hunts, etc. – it's good enough for you and me.

I want to show you how to make as much money as these folks have made – at least on a percentage basis.

In the right market conditions, you could double your money – even make 200% or 300% – with this investment.

These kinds of gains are possible because of a glitch in the system, created by the U.S. government. I'll get into all the details in a bit, but first let me explain why long term, gold is such a safe place for your money...

We're Certain It's A No-Brainer

For me, the starting point is always the same... What is certain? What is known? What can we bank on? And is there an outstanding way to profit that nobody has gobbled up yet?

One thing we're certain of is that the Federal Reserve is going to do its best to prevent deflation (falling prices). The Fed will print money – as much as necessary – to head this thing off. In an effort to calm any fears, the government has been as explicit as possible that it would rather overshoot in this process.

The obvious result is more paper dollars out there. And the next result is that a paper dollar is worthless.

Consider this scenario... Say the supply of gold stays roughly the same. But say the supply of dollars out there increases dramatically. What should happen? It should cost more paper dollars to buy an ounce of gold. And that is exactly what's been happening. Gold rose from a low around $260 per ounce in 2001 to around $1,200 per ounce in 2014.

Chances are the Fed will be "fighting" this battle for a while. And therefore, chances are gold will be an excellent place to profit from this fight in the years to come.

So I went looking for the best way to get into gold... the way that will give us significant upside potential, but will keep our downside risk limited. It's actually hard to find...

We could own gold outright. But if we're right in this Fed scenario, we'd like a little more bang for our buck. We could buy gold futures, but they're risky – why risk losing more than our initial investment if we don't have to? The next logical choice might be shares of mining companies like Newmont Mining, but mining shares are risky, too. I had to dig deeper.

The gold secret is the super-safe way to get into gold and still have big upside potential...

The Glitch in The System

To understand this investment and how it works, we have to back up a little bit...

Before 1933, gold literally was money... gold coins could jingle in your pocket. After 1933, President Franklin D. Roosevelt actually made it illegal for U.S. citizens to own gold or gold coins, upsetting two centuries of stable money...

For most of the 200 years before 1933 (going back to England), an ounce of gold was worth $20.67. Major governments had actually committed to giving you gold for paper money if you demanded it.

FDR changed all that. A month into his new presidency, he ordered all U.S. citizens to immediately exchange all their gold for paper money. His next move was to issue an executive order raising the price of gold from $20.67 to $35, which devalued the U.S. dollar by 69%. In essence, any savings U.S. citizens had were now worth nearly 69% less, by government decree.

Americans were forced to liquidate their investment holdings. Those who failed to do so faced a 10-year jail term, a $10,000 fine, plus a penalty of twice their investment's value. This glitch in the gold system lasted 41 years. Americans were not allowed to invest in gold coins again until December 31, 1974, when President Ford finally re-legalized it.

By 2014, we needed around 1,200 paper dollars to buy an ounce of gold.

Our government wants to pull off what FDR did. It wants to squeeze out of a rough period of debt by creating a massive inflation. The massive devaluation of the dollar worked for FDR: Industrial production rose by 60%, and unemployment fell from 25% to 14% from 1933 to 1937.

Our modern-day government plans to do the same, devaluing our money to stimulate the economy. We can sit back and watch, or we can take advantage of the glitch and pocket gains of 100% or more...

The Secrets of Rare Coins

What I want to tell you about is a way to invest in rare gold coins.

Before you dismiss this idea, remember that this is an investment the most powerful and wealthy families in the world have used for generations.

But it's not just any coins I want to show you how to invest in... It's a very specific group of gold coins.

Let me explain...

Before Franklin Delano Roosevelt, there was his cousin Teddy. Teddy had a thing for coins. He passionately hated America's coins, calling them *"artistically of atrocious hideousness."*

America had become the most powerful nation on Earth. And the president felt that our most valuable coins should be a reflection of our status. So he sought out the foremost sculptor of the day, Augustus Saint-Gaudens...

"Dear Mr. President," Saint-Gaudens replied to Teddy. *"Well! Whatever I produce cannot be worse than the inanities now displayed on our coins, and we will at least have made an attempt in the right direction..."*

Though in poor health, Saint-Gaudens delivered. He designed the gallant $20 "Double Eagle" gold piece, a design that today is nearly unanimously considered the most beautiful coin of all time. It was Saint-Gaudens' last work. He died and never saw the fruits of his labor. (He also designed the $10 Indian Head gold eagle.)

The coins were minted from 1907 until 1933, when Franklin Delano Roosevelt made it illegal for individuals to own gold and melted down many of these gorgeous coins. After gold ownership was banned in 1933, private ownership of gold was not allowed in the U.S. until 1974.

The entire 1933 series of Saint-Gaudens Double Eagles was supposedly destroyed by FDR. But 10 of the coins somehow snuck out of the Mint. Over the years, nine of the 1933-series coins have been recovered and destroyed by the Secret Service.

In the late 1990s, the government seized the 10th coin in New York and made arrests. But the case fell apart, and a compromise was met. The coin would be auctioned, with the proceeds split half and half between the government and the other party. This 1933 Saint-Gaudens $20 Double Eagle sold for $7.59 million, the highest price ever paid for a coin.

Again, a 1933 Saint-Gaudens $20 gold piece would have an intrinsic value of about $1,200 in 2014, since it contains nearly an ounce of gold – yet its value was much higher.

Of course, coin enthusiasts will always pay more than meltdown value for Saint-Gaudens $20 gold pieces – as they are considered to be the most beautiful coins in the world.

We can own a piece of history, and we can own real money with real gold, for a small premium to the meltdown value.

What Kind Of Upside Potential Are We Talking About?

With modest investment in the right coins in the early 1970s, you could cash out and buy a house by 1980, and many did. – David Hall, *Collectors Universe*

Rare coins have experienced a few roaring bull markets since gold ownership became legal again. Coin prices, as measured by the CU 3000 Index (an index of the overall price movement of rare gold coins), were up 1,195% in the 1976-1980 bull market in coins. In other words, a $10,000 investment would have risen to $129,500 in value.

In the 1987-1989 bull market, coin prices (as measured by the CU 3000 Index) rose by 665%.

Coins like the Saint-Gaudens in pristine "Mint State" condition (coins graded "MS65" by the coin-grading service PCGS) were big winners.

Then in 1989, the bottom fell out. Coins were in a horrendous bear market for the next 14 years, which brought the Saint-Gaudens to ridiculous bargain levels. As you can imagine, after 14 years of misery, there were a lot of bitter people in the coin business. After 14 years of people getting burned, it reached the point where "investor" was a dirty word...

The Market That Got So Bad, the FTC Wouldn't Let It Be Called an 'Investment'

If you're contemplating investing, you should know that after the market skyrocketed to its peak in 1989, a bunch of unscrupulous operators entered the coin business, talking about coins as a can't-lose "investment," promising high returns, even guaranteeing profits, and fleecing lots of people in the process.

The Federal Trade Commission (FTC) stepped in, putting a halt to the scammers. The bottom fell out of the market. The FTC was extremely active in shutting dirty operators down in 1992 and 1993.

By 1994, just five years after their peak, coin prices were down about 80%. The bad taste in people's mouths lingered. The FTC even put out a guide to investing in coins to help protect you. Before investing in any coins of any kind, I encourage you to read it here: www.consumer.ftc. gov/articles/0135-investing-bullion-and-bullion-coins.

Our Investment Prospects

When it comes to gold coins, there are three types...

Common gold coins are called "**bullion coins**" because a one-ounce gold bullion coin generally sells at about the same price (or at a small premium to) an ounce of gold. Famous bullion coins include South African Krugerrands and Canadian Maple Leafs.

Rare gold coins are called "**numismatic coins**." These coins, trade based on their rarity, scarcity, and collector demand. Again... in late 2014, the price of gold was near $1,200. But a rare and highly prized one-ounce gold coin could easily fetch tens of thousands of dollars.

Then there is a third type of gold coin... The "**hybrid coin**," we call it. And this is what I like. These coins have characteristics of both of the types above, but they're not really either. The typical Saint-Gaudens is a prime example of the hybrid.

Where to Buy

The $20 Saint-Gaudens is one of the world's most famous coins. Some argue it's the most beautiful U.S. coin ever made. The coin was difficult to mint as it has high-relief designs, which were problematic for production.

Once the coin was produced, it didn't see a lot of circulation at the time of issue, as it was used mostly for international trade and interbank payments. Consequently, most survivors are in lower-grade uncirculated condition (known as "Commercial Uncs" in the trade).

Saint-Gaudens dating from 1924-1928, for example, have a high collectible value, yet they are easy to buy and sell. Like bullion coins, there are enough of them to go around, plus they contain a little less than an ounce of gold (0.87 of an ounce).

Depending on the vintages, the coins are in good supply – coin dealers use the term "common dates" for those. Common dates include 1904, 1908, and 1924.

When buying these coins, you should consider the vintage rarity and the condition of the coin as graded by a professional grading service. I recommend you stick with coins with mint states (MS) between MS-63 and MS-65.

"MS" stands for "mint state," and 65 is the grade, or how closely the coin resembles its "perfect" condition when newly struck. These coins have few blemishes and as such have more collectible value.

Graded coins are packed in a sealed plastic holder meant to protect and authenticate the coin. So be sure you buy this sort of coin. It's usually easiest to do so from reputable sellers.

One of the keys to buying these hybrid coins is to buy them when the ratio to gold bullion prices is low. In 2012, the MS-65 Saint-Gaudens traded at a 40% premium to gold. That was one of the lowest valuations in 50 years. Lower-rated coins like the MS-63 traded at just 25% premiums to bullion value. That was also one of the lowest prices relative to gold in history.

I recommend you buy the MS-65 Saint-Gaudens when they trade for record-low valuations, like they did in 1986. That year, the MS-65s traded at 800% over the melt value of gold, when gold had its extreme run up. At a premium like that – or even just half that – you could easily make 35%-45% on these collector classics.

I wouldn't put more than 5% of your investment in these coins.

Remember, you can always check the live price of gold at www.bulliondirect.com.

— 4 —

A Low-Capital, High-Return Real Estate Investment: Tax Liens

Every year, local municipalities require taxes to be paid on properties – the taxes are for sewer, trash, and police. But every year for many reasons, people don't pay those taxes.

Since the city needs that money, it sells "tax-liens" against the homes of the tax evader. The government regularly auctions these tax liens on the courthouse steps (at least once a year and as often as monthly).

The beauty of this opportunity is the tax collector charges steep penalties and fees for late payments. In 2014, Texas charged 25%, Georgia 20%, Illinois 18%, and Florida 18%. When the property owner pays his taxes and fees, you get your capital back, plus extra fees.

The best part is 95% of these liens are paid off by the property owners within a couple years (sometimes, within months). *Thus, you can easily and safely earn 12%-15% a year on your money by investing in these liens.*

Worst case is the taxes and penalties aren't paid, and the property has to go to auction. Once it's sold, you get your money back. Because taxes are usually only 1%-2% of the value of the property, it's almost impossible to get back less than your initial investment from the proceeds of a foreclosure sale. In some states, you can actually get the property for just the cost of the taxes and penalties you've already paid. But this is rare.

This is how it works: I know of one lot in Florida that was given to the owner as part of a divorce settlement. It wasn't his regular home, and he couldn't be bothered with paying the taxes. So you could bid on the lien at auction.

Within two years of that date, you either pursue a foreclosure on the property – worth close to $200,000 – or you receive a payment of $2,000 plus 15% a year in interest from the owner. Either way, you're sure to get your money back within a year or two. And as I mentioned, most liens are redeemed long before a foreclosure proceeding.

How can you earn 12%-15%? First, find out if your state is a tax-lien state. Not every state handles back taxes through lien auctions. Here's a list of tax-lien states: Alabama, Arizona, Colorado, Florida, Illinois, Indiana, Iowa, Kentucky, Maryland, Michigan, Missouri, Montana, Nebraska, New Jersey, North Dakota, South Carolina, South Dakota, Vermont, West Virginia, and Wyoming.

State law determines the interest, penalties, and fees the owner has to pay to redeem the lien from you, the investor. In some states, the owner pays a minimum penalty (5% in Florida) no matter when the lien is redeemed – even if it's two days later.

If you live in or want to invest in one of the tax-lien states, call the courthouse and find out what time of year and what type of auction it holds. In some states, the auction bidding is for interest rates the investor will receive.

For example, in Florida, bidding starts at 18% and goes down to 0.25%. In other states, potential buyers bid on the nominal amount of taxes owed and go up, but with an interest rate attached to the final balance. In some states, it's a mix of the two. These are local details the court employees can explain.

That's why I love to visit the courthouse and talk with the people in the property departments. They have books and records easily available, although not always understandable. And by hanging out in person in the offices, your questions are quickly answered. A few counties now have online records you can peruse from home, as well.

Once you've picked out the properties, visit all the properties you're interested in bidding on at least a week or two before the auction. Be sure to set the limit you're willing to accept. Once the auction happens, you'll easily lock up returns of 12% on your money and in amounts as little as $500-$1,000. Anyone can invest.

One more thing, I also recommend buying a few books on tax liens a couple months before the auction so you know exactly what to expect. One book I've found useful is *Profit by Investing in Real Estate Tax Liens* by Larry Loftis. He explains the differences between deeds and liens and the various types of bidding across the country.

— 5 —

Dividends Don't Lie

"Dividends don't lie."

It's one of my favorite Wall Street sayings. Accountants can mess with a company's books in all kinds of ways, but they can't fake a cash payment. And if a company can pay a dividend, it's almost always making money.

We've seen Merrill Lynch's Henry Blodgett touting stocks he privately dismissed as crap. (Actually, his term was worse.) We've seen Bernie Madoff mailing out phony account statements to hoodwink $18 billion from clients... and corrupt lenders building a multibillion-dollar firm based on worthless "no-doc," "liars" loans.

That's just a sample. There's nothing new about accounting fraud.

The irony is, protecting yourself from these convoluted shell games is simple... **Demand a cash dividend from your investments**. It's hard to pay shareholders year after year if you're cooking the books.

A dividend is money a company pays its shareholders. Every quarter, the company counts its earnings and pays out some portion to its owners (the shareholders). Essentially, it's your cut of the profits. And it's cold hard cash.

> **❝ Accountants can mess with a company's books in all kinds of ways, but they can't fake a cash payment. And if a company can pay a dividend, it's almost always making money. ❞**

Focusing on dividend-paying stocks is one of the great secrets to building wealth. These stocks should form the cornerstone of your portfolio.

Most investors dismiss dividends. Some alleged "professional stock pickers" refuse to even consider companies that pay a dividend. After all, they argue, the company should be plowing all the money back into the growing business. If the company reinvests the cash in itself, it can grow even bigger, right? Wrong.

Here's what you miss if your sole focus is on capital gains: **Nearly half of your total long-term returns from investing in stocks come from dividends**.

Sure, you want the company to use some of its earnings to grow. But you also want to get your money back along the way. One of the most important rules to investing (along with asset allocation and position sizing) is defining your exit strategy.

How will you get your money back? When you invest in a small startup, you're happy to let your money grow as the business grows. But what happens when the growth slows? Do you sell the stock?

I've Never Bought or Sold a Single Share of Stock. How Do I Start?

At Stansberry Research, we don't recommend or endorse specific brokerages. But I can tell you (and I get no compensation for saying this) I use Fidelity, Schwab, and TD Ameritrade.

I love Fidelity's research functions. But I prefer TD's option-trading functions. Schwab usually offers a little more interest on your cash than the other two.

My assistant uses ShareBuilder. I love her choice, too.

ShareBuilder is a brokerage system created specifically for beginning investors. You can set up an automatic investment plan for only $4 per trade. And if you do more than three transactions a month, you can lower it to $1-$2 per trade. Also, many mutual funds (pooled money invested together in agreed-upon things) don't charge any fees either.

The trade execution is easy. After logging into your account, click on the "Trade" tab, and enter the information – whether you're buying or selling, the stock symbol, number of shares being purchased, order type, and how you're paying.

It only takes a couple minutes to buy or sell stock. ShareBuilder is a simple place to start.

Not if it's still a good business. You don't want to lose out on reaping the success of the business as it evolves into a larger, steadier company. Dividends are a simple way to pay back owners who've invested in the business. By keeping some of the money and paying the rest to shareholders, dividend-paying companies can continue to grow while rewarding shareholders at the same time.

I've seen Wall Street lie and cheat for decades... from Blodgett to Madoff. The simplest, most effective way to fight back is to demand a dividend. Companies that pay dividends are sending you real money – and these dividends don't lie.

$10,000 into $1 million:
The Power of Compounding

In the "Essentials of Asset Allocation" chapter, we discussed one of the great secrets of investment success... one few people ever consider.

Again, asset allocation is how you divvy up your wealth among cash, fixed-income, stocks, and precious metals (what we call "Chaos Hedges"). It's the key to your investment success.

Most folks waste time and money getting burned in IPOs, hot commodities, and risky growth stocks. The rich and sophisticated investor focuses on building an intelligent mix of assets. He focuses on building ironclad wealth vehicles that can sail through any kind of environment.

Now we'll cover another vital aspect of building your wealth...

This cornerstone of investing is the No. 1 strategy for retiring wealthy. The three secrets that make up this strategy are so critical to your investing success that unless you understand them and start applying them today, you'll never get wealthy.

> *66 The rich and sophisticated investor focuses on building an intelligent mix of assets. He focuses on building ironclad wealth vehicles that can sail through any kind of environment. 99*

Embrace this strategy, and you'll be on the road to riches. Ignore it and get lazy about using its power... and you'll never have a chance for the lifestyle you want.

But before I go on, let me warn you: You're probably not interested in what I have to say. It's not some gold stock that's going to the moon. It's not sexy. It's not a quick fix.

Most people just want the quick fix: "Give me the pick, Doc. I wanna make money." Some people actually think retiring wealthy is all about stock picks. But we don't...

We believe in sharing time-tested ideas for wealth, health, and good living. This secret hits home for me personally. Two people close to me got wealthy by following the three simple rules that make up this strategy.

The ideas became apparent to me when I realized my dad learned the secrets unwittingly...

Secret No. 1: The Power of Compound Returns

My dad was a fantastic doctor, bright and kind with his patients. But he was a terrible investor. I watched him get greedy (like most people do). I watched him let his losers run and cut his profits off early (like most people do). Occasionally, he'd buy off some tip at a cocktail party (like most people do)...

Most of the time, he ignored earnings, income, cash flow, or anything when investing in his brokerage account. It was usually a guess or a hot tip for that account... But luckily, his brokerage account was just for play money, and he rarely paid a lot of attention to it.

His retirement savings were a different thing. With that money, he took advantage of the one thing that can make anyone wealthy. You can do it, too. One of my sisters did...

She lives in Bozeman, Montana with her husband and two sons. Their house offers a beautiful view of the mountains. They have the time and money to do most anything they want. I shared secret No. 1 with her about 25 years ago... and she credits me with showing her the way to becoming a millionaire.

The secret is not hard to grasp. You just have to understand a few simple principles. But as you might imagine, it does take some time and a little effort on your part.

And it starts with one simple idea... **compound returns**.

If you're not sure what compound returns are, don't worry. It's easy to understand and a powerful tool when you put it to work.

Simply stated, compound returns are money you make off the money you make. And the more money you make, the more money your money makes off the money your money makes. I hope you're smiling, but here's what happens...

Imagine you're 40 years old, have a $10,000 investment account, and subscribe to my *Retirement Millionaire* letter. In one year, our portfolio's conservative blend of assets returned a fantastic 18%. If you kept reading year after year and kept making consistent 18% annual returns, what would happen to your portfolio by the time you retire at the age of 68?

You'd have earned a million dollars.

The numbers are simple: If you start investing with $10,000, you'll have about $11,800 (not including taxes or fees) at the end of the first year. You made $1,800 on your initial investment.

But in your second year... you're not starting over at $10,000. The $1,800 you earned in the first year will be making money for you, too.

So assuming gains of 18%, you'll have earned another $1,800 on your original capital plus another $324 on the profits from the previous year's $1,800.

You're not just multiplying $1,800 times 25 years. (That only gives you $45,000.) Where does the other $903,000 come from? That's the secret.

The money starts making money on top of itself – your money is compounding.

The money you make in the first year, in this case $1,800, starts making money in the second year, third year, and so on... It continues this way for every stream of money you compound. So the $1,800 you make in your second year also makes $324 in the third (18% of $1,800).

Take a look at the table below and you'll see that by the end of your third year, you'll have $16,430.

Earning 18% Interest on $10,000

	Year 1	Year 2	Year 3
Total Investment	$10,000	$11, 800	$13,924
18% Interest Earned	$1,800	$2,124	$2,506
Year-End Amount	$11,800	$13,924	$16,430

And the money just keeps building. Take a look at the next chart. You can see how much money you'll have at the end of each year. By age 68 (28 years of compounding), it totals nearly $1 million. And if you wait another couple years, until age 70, the compounding effect starts to explode. At that point, you have almost $1.5 million.

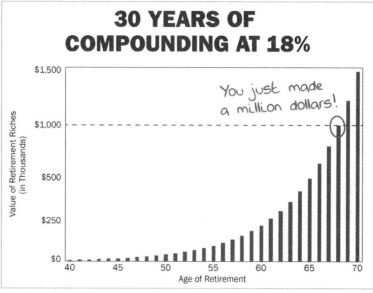

You can see why this secret is so powerful. By plowing your earnings back into your portfolio, you can get your money working for itself and amass a fortune from your initial investments.

But it's not the whole story of how my sister and father became wealthy...

You Can Be A Millionaire Even Sooner

It turns out, the real secret to creating wealth through compounding your profits is to keep adding money year after year...

For example, look at the next chart. You can see how starting with $10,000 and then just putting $5,000 a year for the next 20 years makes a person a millionaire by age 60. That's nearly eight years sooner than the other plan, where you just put in $10,000 at the beginning and waited.

> ❝ *The real secret to creating wealth through compounding your profits is to keep adding money year after year...* ❞

If you continued for just another five years (25 years total), you'd be a multimillionaire. If you maintained this strategy until age 68, *you'd be worth nearly $4 million* ($3.862 million to be exact).

Think about this for a minute. You start at age 40, earning 18% (about what I help my readers earn annually) in a balanced and safe mix of securities. You begin with $10,000 and add a little bit more each year ($5,000). And voila... You're a millionaire at 60.

In the case of my father, he started tucking a little bit of money away each year in the retirement plan his university offered for professors. He wasn't exactly sure how much he was squirreling away (and I couldn't find the records). But it wasn't as much as the initial amount he used to open the account.

My sister applied these same principles in her first job. And she made sure that for every job and raise thereafter, she added a little bit more to the retirement kitty.

Secret No. 2: Start Younger and Get Even Richer

But for her, it was much easier. She started a lot younger and didn't have to put much in (she didn't have much to put in). The chart shows what happens if, like my sister, you start at age 20 with only $2,000 and put in just $300 a year after that... You become a millionaire by age 54.

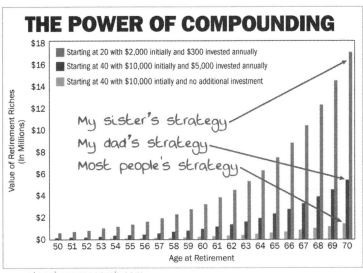

THE POWER OF COMPOUNDING

- Starting at 20 with $2,000 initially and $300 invested annually
- Starting at 40 with $10,000 initially and $5,000 invested annually
- Starting at 40 with $10,000 intially and no additional investment

My sister's strategy
My dad's strategy
Most people's strategy

Value of Retirement Riches (In Millions): $18, $16, $14, $12, $10, $8, $6, $4, $2, $0

Age at Retirement: 50 51 52 53 54 55 56 57 58 59 60 61 62 63 64 65 66 67 68 69 70

At that point, you've put in a total of $10,200 – and earned $990,000 on the original investments. And if you wait five more years, you become a multimillionaire at age 59 – a spectacular return on an $11,700 investment plan. (That's 17,000% if you're scoring at home.)

Secret No. 3: Don't Tell Wall Street About This One

Most people don't know this, but a corporate "loophole" lets you collect $5,000... $10,000... even $30,000 or more in extra income... starting with very little cash.

Some U.S. companies will pay you dividends that grow to five – or even 10 times – bigger than normal over a period of time.

I'm talking about programs that allow you to reinvest dividends and compound your investment in some of the strongest businesses in America.

The key to safely building your wealth is to create a safe and growing stream of investment income. The best way to do that is to invest in a set of American businesses that have reliably distributed income to investors for many decades. In some cases, these investments have been paying out uninterrupted yearly income for decades. **These investments are my favorite super-safe places in the world to put your money**.

However, our Dividend Boost strategy is about more than simply buying stocks with solid dividends. The critical step is to sign up for a program that allows you to funnel that cash into more shares of the company... and that allows you to do it cheaply, avoiding big fees and commissions.

> **66 Most people don't know this, but a corporate 'loophole' lets you collect $5,000... $10,000... even $30,000 or more in extra income... starting with very little cash. 99**

Following this program, I can see investors getting at least 35% of dividend income on their initial cost (so-called yield to cost). And I can see their initial investment easily doubling in 10 years. Put in $1,000 today in this portfolio earning a 3.1% dividend... and you could have $2,000 paying you 17% a year in 10 years... a great start to retirement.

The "Boost" part of our plan is based on a simple – but critical – principle of compounding your income.

It works like this... When the company mails you a dividend check... instead of using it to buy that new lawnmower or take your spouse out to dinner... you simply buy more shares of the company's stock...

That's it... As simple as that sounds, it's an incredibly powerful tool when you put it to work. Let me show you just how powerful...

Let's say you find a stock you like that pays a safe, rich 5% yield. (We'll use round numbers to keep the math in this example simple.) You buy 100 shares for $10 each ($1,000). We'll assume the share price and the dividend stay fixed at $10 and 5%, respectively.

At the end of the first year, you'll receive $50 in dividends (5%). You take that payment and buy five more shares... This increases your position to 105 shares. In Year 2, you earn $52.50 in dividends. You reinvest this, too, adding another 5.25 shares to your position.

You now own 110.25 shares. Repeat this process for 12 years and in the 12th year, you'll make $85.52 in dividends. That's an 8.6% dividend yield off your initial $1,000 investment.

Year	Share Price	Shares	Dividend	New Shares	Total Shares	Yield on Cost
1	$10	100	$50.00	5	105	5.0%
2	$10	105	$52.50	5.25	110.25	5.3%
3	$10	110.25	$55.13	5.51	115.76	5.5%
4	$10	115.76	$57.88	5.79	121.55	5.8%
5	$10	121.55	$60.78	6.08	127.63	6.1%
6	$10	127.63	$63.81	6.38	134.01	6.2%
7	$10	134.01	$67.00	6.70	140.71	6.7%
8	$10	140.71	$70.36	7.04	147.75	7.0%
9	$10	147.75	$73.87	7.39	155.13	7.4%
10	$10	155.13	$77.57	7.76	162.89	7.8%
11	$10	162.89	$81.44	8.14	171.03	8.1%
12	$10	171.03	$85.52	8.56	179.59	8.6%

This is what accountants call "compound" investing. Your dividends turn into stock. This extra stock then produces dividends of its own. That dividend becomes stock, and so on... **Compounding interest or dividends is one of the strongest ways to build wealth in finance**. Warren Buffett built his fortune by compounding dividends.

But we're not finished yet... *The real magic in compounding happens when you pick stocks that pay larger dividends each year.*

Imagine a dividend that grows 10% each year. Your position compounds at twice the speed. The 5% dividend yield turns into a 34.2% "yield on-cost" (as it's called) in the 12th year.

Here's how...

Year	Share Price	Shares	Dividend	New Shares	Total Shares	Yield
1	$10	100	$50.00	5	105	5.0%
2	$10	105	$57.75	5.78	110.78	5.8%
3	$10	110.78	$67.57	6.76	117.53	6.8%
4	$10	117.53	$78.75	7.87	125.41	7.9%
5	$10	125.41	$91.55	9.15	134.56	9.2%
6	$10	134.56	$108.99	10.90	145.46	10.9%
7	$10	145.46	$129.46	12.95	158.41	123.0%
8	$10	158.41	$153.65	15.37	173.77	15.4%
9	$10	173.77	$191.15	19.12	192.89	19.1%
10	$10	192.89	$231.47	23.15	216.03	23.2%
11	$10	216.03	$280.84	28.09	244.12	28.1%
12	$10	244.12	$341.77	34.18	278.30	34.2%

Imagine if you could find a company that increases its dividend by 20% a year. *You'd double your money in Year 8*. And your yield on-cost would be more than 39%.

Compounding to Retirement Wealth

Anyone can compound returns with just a small stash of money... And adding a little more each year (or month) will get you there even quicker. That's secret No. 1.

> 66 *Starting a compounding program could turn out to be the greatest money decision you ever make.* 99

If you're young or know someone who is, please share the story of my sister and how she started with little, added some money every year, and saw it grow to millions of dollars by the time she turned 40.

Secret No. 2 is probably the most powerful. It should be shared among you and your family. If you have children or grandchildren, they need to know about savings and investing.

I know some readers out there will say, "Great idea, Doc... But I don't have 25 years to compound. I need more money NOW." If you're in this position, focus on making regular income if you can still work. And if you're short on retirement money and you are in your 70s or 80s, the biggest key to an enjoyable life is to find a way to live a rich life on the cheap.

I hope you're also intrigued by the power of dividend growth (our third secret). If we invest in solid shareholder-friendly companies, we'll make money over time. And if the companies increase their dividends and we plow those back into the company (without paying taxes early), we've got ourselves a moneymaking machine.

Starting a compounding program could turn out to be the greatest money decision you ever make.

— 6 —

Keep It Simple: How We Pick Stocks for *Retirement Millionaire*

It sounds crazy, but you can know *too much* about a stock.

This is hard for people to accept in our "Knowledge Is Power" society... where the Internet puts thousands of pages of information, data, and news about a company in front of us with a few clicks of a computer mouse.

People like to believe that with enough information, they can make a perfect decision... By adding fact after fact, data point upon data point, their understanding becomes increasingly clear. But it doesn't always work like that.

In the field of behavioral finance – essentially the study of how people make decisions surrounding money – studies have repeatedly shown that humans usually gather too much information... and sometimes get stuck in the process.

Picking a stock, bond, or mutual fund isn't an exact science. Often, it means letting some facts and data go.

Don't misunderstand... I'm not saying you should dive into the market half-cocked, throwing money at every hunch and tip that comes along.

It's true: You need to understand the companies you buy.

I'm saying you shouldn't spend too much time collecting data. People can easily be paralyzed with indecision. At a certain point, investors can get lost in a sea of ratios and statistics that don't add to their understanding of the investment.

For example, you could have a stock that looks expensive based on the past 12 months of earnings, but looks like a steal based on "consensus Wall Street estimates of *future* 12-month earnings." What are those conflicting signals telling us? Which are important? What can we ignore?

Honestly, what does something like the debt-to-equity ratio tell you that net tangible assets growing over three years doesn't tell you? Is that distinction vital to buying the stock? Heck no.

That's why when I analyze stocks, I stick with a time-tested and *simple* strategy...

At *Retirement Millionaire*, we simply search out companies with long histories of growing or stable sales. If a company has endured lean years in the past and has come out strong, it can probably do it again in the future.

We want to see healthy cash flows because they tell us the company is making cold, hard cash and not just reporting accounting tricks with its earnings (like with Enron).

And we want to see a clear pattern of rewarding shareholders with dividends and share buybacks. Dividends compounded over time are the most consistent avenues to big returns. "Dividends don't lie." Companies can't fake a cash payment like they can manipulate other items on the balance sheet. If you're going to cut a dividend check, you have to have the cash to cover it. And a rising dividend is like a magnet drawing shares higher.

That's the heart of picking good stocks. And it has led us to consistent gains.

— 7 —

The 'Loss Aversion' Trap

> **❝ If you're not aware of loss aversion, you'll lose thousands of dollars before you know it. ❞**

I was shocked when my friend showed me her brokerage account.

Sue and I went to medical school together, and she was top in the class (behind me). Her academic record was spotless and impressive. She trained at Johns Hopkins University – probably the most prestigious place you can study. She's a rare – almost unheard of – triple-boarded physician (medicine, hematology, and oncology).

And yet her brokerage account showed $40,000 in losses. And they had been there for a long time, too.

You might think this is nothing for a doctor – especially one as accomplished as Sue. But she's young (early 30s) and still paying off her medical school debt. This was at least half of her savings. (Her face made me suspect it was even more than half.)

The losses highlight one of the most common mistakes (and among the hardest lessons to learn) of investing. They depicted perfectly what behavior finance terms "loss aversion." And if you want to be a successful investor, you must pay attention to this behavior.

Loss aversion is a well-known phenomenon. It's been studied and reported in financial and economic literature. Yet it trips up educated and ignorant people alike. If you're not aware of loss aversion, you'll lose thousands of dollars before you know it.

That's why I want to share Sue's story and teach you how to avoid the greatest trap there is in investing. It takes practice and discipline to protect yourself from loss aversion. But once you learn a few techniques, managing losses will be easy.

As long as you don't fall for the insidious feelings that losses bring, your portfolio will be protected... and you'll sleep well at night.

I want to talk about the nature of Sue's mistakes... why they're so common... and how to keep from falling prey to them. Learning how to train yourself to resist this impulse is far more important to your investing success than simply locking onto another stock recommendation. Here's more of Sue's story...

Bad or Good Advice... It Doesn't Matter

Dr. Sue had been building a savings nest egg, just like everyone should – about eight to 12 months of living expenses. In case an emergency or job issue came up, she'd have the resources to support herself if needed. After graduating from medical school more than $100,000 in debt and earning only the low pay of residency and fellowships, she was slowly building the nest...

Meanwhile, her parents had semi-retired. They had been relatively successful investing in the bull markets of the 2000s and were sharing some of their trading ideas with their kids. It worked well... until the downturn and collapse in 2008.

Like many people, they'd invested and bet on the China boom. A few conversations over dinner convinced me the family was scoring big on micro-cap Chinese businesses. And they had been doing it for a decade...

Their daughter had followed along. With a tip from brother or dad, she'd made some good money along the way. Her savings (and investments) were growing – nearly $80,000. Her debt was declining. She was starting to feel flush and carefree. Investing seemed easy.

But Sue failed to do one critical thing as she kept racking up gains. She failed to protect her gains and prepare to prevent any losses.

When I initially looked at her portfolio stuffed with Chinese-named stocks, she was too embarrassed to even talk about it. "Just take care of it... I don't care anymore," she kept repeating. "Help me get something different."

Her portfolio was a mess. Position after position showed startling percentage losses – 80%, 93%, 95%, and so on. At one point, she looked like she would cry. We closed up the computer and went on to some other fluffy conversation.

Weeks later, she was finally able to sit with me. We explored the issues she faced. The losses should be booked – if only for the tax losses they offered at year-end. And the psychological issues could be discussed and conquered, too.

Loss aversion drives people to simply look away from and avoid booking losses. The impulse is so strong, people are more prone to sell winners early and let their losers run – the exact opposite of what you should do as an investor.

It was first described in the 1970s by psychologists Daniel Kahneman and Amos Tversky. The pair discovered how people feel more pain taking losses than pleasure booking similar-sized gains. Loss aversion is related to a couple other behavioral finance concepts as well – **endowment effect** and **disposition effect**.

Researchers know that once we buy something, we value it more. It's as if the decision adds value to the object, above and beyond its worth the moment before we owned it. This is true not just with stocks but with other things as well – clothes, art, cars, etc...

> **❝ Sue failed to do one critical thing as she kept racking up gains. She failed to protect her gains and prepare to prevent any losses. ❞**

That makes it twice as hard to sell something once we own it, especially if it turns into a loser. This is the endowment effect – we buy it, and it gains more value by keeping it.

> **66** *Loss aversion is easily avoided by using stops and position sizing rules.* **99**

The disposition effect is what keeps people from selling, even when they know they should. People "feel" that by avoiding the act of disposing of the investment (or thing), everything's still OK.

By not selling, we don't have to realize the loss – it's as if paper losses aren't real. Dispose of the stock, and the pain and bad feelings come flooding in. The brain doesn't like those feelings. In Sue's case, it made her physically ill to even think about selling the stocks...

Nearly as harmful... Sue never stuck with position-sizing strategies, either. When her China stocks boomed to 10% or 15% of her portfolio, she never trimmed them back to rebalance the portfolio. Instead of selling the extra 5% or 10% and putting it into undervalued investments, she let them ride. So when they crashed, the losses capsized her entire portfolio.

What can you do to avoid these psychological traps? It's simple... **loss aversion is easily avoided by using stops and position sizing rules**.

In *Retirement Millionaire*, we regularly recommend you use stops of 20%-25%. On most picks, we suggest "trailing" stops... As the prices run up from, say, $50 to $80, you'll sell if the stock drops back down to $64 (20% stop) or $60 (25% stop).

Had Sue stuck to these rules, she'd easily have $30,000-$40,000 more to her name – enough to pay off her remaining medical-school debt. Instead, she let all her gains turn to losses.

Of course, you can also consider simple stops based on your initial entry price. If you bought a stock at $50 a share, you'd sell if the price ever got down to $40 (20%) or $37.50 (25%). I generally prefer the trailing stop. But until the price moves up, the two are identical numbers.

Similarly, there's position sizing. Never put more than 4%-5% in any one investment (single stocks and bonds). The strategy of trailing stops and smart position sizing ensures you never lose more than about 1% of your portfolio on any one investment. (Using a 5% position-size limit with a 20% stop – or a 4% size limit with a 25% stop – works out to about 1% of your portfolio at risk.)

Occasionally, we'll increase the at-risk amount to 10% of your portfolio when we recommend a fund because of the diversification within the mutual fund. When that happens, I sometimes tighten my stop to 15% or so...

I prefer to use Yahoo Finance's e-mail price-alert function – which sends me an e-mail when a stock hits a certain point. But most brokers offer similar functionality on their trading platforms to alert you to a price point.

Whatever you do, I encourage you to **avoid entering the order with your broker**. The orders are "sell on a stop" orders and trigger market orders... which alert the broker to your plans. It's like playing poker, but telling everyone your hand. The effect is probably minimal at the size most of us transact, but I still avoid it.

Avoiding losses is impossible to do... even the best investors have stories to tell about losses. The key is to learn how to limit the losses and avoid the paralysis of loss aversion. Recognizing that it's hard to take losses means setting up a plan for when losses appear.

Loss aversion led Sue to give up more than $50,000 of her hard-earned savings because she fell for the classic problem we all face as investors.

The easiest way to protect yourself is to stick to our trading rules, no matter what. I can count on one hand the exceptions I've made to stop losses. And I'd say that in four out of those five cases, I lost thousands of dollars myself. Don't let it happen to you.

— 8 —

The Facts About Gold (Without the Hype)

In March 2012, the greatest investor on Earth attacked one of the financial world's sacred cows... and an army of bloggers and self-appointed pundits flooded the Internet with condemnation.

Warren Buffett, as you probably know, is an investing legend. He's one of the few people to amass a billion-dollar fortune mostly on his ability to invest in the stock market.

Every year, he publishes an annual letter to shareholders of his holding company, Berkshire Hathaway. It's one of the most widely read commentaries in the financial world.

In his 2011 letter, he included a page-long takedown of one of the most emotionally charged investment choices people make – holding gold.

He ridiculed the idea of owning gold... comparing its buyers to the ignorant folks who were wiped out during the legendary 17th century tulip mania in the Netherlands...

> What motivates most gold purchasers is their belief that the ranks of the fearful will grow. During the past decade, that belief has proved correct. Beyond that, the rising price has on its own generated additional buying enthusiasm, attracting purchasers who see the rise as validating an investment thesis. As "bandwagon" investors join any party, they create their own truth – for a while.

Less than a day after Buffett's critical comments, the Internet "lit up" with rebuttals. Gold lovers (sometimes labeled "gold bugs") called Buffett a moron, a government shill, and a senile old man.

But Buffett had a good point. What I'm about to say might anger you... But hear me out. I like to focus on the facts, not the hype.

Knowing the facts about gold will make a huge difference in your wealth over the long term... And if you own gold, it will help you understand when it's time to hold and when you should diversify into other investments.

If you own gold for one common reason, I'll explain why you're mistaken. And I'll show you a better way to hedge against this very real risk.

Why People Love Gold

For thousands of years, mankind has used gold as a medium of exchange... as money. It was a good choice for a lot of reasons...

First is **scarcity**. The world has only a finite amount of gold, and you can't create any more. All the gold ever mined – about 170,000 metric tons – would fit onto a football field piled to about 6.5 feet high.

In addition, **it doesn't corrode or deteriorate**, **it's easily divisible**, and... relative to other valuable assets you find in the natural world... **it's portable**.

Even after the advent of modern currency, the U.S. government initially "backed" its currency with gold. (The monetary unit represented a claim on some fraction of the government's gold stash.)

Today, that's no longer the case... Our money is not backed by gold. Regardless, our affinity for gold continues.

From early 2001 to late 2012, gold marched from $260 to nearly $1,800... an almost unheard of long-term bull market for any asset. But much of that enthusiasm was built on...

Two Gold Myths You Need to Reject

The fundamental reason people said to buy gold was that it is a great form of savings... that gold is the ultimate "store of value." That belief flows from all the reasons gold was used as money... There's a finite amount, it doesn't deteriorate, etc.

But here's what's wrong with that thinking...

If you own one ounce of gold, no one can tell you whether it will retain its value over time. It depends on the price of gold relative to other things.

You see, gold's fundamental problem is that it is an "unproductive asset." It creates nothing, generates nothing, and does nothing that increases the value of your investment in it.

I don't deny that building up a large supply of gold over your lifetime will probably result in a valuable stockpile. But will it be worth more – or even as much – as you sacrificed to accumulate it? No one can answer that question.

Gold's value depends on someone else paying more for your ounce than you did. As Buffett says, if you want to make money, you're depending on the "belief that others will desire it even more avidly in the future." That means someone else has to pay more for it. Some call it the "greater fool" theory of investing.

On the other hand, land can be farmed and buildings can be rented. An equity stake in a company (stock) can grow more valuable as the company sells more goods. And it can generate cash in the form of a dividend. As a result, you can build financial models assessing things like its present value and future cash flow... giving you the tools to make reasonable estimates of that asset's future value.

Gold does none of that. So you have no way to know its value other than the price you pay.

The other myth that leads people to gold is the belief that the precious metal can hedge you from inflation. (This is the idea that as the price of everyday goods rises, the price of gold increases in lockstep.) This makes some intuitive sense. But in reality, it doesn't work that way...

The next chart shows that over 17 years of rising inflation (1987-2004), gold prices went nowhere...

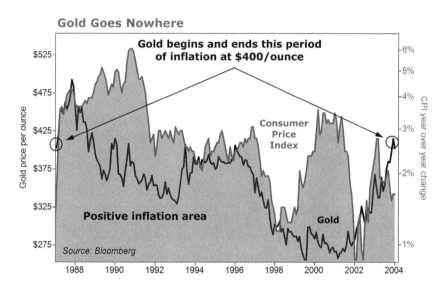

Over my investing lifetime, the only great time to own gold has been when real returns on fixed-income securities turned negative. So for example, imagine investing in a five-year U.S. Treasury note paying interest twice a year. When inflation is more than interest rates on these U.S. Treasurys, gold is a great asset to own.

The next chart shows that. When the real return on a five-year U.S. Treasury note (the interest rate minus the consumer price index) dips and stays in the negative return area, gold thrives.

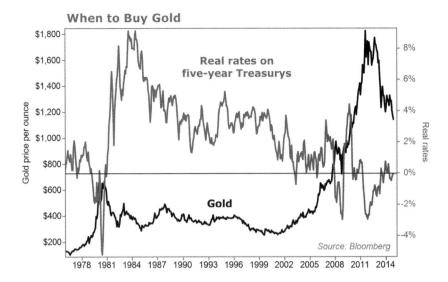

When to Buy Gold

Source: Bloomberg

But that situation is uncommon. As of 2014, it had only happened 16% of the time, since records began. Most of the time, when the five-year Treasury note has paid more than inflation, gold has done nothing.

Gold as a Chaos Hedge

At this point, I'm sure many of you are wondering, "So, Doc, if gold is an unproductive asset... a weak savings vehicle... and a poor inflation hedge... *why do you recommend it?*"

In history, gold has outperformed many other asset classes during times of great economic and political stress. The following chart shows how gold outperformed stocks when the dot-com bubble burst and mortgage crisis sparked a global contraction...

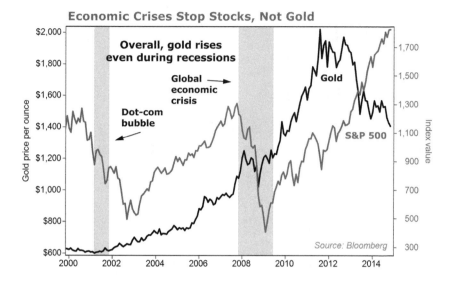

We keep an asset category in the *Retirement Millionaire* portfolio called "Chaos Hedges." This is where we hold investments that will protect us during unusual times. Depending on an individual's circumstances... a person should limit this category to no more than 15% of his assets (and usually much less).

For example, if violence broke out in the streets and the paper currency of the U.S. government was worthless, you'd need to barter with gold or silver coins to get what you wanted. (I don't believe this is likely... but you should always have an emergency plan.)

In *Retirement Millionaire*, we prefer silver coins because the everyday things you'd need to buy (food and gas) would be closer in price to an ounce of silver than an ounce of gold. But you could also a trade on the SPDR Gold Trust Fund (NYSE: GLD), which holds real gold bullion.

You can also own securities called Treasury Inflation-Protected Securities (TIPS). They're issued by the U.S. government.

The Better Inflation Defense

The best way to secure your retirement is to regularly invest in what Warren Buffett prefers: "productive assets." These include everything from farms to businesses.

If you're looking for a good inflation hedge... these productive assets are an excellent choice. Their power to protect against inflation comes from their ability to grow your investment faster than inflation erodes it.

Look for businesses (stocks) that hold pricing power and have brand loyalty. If inflation kicks in, the ability to raise prices right along with input costs helps maintain our wealth. And businesses with loyal customers can usually pass along those price hikes without much loss in volume. That means steady profit margins and more wealth.

> **66 *Investing in blue chips is a winner's game.* 99**

Take a company like McDonald's (NYSE: MCD). The demand for fast food will continue, and Mickey D's will surely be slinging burgers in another five or 10 years. The company regularly responds to consumer demand.

For example, it placated health-conscious parents by offering apples and milk in its Happy Meals. And it sells lattes that compete with local coffeehouses. Some retired friends of mine confess to a daily trip to "their coffee shop" – the one under the Golden Arches.

If prices go up along with inflation, you can be sure MCD will retain its loyal patrons and its profits like it has for the last 50 years. Companies like MCD are perfect inflation defenses.

Many of the blue-chip companies we hold in *Retirement Millionaire* do the same thing. They have quality goods or services, loyal customers, and don't need to spend much to keep making money. Over time, they'll build our wealth and protect us from any possible inflationary pressures.

Investing in blue chips is a winner's game. Names like Johnson & Johnson, Chevron, Wal-Mart, and Walgreens will grow our wealth in almost any condition... something that can't be said for bonds or precious metals. These stocks have proven their ability to make money in some of the toughest times our economy has ever seen.

So if you're at all worried about inflation, you should own these sorts of blue chips for the long term. They are better than gold at fighting inflation... they are better than cash... and they are "all seasons" assets.

The next chart of MCD, gold, and the S&P 500 shows how a great blue-chip company protects you as well as (or better than) gold can during tough times.

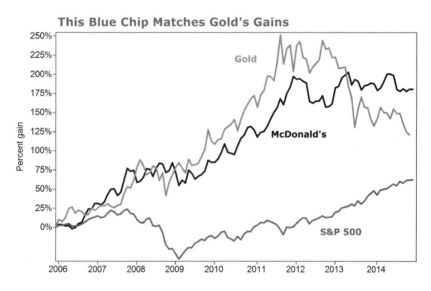

And remember... good stocks can protect you in both short-term and long-term wealth generation. Data from a *Fortune* magazine article says it all. Three $100 investments in 1965 placed in six-month U.S. Treasury bills (short-term interest-bearing securities), gold, and the S&P 500 were worth $1,336, $4,455, and $6,072,

> **" If you're truly interested in an 'all-weather' asset to place a large chunk of your portfolio into, go with the world's best dividend-paying companies... like Coca-Cola, McDonald's, and Johnson & Johnson. "**

respectively by 2012. Stocks beat gold by 36%. This shows the power of long-term investing in good stocks.

Of course, it makes sense to always hold a balanced portfolio of stocks, bonds, cash, and chaos hedges. You could start with around 45% stocks, 35% fixed-income, 15% cash, 5% chaos hedge... and never more than 4%-5% of your assets in any one investment.

In summary... Don't fall for the gold hype. Gold is a good "chaos hedge," but it's not an asset you want to place a large chunk of your wealth in. Store your physical gold on your own property, not with a government-controlled institution.

If you're truly interested in an "all-weather" asset to place a large chunk of your portfolio into, go with the world's best dividend-paying companies... like Coca-Cola, McDonald's, and Johnson & Johnson.

If inflation is a problem, you can depend on these companies to grow your nest egg, while paying cash dividends along the way. If inflation isn't a problem, these companies still grow your wealth and pay ever-rising cash dividends. No one can make those claims for gold.

— 9 —

How to Take Control of Your IRA

One of the joys of investing is watching your money grow...

Putting your money into investments that continuously build your nest egg means all the difference between having a comfortable retirement and just scraping by.

In Chapter 5 of this section, we talked about one strategy that helps grow your wealth: **compounding your savings**. I described how my sister began building her wealth early in life... adding to her savings regularly and reinvesting her dividends and cash distributions. My dad waited until he was older, but followed this strategy as well.

But the real secret is to do this strategy in a tax-sheltered investment account – also known as an Individual Retirement Arrangement (IRA).

Getting money into an IRA allows compounding of returns, without the government shaving off any of the principal. The difference between compounding without paying taxes and paying taxes along the way can be seen in the chart on the next page...

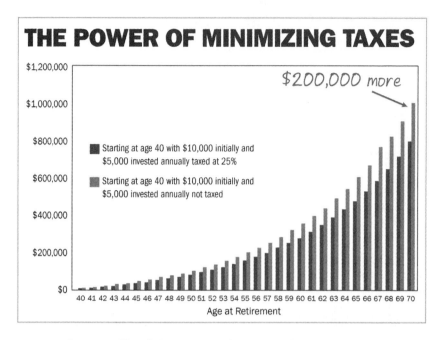

Two people start off with $10,000 each. One put his money in a tax-deferred account. The other did not. Over 30 years, the tax-deferred account would be worth $996,964. The taxed account would be worth $791,347. *That's more than $200,000 extra just by avoiding taxes.*

Today, several forms and types of IRAs exist...

The two main types of IRAs are traditional IRAs and "Roth" IRAs. (The latter is named after Senator William Roth of Delaware, who sponsored the legislation that created these savings vehicles.

When you put money in a traditional IRA, you get a tax deduction for the initial deposit and the government defers taxes on the money until you withdraw the money. As a general rule, you *may* start taking money out at age 59.5... But you *must* start taking money out at age 70.5.

With Roth IRAs, you pay taxes on the money before you put it in. Then when you take out your money in retirement, you don't pay taxes on any of it.

Plus Roth IRAs don't have a required minimum distribution... So you can start withdrawing money when you're 80... 90... or even leave it all for your heirs.

Many people first open their IRA account using the money from their savings account or a certificate of deposit (CD). But when savings accounts and CDs yield less than 1% (like in 2014)... you don't get much for your money by doing that.

Other people have IRAs through a brokerage account. This allows you to invest in stocks, bonds, and options... This is what I recommend.

The best way to manage your IRA is through a self-directed IRA... A typical IRA is managed by the brokerage you hire and limits you to conventional investment choices.

A self-directed IRA is exactly what it sounds like... It puts you in charge of what you invest in. In addition to the conventional investments you can make in a typical IRA – things like stocks, bonds, and options – a fully self-directed IRA allows you to invest in many other things, like real estate (as long as it's not personally used), private stocks, businesses, and even precious metals.

You can invest in just about anything, as long as it's not employed for your personal benefit. For example, you can buy the house next door within your IRA and then rent it to a neighbor. You can also invest in a local small business. Contact the companies we mention at the end of this chapter to learn more.

I use my self-directed IRA to generate income by selling stock options.

> 66 *The best way to manage your IRA is through a self-directed IRA... A typical IRA is managed by the brokerage you hire and limits you to conventional investment choices.* 99

When I use this account for options trading, I have no accounting or tax requirements to follow. I don't pay taxes on that money until I withdraw it.

If you do all your trading inside a retirement account, you won't have to report any trades to the

IRS. The goal is just to maximize your total returns as quickly and as easily as you can.

Two investments not allowed within self-directed IRAs are collectibles – like cars, wines, and stamps – and life-insurance contracts.

To open a self-directed IRA, you need to find a custodian that allows you to make your own investments – usually a brokerage or bank. You can call your current brokerage to see if it offers self-directed IRAs. If not, several companies do.

Below are the names of two places you might consider for doing a self-directed IRA. (I get no consideration from any of them.)...

PENSCO Trust Company
866-818-4472
www.pensco.com

Equity Trust Company
888-382-4727
www.trustetc.com

Always do your research before investing with any custodian. And be sure you're doing it because you have specific investments in mind.

PART IV

The Keys to Investment Success

The Most Important Lesson in Investing: When to Sell

One of the keys to successful investing is **learning how to sell**.

Knowing *when* to sell is half the battle... but you also must have the discipline to follow through on your plan.

Sometimes greed can slip in at the last minute... so *sticking with a plan to sell is critical to protecting your profits*. It also allows you to look for more opportunities to put your capital to work in investments just like the one you closed.

Let's start with my three keys to selling investments...

First... **Whenever you invest in something, write down why you bought it**. This means literally getting out a piece of paper or an index card (or opening a spreadsheet) and writing down your reasons for owning the stock. Maybe you bought for dividend or interest income or for potential growth-driven capital gains.

You should note any data or metrics that support your investment decision. For example, a low price relative to its earnings or cash flow.

Second... **write out when you'll sell the investment**. Do it on the same piece of paper and at the same time you're buying the investment. This includes writing out your expected percentage return and over what timeframe.

This is important as it expresses your plans before you become emotionally attached to the act of purchasing it. Once you own something, "confirmation bias" – the tendency to favor information that confirms your beliefs – can cloud your judgment. It's better to outline your goals ahead of time.

Third... **review your investments at least once a year – preferably every six months**. Make sure the reasons you bought remain valid.

How Do You Know When to Sell?

There's no single rule that will tell you when to sell... That's because there's no rule that tells you when to buy.

The strategy for selling is determined by why you bought in the first place – and should be determined at the time of your initial investment.

It's critical when you buy to know exactly what you expect to get out of the investment and what would lead you to sell...

The simplest way is to set a simple stop loss or trailing stop loss. Both kinds of stop losses take the emotion out of the decision when an investment works against you.

With a **simple stop loss**, you set a fixed point at which you'd sell... essentially setting the maximum amount you're willing to lose if you're wrong on an investment. So for example, if you buy a stock at $100 per share, set a 20% stop loss, and it falls to $80 per share... you'd sell no matter what.

The principal criticism of this kind of stop is that you've only committed to selling at a loss... Theoretically, your investment could rack up huge paper gains, and you could give them all back if the stock fell all the way to your fixed stop loss.

> *The strategy for selling is determined by why you bought in the first place – and should be determined at the time of your initial investment.*

> ### *DO WHAT I DO*
>
> **Create a sell level on a chart by marking an expected return one year out and then using that as the technical trigger.**

Trailing stops address that problem... They're a simple, easy-to-understand way to eliminate your emotions and get out of losing positions before they get too large... as well as capture gains when paper gains get to large.

With a trailing stop loss, you raise your selling price every time the stock hits a new high. Say you buy a stock at $50 a share and set the trailing stop at 20%. If the stock price falls straight down, you'd sell at $40 a share. But if it rises to $80 a share, you would sell on a decline back to $64 (20% below the high of $80). That way, you've protected yourself and pocketed a 28% gain.

You can also use fundamental analysis to determine when you might sell a stock. For example, sell when the shares become overvalued relative to the company's earnings or cash flow and compared with other potential investments.

Or you can do what I do... **Create a sell level on a chart by marking an expected return one year out and then using that as the technical trigger**.

For example, say I buy a stock at $100 per share. If my plan is to make 12% a year, I'll mark $112 and $124 on the chart. If in one or two years the stock hasn't traded above those levels, I'll sell. This sort of technical analysis can also incorporate moving averages or price support and resistance levels to guide you. (I don't use this much for selling, but I do when buying.)

Here's an example where using buying and selling rules help protect gains... I heard about three guys who bought land for $1 million. Six months later, they were offered $2 million for it. Doubling your money over three years is a good goal for an investment in raw land... To get there in six months is fantastic.

However you determine your sell prices, it's important to write things down. This teaches you discipline. It helps illustrate when investments are working out and when they aren't. That way, when it's clear they aren't working the way you envisioned, you can change things.

One trick I use to make sure I stick with my discipline is to ask myself whether I'd buy more right now or recommend it to friends or family members. If the answer is no, it's probably time to sell.

> *66 However you determine your sell prices, it's important to write things down. This teaches you discipline. It helps illustrate when investments are working out and when they aren't. That way, when it's clear they aren't working the way you envisioned, you can change things. 99*

Also, if I'm really worried I'm making a mistake about selling... I remind myself that I can always open a new position after a 30- or 60-day break. There's nothing magical about the time frame. It just serves as a cooling-off period for my emotions. Most likely, a good investment will still be attractive at that point. In many cases, I've found better opportunities by then.

Knowing When to Sell: There's No Place for Emotion

Let's say stocks are trading at record highs – and stops don't apply. When should you take your money off the table?

The key is to be aware of the power of your feelings. When emotions are involved, **buying investments is easy, selling is much harder...**

With most people, psychology usually works against your investments. So I'm going to show you a few pitfalls to be aware of when thinking about selling stocks.

This Is a Universal Impulse... and a Terrible Choice

Imagine this simple scenario...

Say you own two stocks. You bought each at $50 a share. Over the course of your investment, one has risen to $75 per share. The other has fallen to $25.

Suddenly, you and your spouse decide you need to raise money for something immediately. Perhaps a car you've wanted is on sale at the local dealer or a cabin on a lake where you want to retire is suddenly on the market. You need to raise some cash. You decide to sell one of your investments. But which stock do you sell?

If you're like most people, you choose to "capture" your gains... sell the $75 winner and keep holding the $25 loser. You may think the loser stock seems to have more upside potential, and you've probably been waiting to "get even" on the position...

It's a nearly universal impulse... but it's a terrible investing choice.

People love to sell their winners too soon and ride their losers too long. A slew of behavioral finance studies show it. One, by University of California at Berkeley professor Terry Odean, found investors are almost twice as likely (1.7 times) to sell a winning stock as they are to sell a losing stock.

> *66 Let your winners run, and cut your losers short. 99*

Following similar logic (urges, really), investors held losing stocks for 124 days and unloaded their winning stocks after 102 days.

You may say, "Maybe the winning stock had grown overvalued, and its gains were behind it."

It turns out, the winning stocks (which had been sold) subsequently outperformed the losing ones (which investors were still holding).

It depends on what timeframe you look at. But the general consensus is that in six- to eight-month periods, stocks that are moving up tend to keep moving up, and stocks that are falling tend to keep falling. It's a phenomenon called "**autocorrelation**."

This confirms the old adage: "Let your winners run, and cut your losers short."

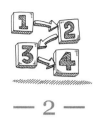

— 2 —

Four Key Numbers I Look at Every Time I Evaluate a Business

One of the best ways to build long-term wealth is by regularly investing in businesses.

Historically, stocks should return around 7%-9% a year. This is far above the average of inflation. So by saving money in stocks, you're almost guaranteed to increase your net worth over time. If you earn 8% and inflation is 3%, you're making "real" wealth... about 5% a year.

But it's vital for investors to know when to buy and sell individual securities. We start with four simple metrics when deciding to invest.

We look for relative values. So we're not just looking at the rock-solid, absolute numbers. We also want to look at those numbers relative to the market, the industry, and the security's own historical record. Our four metrics are...

1. Price-to-earnings (P/E) ratio

2. Price-to-book (P/B) ratio

3. Price-to-sales (P/S) ratio

4. Dividend (or interest) yield

Price-to-Earnings Ratio

The price-to-earnings (P/E) ratio is simply the stock's price per share divided by its earnings per share.

$$P/E \ RATIO = PRICE \ PER \ SHARE / EARNINGS \ PER \ SHARE$$

The P/E is often what you'll read about when professionals consider a stock. A low P/E often means you're getting a good price. A high P/E means the stock is expensive. I compare a company's current P/E with the market average, the stock's long-term average, and its competitors' averages.

Price-to-Book Ratio

The price-to-book (P/B) ratio is the stock's price per share divided by the book value per share.

$$P/B \ RATIO = PRICE \ PER \ SHARE / BOOK \ VALUE \ PER \ SHARE$$

Book value is determined by subtracting liabilities from total assets. Think of it as the corporate equivalent of a person's net worth. Divide that by the number of shares outstanding to get a book-value-per-share number.

The P/B is useful for valuing an asset. It gives you a realistic idea of the relative value of your investment dollar when considering another asset. If you buy at a P/B value of less than "one times book" (or "1x book"), you're getting a bargain. At 0.8x book, you're buying assets for 80 cents on the dollar.

When P/B is greater than 1x, you're paying more than the "net worth" of the company's assets. That's not necessarily a bad deal. But if you start paying 3x-4x book value, you're entering dangerous and rarefied air. You're paying a lot for assets that may not be worth so much.

Price-to-Sales Ratio

The price-to-sales (P/S) ratio is a stock's share price divided by its sales per share.

$$P/S \ RATIO = PRICE \ PER \ SHARE / SALES \ PER \ SHARE$$

This measures how much in sales you are buying for every $1 you spend on the stock. As with the P/E, I compare a company's P/S with its competitors' to see how it's valued relative to others in the same industry.

Dividend Yield

An investment that's generating cash and returning some of that cash to shareholders (in the form of a dividend) is what I call "shareholder friendly."

Companies with long histories of dividend payments top my list of potential investments. You can't use accounting schemes to fake a dividend for very long... So a solid dividend is often a sign of a great company.

> 66 *An investment that's generating cash and returning some of that cash to shareholders (in the form of a dividend) is what I call 'shareholder friendly.'* 99

— 3 —

Four Rules of Thumb to Collect Income and Grow Your Wealth Safely

When it comes to science, medicine, and investing... nothing works better than good rules of thumb.

"Eat your vegetables" and "an apple a day keeps the doctor away" may seem like hackneyed or simplistic advice. But they are two of the best health guidelines ever uttered. Advice to "walk 15 minutes a day" has now been shown to decrease risks of cancer and diabetes...

These rules of thumb will bring easily gained benefits.

The same is true for investing. Simple rules of thumb can take much of the human error out of your decision-making...

For example, one dangerous phenomenon it helps you avoid is the "**recency bias**." People place too much importance on the most recent events. That forces them out at the bottom of markets and in at the top.

To see the recency bias at work, just think about 2012... People were afraid of another 2008-2009-type collapse. Record numbers of mutual-fund investors were piling into bond funds and, worse, buying U.S. Treasury securities.

Interest rates were near all-time lows, but investors followed the crowd into bonds. They were overly concerned about the past and were dumping stocks. But in *Retirement Millionaire*, we weren't.

We stuck with the simple rules for evaluating opportunities... And we made a lot of money in stocks.

You may be among those stuck with tons of cash at the local bank or credit union, earning 0.05% on your money. If you're wondering what to do... learning a few rules of thumb for investing will immediately help you.

In this chapter, I'm going to outline a few simple rules that will help you know when an individual stock represents a great opportunity to collect income and grow your wealth safely... or when an investment may have run its course.

Even if some of these ideas seem familiar or simplistic, I urge you to incorporate them into your investing as you build a long-term portfolio... It's a time-tested formula for success.

Rule No. 1: Look for price-to-earnings ratios below the long-term average of the S&P 500, generally below 17x. A low P/E ratio suggests the company is trading below its value, making it cheap.

Rule No. 2: Look for stocks trading for a price-to-book ratio below 1x. A low P/B value suggests the company is undervalued, and you could be getting into a great company at a discount.

Rule No. 3: Try to avoid paying more than a price-to-sales ratio of 3x for the stock of a solid, reliable business.

In the private markets, businesses usually get bought and sold at prices that are between 1x and 2x sales. Of course, some well-established businesses with reliable sales can command a higher ratio.

Rule No. 4: Look for stocks that pay a dividend representing at least 2% of the share price. I also like to see a history of growing dividend payments. And I like the dividend yield to exceed the five-year Treasury note.

I prefer companies with a payout ratio of less than 50%... The payout ratio is the percent of earnings needed to support the dividend. In theory,

> **These four simple rules for valuing a company make investing easier. Following them is a great way to invest in safe and solid opportunities. In fact, most of the times I've lost money, I violated these rules.**

at a 50% payout, a company's earnings could fall in half and still cover the dividend. This is an extreme. But by limiting ourselves to payout ratios of 50% or lower, we feel safer at night knowing our income is reliable.

A strong, consistent dividend almost always indicates a healthy business. The company is generating cash and wants to say "thank you" to shareholders.

Rising dividends also shore up stock prices in bear markets. Thus, dividend stocks are defensive stocks by nature. A rising dividend acts like a pontoon float and prevents the stock price from falling much.

These four simple rules for valuing a company make investing easier. Following them is a great way to invest in safe and solid opportunities. In fact, most of the times I've lost money, I violated these rules.

— 4 —

The Single Biggest Financial Mistake You're Probably Making

If you're like the vast majority of Americans, chances are good that you're flushing money down the drain right now.

Most U.S. employers offer a simple way for workers to immediately boost their income. It takes no effort beyond filling out a simple form. Yet nearly two-thirds of Americans say, "Thanks, but no thanks."

> *66 One of the easiest decisions you can make in retirement investing is enrolling in your 401(k) plan. If your employer offers any sort of matching plan, this is an investment that simply can't be beat. It's literally free money. 99*

It's pure laziness...

One of the easiest decisions you can make in retirement investing is enrolling in your 401(k) plan. If your employer offers any sort of matching plan, this is an investment that simply can't be beat. It's literally free money.

There is no better strategy out there than letting someone else enlarge your deposits and compounding it tax-free. At my company, employees earn an immediate 50% return on the first 6% they tuck away for retirement.

Many companies across the country work the same way. Yet many Americans balk at the opportunity. According to the nonprofit National Bureau of Economic Research, only about one-third of American workers enroll in 401(k) programs. (I've seen numbers that say a measly 23% participate.) Yet when employers install automatic enrollment programs – which allow employees to opt out rather than opt in – enrollment jumps to more than 85%.

It's not usually a calculated, intentional decision that keeps employees from saving in their 401(k)s. It's just inertia that prevents people from making what's clearly the best financial decision for their future.

And the inaction isn't limited to just 401(k)s, either.

Rather than spend a few hours per year keeping our financial house in order, we procrastinate... We promise ourselves that we'll figure it out next month or the month after that. In part, we're frozen by the fear of making the wrong decision. And if we know mistakes lurk within our statements, admitting it and changing course is even harder.

I've spent decades in medicine and finance. I've worked for the "best" on Wall Street and studied at two of the top medical schools in the country. I've been inside these industries and seen the personal risks that people take on when they mindlessly trust these institutions to take care of them. Don't. Your wealth and your health depend on it.

Many people entrust their entire future to their broker, bank, or other institution... and pay exorbitant fees in the process. They assume they don't have the intelligence, education, or intuition that a Wall Street big shot has. Believe me, you do.

Take the "smartest" guys on Wall Street: hedge-fund managers. Hedge funds are fantastic at making money... for themselves. From 1998 to 2010, hedge-fund managers pocketed $379 billion in fees. But their investors gained just $70 billion. In other words, *hedge funds made five times more money for themselves than for the people who entrusted them with their money.*

This just doesn't make sense... especially when you realize that most funds underperform the market. For example, on average, hedge funds have made about 5% for their clients this year, lagging behind the S&P 500 benchmark index's 15% gain, according to a recent Goldman Sachs report. That kind of performance is typical.

Now, it's true that you need a little bit of knowledge in economics and finance to truly stay ahead of the game. That's what we're here for: to teach and empower you. Despite what the Wall Street fee machine will tell you, it only takes a little bit of common sense and attention to the things you're investing in to take control. And today, we're going over a couple ideas that will help you.

But as we do our part, you need to do yours and take your financial future into your own hands. Don't let your future quality of life be determined by whether your employer does an opt-in or opt-out of your 401(k). And don't pay exorbitant fees to arrogant fund managers who lag the market. Remember... you determine your future.

The Safety of Municipal Bonds

Almost every finance guru I know of has one person he uses as the "perfect indicator"...

Contrarian thinkers like me – folks who find opportunity by challenging conventional wisdom and investing against the crowd – often seek out that one person who always seems to be running with the herd. That person is most valuable when uncertainty starts swirling.

In 2013, I got a note from my favorite contrarian indicator. She's an old friend from my days living in New York City and a subscriber to several Stansberry Research newsletters... who sometimes follows my advice. She wrote to me in a panic about the drop in her municipal-bond fund prices. I told her what I tell everyone: Read my newsletter and e-mails over again.

I can't give individual advice to *anyone*. (Not even to my family.) The government's "publishers exemption" (freedom of speech aside) allows me to write about securities, but prevents me from giving individual advice.

But the broad message I would give my family, my friends, and my subscribers is the same. And it's very simple...

Municipal bonds are one of the safest income-paying securities I know. The historic default rate on these securities is minuscule. Investment-grade municipal bonds (those ranging in grade from A to triple-A) had a default rate of only 0.017% from 1974-2014, according to *Forbes* magazine.

Muni bonds are loans to local governments. By buying a muni bond, investors give a locality cash to build roads, schools, or other public buildings. In exchange, the government promises to send investors regular interest payments and return the initial "principal" investment at the end of a set period of time.

With many "muni bonds," the local government uses its taxing authority as a promise to pay back investors. Essentially, investors don't have to worry about where the municipality is getting its money... If things get tight, it'll raise taxes.

And if the locality does get in trouble... these bonds are among the first things it has to repay in any default case. So the interest and principal repayment on these securities is nearly certain.

But when Detroit filed for bankruptcy in 2013... writers speculated that it could rewrite the laws governing bankruptcies and the assumptions that support the muni-bond market.

> *66 Municipal bonds are one of the safest income-paying securities I know. 99*

For example, I've heard conjecture that the hopes and wishes of other unsecured creditors may be equally relevant in a bankruptcy court.

It's unlikely that any one bankruptcy – even Detroit's $20 billion filing – will cause more than a blip in the immense $3.7 trillion muni-bond market.

Also... no creditor's claims can take precedence over the senior debt. This will remain a fundamental tenet of both capitalism and the rule of law. You cannot make promises to me and sign documents that agree to the terms, then come crying later that you don't want to pay... or that you want to pay someone else what you pledged to me.

Almost all municipal debt is safe. The bonds (and our funds, which hold muni bonds) are trading at cheap levels compared with other debt. And they pay tax-free interest income. Muni bonds should be a part of nearly everyone's portfolios.

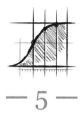

— 5 —

How to Make 50%-100% Gains Outside the Financial Market

I spent 10 years on Wall Street as a professional trader for some of the largest investment banks in the world – Goldman Sachs, Chase, and Yamaichi (the "Goldman Sachs of Japan")…

I learned – and contributed to – strategies that helped these firms make billions.

However, there's a way to make money for your retirement that those banks likely wouldn't tell you about. It's something I've called "Thrift Arbitrage." And it has nothing to do with stocks, options, or any other conventional financial strategy…

Instead, it's a way you can invest directly in a company's most successful product lines without having to buy a stake in an entire business.

Imagine investing not in Apple, but the iPhone line – its most profitable product by far. Or imagine investing in Microsoft's Windows operating system software, while ignoring failed products like the Zune music player.

I know that sounds confusing. But as you'll see, this strategy is simple. It requires no trading experience… you just need to be prepared to do some extra homework. And you only need to "invest" a little capital in each transaction. (As you'll see, the gains are large in percentage terms, but you can only use a little money each time.)

This strategy is fun, carries little risk, and is highly effective if done the right way.

I realize this probably sounds too good to be true. I'll explain exactly what you need to do.

First things first let me explain...

What Is 'Thrift Arbitrage'?

The strategy I'm about to share with you is not a traditional financial investment. You're not investing money into a particular security and profiting from the increasing value of that security.

Instead, you can use this income strategy *outside* the world of finance.

Like I said, some of the percentage gains you can make using this strategy are larger than traditional stock market returns. However, when using this strategy, you can only allocate a small amount of money in each transaction – usually just a few hundred dollars at a time.

I call this strategy "thrift arbitrage." It helps you safely generate extra income regardless of which direction the markets move.

Arbitrage is the art of taking advantage of price anomalies in order to make a profit. To do this, you typically buy something in one market, immediately sell it in another market, and profit from the difference.

For example, let's say you buy a chair for $100 that someone else out there is willing to buy for $150. That means you can immediately sell the chair for a 50% return. When you execute deals like these, you are earning guaranteed profit. This is arbitrage.

In the stock market, people try to find arbitrage opportunities all the time by looking for price discrepancies on stocks. For example, a trader may buy a stock in a foreign market where the price has not yet adjusted for the exchange rate. He knows he can immediately sell for more in the New York markets.

These situations often happen in merger or acquisition deals. It's not unusual to see shares of the companies involved trade for less than the value the merger deal places on them. Investors who can buy and hold on through the deal's closing often do very well...

However, you can take advantage of the same phenomenon without venturing into the stock market. The second-hand market, where people trade thousands of different products every single day, offers endless arbitrage opportunities.

I call this "thrift arbitrage" because you'll literally be taking advantage of price anomalies you can find in thrift stores, garage sales, and other second-hand markets. The key to thrift arbitrage is, just like the stock market, you have to know which products you can buy and immediately sell for a profit.

Every day, millions of Americans attempt thrift arbitrage. They buy products for one reason or another and then try to sell those products to make a little extra cash.

The problem is most people have no clue which goods to trade. So I investigated this market to identify exactly which product lines fetch high prices in the second-hand market and how individuals can capitalize on discrepancies between the prices they find at local thrift stores and those in the national marketplace.

I've even personally used this strategy. My brother and I helped to clean a family member's home. While organizing the home, we found a long-forgotten antique lamp. We put the lamp up for sale on the Internet auction website eBay. Within 24 hours, we received an offer of $450... with little work on our part.

Of course, your attic offers a limited "inventory." To take full, ongoing advantage of thrift arbitrage, you'll need to continue to scout for new items to sell. Thrift stores and Goodwill centers are great places to find items of value. You can also find plenty of discount shops near your house that carry goods, which you can buy and then sell for a profit.

These opportunities don't crop up all the time. But by dedicating a few hours out of your week, you could safely generate extra income no matter what is happening in the financial markets.

> *Thrift arbitrage will not make you rich. And some days, you won't find any opportunities. But if you keep on the lookout for the right products, thrift arbitrage can be a great way for you to generate extra income with just a few hours of work.*

Think about it...

What are people spending their money on right now? Maybe your friends are buying new brands of clothing or paying a lot of money for vintage electronics. Can you buy these same goods at a lower price at a local store? If so, you can use the thrift-arbitrage strategy.

Again, thrift arbitrage will not make you rich. And some days, you won't find any opportunities. But if you keep on the lookout for the right products, thrift arbitrage can be a great way for you to generate extra income with just a few hours of work.

Keep in mind though, this strategy does involve a certain degree of speculation... especially if you're unfamiliar with the products you want to sell.

So what products do I believe you should buy and sell in order to achieve thrift arbitrage right now?

In our research, we found several companies that regularly provide opportunities to use my thrift-arbitrage strategy successfully.

These goods give you the best shot at profiting from price discrepancies in the market. Just remember, just like any market, the second-hand market offers no guarantees.

Thrift Arbitrage Brand No. 1: Allen Edmonds

Allen Edmonds is a high-quality American shoe manufacturer. A new pair typically costs around $300.

Founded in 1922, the Wisconsin-based company became famous for providing shoes to the Army and Navy in World War II.

In addition to the high quality of its shoes, Allen Edmonds is a sought-after brand in the second-hand market because of its "recrafting" program. For a small fee, the company restores any pair of Allen Edmonds shoes, so you don't have to replace them. For example, you can get a new set of heels put onto an existing pair of shoes for $50. For $125, you can replace the soles, heels, welting, cork layer under the insoles, and laces.

On auction sites like eBay, you may see Allen Edmonds shoes selling for $250-$400 depending on the style. However, you can find these shoes for much less at outlets and other discount stores.

And remember, by taking advantage of the company's recrafting policy, you can buy any used pair of Allen Edmonds shoes, replace any needed parts, and then resell them on the national markets... often for twice what you paid for them.

In February 2012, for example, a woman named Susan bought a pair of Allen Edmonds shoes at an estate sale for $2.50 and sold them three days later for $91. In May 2013, she purchased another pair of Allen Edmonds (ankle dress boots) for $2.50 and resold them for $80 plus shipping. In both instances, Susan made more than 3,000% on her money.

A good place to start looking for used Allen Edmonds is your local Goodwill or Salvation Army stores. In the past, I've seen several new pairs selling at Nordstrom Rack for around $50 to $80. A few other websites where I've found good deals on these shoes include:

- www.amazon.com
- www.6pm.com
- www.zappos.com
- www.shoebuy.com
- www.ebay.com

When bidding on used Allen Edmonds, never pay more than $100.

Also keep in mind that Allen Edmonds is one of the only shoe companies that make shoes in half-sizes, increasing the company's popularity. Be on the lookout.

Thrift Arbitrage Brand No. 2: Pendleton

Thomas Kay, an English weaver, founded wool manufacturer Pendleton in Oregon in 1863. It sells men's and women's clothing and home goods – all made of wool. Pendleton controls every step of the manufacturing process of its goods.

This attention to detail is one reason why Pendleton's products sell in high-end retailers like Nordstrom and Lord and Taylor (alongside better-known designer brands like Burberry and Gucci).

Unlike other fashion designers, Pendleton shirts appeal to the everyday man. They are simple and "classic" in design, giving them longevity not found in other "trendier" designer brands. I personally own several Pendleton shirts.

More importantly, due to high demand and popularity, the chance of you finding Pendleton shirts in a discount store or goodwill center is much higher simply because most people have no idea that the Pendleton brand name carries a lot of weight with its customers.

These are excellent goods that you can find for $5 or less and resell for a significant profit. These shirts typically resell for anywhere between $30 and $60, depending on the style, color, and design. But never pay more than about $10.

I know a man who bought five of Pendleton's thick wool shirts in mint condition for $1.99 each at a thrift store in July 2013. He sold three for $29.99 each, giving him a 1,400% return on his money.

Thrift Arbitrage Brand No. 3: Levi Strauss & Co.

Levi's is the epitome of a long-lasting, household name.

Jacob David and Levi Strauss secured a patent for "blue jeans" on May 20, 1873. It's still the signature fashion choice the world associates with Americans.

Consumers worldwide love blue jeans – taking home more than 450 million pairs of jeans each year. High-end brands like Roberto Cavalli cost $1,200 per pair. Levi's sells jeans for between $20 and $40.

Levi's is probably the easiest jean brand to find and sell for a profit. It's realistic to find a pair of Levi's jeans at a yard sale or in your local thrift stop for just a few dollars. But you can sell them for closer to the regular retail price (depending on their condition).

In 2011, for example, Paila B. of Saint Paul, Minnesota bought a pair of Levi's jeans in a church rummage sale for $1 and sold the pair for $14.80.

Other notable jean brands you can generate second-hand returns on include True Religion, Rock & Republic, Seven for all Mankind, Miss Me, and Citizens of Humanity. These brands are big sellers on eBay when it comes to name brand jeans. However, remember fashions change, so the demand for these kinds of brands will come and go. Levi's is a brand that has held its reputation for generations.

Also, be sure that the jeans you're buying don't have stains, rips, unintentional tears, or any personalized modifications. In addition to yard sales and Goodwill stores, you can find "thrift arbitrage" bargains at discount retailers like T.J.Maxx, Filene's Basement, and Marshall's.

According to the *Wall Street Journal*, online sample sale sites like www.gilt.com, www.ruelala.com, and www.editorscloset.com offer sales of 50% off overstock jeans from a particular designer. Sales often last just 24 hours, and coveted items sell within minutes. Members get advanced notice of approaching sales.

Thrift Arbitrage Brand No. 4: Nintendo

If you didn't grow up playing video games, you may have a hard time believing this industry is one of the fastest-growing sectors of the U.S. economy.

From 1996 to 2013, video-game sales grew from 74 million to 188 million. That's growth of about 154%. And Nintendo is one company that's enjoying a healthy portion of that growth.

Nintendo has produced some of the most influential video-game series of all time, including Mario, Zelda, and Metroid. It has also produced some of the best-selling video game systems of all time, including the Nintendo Wii, the Nintendo DS, Nintendo GameCube, Nintendo 64, SNES, and the original Nintendo Entertainment System (NES).

The NES' American release in 1985 helped revive the video-game industry. In 2009, IGN – an entertainment website – rated NES the greatest gaming console of all time. More than 700 games were created from 1985 to 1994 for the NES. That's our thrift arbitrage opportunity.

Like most computer technologies, new video games are much more advanced than their 30-year-old counterparts. But many young adults who grew up playing video games have a strong sense of nostalgia for the older games (no different than the nostalgia most people feel for childhood toys of any kind).

So a huge market exists for "retro" video games of the past. Some gamers are willing to pay thousands of dollars for many of these vintage titles.

A game called "Stadium Events" by Bandai sells for about $41,300 new and about $1,000 used. Many other titles like Cheetahmen, Hot Slots, and Caltron 6 in 1, sell for more than $500 used.

Even more common titles – like Snow Brothers, Bonk's Adventure, Menace Beach, and Megacom 76 – are worth more than $50 used. The public doesn't realize the value in some of these older games and will often discard these titles, donate them to Goodwill, or sell them at yard sales. (You may even have some in your basement from when your kids were young.)

One of my former colleagues made an average of $10,000 a year in extra income through buying and selling old Nintendo video games. He spent around five hours a week shopping for different titles online or at local thrift shops and then resold these games to collectors on the open market.

If you're interested in generating gains through trading NES games, I suggest you ONLY try to find these games at local garage and yard sales. Some thrift stores sell these games at higher prices due to increased popularity. Just remember, no matter where you are, be on the lookout for these old Nintendo games. You never know when or where you can find one.

The pricing for these games varies widely, based on scarcity and original popularity. For a pricing guide of NES games, I recommend using the website: videogames.pricecharting.com/console/nes?sort-by=name.

Thrift Arbitrage Brand No. 5: Nike

Nike is a name that's synonymous with sports and athletic wear. It's one of the most recognizable clothing brands in the world.

The company sells around 120 million pairs of shoes each year in 160 countries and has captured nearly 40% of the global sport footwear market since it was founded in 1978.

It has thousands of different products on the market and is teeming with memorabilia coveted by Nike fans all over. In particular, Nike makes the world famous Air Jordan shoe-and-clothing brand (named for legendary basketball player Michael Jordan).

Because of the public's demand for many of Nike's products – including its golf clubs and blazers – these kinds of items sometimes sell for a slightly higher premium than other name-brand goods.

One woman I learned about, Rebecca, bought a Nike cycling jersey for $5 and sold it for $53.99. That's an almost 1,000% return.

As with any popular product line on the market, there is no guarantee that you can resell every Nike product you find at a higher price. But my research shows Nike is one of the best product lines you can search for – whether it's a sports bag, jersey, or pair of sandals.

Due to the sheer quantity of goods on the market, you can usually find Nike shoes and apparel in discount stores such as Ross or T.J.Maxx, and in most Goodwill stores close to your home... although you're more likely to find the vintage items in thrift stores.

Thrift Arbitrage Brand No. 6:
LEGO

You're likely familiar with LEGO's brightly colored, interlocking building blocks... Many of us spent a good part of our childhoods building with LEGO bricks... and bought the popular sets for our children (or grandchildren).

The LEGO group was founded in Denmark in 1932 by Ole Kirk Christiansen, who became the richest man in Denmark.

LEGO products are immensely popular today. The company sells about seven sets every second in more than 130 countries. Valued at $15 billion in 2014, LEGO is the world's most valuable toy company.

In 2012, it generated $4.1 billion in revenue, a year over year increase of 25% (nearly triple its 2007 sales). That was the fifth consecutive year the firm had annual revenue growth of over 15%. And as of 2013, LEGO constituted 85% of the building-block market.

Sounds like a great investment. Unfortunately, you can't buy LEGO stock. The company is private, so the general public can't buy shares.

But you can profit from LEGO's success through thrift arbitrage...

LEGO regularly creates special sets, often based on successful movies or television shows. These sets aren't in production for more than a few years. So a large – and growing – number of collectors covet these limited LEGO sets.

Let's say you purchased LEGO's Millennium Falcon set back in 2007, which at the time sold for $500. (The Millennium Falcon is a spaceship featured in the hugely successful *Star Wars* franchise.) By 2013, that particular Millennium Falcon set sold for more than $12,000 on eBay.

Keep in mind, LEGO regularly produces different *Star Wars* sets (including the Millennium Falcon.) So not every set will yield the same results. You have to know which were produced in limited numbers.

In June 2013, a fellow named Arthur M. wrote on Brick Picker (a LEGO price and investing guide) that he made a 400% return in less than one day on the *Star Wars* robot LEGO set. Arthur says that he averages a little more than 100% on all his LEGO investments. "It comes out to about a 30% annual return," he says.

Buying and selling LEGO sets is a great way to generate extra income... if you do your research and stay informed on which limited edition sets are likely to rise in value.

There is one crucial rule to trading LEGO sets you need to know. *An opened LEGO box is worth nothing.* Collectors often demand that these sets be in "mint condition," meaning the box is unopened and shows no sign of wear and tear.

My suggestion for generating income is to only focus on specific LEGO sets. The most coveted sets are based on popular movies and comic books. One LEGO set sold on eBay for $3,200 because it featured a pair of figures from the Marvel movie, *The Avengers*.

Where Can You Buy LEGO Sets?

Typically, I suggest you avoid shopping for LEGO sets at regular retail stores like Toys-R-Us. The markups are too high.

Instead, go to your nearby discount chain stores first. Places like Ross, Marshall's, Five Below, Big Lots, T.J.Maxx, and Target. Just remember, *an opened LEGO set is worth very little in the second-hand market.*

Make sure that the box is in good condition and unopened.

Thrift Arbitrage Brand No. 7: Disney

In 2012, approximately 126.5 million people traveled to Orlando, Florida to visit Walt Disney World. The second-most popular park in America by attendance was Universal Studios, which had just 34 million attendees. From Mickey Mouse to Snow White, Disney characters have become an integral part of American culture.

Since its founding in 1923, The Walt Disney Company has grown from a small animation studio to one of the largest corporations in the country. Disney has branched into every entertainment medium including movies, books, and toy production.

Through several acquisitions, the company now owns three of the top-grossing movie studios including Pixar, Marvel, and Lucasfilm. Disney even owns video-game developer Electronic Arts and sports cable network ESPN.

But what's useful about Disney is the nostalgia it generates in so many Americans. Millions of Americans grew up with animated classics like Snow White, Cinderella, and Pinocchio... And they cherish their memories of those films.

In an effort to sustain the collectible idea of these films, Disney created the "Disney Vault," periodically taking copies of these movies off the market. This way, the iconic titles are available for a limited time, after which they are put "in the vault" and not made available for another 10 years.

This is why Disney films have become instant collectibles and sell in excess of their original retail price.

Hundreds of Disney products draw big dollar figures from collectors. Finding these items can be a challenge. But based on my experience, you can find them in most thrift and Goodwill stores. You just need to know which items to shop for...

I've found that when it comes to trading on the demand of Disney's products, you always want to look for older, vintage pieces. ALWAYS be on the lookout for enameled Disney pins.

Disney pin-trading began in 1999. These colorful metal pins – usually featuring one of the company's famous animated characters – became the most popular merchandise and collectibles in all of Walt Disney World and Disneyland.

Keep an eye out for "retro" pins from the first year or two of production.

Many of them sell for hundreds or thousands of dollars on eBay. You can find some pins on Amazon. But I suggest first looking at second-hand stores. These are usually the best places to find deals on pins.

Plush dolls are another Disney product with high demand and resale value. The company has been producing plush dolls for decades. Many older dolls list for several hundred dollars. Others sell for anywhere from $10 to $50.

In May 2013, for example, a woman named Grace bought a Winnie the Pooh Heffalump plush doll for $1 and resold it for $30. She also bought a Disney dress-up costume for $1 and resold it for $46.

Finally, Disney posters are among the most sought-after items on the market. Many posters from the 1930s and 1940s sell for thousands of dollars.

The key with Disney is to look for vintage items and always check the value of these items before purchasing them. Check websites like eBay and Craigslist for an idea of their resale value.

The Advanced Strategy

One of the advantages of these thrift-arbitrage opportunities is they are short-term trades. You don't need to hold onto a pair of Allen Edmonds shoes for years waiting for them to accrue value. The market already exists.

However, once you're comfortable with the idea of scouting out discount stores and yard sales for these thrift-arbitrage opportunities... you can try a more advanced strategy.

If you're willing to wait for a return on your money and work a little harder, the return on your effort can be even greater...

Instead of looking for valuable items selling cheaply at stores or estate sales, you can buy items brand new from regular retailers like Wal-Mart. The catch is... you have to hold onto them for a few years while they accrue value.

Let's use Nike as an example...

As I said previously, you can find Goodwill selling Nike shoes or sweatshirts for just a few dollars. And you can resell them online immediately for at least twice what you paid.

But Nike also has "limited edition" items that increase in value over the years. Some versions of the Air Jordan basketball sneaker have limited production runs. Because of the small number produced (and the potential to become a vintage collector's item), the value of the shoes could increase substantially over several years.

All you have to do is buy the shoes when they're first released and sit on them for a few years as you wait for the value to rise. In the cases of these limited-run products, you can buy them at retail prices from stores like Wal-Mart and Target.

There are several risks here. The shoes, for various reasons, may not increase in value. Or you decide to sell them at a time they have become unpopular. This makes the strategy speculative and strongly correlated to sentiment.

So don't spend more than a small amount of money on these products. And take your time learning the market for these items. Still, if you buy the right item at the right time, you could see huge returns.

Getting Started

One of the best places to sell the items you find is eBay. It's the largest online marketplace, with more than 100 million active users.

Using eBay is simple... To sign up, you need to provide personal information like your name, mailing address, e-mail address, and a payment method.

When you've set your account up, you can start selling.

With any product you want to resell, it's important to first go online and see what similar goods are selling for. Check current eBay listings.

You can look up recent completed eBay sales on www.watchcount.com. Just copy and paste the eBay listing number into the homepage search box, and you can view the item info – including the actual best-selling price.

When you've decided on a price to list your item at, take some pictures. My assistant, who regularly sells items online, recommends these steps:

1. Take several pictures from different angles.

2. If the item has a flaw, don't hide it.

3. Use a neutral background like a white sheet.

4. Natural lighting is best for good photo quality.

Once you've gotten photos, write up a good description of the item. If you're selling clothes, note the size, the fabric, how often the item was worn (if you know), and if there are any issues with the item. For example, a shirt that's missing a button.

If it's an item like a LEGO set, you can give a little history on the item. Describing the original manufacturing date, the condition, and the item's rarity can help improve your sales.

It's hard to give too much description when you're selling something. But give too little, and people may pass on the purchase.

Also, it's important to remember that people you sell to can rate the transaction. (You can rate buyers as well.) If you have a poor reputation on eBay, people will be less likely to buy from you. You don't want people returning items because you weren't 100% honest.

Remember... for some items, you have to buy and hold. I prefer companies whose products you can find and sell immediately for a profit. If you sell on eBay, don't forget to include shipping and handling, and eBay's listing fee. These can lower your profit.

If you really don't want to get your hands dirty, go to an eBay consignment shop. These shops take care of the selling and shipping for you. You won't make as much, but you won't have to do the hard work, either.

You can also do this on Craigslist and Amazon. These sites don't allow bidding. As the seller, you simply list your price. Craigslist also limits your selling to the local area where you live and work.. This can save you on shipping and handling (especially important for large items like furniture), but you'll lose the large pool of buyers you'd get using Amazon or eBay.

You can also use the Internet to help you find products to sell. There are several websites that can help you find some of the best products you can buy to sell for a profit.

- www.latenight-coffee.com/category/flippin-friday-stories/

- thriftaway.wordpress.com/

- goodwillhaunting.blogspot.com

- thriftshopfinds.wordpress.com

It takes a little legwork to know the value of popular items and find them for sale. But many people say hunting is part of the fun.

As I said, using thrift arbitrage, the percentage gains you can make buying and selling second-hand items can be large. Although the nominal amount you make isn't always eye-popping, regularly reselling popular items you find in second-hand shops and yard sales can turn into a healthy stream of supplemental income...

— 6 —

How to Buy Securities

When it comes to buying securities, you have two broker options: full-service or discount.

Full-service brokers work for firms like Merrill Lynch, Wells Fargo, and Edward Jones. They interact directly, person to person, with clients. They frequently call customers with buy-and-sell recommendations.

Full-service brokers can be useful if you need a lot of hand-holding. The problem is brokers who take care of everything also charge fees and commissions for that hand-holding. It can add up to as much as 1%-2% of your assets every year.

Decades ago, almost every broker was full service. They charged enormous commissions. I used to pay $75 to put on trades of less than $5,000. That means I lost 3% just by entering the position (1.5% to buy and 1.5% to sell). Full-service broker commissions are still relatively expensive – commissions on 100 shares can run $25-$35.

The commissions may be worth it to you. But I generally do not recommend (nor do I use) full-service brokers... On top of the costs, many brokers lack critical experience trading securities. Many are newly graduated. Most have zero net worth.

Mostly, they're relaying advice that comes from headquarters. The big firms have a centralized "strategist" who generates investment ideas and shares them with the brokers at weekly meetings. The brokers/salesmen parrot the picks to clients.

I prefer to use **discount brokers**. You interact mainly with their websites. These brokers normally don't talk with you on the phone unless absolutely necessary. (And they charge more if you transact with them over the phone.)

In exchange for accepting less human contact and spoon feeding, discount brokers lower your transaction costs considerably. The fees and charges are small, which means more money for you.

Most of them offer access to an array of worldwide markets and securities. Their services are easy to use and include education and research materials. I use these as a substitute for broker advice.

Top Online Discount Brokers

Every year, we've ranked seven online discount brokers.

We used information from *Barron's* (my favorite weekly business newspaper), personal interviews, and actual trading experiences. Every year, *Barron's* ranks the top online brokers, but not all the firms it details are suitable for *Retirement Millionaire* recommendations.

In the next table, I've broken out several categories to evaluate the brokerages. You'll need to decide which of these factors is more important to you. But the good news is that all seven of these brokers do a good job. They all execute well, offer good prices, and provide reasonable amounts of research.

You should know that we aren't compensated financially for mentioning *any* of these brokers. Although I like TD and Fidelity, I've heard wonderful things about Interactive Brokers and TradeKing. We've included the websites and phone numbers for you to get started with any of them.

You can use the following table as a basis for finding the broker that's right for you. You may not meet the minimum annual income for a specific broker, or you may want a broker that's more willing to walk you through trades. Simply use this list as your starting point.

Brokerage	Fees	Cost Per Option Trade	Phone
TD Ameritrade	Internet stock trades: $9.99 + $0.75 per option contract Telephone trades: $34.99 + $0.75 per option contract Options assignments: $19.99 commission	$10.74	800-454-9272
Interactive Brokers	$1.00 minimum per option contract $0.15 – $1 commission per contract (U.S.)	$1.15	877-442-2757
OptionsXpress	35+ Trades/Quarter: $12.95 for one option contract 0-34 Trades/Quarter: $14.95 for one option contract	$12.95 $14.95	888-280-8020
Fidelity Investments	$7.95 + $0.75 per option contract	$8.70	800-343-3548
TradeKing	$4.95 per stock trade + $0.65 per option contract	$6.25	877-495-5464
E*TRADE Securities	$9.99 + $0.75 per option contract Options Exercise: $19.99	$10.74	800-387-2331
Charles Schwab	Internet trades: $8.95 + $0.75 per option contract Telephone trades: $8.95 + $5.00 per option contract Options assignments: $8.95 commission	$9.70	866-232-9890

Trading Options With Your Broker

When you request broker approval to trade options, the broker will assign you a "level" of authorization, typically 1-5. The levels relate to your trading experience, the varying degrees of risk carried by different options trades, and the firm's desire to limit people from losing lots of money in riskier trades.

By limiting the access to advanced trading strategies, the brokerages better maintain their risk to losses as well. Once you show your ability to handle certain trades and transactions, the brokerage raises your "level."

You'll need to get approved to do covered-call options for some of the strategies. In most firms, that's Level 1. The levels can vary from broker to broker. But if you're new to options, you should start by seeking "Level 1." This entry level authorization allows you to perform covered-call trades.

The Best Books on Options Trading

The best book out there is probably Lawrence McMillan's classic *Options as a Strategic Investment*. I grew up on McMillan's stuff... And this book is the bible of options.

However, there are simpler books like *Stock Options For Dummies*. And McMillan has a few shorter, simpler books, like *Profit With Options* (which is really just a subsection of his bigger book).

Here's how the levels breakdown...

Level 0: You can have long positions on stocks, bonds, and mutual funds but you can't trade options.

Level 1: You can write covered calls or sell stocks short.

Level 2: You can buy call and put options. You can also write covered puts.

Level 3: You can create a debit spread.

Level 4: You can create a credit spread. You can also sell naked puts.

Level 5: You can sell naked calls. You can also write naked index puts and calls.

Only advanced traders need to consider Level 3 or higher...

I've used Fidelity, TD Ameritrade, and Schwab. Plus I've seen Interactive Brokers in action, and it's easily the least expensive broker from a transaction and cost point of view.

In 2009, TD Ameritrade acquired a company called thinkorswim. *Barron's* rated thinkorswim the No. 1 broker for several years. That acquisition and the ease of using its website made TD Ameritrade my favorite online broker in 2014.

Again, <u>do not consider anything in this note a recommendation for any one firm</u>. This is simply a list of brokerages that receive excellent ratings for providing a great discount brokerage platform... plus a few I have personally tried and had good experiences using. You'll have to choose a brokerage that suits your needs.

— 7 —

Mutual Funds: Misunderstood and Ideal for Beginners

When my mother passed away, she left some money to my sister and me.

My sister confessed that she needed my help. She wanted to protect the money she was getting from our mom and make it work for her. She wanted to learn how to invest for income and capital gains. But she didn't know how to take even the first steps to set up an account and get started.

I decided to write on the topic. What would I want a novice investor to know about getting into the investing world... safely and enjoyably?

No matter if you're starting out with a small inheritance or simply want to start investing, this message is for you. If you've never invested but you can take $25 or $50 a month and put it into the market, this message is for you.

I'm going to show you how to use one of the most maligned and misunderstood investing vehicles in the market. Ironically, it's also one of the most accessible and easy to use. And when you understand its benefits, it's an ideal way to quickly diversify your portfolio and begin compounding your capital...

Even if you're an experienced investor, read on... thinking about the fundamentals of investing can help remind us of what's important.

The Easiest Place to Start Investing

The simplest way to start investing is through something called a "mutual fund."

A mutual fund is a company that pools the assets of multiple investors and – with the help of a manager – invests the money. It issues shares that you own just like a small company. The large pool of money makes it easier for individuals to invest in many stocks. That keeps the portfolio diversified because no one position takes up too much of the capital.

For a simple example, 100 people could invest $1,000 each... leaving the fund with $100,000 in assets. The fund manager could then buy a large basket of stocks. If the manager followed our position-sizing rule of limiting investments to no more than 5% of the portfolio... $100,000 would be enough to buy 20 or so stocks.

So instead of an individual needing $100,000 on his own to invest, he can pool his resources and invest in an array of securities resources with only 1% of that.

If you don't want to pick individual securities or if you want easy and instant diversification, mutual funds are great places to start. The buying power of pooled money also means better prices on the securities than if you tried to buy all the individual securities by yourself, having to pay commissions and fees on each transaction.

There are two types of funds – closed-end and open-end funds.

Use **closed-end funds** when you're buying municipal bonds and making other fixed-income investments. Closed-end funds issue a limited number of shares. So the share price can fluctuate based on investor demand. This means that a closed-end fund can trade above or below the value of the fund's assets – called the net asset value (NAV).

That fluctuation also gives us easy opportunities to make money when the price of the shares moves up from a discount and closer to the NAV. **Buying closed-end funds for less than NAV is one of my favorite secrets for making money in the markets.**

Most mutual funds are **open-end funds**. This type of fund can issue as many shares as investors want to buy. Because your money is almost immediately invested, open-end funds always trade at their NAV.

Funds invest in just about anything... Some focus on specific strategies or types of investments. For example, some funds hold only blue-chip stocks, some invest in emerging markets, and others specialize in bonds.

Each fund has a charter that it must adhere to, meaning a fund can only invest in what's mentioned in the fund's charter.

Some investors look down on mutual funds, viewing them as simplistic options for "little league" investors. I urge you to put aside these prejudices.

We've had lots of success using big diversified funds including Vanguard Inflation-Protected Securities Fund (VIPSX) and Fidelity Select Medical Equipment and Systems Fund (FSMEX).

Other people say when you invest in mutual funds, your returns are undermined by the fees they charge. This is a legitimate concern... but one you can manage.

When it comes to fees... you need to know the difference between "load" and "no load" funds. "Load" funds are essentially charging you commission fees. And the charge can range from 3% to 9%. It means that for every $100 you want to invest, the fund takes up to $9 and you're only investing the other $91. You'd have to make 10% on your investment just to break even.

Don't Ever Buy a Load Mutual Fund.

The no-load funds don't sap your principal this way. Also, research shows that both types of funds have equal returns on your assets, so why start from behind with a load fund?

But you also need to watch annual management advisory fees, which both load and no-load funds charge. When you're looking for a no-load fund to invest in, stick with ones whose management fees are less than 1%.

The fees also raise another caution about mutual funds... They are not for trading. Mutual funds are designed for investors who intend to hold for a long period of time. If you plan to hold for less than three years, mutual funds aren't for you.

Winnowing Down the Choices

One problem that often overwhelms folks venturing into mutual funds is the seemingly endless universe of funds. The mutual-fund industry is immense. In the U.S. alone, it totals $13 trillion in assets managed, as of 2014.

The first thing you need to know to sort through the options is this: There are "families of funds" – financial firms that specialize in offering investors a variety of funds for investment... Some common names you may have heard are...

- Vanguard

- BlackRock

- Invesco

- Nuveen

- Charles Schwab

- Fidelity Investments

Fidelity was a client of Goldman Sachs when I worked for the investment bank... I virtually lived on the New York-to-Boston airplane shuttle for a couple years, making weekly trips to teach Fidelity managers about using futures and options to improve their returns.

(Rest assured, my relationship with Fidelity ended when I left Wall Street in 1995... I get no remuneration in mentioning it here as an example.)

Let's take a look at Fidelity's funds... All of the funds I'll describe are no-load with low management fees.

Fidelity manages more than 200 funds: stock funds, bond funds, index funds (which follow a specific index, like the S&P 500), "target" funds (which balance the allocation in the fund based on your age), and many others.

When you buy shares of a fund, a manager uses your money to invest across a wide spectrum of investments depending on the fund's charter. Fidelity's website lists the funds depending on your needs.

The simplest way to start is to invest in a so-called "balanced" fund. Fidelity calls them "asset allocation" funds. The goal of these funds is to be a one-stop shop for investors who want instant access to a diversified portfolio. This type of fund is comprised of several types of investments, including stocks (from small- to large-cap), bonds, interest-paying money-market accounts, and international investments.

Two simple examples of balanced funds Fidelity offers are the Fidelity Asset Manager 60% Fund (FSANX) and the Fidelity Asset Manager 85% Fund (FAMRX). You just need $2,000 to invest in either of them.

The Fidelity Asset Manager 60% Fund keeps 60% of its assets in stocks, 35% in bonds, and 5% in short-term and money-market investments. The stocks are a mix of domestic and international equities. So not only are you diversified across assets, but you also get global diversification.

The Fidelity Asset Manager 85% Fund keeps 85% of its assets in stocks and 15% in bonds and short-term and money-market investments. Like the 60% fund, the stocks are a mix of domestic and international equities. However, the higher percentage of assets in stocks means this fund is a little riskier. This is a better choice for someone not nearing or in retirement.

As I mentioned before, some funds invest in specific investments. So instead of investing in just one fund, you could invest in several funds to diversify your portfolio. For example, you could invest in two or three different stock funds and two or three different fixed-income funds.

The Fidelity Large Cap Stock Fund (FLCSX) invests more than 80% of its assets in large-cap stocks. Three of its top 10 holdings are positions I've previously recommended in my *Retirement Millionaire* newsletter:

Microsoft (Nasdaq: MSFT), Wells Fargo (NYSE: WFC), and Chevron (NYSE: CVX).

The Fidelity Nasdaq Composite Index Fund (FNCMX) follows the aggregate performance of the more than 3,000 stocks listed on the Nasdaq exchange. Three of the fund's top 10 holdings include Microsoft, Cisco, and Intel... all companies I've recommended.

Fidelity also has municipal-bond funds similar to those we've held in my *Retirement Millionaire* portfolio, including its Fidelity Intermediate Municipal Income Fund (FLTMX) and the Fidelity Tax-Free Bond Fund (FTABX). Both funds seek to make income from investment-grade municipal bonds.

When to Build Your Own 'Mutual Fund'

If you are just getting started investing but want to quickly deploy a large amount of capital that you're counting on for the future... mutual funds are ideal.

There's no hard rule for what qualifies as a "large amount"... That depends on your needs, income, and tolerance for risk. But in general, if you have $100,000 or more to work with... it would be a full-time job trying to quickly create a portfolio that is sufficiently diversified across conservatively sized positions (none accounting for more than about 5% of the portfolio). For immediate exposure to stocks, you could put 30%-60% into a stock mutual fund.

But if you're talking about starting with, say, a $5,000-$10,000 bonus from work or a smaller inheritance, you may want to do the same thing for ease and to lower transaction costs as a percent of your total assets.

PART V

Foods to Seek Out, Foods to Avoid

— 1 —

Coffee Will Help You Live Longer

The Arabian physician Avicenna is credited with brewing the first cup of coffee around 1,000 CE. And the earliest concrete evidence of commercial coffee was found in Constantinople, where the first coffeehouse opened in 1475.

The first English coffeehouses opened in the 1650s. They were called penny universities. Yep, the price for a cup was a penny.

Once thought to be a drink of the devil, the pope finally approved coffee as a miracle cure. By 1765, there were close to 300 coffeehouses in Venice alone. Move over, Starbucks!

The wild popularity of coffee offers plenty of evidence of human addiction – in this case, to coffee's naturally occurring compounds, including caffeine. Natural coffee is a mix of many substances, some of which contain antioxidants.

Among its benefits, coffee has been shown to:

- Dilate blood vessels.

- Reduce the amount of LDL (the so-called "bad" cholesterol).

- Decrease risks for Parkinson's and Alzheimer's disease.

- Decrease risk for colon cancer (decaf doesn't do this).

- Lower the risk for Type 2 diabetes.

- Reduce heart rhythm problems.

What about the nearly ubiquitous conventional wisdom that coffee is bad for you? Doesn't coffee cause cancer? Is caffeine harmful?

In the late 1970s, studies associated coffee with bladder cancer. But well-controlled studies later attempted to duplicate the association and failed to confirm any of the earlier reported studies. The reason? Mr. Coffee machines had hit the market, and the paper filters remove several of the toxic volatile oils related to cancer. [But don't worry about your espresso or French presses... unless you're downing the equivalent of two or three *pots* a day.]

There's little evidence that caffeine, in moderate doses, does any harm.

One exception may be if you suffer from thyroid disease. Thyroid disease often shows up as intolerance to temperature changes, feeling hot or cold when everyone else is fine. Frequently, suffering from severe dry skin is also thyroid related.

Studies remain inconclusive. But my hunch is some people who are predisposed to thyroid disease aggravate the condition by drinking coffee. If you worry you have thyroid disease, try laying off the caffeine for a while.

Oh and don't forget the most important part of coffee... the aroma. Just smelling coffee lowers the risk of cancer in animals. And the stuff actually changes genes in humans, makes us less sleepy, and lowers blood pressure.

But these aren't the only benefits...

Several new studies show coffee lowers your risk of heart disease, dementia, and Alzheimer's. One study showed that people who drank at least one cup of coffee per day lowered their odds of dying during the next year by 37%. Even drinking up to four cups per day is beneficial – making you 56% less likely to get Type 2 diabetes.

And if you can, drink caffeinated coffee. Caffeine gives most of the benefits in a cup of coffee. It's used to treat asthma and headaches (although some people do actually get headaches when they consume caffeine).

The next time you have an upset stomach, try drinking coffee. We've been told for years that coffee leads to an upset stomach. But roasting coffee beans actually creates a compound, N-methylpyridinium (NMP), that helps lower stomach acid. Researchers don't completely understand how it works, but they know NMP lowers acid secretion in the stomach.

The darker the roast, the better the coffee is for your stomach. For years, Eight O'Clock Coffee Colombian roast has consistently earned the top spot in the *Consumer Reports'* annual coffee tasting. It's the one I brew at home.

A 2012 study from Boston's Brigham and Women's Hospital found that regular coffee consumption (in addition to exercise) reduces inflammation... a body reaction that fosters skin cancer. Women who drank at least three cups a day had a lower risk of developing skin cancer than women who drank just one cup a month.

And caffeine seems to be necessary. No link was found between drinking decaf coffee and lowering cancer risk. Researchers found that other items with caffeine (like tea and chocolate) also decreased skin cancer risk. Just don't drink too much coffee later in the day... For most people, too much caffeine can cause insomnia.

This is just one more study showing the great benefits of coffee. Over the years, we've found that coffee lowers your risk of heart disease, dementia, and even Alzheimer's. But it also reduces the likelihood of women developing depression and breast cancer.

Just don't drink too much coffee... It can raise your blood pressure. Stick with a couple cups a day. Moderation is always a good choice.

— 2 —

Two Tablespoons of Oil a Day for Better Health

One of the most delicious tastes in the world is the first press of extra-virgin olive oil.

I use olive oil whenever and however I can. I cook my eggs with it in the morning, and I cook my meats with it in the evening. And besides tasting so good, olive oil prevents disease.

For centuries, the therapeutic benefits of olive oil, particularly the first press – the so-called extra virgin – have been touted.

Hippocrates, considered by many to be the father of Western medicine, prescribed olive oil for almost every ailment. The people of the Mediterranean region recognized early on the uses of olive oil for nutritional, cosmetic, and medicinal purposes.

Evidence shows a Mediterranean diet, which includes tons of olive oil, lowers harmful cholesterol. The mechanism for this is not fully known, but simple micronutrients within olive oil may bestow the benefits. The chemical structure and function of olive oil also protects other cholesterols in your body from oxidation. Thus, olive oil discourages many diseases of inflammation, including heart disease, arthritis, and even high blood pressure.

Among the other reasons to follow the Mediterraneans and use olive oil...

- It's a mild laxative.

- It may protect the stomach from ulcers.

- It helps dissolve clots in capillaries (the small vessels in your body).

- It has been found to lower the degree of absorption of other edible fats, thus lowering caloric intake.

- It helps with the proper modulation of pancreatic and intestinal hormones.

Taking two tablespoons of olive oil a day is all you need to reap the health benefits. I easily get this much and encourage you to do the same. Don't be lazy and take it like cough syrup... at least have some fun with it.

Use it in place of fats like butter and other oils every time you eat and cook. You can flavor the oil with simple things like basil or garlic or more complicated mixtures like the restaurant Carrabba's does for dipping bread.

Better yet, toss out your "fake" high-fructose corn syrup salad dressings and simply mix a little vinegar (flavored if you like) with olive oil for your salad dressings and marinades.

By the way, olive oil is wonderful on the skin. My girlfriend and I often exchange a hand or foot massage with olive oil.

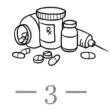

— 3 —

Beware of Fiber Supplements

Most doctors will tell you that fiber supplements are good for you and can help ward off colon cancer. But be careful, this is hardly gospel truth.

In fact, one study using a common fiber supplement, psyllium, actually found an *increase* in precancerous colon tissue – called polyps. And the whole idea that fiber fights cancer comes from old (1971) circumstantial evidence from Africa.

Fiber does offer some verified benefits – mostly helping to regulate blood pressure and normalize bowel movements. So to keep things moving and improve your health in other ways, make sure you get your fiber from your regular diet, NOT in a supplement.

Specifically, you should eat lots of raw fruits, vegetables, whole grains, and beans. Some great sources of healthy fiber are: apples, oranges, root vegetables, pinto beans, oatmeal, berries, rye bread, pears, popcorn, and brown rice.

— 4 —

Reduce Serious Health Risks When Grilling

Most Americans own a barbecue grill. More than half grill year-round. Many barbecue at least twice a week during the summer.

But as popular as grilling is, it comes with a number of health hazards. People have studied the science behind grilling, and I've researched these things as well. There are healthy ways to grill, and ways that are hazardous to your health. So read on, and enjoy your grilling on the Fourth of July.

The terms "barbecue" and "grilling" are frequently used interchangeably. But they're actually two different cooking methods. **Grilling** involves cooking food directly over a heat source using a "grill" to keep the food away from the coals or wood.

To **barbecue** means cooking food at low temperatures (about 350 degrees) for a longer period of time over indirect heat that produces lots of smoke. This method is best for larger pieces of meat, like thick steaks, whole roasts, and ribs.

So what could possibly be dangerous about these ancient methods? After all, humans were cooking meat over open flames long before we invented the Jenn-Air.

It turns out, grilling and barbecuing create heterocyclic amines (HCAs) and polycyclic aromatic hydrocarbons (PAHs). The U.S. Department of

Health and Human Services lists HCAs as known carcinogens.

HCAs are produced when creatine – an amino acid found in muscles – combines with the natural sugar in meat and is heated during cooking. High heat and long cooking times causes grilled meats to produce high concentrations of these HCAs. The five foods yielding the highest levels of HCAs (when prepared well-done) are chicken breast, steak, pork, salmon, and hamburger – all common items to cook on your backyard barbeque grill.

Since HCA concentration increases with heat and time, it stands to reason that the production of HCAs in meat increases the longer and hotter the meat is cooked. And to make matters worse, if the HCAs don't get you, the PAHs will.

Close your eyes and think about that luscious cloud of smoke that rises when you open the top of your grill or when a piece of fat from your steak falls into the fire. Aaaahhhhhh, mmm... Makes your mouth water, doesn't it?

Well, that cloud you just inhaled is packed full of PAHs – which are simply the not-yet burned up residue of fuel, like wood or gas, that sticks to the surface of food (and also adds flavors).

Whereas HCAs are formed by any high-heat cooking method, PAHs are more closely related to the smoke in barbecuing. Polycyclic aromatics have long been thought to trigger some cancers and many other diseases. The best example of damage linked to PAHs is lung disease in smokers.

Almost makes you want to throw away your tongs, your kiss-the-cook apron, and your fancy chef's hat.

Well, all is not lost. While several studies find consuming well-done meat with crispy outsides is a risk factor in certain cancers, other studies find little relationship between cooking methods and cancer risks. So what's a tong-carrying, apron-swathed, chef-hatted, red-blooded male to do?

Here's what I do when grilling or barbecuing to lower my production of HCAs and PAHs...

I don't overcook. Rare or medium-rare meats taste better and have fewer of those nasty HCAs and PAHs.

I trim the fat if it's burning. This cuts down on the PAH-filled smoke.

I use a gas grill whenever possible. Gas grills cook at a lower and more even temperature than charcoal. They also produce less smoke.

I use thinner cuts of meat. This cuts down on the total cooking time needed, but still gives me some of that grilled flavor.

When I absolutely have to have a thick steak, I'll do a quick flash over higher heat to lock in the juices and then slowly cook it over indirect heat with the top open to avoid smoke and high temperatures. This adds a little bit of extra time on the grill, but it keeps that grilled flavor without smoke, burning, and char.

I don't eat the blackened or burnt parts. OK, I do cheat once in a while on this because I am a mere human and only have so much will power. But I do this very rarely... maybe once or twice a year. OK, three times.

I often have an enormous salad after I eat grilled meat. I even add fresh vegetables or fruits to the racks when I grill. The vegetables and fruits are low in fat and high in fiber, which helps keep digestion regular. They also contain many cancer-fighting substances, like vitamin C.

I love mushrooms, onions, carrots, zucchini, broccoli, corn, potatoes, and green and red peppers. For fruits, I use peaches, papaya, pineapple, and mangos.

I love to use marinades. One of my favorites is just olive oil and balsamic vinegar with some rosemary and pepper. The acid in marinades (vinegar for example) helps reduce the formation of carcinogens on your grilled foods. In one study, it lowered the HCA production by 90%.

— 5 —

Three Foods to Instantly Improve Your Health

Summer is one of the best times of year to get fresh fruits and vegetables.

I love to hit local farmer's markets on Saturdays to pick up fresh produce, especially things I don't grow at home. I have a garden full of nutritious foods like blackberries, raspberries, peaches, rhubarb, tomatoes, and many different kinds of herbs.

Eating the right foods is a simple way to improve your health. The right foods increase your energy levels, help you sleep better, decrease your risk of cancer, and deliver myriad other benefits. Three foods stand out above all the rest... berries, avocados, and broccoli.

Berries

I buy Cinnamon Life cereal for one purpose and one purpose alone: to eat with the world's best fruit.

I eat fruit with everything – chocolate ice cream... a bowl of milk... yogurt... waffles. What is this super fruit I love so much? **Blueberries**!

Blueberries taste sweet and tart but have texture and tannins to balance the sugars. The skin's color provides much of their health benefit... I call blueberries the "perfect blue food." They can help lower cholesterol, fight cancer, and improve digestion. They even aid your metabolism.

One study shows that probiotics, in food like yogurt, help break down the antioxidants in blueberries (called polyphenols) to more usable forms. This allows your body to absorb more of the nutrients and reap more benefits.

Blues (and actually many other kinds of berries) improve health because of their so-called antioxidants, flavonoids, anthocyanins (which gives the skin the blue color), and other chemicals.

Blues are No. 1 on my list of superfoods – mainly because they have the highest amount of those antioxidants, more than any other fruit. Plus, these little buggers are full of vitamin C, vitamin E, beta-carotene, and manganese. This has to be a fruit served in heaven.

A good breakfast is a blueberry smoothie with protein powder, vanilla, cinnamon, plain yogurt, and ice. It's about 350 calories balanced between fat, carbohydrates, and protein, so my blood sugar stays steady.

Blueberries truly have many health benefits. For just a few examples, they...

- Improve digestion and relieve constipation

- Lower cholesterol

- Slow aging

- Improve eyesight

- Reduce inflammation

- Fight cancer

- Relieve diarrhea

- Fight urinary-tract infections

- Improve recovery from strokes

When it comes to the blues... What do I do? I make sure to buy two-for-one blueberries by the ton. They freeze well. And they last for weeks in the fridge. Don't wash the berries until right before eating them or the skins get soft and moldy. (This tip is true for other berries as well.)

Raspberries (probably my second-favorite after blues) are packed with flavonoids like ellagic acid. Research shows ellagic acid inhibits tumor growth in certain cancers. And according to the American Cancer Society, it kills cancer cells without harming healthy cells.

Strawberries are also full of ellagic acid. Like all berries, they have lots of cancer-fighting antioxidants and anti-inflammatories. They relieve many of the symptoms of rheumatoid arthritis – especially pain.

> ## *DO WHAT I DO*
>
> Mix a little white vinegar with water and soak your produce before eating. Then, rinse the stuff off with water.

One drawback: Store-bought strawberries and raspberries tend to be highly contaminated with pesticides. Do what I do... Mix a little white vinegar with water and soak your produce before eating. Then, rinse the stuff off with water.

Blackberries also help lower cholesterol and fight cancer. And they improve your immune system because they're packed with vitamin C. Their high amounts of potassium and salicylate (an ingredient in aspirin) may help protect you from high blood pressure.

All berries are great for eye health. Science shows unique micronutrients that make berries high in antioxidants offer special benefits for the eye.

Avocados

Avocados are another amazing food, but they've gotten a bad reputation over the years. Many people avoid avocados because they're high in fat. It's true... A medium-sized avocado is loaded with 30 grams of fat. But much of the fat is monounsaturated fat – known to lower LDL "bad" cholesterol.

Avocados also contain a sugar called mannoheptulose, which inhibits the secretion of insulin. If you have hypoglycemia – low blood-sugar levels – eating avocados is a healthy source of glucose. But because glucose inhibits insulin, avocados can cause "instant diabetes" – a rapid increase in blood sugar levels.

Most people with healthy blood-sugar levels don't have to worry about this. But if you're diabetic, monitor your blood sugar when eating avocados.

I love to eat avocado wedges in a salad or as guacamole.

Broccoli

Broccoli is one of the best cancer-fighting foods. It includes a compound called isothiocyanate and a phytochemical known as sulforaphane, both of which are shown to help fight cancer. Broccoli also contains an antioxidant known as indole-3-carbinol. Some studies link this antioxidant to a lower risk of breast and cervical cancer.

> ### *DO WHAT I DO*
> Steam the broccoli and add a little lemon juice and olive oil. But don't overcook it. Boiling or over-steaming broccoli reduces some of the nutrients, like sulforaphane and vitamin C.

The vegetable also has more vitamin C than a medium orange and is one of the best sources of vitamin A.

Eating just four servings of broccoli a week can cut your risk of prostate cancer in half. One cup of raw broccoli or one half-cup of cooked is equal to one serving.

Do what I do to improve the taste... steam the broccoli and add a little lemon juice and olive oil. But don't overcook it. Boiling or over-steaming broccoli reduces some of the nutrients, like sulforaphane and vitamin C.

If you want to start living a healthier life, make sure berries, avocados, and broccoli are part of your weekly diet.

— 6 —

'Good Bugs' Abound in One of the Healthiest Foods on the Planet

If you've ever opened a yogurt container and been tempted to pour off the liquid swishing around on top, don't. That liquid is swimming with millions of bacteria that provide yogurt's key benefit.

The bacteria are called "probiotics" – literally "good bugs."

Probiotics have mean-sounding names like Lactobacillus bulgaricus and Bifidobacterium bifidum. But they work to improve digestion and enhance your immune system.

Eating yogurt regularly helps to moderate your immune system's responses – almost like the tune up of a car. Some research shows yogurt reduces allergies and autoimmune diseases. Yogurt also lowers the risk of certain cancers like bladder cancer.

One other benefit I've discovered is eating yogurt saves money on toilet paper. Yogurt improves the quality of stool formed and makes bowel movements much easier.

You can choose from several kinds of yogurt – plain (which can be organic or not), "Greek," or one of the specialty kinds, like Activia. The specialty brands claim to have an extra probiotic called Bifidobacterium animalis. (Each brand has a different name for it. It's intestinal bacteria commonly found in pigs.) This is just another type of probiotic that helps your digestive system.

I prefer to buy (and even make) good, old plain yogurt. Plain yogurt is lower in calories than Greek yogurt (though it has less protein). Best of all, plain yogurt is the cheapest. Specifically, I like Dannon and Stonyfield Farms plain yogurt.

I avoid all the flavored "fruit on the bottom" or "blended" yogurts. They're loaded with sweeteners I don't need. Instead, I swirl in a few blueberries for a sweet, healthy snack.

If you're not a fan of eating yogurt (texture or taste), you can also take supplements containing acidophilus. These capsules contain the identical probiotics as most yogurts.

> ### DO WHAT I DO
> **Swirl some blueberries into yogurt for a sweet, healthy snack.**

— 7 —

The Dangers of Taking Fish Oil

Stansberry Research Editor in Chief Brian Hunt – an avid fitness sage – came into my office once after reading the claim that athletes should take 30-45 grams of fish oil a day. He's not alone...

Conventional wisdom says fish is good for you. Studies from Harvard and the Journal of the American College of Cardiology found people who eat at least two servings of fish per week were 36% less likely to die from heart disease.

Those claims led to nutrition research that pointed to fish oil as the probable mechanism. Like most things though, more isn't necessarily better.

As a food, fish is low in carbohydrates, high in protein, and moderately high in fat. The fat composition of fish is the important issue. Fish meat is low in saturated fats. This is good because too much saturated fat is thought to be harmful.

The two fats providing benefits in fish are the monounsaturated and the polyunsaturated fats. Monounsaturated fat is what makes up olive oil and is well-known to aid heart health.

The polyunsaturated oils have special chemical bonds along the chain of carbon atoms (oils are just strings of carbon atoms of various lengths). When the bond is on the third carbon, we call it an omega-3 fat.

Although the reasons aren't clear, omega-3 fats (from fish as well as other sources) reduce inflammation and thus offer health benefits.

Inflammation can increase your risk of heart disease, diabetes, and aging. Eating fish inhibits these things.

Since not everyone loves seafood, the dietary supplement industry has an alternative: fish-oil pills.

Fish-oil supplements are marketed as miracle pills. Some research suggests the supplements can ease depression, high blood pressure, and even arthritis. However, despite the miracle-cure claims of fish oil, serious health concerns surround taking fish oil, especially in such large amounts.

Here's why: One of the omega-3 fats in fish oil is known as DHA. Studies have shown DHA lowers total cholesterol. On the surface, this sounds good. But total cholesterol is made up of multiple components. Two of the most important are LDL and HDL.

LDL is thought to create arterial plaque and is labeled a "bad cholesterol." On the other hand, HDL is the "good cholesterol." DHA slightly increases HDL and LDL (the bad kind).

But the real problem I've discovered is some of these pills can be tainted with chemical killers like PCBs, mercury, and dioxin. These poisons concentrate in fish higher in the food chain. Thus, small fish have less poison in their flesh. Each larger fish up the chain eats the smaller fish and concentrates the poisons. Mercury is known to cause neurological problems in babies and the elderly.

In 2010, the Mateel Environmental Justice Foundation and FishOilSafety. com filed a lawsuit against manufacturers of certain fish-oil supplements, including RiteAid, Nature Made, and CVS. These watchdog groups tested 10 supplements and found each one contained some level of PCBs, a once-common component of plastics. Congress banned PCBs in 1979.

Of course, the supplement makers claim to have a solution... making omega-3 pills from a plant called flaxseed. According to a study in *The American Journal of Clinical Nutrition*, flaxseed oil demonstrates the same benefits as fish oil. Although it lacks the two omega-3 fatty acids – DHA and EPA – flaxseed contains oil known as ALA. Your body naturally converts ALA into DHA and EPA, albeit inefficiently.

The downside to flaxseed oil? Very little has been done to study the long-term effects of taking flaxseed. Plus, the oil goes rancid quickly. I don't like fat soluble, oil-filled vitamins. Fat-based chemicals can build up in human tissues. I avoid taking too many fat-soluble vitamins like A, D, E, and K. You should, too.

Yet supplement makers are stuffing pills, baby foods, and even milk with these Omega-3 oils based on health claims that are equivocal at best. At worst, we're discovering supplements lack the natural balance of oils and micronutrients that exist in the "whole" food (like actual fish meat).

Seafood likely contains other health-giving chemicals and molecules not yet measured.

The key is to eat fish lower in mercury... like salmon, light tuna, herring, mackerel, and anchovies. Plus, most of the good research showing clear benefits of fish involved whole fish, not fish oil.

Finally, fish oil is dangerous in that it alters your bleeding and coagulation functions. Too much and you could induce strokes from bleeding into your brain. Until high doses of fish oils are studied and the mechanism of action is better understood by hematologists (blood doctors), I wouldn't take more than one or two pills a week, or 1,000 mg of oil. The amounts my Editor in Chief talked about are just plain dangerous.

What do I do? I prefer eating real fish. I eat salmon or light tuna (lowest amount of mercury among tunas) three to four times a month and take an occasional fish oil pill of 300mg from GNC. With moderation, a mix of whole food, and a minimum of pills... I get nearly all the health benefits without having to worry about the risks.

The important part is to eat fish and pills that are low in mercury.

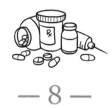

— 8 —

The Dangers of Fat-Soluble Vitamins

If you're not careful, you could be killing yourself... inviting cancer or other problems.

A Finnish study about a decade ago showed the combination of vitamins A and E to be deadly... And yet a brand-name nutraceutical manufacturer created the combination because it could combine two "antioxidants" and marketed the pill as being healthy.

The problem is that because there's no regulation, supplement marketers and manufacturers aren't required to run their pills through rigorous (and expensive) scientific studies. The Dietary Supplement Health and Education Act of 1994 exempts them from needing to test safety and effectiveness.

The act allowed anybody to combine anything that is a vitamin, mineral, herb, botanical, or amino acid into a pill and sell it as healthy for you. Now, the marketers (and many doctors) are touting pills with clear health risks, making scientifically shaky (at best) claims...

Several years back, the over-the-counter (OTC) supplement market surpassed the prescription market in dollar sales. Research shows nearly 80% of people take supplements occasionally. No problem there. Many supplements have proven benefits...

The thing is, research shows close to 60% of people think supplements are safer than prescription or OTC medications and that supplements sold in "health" stores and online are proven safe... That's a dangerous – potentially fatal – assumption.

I take vitamin C daily and also take an occasional multivitamin. But I'm careful about what I take and how much of certain vitamins I consume. You should think twice about adding unproven pills to your body.

Fat-Soluble Vitamins Can Build Up in Your Body

In the case of vitamins A and E (and two others we'll discuss in a moment), the real danger is these vitamins are fat soluble. If you're overdosing on fat-soluble vitamins, they build up over time in your fatty tissues.

At high concentrations, these vitamins create serious health problems. That means you could easily be overdosing on what's marketed as a perfectly safe supplement. The fat-soluble vitamins are A, D, E, and K.

Water-soluble vitamins – like vitamin B and C – don't collect in your tissues. So it's hard to overdose on them. Most times, if you take too much of a water-soluble vitamin, you'll simply urinate it out.

And yet while the fat-soluble vitamins might have some benefits, they can also have dangerous consequences if levels rise in the body, especially from taking them in concentrated pill forms.

Let's run through the commonly touted fat-soluble vitamins:

<u>**Vitamin A**</u>

The Good News: Vitamin A helps promote bone and tooth growth, as well as improve night vision. If you've heard of the nutrient beta-carotene, it's a naturally occurring form of vitamin A that appears in vegetables like carrots and sweet potatoes. You can also get vitamin A from dairy products, leafy green vegetables, and several other foods.

The Bad News: An overdose of vitamin A can cause blurred vision, hair loss, headaches, and even bone pain. In infants and young children, too much of it causes growth retardation.

Proper portions: An adult needs about 3,000-5,000 international units (IU) a day of vitamin A. A carrot has 4,000 IU of vitamin A. Throw a carrot in your lunch bag every day, and you're doing fine. Unless you're a starving African villager, you have no reason to supplement your diet with this fat-soluble vitamin. The dangers far outweigh the benefit.

Vitamin D

The Good News: Your body naturally converts sunlight to vitamin D, which hardens bones and teeth and helps you absorb calcium (also critical to bone structure and function).

The Bad News: Too much vitamin D can cause kidney failure, kidney stones, and painful muscle spasms. Worse, a review in *The New England Journal of Medicine* (*NEJM*) linked vitamin D to increased pancreatic and esophageal cancers.

People with little knowledge of the science tout vitamin D as the cure for depression, osteoporosis, and cancers alike. The *NEJM* study showed no indication that higher serum concentrations warded off some of the more common cancers like endometrial, esophageal, gastric, kidney, ovarian, and lymphomas.

Proper portions: The maximum amount of vitamin D you need is 400 IU a day. You can get most of this amount by spending a few minutes outside. Even better, your body self-regulates this process... So you can spend hours outside and still get just the right amount.

People who live in areas with limited sun in the winter can become deficient in vitamin D. In those cases, dietary supplements are warranted. But be careful...

Several commercial vitamins are stuffed with 600-1,000 IU in each pill. Also, you can find vitamin D in dairy products "fortified" with it, as well as over-the-counter fish-oil pills. I've seen bottles of vitamin D pills with a 5,000 IU megadose.

If you're vulnerable to vitamin D deficiency, be mindful of the dosage you're taking and give your body the time to process the chemicals you're feeding it. You only need 400 IU, so I wouldn't take that 5,000 IU pill more than once every 12 days (5,000 divided by 400).

That assumes you don't get any sunlight or eat any foods with it for those days – an absurd assumption. One bottle should last about four years.

Vitamin E

The Good News: Vitamin E is found in whole grains, nuts, and leafy green vegetables. It's a well-known antioxidant and prevents damage to cell membranes.

The Bad News: Studies are mixed on the benefits. This is due in part to the fact that vitamin E exists in eight different structures in nature. That makes designing reliable studies tricky at best.

Proper portions: The most an adult needs is around 60 IU per day.

Vitamin E in high doses can be deadly. If you take much more, you can experience fatigue, muscle weakness, headaches, and excessive bleeding. Some people take 1,000-2,000 IU a day, at great risk to their health.

Vitamin zealots claim E is the fountain of youth. Again, it isn't. And no amount of name-calling or anecdotal claims should convince you otherwise.

Vitamin K

The Good News: Vitamin K is critical in blood clotting as well as bone metabolism. A shot of it is given to every U.S. infant at birth to prevent a rare but fatal brain bleed. (Only five in 100,000 infants now experience such brain bleeds.) New research shows vitamin K is important for bone health.

The Bad News: Not much... Vitamin K taken orally – even in large doses – is rarely toxic.

Proper portions: The human body uses about 100 micrograms per day. You can easily get most of the vitamin K you need in a single serving of green vegetables. A cup of broccoli has 629 micrograms. A teaspoon of parsley carries 75 micrograms. One study showed eating lettuce once a day cuts your risk of hip fractures in half. And vitamin K is readily recycled in the body's cells.

With an adequate diet, you don't need extra supplementation. Mega dosing hasn't shown any ill effects... but it is unnecessary.

If you're concerned about a vitamin deficiency, do what I do...

My diet is varied, and I eat nuts and green leafy vegetables regularly (weekly at a minimum) for natural doses of vitamin E. For my vitamin A, I eat carrots, sweet potatoes, and green leafy vegetables. When you consume these vitamins in whole foods, you're getting much lower doses and avoiding the risks of toxicity and long-term dangers of cancer.

Of course, I'm human... Like anyone, I fall short of those dietary goals from time to time. To cover myself in those cases, I take a vitamin supplement once a month. *Most people don't need to take a supplement containing fat-soluble vitamins any more often than that.*

Your body needs small amounts of these vitamins to function well. If you're eating greens and colored fruits and vegetables weekly, you're putting all the fat-soluble vitamins you need into your system. Your liver and the fat in your body store these vitamins and can get them when they're needed.

DO WHAT I DO

My diet is varied, and I eat nuts and green leafy vegetables regularly (weekly at a minimum) for natural doses of vitamin E. For my vitamin A, I eat carrots, sweet potatoes, and green leafy vegetables.

— 9 —

Three White Foods That Kill... and Three That Cure

I call them "**white killers**"...

Every time you reach into your refrigerator or cabinet, you might be grabbing these killers... foods that are processed, refined, and essentially stripped of their natural nutritional benefits.

The three worst white killers are sugar, white rice, and white bread...

These three white foods (called "high glycemic index" foods) are known to significantly increase your blood-sugar levels. When you eat high-glycemic-index foods, your body senses the extra sugar (what we don't need for energy) and produces extra insulin in the pancreas.

The insulin secreted into the blood stream triggers a host of things – a decrease of magnesium and an increase of sodium in the blood. Insulin also increases pro-inflammation molecules (like homocysteine) in the blood.

Insulin even triggers the production of fat. The extra fat leads to high blood sugar and keeps metabolism "stuck" in storage mode. Lots of insulin causes the vessels to get oxidized and stiffen... leading to higher blood pressure. Over time, this could cause strokes and heart disease.

Bottom line: Avoid eating high-glycemic-index foods.

Everyone has heard **sugar** is bad for them. But most of America can't stay away. On average, Americans consume 355 calories of sugar per day. The American Health Association recommends women get less than 100 calories from sugar and men get less than 150 calories from sugar.

> ### *DO WHAT I DO*
> Avoid sweeteners. If I do want some "sweetness," I'll use molasses or turbinado sugar – a natural brown sugar that's only partially refined.

Yet the average American probably consumes more than double the recommended amount.

Studies show eating lots of sugar lowers your good cholesterol (a so-called high-density lipoprotein, HDL). HDL cholesterol is important because it inhibits excess levels of harmful fats and "bad" cholesterol (low-density lipoprotein, or LDL) from sticking to arteries. That keeps your blood flowing easily. Low levels of HDL increase your risk of heart disease.

Elevated blood glucose leads to immune-system problems, including white blood cell dysfunction and clotting problems.

Do what I do... Avoid sweeteners. If I do want some "sweetness," I'll use molasses or turbinado sugar – a natural brown sugar that's only partially refined.

Two other white foods that must also be avoided are white rice and white bread... Both are carbohydrates stripped of their natural health benefits.

White rice is brown rice stripped of the outer layers (husk, bran, and germ). These parts contain most of the benefits of rice... like fiber. The rice is bleached to give it the perfect white look you're used to.

White bread is loaded with calories and sugar... and offers little nutritional benefit because it lacks whole grains. And like rice, it's full of chemicals to make it look pristine and appetizing.

I prefer to eat brown and wild rices and whole-grain breads. Some of my favorite breads have 12 grains or more. But if you don't like the texture or taste of fully whole-grain bread, look for some with just three grains.

(They have a softer, less grainy texture.)

These three white foods are full of chemicals and lack nutritional value. But that doesn't mean you need to avoid all white foods.

Three white foods packed with nutrients are cauliflower, white onions, and white beans. These whites won't kill – they can cure.

That's because they're all low-glycemic-index foods. Plus...

Cauliflower is a good source of potassium. Potassium helps keep your organs – especially your heart and kidneys – working properly. Cauliflower also has vitamin C and omega-3.

Vitamin C is my go-to vitamin when I'm feeling a cold advancing. And as we've discussed, omega-3 fatty acids lower your risk of cancer, reduce blood pressure, and improve mental health (along with many other benefits).

White onions are another food high in vitamin C. They have cancer-fighting flavonoids – antioxidants found in plants. White onions also have allyl propyl disulphide. This chemical is what makes you cry when you cut an onion. But it also lowers blood sugar and aids in lowering cholesterol.

Another favorite is the **white bean**. White beans act like an antidiabetic medication by lowering and stabilizing insulin release. White beans are also loaded with fiber, which helps lower your overall cholesterol levels. They also contain folate – a B vitamin that reduces your heart-attack risk.

Avoid the white killers... but make these three beneficial white foods staples in your diet.

I rarely eat any of the white killers on my list. And I make sure my diet contains the healthy white foods. They help control the insulin levels in my body and can keep me feeling fuller than most foods. They also help me maintain energy, my immune system, and cardiovascular processes.

So cut out white sugar, white bread, and white rice... Fill yourself up on cauliflower, white onions, and white beans. You'll be amazed at how much better you'll feel throughout the day.

— 10 —

You Won't Believe How Much Food Labels Don't Tell You

The next time you're clinking wine glasses over a bottle of cabernet, remember... you could be sipping fish-bladder extract.

If you're like most people, you assume when you buy wine, you're buying a bottle of fermented grapes. But there's more to it than that.

One common ingredient in wine is isinglass – a fish-bladder extract. It's used to clarify the wine. Other regularly used ingredients are gelatin, egg whites, yeast, clay, various color enhancers, and even food flavorings.

A quick poll I did in the office confirmed that few people realize wine contains such extra ingredients.

And this isn't just a problem in the U.S. If you think you can avoid these ingredients by sticking with European wines – thanks to their centuries-old wine standardization laws – you're wrong.

Those laws focus mostly on the types of grapes makers can use. But the European Union (EU) does not require the wine industry to include ingredient labels. Most of the additives allowed in the U.S. are also allowed in the EU. So can you be sure that Burgundy is mostly Pinot Noir... but a little fish-bladder extract? Maybe, maybe not.

Some winemakers in the U.S. are deciding to list ingredients. Bonny Doon Vineyard in Santa Cruz, California decided to include an ingredients list in 2007. A few other vineyards followed.

I'm not too concerned about isinglass itself... The point is, it's shocking to discover some of the things in our food that aren't disclosed on labels.

The Alcohol and Tobacco Tax and Trade Bureau regulates wine labeling. But the requirements focus only on the brand, alcohol content, location of origin, and time of bottling (plus a generic health warning).

When I began creating my own label for my first vintage of wine (a 2009 Cabernet called "Eifrig"), I was shocked to learn that there are no requirements to disclose much about the wine.

And some common ingredients concern me... Velcorin, for example, is used as a preservative or sterilizing agent. The FDA and the EU Scientific Committee both say velcorin is safe in tiny quantities to use in beverages. Yet people who handle the chemical in large quantities must wear Hazmat suits.

And of course, it's not just an issue with wine... The FDA allows for a 20% margin of error on food labels. So for example, if you're eating food that claims to be 100 calories, it could actually be 80 or 120 calories. The same margin of error applies to the daily values you'll see on labels...

Worse, many food makers aren't even living up to the 20% margin-of-error rule. Over the years, numerous other studies have documented the inaccuracy of food labels.

In 2008, the ABC television program *Good Morning America* conducted a study that found Ritz Crackers had 36% more sodium than advertised on the label. Wonder Bread had 70% more fat than the label claimed. Several other foods were well out of the FDA's 20% margin.

At *Retirement Millionaire*, we're all about empowering people with information... which is why I've taken an interest in another hot-button issue...

Genetically modified organisms (GMOs) are organisms that have had their genetic material changed using genetic engineering techniques. GMOs are found in crop seeds like soy and corn and whole products like tomatoes. Even salmon can contain GMOs as a result of runoff into rivers. GMOs are meant to protect crops from insects, diseases, and pesticides, which would improve crop yields and make crop quality more consistent.

But GMOs attract a lot of controversy. Some people claim they decrease the nutritional value of foods and increase the use of herbicides and pesticides. There are also theoretical dangers to humans.

I'm not saying GMO foods are good or bad... The science and research on both sides of the GMO debate are equivocal at best. But whatever your view of GMOs, *you should have the information you need to make an educated decision about what you choose to eat.*

As of 2014, a warning (or even a label) was not required on foods that contain GMOs. But several states tried to change that. The Vermont Right to Know Genetically Engineered Food Act became a hot issue in 2013. More than 96% of voters in Vermont supported the bill. But the movement stalled... after the state faced legal pressure from some agricultural industry giants.

If you have the opportunity to vote on a labeling or disclosure initiative... I urge you to vote in favor of transparency. It's the only way we can make informed decisions for ourselves about our health and wealth...

Otherwise, we're left trusting that government and industry are acting in our best interest. And that means people in Hazmat suits dumping chemicals into our food without our knowledge.

How Can You Know What's in Your Food and Drink?

One way to be sure of what you're getting in your food... bypass processed foods as often as you can. Manufacturing adds unknown ingredients, and the nutritional information of processed foods is largely unbelievable.

But when you pick up an apple grown in your backyard or by a trusted neighbor or local vendor... you can be sure what you're getting is an apple and little else.

Do what I do... Ask manufacturers whenever you have specific questions. Call customer service phone numbers and ask. If they don't tell you (or won't), don't buy.

> ### *DO WHAT I DO*
> **Ask manufacturers whenever you have specific questions.**

— 11 —

Is Organic Food Really Better?

Every time I walk into a grocery store, I see signs and labels trying to convince me of some food's healthy qualities.

Everything from cereal to meat to beverages to produce can be labeled as "organic," "all natural," or "local." Hundreds of food products are labeled and marketed this way... trying to convince the consumer that the food is healthier.

But here's the catch... The "all natural/organics" fad obscures a real problem in America's food supply.

The issue is pesticides. Foods containing pesticides have been linked to Parkinson's disease and human thyroid dysfunction. These poisons are also known to alter human liver and brain function. And the effects happen indirectly from just minute amounts of these chemicals. In the smallest amounts, they contaminate water supplies, which can kill animals and result in human birth defects.

Consumers are being conned into thinking these "organic" or "all natural" foods eliminate this risk, when really, none of these terms ensure the overall healthiness or safety of the food.

First... let's dispense with "all natural" and "local." When it comes to health, these terms are virtually meaningless.

Calling a food "all natural" means nothing. As of 2014, the FDA had no formal definition of when a product can be called "all natural" (unless a food is a meat or an egg). The U.S. Department of Agriculture (USDA) requires meat, poultry, or eggs to have "no artificial ingredients or added color and be only minimally processed" before the product can be called natural.

The term "local" varies from state to state. Local can be food grown in a certain radius or simply food grown somewhere within your state. Local doesn't reflect how the product was made (if pesticides or artificial ingredients were used). Like the "all natural" label, the *government does not regulate the use of this term.*

Finally, there's "organic"... Products bearing this label must be made with organic ingredients, which are USDA-certified. "Organic" suggests the product is made without the use of synthetic or chemical pesticides or herbicides.

But remember... organic farms still use pesticides. They just use pesticides that are labeled "organic" and certified by the National Organic Standards Board. Two of the most common organic pesticides are rotenone and pyrethrin.

Rotenone is toxic to aquatic life. A study published in 2011 from the National Institute of Environmental Health Sciences found people who used this pesticide were 2.5 times more likely to develop Parkinson's disease.

Pyrethrin has its risks as well. From 2003 to 2007, 20 deaths linked to the pesticide were reported to the U.S. Environmental Protection Agency. It's also extremely toxic to dogs and cats.

Not only that... But foods can consist of up to 5% nonorganic chemicals and still bear the organic label.

At *Retirement Millionaire,* we're all about finding ways to live a better life on less. That means knowing which veggies and fruits have the most and the least chemicals.

Every year, an organization called the Environmental Working Groups updates its list of the "Dirty Dozen" – the 12 foods that have the highest amounts of pesticides. You can see the 2013 version of this list below.

We've also added in the far right column the 12 foods that have the least amount of pesticides. Write it down and post it on your fridge. Take a copy with you to the grocery store.

Rank	Highest in Pesticides... The Dirty Dozen	Lowest in Pesticides... The Clean 12
1	Apples	Asparagus
2	Celery	Avocados
3	Cherry tomatoes	Cabbage
4	Cucumbers	Cantaloupe
5	Grapes	Sweet corn
6	Hot peppers	Eggplant
7	Nectarines – imported	Grapefruit
8	Peaches	Kiwi
9	Potatoes	Mangos
10	Spinach	Mushrooms
11	Strawberries	Onions
12	Sweet bell peppers	Papayas

To protect yourself, do what I do...

When buying foods from the Dirty Dozen list, buy organic. The restrictions reduce some pesticide exposure and are better than nothing. (When buying produce on the "clean" list, save a few bucks and skip the organic offerings.)

More important... *wash all your produce with a mixture of white vinegar and water.* I let everything soak for a bit and then rinse the fruits and vegetables off with just water. This method is effective since most of the pesticide residue sits on the skin.

> ## DO WHAT I DO
>
> **When buying foods from the Dirty Dozen list, buy organic. The restrictions reduce some pesticide exposure and are better than nothing.**

— 12 —

17 Foods, Supplements, and Personal Products to Avoid

Soy

Real men don't eat soy. Not unless they want to grow fatty breasts...

I used to drink about 15 cartons of Silk brand soy milk a year. But now it's down to just a couple in six months. The reason? Soy protein contains genistein and daidzein, which are known phyto-estrogens (plant-produced estrogens).

High levels of estrogen (the hormone that makes women look and act like women) in men causes reduced levels of testosterone, loss of muscle tissue, increase of body fat, and a decrease in libido and sexual function.

Sushi

Don't eat sushi on Mondays.

> **DO WHAT I DO**
> Opt for well-cooked fish.

Unless you're at a highly touted seafood restaurant on the water, I'd recommend you avoid all seafood early in the week. The freshest fish is usually delivered later in the week, right before the busy weekend. So what you get on a Monday night is usually just the leftovers, which means the fish is four to five days old. If you can't hold back, do what I do and opt for well-cooked fish.

Teeth Whiteners

Stop using harsh teeth whiteners.

The next time you have a drink that stains your teeth (like red wine or coffee), do what I do... have a few sips of water. The water washes away the acidic residue that harms enamel and stains teeth.

> ### *DO WHAT I DO*
> Have a few sips of water. The water washes away the acidic residue that harms enamel and stains teeth.

And whatever you do, wait at least 30 minutes to brush your teeth after drinking acidic beverages. The damage caused by whitening toothpastes is worse after eating or drinking something acidic. Waiting allows your saliva to rebuild tooth enamel.

Antibacterial Soaps

Stop using harmful antibacterial soaps.

These soaps won't fight germs much better than regular soap. While regular soap doesn't kill all of the bacteria on your hands, you don't need it to. Simply removing some of the germs will keep you healthy – especially during cold season.

Antibacterial soaps can also be dangerous. Early studies show triclosan – the main antibacterial ingredient in the soaps – can alter your hormones. This can cause developmental and reproduction problems. Trust your body to do what it's made to, and it will fight off germs just fine.

In addition, a 2005 study of 224 households from the University of Michigan School of Public Health found that families using antibacterial soap were no healthier than families using regular soap.

Unless you're a doctor, you don't need antibacterial soap.

> ### *DO WHAT I DO*
> Use plain, ordinary soap. As long as you wash thoroughly – 15-20 seconds at least – the soap will separate bacteria from your skin.

So do what I do... use plain, ordinary soap. As long as you wash thoroughly

– 15-20 seconds at least – the soap will separate bacteria from your skin.

And speaking of washing your hands, stop using so much hand sanitizer. Hand sanitizer does not significantly reduce how often you catch a cold or the flu. Study volunteers applied hand sanitizer every three hours, but experienced colds and the flu almost as much as people who used no hand sanitizer.

Tap Water

You could be drinking contaminated tap water.

About 20% of the U.S.' water supply has dangerously high levels of arsenic. Arsenic is a chemical naturally found in rocks, soil, and water. Exposure to high levels of arsenic is known to cause cancer.

Moderate levels of exposure can increase your risk for high blood pressure and Type 2 diabetes. Arsenic in your drinking water could also put you at higher risk of having a stroke.

According to the Environmental Protection Agency (EPA), an arsenic level of 0.01 parts per million (ppm) or lower is safe for people to drink. But in 2009, the advocacy organization Environmental Working Group found dangerously high arsenic levels in several states' drinking water supplies.

In both Maine and California, all 10 water supplies tested had arsenic levels greater than 0.01 ppm. Several water systems in Florida had high levels of arsenic, some up to 0.023 ppm. In California, one water system had arsenic levels as high as 0.29 ppm.

Your local water utility is required to report on all toxins found in water. If your water has high levels of arsenic – more than 10 parts per billion – ask your local health department for a list of treatment specialists. Treating arsenic in drinking water can be a complicated process, and a specialist will know the treatments that are best for you.

Baby Products Containing Chlorinated Tris

A 2011 study found eight out of 10 common baby products contain a suspected carcinogen called chlorinated tris.

Chlorinated tris is a flame-retardant chemical commonly found in the padding of car seats, strollers, and high chairs. Infants breathing or absorbing the chemicals are at higher risk of developing cancer. Chlorinated tris can also permanently damage an infant's developing brain.

Look for polyester or cotton filling in mattresses, car seats, and high chairs. Some retailers, like Babies "R" Us, have organic sections where you can find mattresses made from cotton. Also, the manufacturer Orbit Baby offers a wide selection of flame-resistant strollers and car seats that don't use the harmful chemicals.

Zicam

You may be ruining your sex life with this cold remedy.

Aromas make my "Top 12 Ways to Improve Your Health" list every year. That's because different smells can relax you, invigorate you, and improve your mood. Some aromas like pumpkin and lavender (mixed together), can even improve your sex life.

But your cold medicines may be damaging your sense of smell without realizing it. In 2009, the FDA warned that zinc sprays could lead to a loss of your sense of smell. One of the most well-known manufacturers of zinc sprays is Zicam.

Despite the FDA's warning, Zicam assured its customers zinc sprays are safe. And the company continued to distribute them.

> **DO WHAT I DO**
>
> When I have a stuffy nose from a cold or allergies, I use my Neti pot.

But more studies show the dangers of using zinc sprays... especially ones that put liquid directly into your nose. Zinc can cause you to temporarily – or permanently, in some cases – lose your sense of smell if the chemicals get up into your olfactory bulb.

And besides, several studies show zinc probably doesn't shorten or prevent colds.

So do what I do... When I have a stuffy nose from a cold or allergies, I use my Neti pot. The Neti pot is a device used to rinse the sinuses out. You can buy one at your local drug store for about $10. I use mine once a day when I have a cold or when my sinuses are clogged from allergies. But follow the instructions carefully, and don't use tap water.

Fish-Oil Supplements

Anyone receiving cancer treatment needs to stay away from fish-oil supplements...

Fish-oil supplements can be high in mercury and increase the risk of bleeding, including inducing strokes from bleeding in your brain. They also reduce the effectiveness of cancer chemotherapy.

A 2011 study found that certain fatty acids – called platinum-induced fatty acids (PIFAs) – in fish oil make cancer cells resistant to different types of chemotherapy. One of the chemotherapies PIFAs inhibit is cisplatin, which is commonly used to treat lung and ovarian cancer (and derived from platinum). The fats shield cancer tumors from chemo treatments.

Researchers aren't sure whether PIFAs interfere with all types of chemotherapies. But if you're going through chemo, tell your doctor about all the nonprescription drugs you might be taking. In this case, be sure and ask whether fish oil can hinder your cancer treatment.

Ginkgo Biloba

Ginkgo biloba – the fifth best-selling supplement in the U.S. – is often touted as a memory aid and a tool for preventing dementia. But many studies show no difference between people taking a ginkgo biloba supplement versus a placebo.

And taking ginkgo can have dangerous side effects... Chemicals in ginkgo help to open up blood vessels, which improves your blood flow. But the chemicals also thin the blood... creating an increased risk of bleeding.

I tried it a few times, and it made my cheeks and ears flushed, like I came in from a winter storm and guzzled red wine.

Consistent with my experience, research suggests it may benefit those with peripheral vascular blood flow disease. But as with all supplements, be careful of the hype, and carefully monitor how much you consume.

Sleeping Pills

Stop taking sleeping pills, immediately.

A 2012 study tied the use of prescription sleeping pills to an increased risk of cancer or death. People who took just 18 sleeping pills a year had a 3.5 times higher risk of dying during the study period compared with people who didn't take any.

That risk increased to five times for people who took 132 pills a year or more. The latter group also had a 35% jump in cancer risk. The greatest risks were for people less than 55 years old.

So before you resort to sleeping pills, I urge you to try these sleep aids (all of which I've used to improve my sleep)...

Drink a glass of whole milk... It contains a type of vitamin B that promotes rapid-eye-movement (REM) sleep. Keep your bedroom dark, quiet, and free of electronics. Get rid of chargers and clocks... they emit electromagnetic radiation. Turn off all electronics like iPads and PCs an hour or so before heading to bed. The light emitted disrupts sleep patterns.

Headphones

Your headphones are ruining your hearing.

Researchers in Belgium studied 4,000 Flemish high school students. One in five of those students heard constant ringing in his ears. This ringing – known as tinnitus – hinders sleep, concentration, and communication.

Almost 75% of the students experienced temporary tinnitus. These findings indicate some of these students with tinnitus could experience hearing loss as they age. Teens aren't the only ones with these problems. It occurs in adults as well.

At my office in Baltimore, dozens of people wear headphones at their desks every day. The biggest problem is wearing headphones with the volume too high.

Once on a bus in California, I could hear a girl's music even though she was wearing headphones. I was sitting two rows away from her, on the opposite side of the extremely noisy bus. I have no doubt she seriously harmed her ears.

So what can you do to protect your teenagers and yourself? The most obvious answer is simple... Turn down the volume in your headphones.

You can test the volume at home. Just turn on your phone or mp3 player with the headphones plugged in. Then walk 10 feet away. If you can still hear the music, the volume is too high.

Mosquito Repellant

During mosquito season, remember that studies show chemical repellant diethyltoluamide (DEET), found in most commercial bug sprays, can be toxic to humans.

I try to use the lowest concentration of this stuff. Most people do the opposite, which risks long-term health problems, just like using high concentrations of sunscreen does.

Instead, try healthy and natural alternatives like oil of lemon eucalyptus to keep bugs away. I use a brand called Repel. Also, if you have an outside space at home you enjoy, try planting natural repellants like geraniums, mints (of all kinds), lavender, and pennyroyal. These plants are known to keep away all sorts of critters.

Soda

Sodas are about the worst thing you can drink on a regular basis.

Sugary drinks, like soda, increase inflammation in your body, which increases the risk of heart disease. Worse, research from the U.S. Department of Health shows drinking one can of soda a day leads to 10 extra pounds of weight per year.

And switching to diet sodas isn't any better. Among other things, diet sodas typically contain aspartame, a no-calorie sugar substitute that, along with caffeine, can cause headaches.

Do what I do... Drink green tea. Green tea is calorie-free, lowers cholesterol, fights cancer, and keeps immune systems strong. One of my favorite brands is Bigelow.

Lots of people load up on fruit juices as a "healthy" alternative to sodas and other sweet drinks. And many manufacturers market them as healthy super-foods. What they really are is a great way to pump your body full of unnecessary sugar.

A 2011 study found that people who drink three or more glasses of fruit juice per day are 74% more likely to develop colorectal (colon) cancer. And colon cancer is pretty common. More than 130,000 people are diagnosed with colorectal cancer in the U.S. annually. Why risk it?

> **DO WHAT I DO**
>
> Drink green tea. Green tea is calorie-free, lowers cholesterol, fights cancer, and keeps immune systems strong. One of my favorite brands is Bigelow.

Fruit is a valuable part of any diet. But juice is not the same. Fruits are loaded with both cancer-fighting antioxidants and fiber. Fruit juices lack the fiber of whole fruit. And worse, fruit juice is high in sugar, which causes spikes in glucose that increase your risk of contracting diabetes and cancer.

If you want fruit juice, make your own. Use the entire fruit, pulp and all. You'll still get gobs of sugar into your bloodstream, but the fiber will slow down the sugar's absorption and help you feel a little fuller sooner.

Calcium Supplements

A 2010 study showed taking calcium supplements can raise your risk of heart attack 30%.

Taking calcium supplements raises the calcium in your blood to dangerous levels. High blood calcium causes plaque buildup in your blood vessels, leading to heart attacks.

Women (more so than men) lose bone density as they age. Women are also at higher risk of developing osteoporosis. Doctors and websites like Webmd.com often recommend taking calcium supplements. What do I recommend?

Women should walk every day and do weight-bearing exercises to build bone density. Eat healthy foods to fulfill your calcium needs. When calcium comes from food, the body absorbs it slowly to keep your blood calcium levels from rising.

Yogurt is an excellent source of calcium. Yogurt is one of my favorite foods with several other benefits (as I discussed in Chapter 6).

Laundry Detergents With Strong Odors

Beware of detergents that smell "clean."

A report from the National Academy of Science showed that detergents, fabric softeners, and dryer sheets with strong odors are full of harmful chemicals. One of these chemicals is a petroleum-based synthetic that's been shown to damage lungs and the nervous system, as well as cause cancer.

Switch out your laundry cleaners for nontoxic, natural products, like the brands Seventh Generation or Method. Both use all-natural ingredients in their cleaners and won't cost you an arm and a leg.

You can also do what I do... Run your washer with half the amount of detergent that's called for, and use the extra-rinse cycle.

> ### DO WHAT I DO
> **Run your washer with half the amount of detergent that's called for, and use the extra-rinse cycle.**

Processed Meat

A 2012 study by Sweden's Karolinska Institute published in the *British Journal of Cancer* found that eating too much processed meat increases your risk of developing pancreatic cancer by 19%.

Just eating one sausage link a day (about 50 grams of processed meat) raises your risk. Even with the elevated risk, pancreatic cancer is rare. (Only one in 7,200 people get it in any given year.) Still, eating processed meats has other consequences. Eating just one serving of processed meat a day raises your risk of heart disease and stomach cancer.

Hot dogs, bacon, sausage, and cold cuts are all on the list of processed foods to avoid. Do what I do... Try to keep your processed-meat intake to once or twice a week at most... And always take vitamin C (500 mg to 1,000 mg) after eating it. It's thought that the bad chemicals – like nitrates – are countered by vitamin C's antioxidant properties.

> ### DO WHAT I DO
> **Try to keep your processed-meat intake to once or twice a week at most... And always take vitamin C (500 mg to 1,000 mg) after eating it.**

Acetaminophen

Acetaminophen is the generic name of drugs like Tylenol (which you probably have in your medicine cabinet). People think this drug is so safe, it's given to kids and nursing moms.

In late 2012, the FDA linked acetaminophen to three rare and potentially fatal skin diseases – Stevens-Johnson Syndrome, toxic epidermal necrolysis, and acute generalized exanthematous pustulosis.

Due to these dangerous reactions, the FDA requires any prescription drugs containing acetaminophen to add a warning label.

This isn't the first time the dangers of acetaminophen have come to light. Previous studies showed acetaminophen can increase blood pressure and cause liver damage (especially in large doses).

> ### *DO WHAT I DO*
> Stretching, massage, and using a tennis ball to help massage muscle pain are some of my favorites. If you absolutely feel you need pain relief, try Excedrin.

For years, I've told readers to moderate use of these types of painkillers. There are healthier ways to reduce pain. Do what I do... Stretching, massage, and using a tennis ball to help massage muscle pain are some of my favorites. If you absolutely feel you need pain relief, try Excedrin. It contains a combination of low amounts of acetaminophen, aspirin, and caffeine.

Products containing acetaminophen (like Tylenol) will have lower recommended dosages and may become prescription only. Others will be banned. Two medications likely to be banned are Vicodin and Percocet, as they combine acetaminophen with narcotics and easily lead to dependence.

If you're on a daily regimen of a medication that contains acetaminophen (check the bottle if you're unsure), decrease your daily dosage to no more than 650 milligrams.

— 13 —

19 Foods That Can Help Small Everyday Ailments, and Some Big Ones

Oysters

Some men who suffer from impotence could find help from a surprising source... oysters.

Raw oysters act like an aphrodisiac. There's no scientific evidence to support oysters providing any benefit to people

> **DO WHAT I DO**
>
> Only eat oysters harvested during months that have an "R" in their name (the colder months).

with a normal and healthy sex life. But raw oysters contain high amounts of zinc. And zinc deficiency can cause impotence.

Six oysters contain five times your daily zinc needs. So oysters could help if your libido suffers from a zinc deficiency.

But be careful when eating raw oysters. Some contain bacteria that cause a blood infection called vibrio vulnificus septicemia. Depending on how much you ingest, vibrio vulnificus septicemia can cause a simple stomach upset or it can be fatal.

To avoid the health risks, eat raw oysters that are pasteurized or oysters harvested from cold waters. (The bacteria thrives in warmer waters, like the Gulf of Mexico). Do what I do... Only eat oysters harvested during months that have an "R" in their name (the colder months).

Eating oysters also lowers blood pressure. Oysters are rich in magnesium and a set of proteins called amino acids. The magnesium relaxes muscles that control blood vessels.

Interestingly, the amino acids look and act just like a popular drug already used to treat high blood pressure – Captopril. This drug inhibits a chemical produced by the lungs and kidneys, called ACE, that increases blood pressure.

Beans

A 2012 study found diabetics who eat one-half cup of beans per day had lower levels of glucose, insulin, and hemoglobin A1 C (a long-term measure of how high blood sugar gets in your body).

The study used garbanzo, black, white, and pinto beans. Regularly eating beans lowered participants' hemoglobin A1 C levels by 0.48%, which is equivalent to antidiabetic medications.

Even if you're not diabetic, beans should still be part of your regular diet. I love to eat black beans with eggs in the morning for breakfast. Not only do I get the insulin-reducing power of the beans, but I also get a huge boost of protein and fiber to start the day.

Chewing Gum

Chewing gum can cut your risk of heart disease.

Certain sugarless gums kill mouth bacteria. Plaque caused by excess bacteria in your mouth leads to gum disease. And more than 17% of people older than 65 have gum disease. Worse, people with gum disease are three times more likely to have a heart attack than those without it.

Chewing sugarless gum with xylitol is a simple way to cut your risk. Xylitol is a sweetener that suppresses mouth bacteria. One of the most popular sugarless gum brands with xylitol is Trident. Another is the European gum brand Stimorol.

Sugar-free gum also helps prevent heart burn.

When gastric acid is regurgitated, your esophagus inflames. This causes the burning sensation you feel in your chest. It's a common issue. More than 40% of Americans suffer heartburn once a month, and 7% have heartburn weekly. Fatty meals, alcohol, stress, and certain acidic foods like grapefruit are common causes of heartburn.

Antacids – like Tums – are a popular way to fight heartburn. Since it can occur at any time, you may not always have them with you. So when you start to feel heartburn coming on, grab a piece of sugar-free gum.

Chewing gum causes your mouth to produce saliva, which can help keep the acid from rising. But don't chew gum with sugar. It will just make the heartburn worse.

And keep the gum away from Fido. Xylitol is toxic to dogs and can cause acute liver failure.

Kale

Eat kale for better-looking skin.

> ### DO WHAT I DO
> Add a little bit of kale to your salad (when in season) to get the amazing skin benefits.

Kale is packed with vitamins A and K. Vitamin A is essential for your skin tissue to repair itself. Studies show vitamin A controls acne, reduces wrinkles, and corrects flaky skin. Vitamin K helps maintain skin's elasticity, which keeps your skin from sagging and developing wrinkles.

Kale is an easy food to add to your diet. This dark green, leafy vegetable looks similar to lettuce, but the taste is slightly bitter. Do what I do... Add a little bit to your salad (when in season) to get the amazing skin benefits.

Nuts

Improve your mood just by eating walnuts.

Walnuts are packed with serotonin – what I call the "molecule of happiness." The neurotransmitter plays a role in regulating a diverse array of the body's functions, including sleep, sex drive, appetite, and mood regulation. Serotonin also creates feelings of calm and happiness.

A 2011 study from Spain found that people who ate a one-ounce combination of walnuts, hazelnuts, and almonds a day had more serotonin than people who did not.

In addition, walnuts also improve the fats in your bloodstream. They lower LDL (bad cholesterol) and raise HDL (good cholesterol). So do what I do... Eat a couple handfuls of nuts daily.

> ## *DO WHAT I DO*
> **Eat a couple handfuls of nuts daily.**

Many other nuts have health benefits as well...

Almonds protect against dementia with natural vitamin E. Pecans protect against cardiovascular disease. Peanuts (OK, OK I know they're legumes) contain resveratrol, which prevents heart disease. Pistachios lower cholesterol and have chemicals similar to those in leafy green vegetables – lutein, for example. Cashews help support your immune system.

But be careful about how many nuts you eat. These foods are calorie-dense because they're so high in fat. (Fats have more calories per weight than carbohydrates and protein do.) So do what I do... Eat only a couple handfuls a day of mixed nuts.

Berries

Berries can slow mental decline in women... according to data published in the *Annals of Neurology.*

Researchers from Brigham and Women's Hospital found that women who ate one cup of strawberries or a half-cup of blueberries each week delayed cognitive aging the equivalent of up to two and a half years. It's believed that the flavonoids in the berries reduce inflammation that can cause cognitive impairment.

Berries have long been a favorite food of mine and one of my top health secrets. They help lower blood pressure, lower cholesterol, fight cancer, and improve digestion. I eat berries almost daily... in my yogurt, oatmeal, smoothies, or just on their own. I strive for two-and-a-half cups of berries a week to reap the full benefits.

Cherries

Cherries have an added benefit... A chemist at Michigan State University found that they can act like a pain reliever similar to aspirin or naproxen. They can block inflammation and pain enzymes to help relieve pain. Studies found just one bowl of cherries a day can help lessen pain from diseases like arthritis.

Cherries also help reduce muscle pain. One 2010 study from Britain's Northumbria University showed that runners who drank cherry juice twice a day, five days before a marathon experienced less muscle inflammation and recovered their strength quicker than runners who drank a placebo.

Tumeric

Add a little turmeric to your diet the next time you have achy joints.

Turmeric is a spice used in curry. It also gives mustard its yellow color. Turmeric acts as an anti-inflammatory, which can relieve joint pain, improve digestion, and protect against memory loss. The benefits come from curcumin – a primary chemical in turmeric.

The spice has been used for centuries for its medicinal qualities. A 2012 study from the journal *Diabetes Care* found that regular use of turmeric can prevent Type 2 diabetes. Participants in the study were pre-diabetic. Those who ate turmeric still had not developed diabetes after nine months.

So how can you add turmeric to your diet if you're not a fan of curry? You can use it as a spice on salads, in soups, and on rice. And if you use it with black pepper, you'll get even more of the benefits, as pepper helps your body absorb more of the nutrients from the spice.

Oregano

Another beneficial spice to keep in your pantry is oregano.

In 2012, Long Island University researchers found that a chemical in oregano – called carvacrol – kills prostate cancer cells. Carvacrol triggers a reaction known as apoptosis, which causes a cell to kill itself. For years, the health benefits of oregano have been studied, including its anti-inflammatory properties. But this research could be life-changing for men with prostate cancer.

If not caught, prostate cancer is a deadly disease… it kills 30,000 men a year. While you're more likely to die of something else even when you have prostate cancer, the treatments used for it are harsh (as I cover in Part VII, Chapter 7).

They can damage your quality of life more than the cancer will.

The treatment options can come with some discouraging side effects: sterility, urinary incontinence, and even impotence. Prevention is key. Add oregano to your diet whenever you can.

Tomatoes

Here's a simple way to lower your stroke risk... eat tomatoes.

Several chemicals inside the tomato – like lycopenes, coumaric acid, and chlorogenic acid – make it healthy. These chemicals are strong antioxidants and help keep your cellular function and immune system healthy. Tomatoes also provide other micronutrients like potassium, iron, and vitamins A and C (even more than oranges).

> ### DO WHAT I DO
>
> **During the summer, I grow my own tomatoes so I have them whenever I want. I like to put them on salads, sandwiches, or in different soups and stews. You can even eat them on their own with a little bit of pepper.**

According to a 2012 study out of the University of Eastern Finland, men with the highest levels of lycopene in their blood were 55% less likely to have a stroke than men with the lowest blood levels of lycopene. Lycopenes neutralize free radicals, preventing them from damaging blood vessels.

If you want to get more lycopene in your diet, do what I do... During the summer, I grow my own tomatoes so I have them whenever I want. I like to put them on salads, sandwiches, or in different soups and stews. You can even eat them on their own with a little bit of pepper.

You can also find lycopene (although in lesser amounts) in watermelon and grapefruit.

Brown Rice

Eating brown rice and beans can lower your risk of developing colon polyps.

Colon polyps are a precursor to colorectal cancer, the third-most common cancer in both men and women. A study from Loma Linda University in California found that eating a serving of brown rice just once a week lowered the risk of colon polyps 40%. Eating legumes three times a week lowered the risk 33%.

These foods have high fiber content and anticancer properties. And fiber helps to keep your bowel movements feeling normal.

Do what I do... Try to eat brown rice once a week. Be careful about taking fiber "supplements" instead of real food. Some of these supplements might actually increase your risk of polyps.

> ### DO WHAT I DO
>
> **Try to eat brown rice once a week. Be careful about taking fiber "supplements" instead of real food. Some of these supplements might actually increase your risk of polyps.**

Peppermint

The next time you have an upset stomach, take a little peppermint.

More than just giving you fresh breath, peppermint has been used for thousands of years to improve digestion, lessen cold symptoms, and cure a sore throat. It's a great, all-natural way to make your stomach feel better.

It reduces symptoms of irritable bowel syndrome – like bloating, gas, diarrhea, and stomach pain. It also calms the stomach muscles and helps food move through your stomach more quickly... helping with indigestion and nausea.

You can keep some peppermint tea handy or you can just boil peppermint leaves for a few minutes with water. Just strain the water to remove the leaves before your drink it.

Don't have any peppermint handy? Try coffee instead. A compound in brewed coffee – N-methylpyridinium (NMP) – helps upset stomachs, too. It lowers stomach acid to help you feel better.

Rosemary

The next time your brain needs a boost, take a whiff of rosemary. A 2012 study out of the University of Northumbria in Newcastle, U.K., found people performed better on memory tasks in a room that smelled of rosemary than people in a room without the smell.

This study gives more evidence to what people have known for years. The ancient Greeks used rosemary to improve memory. It's believed that rosemary promotes blood flow to the brain and helps maintain the nervous system neurotransmitter acetylcholine... keeping your memory intact. I've written about the powerful reactions people have to different aromas... including lavender and pumpkin in Chapter 13.

Green Tea

Drink green tea three times a week to lower your risk of digestive cancers.

In 2012, *The American Journal of Clinical Nutrition* published a study that found women who drank three cups of green tea a week were 14% less likely to suffer from stomach, colon, and throat cancers. Women who kept this routine for 20 years saw a 20% drop.

The anticancer properties likely come from the antioxidant epigallocatechin 3-gallate (EGCG). Green tea also lowers your risk of prostate cancer, lung cancer, and pancreatic cancer.

Chocolate

A study out of the Science and Technology Institute of Food and Nutrition in Spain found chocolate can lower your risk of colon cancer.

> **DO WHAT I DO**
>
> **Eat about one or two small pieces of chocolate per day.**

The cocoa in chocolate contains polyphenols, known cancer-fighting compounds. Over an eight-week period, researchers found cocoa prevented the growth of pre-cancerous colon tumors in rats.

If you want the best benefits, stick with dark chocolate. The darker the chocolate, the better the benefits, as the higher cocoa content (at least 70%) packs more polyphenols. But as with most things, moderation is important. Do what I do... Eat about one or two small pieces per day.

Chili Peppers

Looking for an all-natural aphrodisiac to help your libido? Two of the best foods are chili peppers and dark chocolate.

Chili peppers are filled with capsaicin, a chemical that creates an effect similar to what a body experiences during arousal by speeding blood flow and spurring an endorphin release. Dark chocolate contains a chemical, nitric oxide, which is believed to improve sexual function in men and women.

Always exercise regularly as this helps sexual function as well.

Ginger

Take ginger to ease muscle pain. Ginger has been used as an anti-inflammatory in other cultures for centuries. Taking a daily supplement with two grams of ginger can reduce muscle soreness. Daily use, after 11 days, also increased participants' range of motion in their muscles.

Ginger has been used to treat pain for thousands of years. Several studies over the past few years have found ginger can relieve sore muscles, migraines, and even arthritis. Two active ingredients in ginger – zingerone and shogaol – act as anti-inflammatories.

Studies found ginger inhibits pain in a way similar to medications like Advil and Motrin. But unlike those medicines, fresh ginger is a natural pain remedy with fewer side effects.

I love to eat ginger whenever I eat sushi. But you can also find ginger supplements that offer the same benefits. You can get ginger supplements at Target or GNC. Research shows that about two grams a day reduces inflammation.

Comfrey Root

Comfrey root, an herb that's been long used for fertilizer and medicinal purposes, relieves acute back pain.

A study from *The British Journal of Sports Medicine* found that a comfrey-root ointment relieved pain for 95% of participants. Comfrey contains allantoin, a chemical that speeds up the replacement of body cells. This replacement of cells helps to soothe inflamed tissue and relieve pain.

However, comfrey root can cause liver damage if overused. Limit use to 10 days or less at a time and only about four grams each day (most containers have about 50 grams total). The brand used in the study, Kytta Salbe, is made by global health care company Merck.

A lot of back pain is stress related. Try yoga to help relieve some of the stress pain before using pills or ointments.

Broccoli

Eating just four servings of broccoli a week can cut your risk of prostate cancer in half.

> **DO WHAT I DO**
>
> **Steam the broccoli and add a little lemon juice and olive oil.**

A compound found in broccoli, isothiocyanate, can stop the cause of cancer and inflammation (which plays a role is several types of cancer). One cup of raw broccoli or one half cup of cooked broccoli is equal to one serving. You can do what I do to improve the taste... Steam the broccoli and add a little lemon juice and olive oil.

Watermelon

Watermelon is my next miracle food... Eating watermelon helps reduce inflammation.

Inflammation is probably the biggest (and most underappreciated) health risk people face. Diseases directly linked to inflammation include heart disease, arthritis, and high blood pressure.

Watermelon is loaded with inflammation-fighting antioxidants, including vitamins A and C. And it's a great source of lycopene – a carotenoid (antioxidant than gives carrots their color) well-known for reducing the risk of prostate cancer.

As an extra benefit, watermelon is 92% water. So it's low in calories and fat. One wedge (about one-sixth of a typical watermelon) contains just 86 calories.

A Good Reason to Eat Fruit

Women who eat citrus fruits have a 19% lower risk of having an ischemic stroke. Citrus fruits – like oranges and grapefruits – contain a type of chemical called flavanone that improves blood vessel elasticity and reduces inflammation.

While researchers didn't recommend a specific amount of citrus fruits, the higher a woman's flavanone levels were, the lower the risk of stroke. But beware... if you're on medications of any kind, check with your doctor before you start eating a lot of grapefruit. Citrus fruits can increase the concentrations of many drugs due to the interaction with some of your cellular metabolism.

— 14 —

Myth: Fat Is Bad for You

Products claiming to be "fat free" or have "zero trans-fat" are big sellers in supermarkets. Diet plans declare that to lose fat, you have to stop eating fat. But the truth is, not all fat is bad for you.

Our bodies need fat as fuel. Fat also transports fat-soluble vitamins and provides cells with essential fatty acids (EFAs), like omega-3 and omega-6 fats. You need a balance of both to keep your body functioning... But omega-3s seem to get much more publicity than omega-6s.

Marketers love this because of the claims they can make that omega-3 fats...

- Lower cancer risk
- Stabilize heart rhythms
- Improve heart function
- Reduce blood pressure
- Lessen musculoskeletal pain (omega-3 fats are as powerful as ibuprofen in decreasing pain)
- Enhance the immune system
- Lower inflammation
- Improve mental health
- Decrease risk of Alzheimer's

Several studies have also shown that babies fed formula containing omega-3 score higher on mental development and visual acuity tests. Omega-3s are thought to be important to our mental and eye health because the brain and eye tissues hold the highest concentrations of omega-3.

Given the apparent benefits, what can you do to get more omega-3 fats in your diet other than eat fish?

Eggs, butter, and even plants and some baby formulas are major sources of omega-3s. You can also find omega-3 in walnuts, cauliflower, broccoli, kidney beans, and spinach. But fish has the highest concentrations and the most benefit because of the longer-chain fatty acids (DHA and EPA).

Unfortunately, the average American diet lacks omega-3 fats. This is in stark contrast to the Japanese, who consume large amounts of omega-3s (mostly from fish). And it's thought that Japan's extremely low cardiovascular disease rate is mainly due to these fats.

Americans consume about one-third the omega-3s as the Japanese... and have four times the heart disease rate as Japan.

As the American diet has changed from plants to meat, we've had a harder time getting adequate amounts of omega-3. The animals we eat rarely graze on plants in the field (grasses)... Animals are often fed corn because it helps them become fat quickly.

Some statistics claim 99% of Americans are omega-3-deficient. There are several ways you might suspect you're deficient in omega-3. Signs of an omega-3 deficiency include...

- Depression
- Fatigue
- Dry skin
- Brittle hair and nails
- Constipation
- Frequent colds
- Poor concentration

To make sure I get enough omega-3, I try to consume cold-water fish once a week. I usually get a tuna salad sandwich, but I much prefer grilled salmon. I also like to fill my diet with eggs and vegetables that contain omega-3 fats. I'll occasionally take a 300 mg fish oil supplement. Use some common sense and focus on whole foods: fish and plants.

— 15 —

Question the 'Conventional Wisdom'

Please, always push your doctor to back up the "conventional wisdom"...

For example, doctors have long told pregnant women to avoid eating peanuts and tree nuts, and that children should avoid eating peanuts until after age three to prevent a peanut allergy. The American Academy of Pediatrics (an organization of 60,000 pediatricians with the goal of improving the health of children) has supported this claim for decades.

As of 2014, about 1% of Americans (adults and children) have a peanut allergy. Between 1997 and 2007, the number of peanut allergies tripled. But there's no proof linking peanut-eating pregnant women to childhood nut allergies.

And researchers at Boston Children's Hospital refute the old guidelines. They studied more than 8,000 children and their mothers. Children whose mothers ate peanuts during pregnancy were no more likely to have a peanut allergy than children whose mothers avoided peanuts.

So moms, don't worry about snacking on nuts... they're one of my favorite ways to sate hunger and a great source of protein.

PART VI

You and Your Doctor

— 1 —

Five Things to Ask an Eye Surgeon

The first time I met Rebecca Bobo, I knew she was the kind of doctor I would send my mom to...

I was attending a seminar for residents and fellows at my hospital, where we all shared our research and listened to lectures from a few distinguished guests. Dr. Bobo, my peer at the time, presented research on 10 years of eye surgery data at a Georgia hospital.

Her research showed wide discrepancies in the success rate of eye surgeries performed by doctors in training. Some worked on several patients who suffered severe complications (ones that can lead to blindness). Others experienced zero complications.

Some doctors are good at what they do and some aren't. The key point is that in a year, all these young surgeons – good and bad – would be turned loose on patients, and *no one was paying attention to whether they were helping or hurting the people in their care.*

Hers was the best research of the day – a blend of common sense and practicality. And it is the absolutely most important thing doctors should do in medicine – measure the rates of success. Sadly, this sort of work is rarely done. What she presented was not surprising, but it's not talked about.

Dr. Bobo moved to Stuart, Florida to a thriving ophthalmology practice. I called her up to see how she was doing. As we talked eyeballs, it was clear patients often lack critical information when contemplating surgery.

Together, we came up with this list of five things you should ask your eye surgeon before going under the knife for cataract surgery. Your doctor should give simple answers, too. If you sense any hemming and hawing, find another doctor. Here are the questions to ask:

1) "**Do I really need cataract surgery?**" I am amazed at how many people are told they need cataract surgery when they don't. Cataract surgery is elective surgery. The cataract should come out when *you* feel you are having problems, not because your doctor wants to do surgery.

First, your doctor should do a "glare" test – with a bright light – before determining the need for surgery. A bad cataract distorts the bright light and makes it nearly impossible to see with this test. But if your vision only "glares" to 20/40 or even 20/50, you probably don't need surgery.

As Dr. Bobo told me...

> I can't tell you the number of people who come to me for a second opinion with 20/20 vision and no visual complaints. They are ready to have their cataracts removed, when in fact, they're not even close to ready for removal.

Don't get surgery until you need surgery!

2) "**Do you keep surgical statistics? If so, what are they?**" Eye surgery is the safest surgery there is. Your surgeon should be able to tell you how many cases he has performed, what percent of those have had a complication (it should be less than 2%), and what percent required a different lens due to complications (it should be less than 1%).

Most "complications" are minor and go away after a day or two – but make sure your doctor's numbers are low.

Also, he should be able to tell you the *number* of patients who contracted endophthalmitis. An acceptable answer is either zero or one. This is a dangerous infection that leaves people blind. It's rare, and you have no reason to get surgery from someone who's had more than one in his career. I know several cataract surgeons who have performed more than 10,000 cases without an infection.

Ask your surgeon for a printout of his statistics. He should keep them on a computer. If not, run out of there.

3) **"Do you use the support of an anesthesiology team during the surgery?"** If your doctor says no, go elsewhere. The last thing you want is a problem with your medication, heart, or breathing while your surgeon is working inside your eyeball. Imagine if something were to happen to you, and your eye surgeon has to STOP taking care of your eye to manage your vital signs.

If your doctor tries to convince you that he can handle it all... tell him thanks but no thanks. Sure, the odds of a problem are slim. But why take the chance when so many good eye surgeons work with an anesthesiologist or a nurse anesthetist (half-doctor, half-nurse who specializes in anesthesia and works under the authority of an anesthesiologist).

4) **"Do you use antibiotics before and after surgery?"** Make sure your doctor uses antibiotics liberally before and after surgery. A regimen of three days before surgery and a week or two afterward is the minimum. The worst infection you can get is one in the eye after cataract surgery. It's a blinding infection. But it's almost impossible to get if you take antibiotics.

Also, be sure you wash your head and face the day of surgery. The less bacteria in the area, the lower the chances of a devastating infection.

5) **"What do you use to numb my eye?"** The answer might be "topical" or a "nerve block." Topical means simply using eye drops on top and a little anesthetic inside. The nerve block requires a needle to inject anesthetic around the eye.

If your surgeon is up-to-date on his technique and skills, he has no reason to be sticking needles around your eye for surgery. Why risk bleeding and other complications needles can create? Sure, some old-school doctors stick with nerve blocks because that's what they're used to. But if it were my mother, I'd make sure the surgeon's statistics were that much better before telling her to take the extra risk of another needle.

I hope your doctor can answer these questions honestly and with confidence.

Cataract surgery can be one of the most rewarding surgeries there is. Both patients and doctors get a lot of benefits from a successful case. In minutes, you'll be seeing better, and the results are easily measurable.

But make sure your eye surgeon is open to sharing information with you before you have the cataracts removed. Take the time to get to know your doctor by asking these five questions.

— 2 —

Five Medical Tests to Avoid

Never forget... the medical industry is a business.

Despite his insistence that he's just there to help you... your doctor isn't just working for you. Pharmaceutical companies are paying your doctor thousands of dollars – hundreds of thousands, in some cases – to push their drugs. Allergan, for example, paid one Florida doctor more than $160,000.

This is a serious conflict of interest. And it contributes to an epidemic of overtreatment.

Worse... many doctors know they're overtreating patients. A 2011 survey found 28% of doctors say they treat patients too aggressively. Only 6% think their patients don't receive enough medical care.

This doesn't surprise me... I worked in the industry for years. After I left Wall Street, I went to medical school and became a board-eligible eye surgeon. I've published research in peer-reviewed journals. (You can even find me in PubMed, the National Institutes of Health's clearinghouse for medical research.) I saw this overtreatment firsthand.

Of course, not all medications are useless... and some medical exams are critical. But some commonly prescribed exams are harming your health more than helping it. And they're wasting your hard-earned time and money.

What can you do? Without spending hours doing research, how do you know whether to follow your doctor's advice to get whatever "oscopy" or "ostomy" he's recommending?

To help you, my research team and I have created a list of medical exams you should avoid.

Here are the five exams we chose:

1. Prostate Specific Antigen test (Grade D)

2. Carotid Artery Stenosis screening (Grade D)

3. Pancreatic Cancer test (Grade D)

4. Peripheral Artery Disease screening (Grade D)

5. Dental X-rays

We'll get to the specifics of each test in a moment... But first, know that these tests (except dental X-rays) received a "D" grade from the U.S. Preventative Services Task Force (USPSTF).

The USPSTF is a panel of 16 MDs and PhDs whose specialties range from behavioral health to pediatrics. These experts make recommendations on the usefulness of screenings, counseling services, and preventative medications.

Its grades range from A to I.

A "D" means the USPSTF recommends against getting the exam. If the task force feels there's not enough evidence to either recommend or advise against a service, it could opt to assign the service an "I" for inconclusive.

The reasons for the five tests I listed vary... Some of these tests are just useless when the patient is actually free of the disease. Others are harmful. The largest issue we found in our research on these exams is the potential to receive a false-positive result.

The next time your doctor tells you that you need a specific exam (or treatment), make sure to question him about the reasons and the usefulness of the test. And if a test is positive, confirm it before dangerous treatment begins.

To help you, we've created this list of five exams that most healthy adults won't need (but doctors try to perform anyway)...

1. **Screening for Prostate Specific Antigen (PSA)**: We already discussed the dangers of PSA tests in Chapter 6. So we won't spend much time on it here.

Studies show the PSA is unlikely to reduce your chance of dying from prostate cancer. A positive PSA test can also lead to overtreatment. The treatments for prostate cancer can lead to worse side effects than the cancer itself... including impotence and heart problems.

2. **Screening for Carotid Artery Stenosis (CAS)**: CAS is a narrowing of the carotid arteries due to a buildup of plaque. Some research suggests the buildup of plaque increases the risk of stroke.

Other evidence shows only a small portion of severe strokes are related to CAS, with only 1% of people 65 and older having a severe case of CAS (where 60%-99% of the arteries are blocked).

Like the PSA, screening for CAS using an ultrasound test is well-known for yielding false positives – meaning the test shows artery blockages when there are none.

A false-positive result often leads to more invasive – and dangerous – procedures. And since studies show screening for the disease does little to nothing to reduce risk (especially for people who have no symptoms of CAS), don't do it.

3. **Screening for Pancreatic Cancer**: When I trained as a physician, a pancreatic-cancer diagnosis was a six-month death sentence. And not much has changed. According to the American Cancer Society, only 20% of patients diagnosed with pancreatic cancer live longer than one year after being diagnosed.

Imagine getting a false-positive result for a cancer that likely means you have less than a year to live. Thankfully, false positives aren't common. The problem is, the current tests available to screen for pancreatic cancer aren't able to catch the disease in early stages.

Doctors sometimes use an endoscopic ultrasound on individuals with a high risk of developing the cancer. The usefulness of this is currently in testing stages. But due to the short lifespan of people after diagnosis and the inability of current screenings to catch the cancer in early stages, screening has no effect on the mortality rate from this cancer, according to the USPSTF.

4. Screening for Peripheral Artery Disease (PAD): PAD occurs when arteries (typically in the pelvis and legs) narrow. This reduces the blood flow to your legs, leading to pain in your hips and legs. The narrowing of the arteries could be a sign that fatty deposits are accumulating in your arteries, reducing blood flow to your heart and brain and leading to an increased stroke risk.

However, the USPSTF found that screening for PAD doesn't result in any medical benefit (like reducing stroke risk). So don't waste your time and money on it.

5. Dental X-ray: Regular X-rays are common in the medical world for a variety of health reasons. If you hurt your ankle and it's painfully swollen, a doctor might recommend an X-ray of the bones. If you have pneumonia, you might get an X-ray of your lungs to check the severity of the case.

While they're useful, X-rays come with a big risk in the form of radiation. Any amount of radiation leads to an increased risk of developing several different cancers.

Despite the risks, dentists often recommend their patients have regular dental X-rays (usually annually). I stopped getting dental X-rays in 1996 when I realized the increased risks of thyroid cancer and brain tumors. And I haven't had an X-ray (of any kind) since.

A good dentist doesn't need X-rays to find problems. So if you're not having any dental issues (like pain) or having a procedure like braces, don't bother with the X-ray.

These aren't the only overused procedures. In 2012, the American Board of Internal Medicine – a nonprofit that certifies health professionals –

helped start a campaign called "Choosing Wisely." The campaign helps doctors and patients make better decisions regarding 45 of the most overused treatments and procedures.

With most health problems, the key is prevention.

For the first four diseases – prostate cancer, CAS, pancreatic cancer, and PAD – eating a plant-based diet, cutting out processed meats, and maintaining a healthy weight are all ways to cut your risk. Keep your teeth and gums healthy by making sure you brush your teeth at least twice a day. And most important, floss regularly.

— 3 —

Five Essential Medical Tests for a Healthy Life

Some medical warning signs shouldn't be ignored...

George was 85 years old when his wife noticed some strange moles on his face. At his wife's insistence, he went to the doctor to have the moles checked.

After a biopsy, the doctor found George had an early stage of skin cancer. Within a few weeks, he had surgery to remove the cancerous moles.

I regularly criticize the medical industry. A lot of my criticism might lead you to believe I'm anti-medicine. But I'm not... I'm all about common sense, science-based tests and treatments.

As a medical doctor, an insider to one of the country's biggest industries, I've seen the benefits of medical procedures and drugs... when used appropriately.

In Chapter 2, I told you about five dangerous tests that are overused. However, some tests are useful and necessary – likes George's skin-cancer screening.

In this chapter, we'll discuss the medical tests you should get. The five tests that are critical to your health are:

1. High blood pressure screening

2. Colorectal cancer screening

3. Skin cancer screening

4. Lipid disorder screening

5. Eye disease screening

Most of these tests received an "A" grade from the U.S. Preventative Services Task Force (USPSTF). The USPSTF is a panel of 16 MDs and PhDs whose specialties range from behavioral health to pediatrics. These experts look at the research data and make recommendations on the usefulness of screenings, counseling services, and preventative medications.

Its grades range from A to D.

A "D" means the USPSTF recommends against getting the exam. An "A" grade means the USPSTF recommends the exam. Screening for high blood pressure, colorectal cancer, and lipid disorders all received "A" grades.

If the task force feels there's not enough evidence to either recommend or advise against a service, it could opt to assign the service an "I" for inconclusive. Skin cancer and eye screening received "I" grades.

But as I'll explain... I've studied the research, looked at the facts, and found these to be among the five most important exams to maintain your health...

1. **Screening for High Blood Pressure**: High blood pressure has earned its nickname "The Silent Killer." Symptoms often emerge too late to avoid dire (even fatal) health consequences. One of the first signs can be a stroke.

If your blood pressure is 140/90 or higher, then you have high blood pressure. The problem is, you can't detect high blood pressure without screening. Your pressure can slowly rise over time, doing damage to your internal organs, including your brain... This makes screening for high blood pressure essential.

Fortunately, you don't need to spend time at a doctor's office to monitor your blood pressure. Many stores like Rite Aid, Walgreens, and many Wal-Mart pharmacies have blood-pressure monitors in the store. I regularly roll my sleeve up and use these monitors to check my blood pressure.

> ### *DO WHAT I DO*
> **Meditate regularly. This can quickly relieve sensations of stress, a leading cause of high blood pressure.**

Factors like caffeine and anxiety can also raise your blood pressure. So be sure to avoid these before the test. Some people actually have "white coat" syndrome – where anxiety over visiting the doctor sends their pressure up artificially.

Also, try to sit calmly for a few minutes before you take the test. If one of your readings shows your blood pressure is high, don't panic. Take the test again in a couple days or at a different store. If it's still high, ask someone at the pharmacy how often they calibrate the machine. (They should at least once per year.)

If you find you do have high blood pressure, there are plenty of ways to take control of it without immediately going on medications. Make sure you exercise regularly and eat the right foods. Four foods that lower blood pressure are dark chocolate, eggs, wine, and olive oil... as well as foods high in potassium.

And do what I do – meditate regularly. This can quickly relieve sensations of stress, a leading cause of high blood pressure. After a few months of regular meditation, research shows you can lower your blood pressure by at least 10 points without visiting a doctor or using medications.

2. **Screening for Colorectal Cancer**: Colorectal cancer can strike both the colon and rectum. It typically begins as benign clumps – called adenomatous polyps. These polyps are small and don't often produce symptoms early on, making the cancer hard to detect without screening.

> ### *DO WHAT I DO*
> Take one baby aspirin a day
> or one 325-milligram aspirin
> every week.

Of course, not all polyps develop into cancer, but they can. And the cancer can even spread to other organs throughout your body. Symptoms of this usually show up in the later stages. Screening can catch the polyps before they're cancerous. So it's wise to have them removed.

The USPSTF recommends screening for adults aged 50 to 75 years. If there is a history of cancer in your family, be sure to have screening done starting at age 50. The types of screening include fecal occult blood testing, sigmoidoscopy, and colonoscopy.

Fecal-occult testing requires stool samples which are tested for blood – a sign of colorectal cancer. It's a little annoying but has fewer side effects. A sigmoidoscopy looks for unusual growths in the rectum and lower colon. A colonoscopy examines the entire rectum and colon. Growths can be removed or biopsied during a colonoscopy, but the colonoscopy is slightly riskier than a sigmoidoscopy.

There's no way to prevent colon cancer, but you can reduce your risk. Most important, keep your weight in check. People who are overweight or obese have a higher risk of colorectal cancer. This is especially true for people with large waistlines.

To lower your risk, limit your intake of alcohol and processed meats. Also, some studies show regular use of aspirin lowers your risk. Do what I do... take one baby aspirin a day or one 325-milligram aspirin every week.

3. **Screening for Skin Cancer**: The three main types of skin cancer are basal-cell skin cancer (the most common), melanoma, and squamous-cell skin cancer.

Basal-cell skin cancer is found on the face and other areas that get regular sun exposure.

Melanoma occurs anywhere on the skin's surface. It can even occur on the eye and in the intestines. Both basal-cell skin cancer and melanoma are more common in people with fair skin.

Squamous-cell skin cancer is the most common type of skin cancer in people with dark skin and is usually found on legs and feet. For fair-skinned people, squamous-cell cancer usually appears on the head, face, ears, and neck.

Skin cancer looks like a slightly strange mole. Some benign moles can turn cancerous. There are ways to tell potentially cancerous moles from benign ones. Cancerous moles are asymmetrical, have irregular borders, uneven color, changing size or appearance. The only way to identify if a mole is cancerous is through monitoring and screening.

Screening with a doctor is generally simple. A quick look by a dermatologist is enough to know if a biopsy is needed. The doctor biopsies the lesion, taking a small tissue sample to test and examine for cancer cells. Biopsies are often done in a doctor's office or as an outpatient at a hospital. The doctor uses a local anesthetic on the biopsy area to lessen pain from the procedure.

The easiest way to prevent skin cancer is to protect your skin from excessive sun. Avoid going outside during prime burning times of 11 a.m. through 2 p.m. If I have to go out midday, I wear a long-sleeved shirt and a hat. I also wear sunglasses to protect my eyes.

Avoid sunscreens. They're loaded with known carcinogens. (Think of them as cancer-causing chemicals you'd never put on a baby.) I try to avoid lotions stronger than SPF4.

4. **Screening for Lipid Disorders**: Lipid disorder is a broad term used for excess fat in the bloodstream. The most common lipid disorder is from excessively high cholesterol and triglycerides (another type of fat).

Many components make up total cholesterol. But the two most important are considered "bad" cholesterol (low-density lipoprotein, or LDL) and good cholesterol (high-density lipoprotein, or HDL).

LDL is "bad" because it's thought to catalyze arterial plaque formation, clogging arteries. HDL cholesterol inhibits excess levels of harmful fats and LDL from sticking to arteries. High cholesterol and especially triglycerides increase the risk of heart attack and stroke. Unfortunately, high cholesterol has no symptoms. So you may not know you have it until it's too late.

Screening for cholesterol is simple... A patient fasts for nine to 12 hours before a blood test, called a lipid panel. The test measures the levels four common types of lipids in the blood – total cholesterol, LDL, HDL, and triglycerides. A doctor determines if you have high cholesterol based on the quantities of these lipids.

High cholesterol is preventable in most cases. The simplest ways to prevent high cholesterol are exercising regularly, eating a diet packed with vegetables and fruits – high-fiber foods – and maintaining a healthy weight. Also avoid simple carbohydrates whenever possible (bread, rice, and mushy vegetables).

5. **Screening for Eye Diseases**: Two of the most common eye diseases (except general vision problems like near- or farsightedness) that occur as we age are age-related macular degeneration (AMD) and glaucoma.

AMD is an eye disease that damages the macula – the part of the eye that provides central vision. Glaucoma is a group of eye problems that damage your eye's optic nerve (which carries images from the retina to your brain), resulting in vision loss and blindness.

To test for AMD, your doctor should examine the back of your eye, test your central vision, even perform an angiogram that uses a colored dye to highlight abnormalities in the blood vessels in your eye, or use an optical coherence tomography (OCT). The OCT discovers thinning or thickening of areas around the retina nerve fiber layers.

To test for glaucoma, a doctor may measure the thickness of your cornea, examine the back of your eye, test your distance and peripheral vision, and measure the pressure in your eye using a tonometry test. Most of us get the "puff of air" test when we go to the eye doctor... That's one type of tonometry test.

Factors like cardiovascular disease or high blood pressure increase your risk of AMD... as does smoking. So keep your health in check and quit smoking. The best way to prevent both AMD and glaucoma is through a diet rich in foods with vitamin C, vitamin E, zinc, copper, and omega-3 fatty acids.

If you have AMD in your family or have been diagnosed with it, be sure to discuss the pros and cons of supplements containing these substances.

In the case of AMD, supplements with omega-3 and these vitamins and chemicals have been shown to change the course of the disease. But as always, consider getting the chemicals in the form of whole foods – like fresh vegetables, nuts, and fish.

While these five tests we've described don't eliminate your risk of overtreatment or even disease, it's likely you can improve the quality and length of your life by considering these tests sooner than later.

If the results of these exams come back positive, please research the possible treatments with your doctor and get a second opinion if you're in doubt. Always weigh the benefits and risks. And feel free to ask your doctor about the scientific proof for his recommendation. If he can't show you the proof, get a new doctor.

— 4 —

The Months to Avoid Hospitals If You Possibly Can

Don't go near a hospital during June, July, or August.

If you or a loved one are considering any sort of hospital visit for an elective or nonemergency procedure, you absolutely should stay clear of any medical facility with residents during the summer.

Doctors in training, so-called residents, switch over every year on July 1. In June, the senior residents, who are about to leave, couldn't care less about taking care of you. They are thinking about getting out of there, finding a real job, and starting to pay down their debt (average debt is $139,517).

The new ones coming in on July 1 can't find their way out of a paper bag and are scared to death. The senior staff members – supposedly supervising them – are taking their summer vacations.

The problem is temporary. Once September hits, the new doctors have a couple months of experience under their belts and the seniors are back at work supervising again... It's as safe as it gets by then.

— 5 —

Your Doctor's Advice Could Kill You

It's one of the most common orders doctors give their patients... especially those with high blood pressure. But this widely accepted piece of advice is not just misguided, it endangers patients.

I'm talking about **cutting back on salt**.

For years, doctors have advised patients to lower their salt intake... especially patients with high blood pressure. And doctors aren't the only ones.

In January 2010, New York City Mayor Michael Bloomberg took the anti-salt propaganda to a new level. He was part of the creation of the National Salt Reduction Initiative, which proposed to reduce salt in restaurants and packaged products by 25%.

At *Retirement Millionaire*, we pride ourselves on debunking myths. After checking the facts, we found this advice from doctors and the "Nanny State" may be killing you.

Salt, it turns out, is actually essential to life.

One of the most common salts in our diet is made of the ionic compound sodium chloride (NaCl). Sodium is a positively charged ion and chloride is a negatively charged ion. Salt dissolves well in water, but due to the strength of attraction between sodium and chloride, it doesn't dissolve in much else.

When people think of salt, they tend to picture white stuff in a blue cardboard cylinder container. But salt is much more complex than that. Salts come in different tastes, odors, and colors. Blue salt, for example, contains copper and iron.

Many people put edible salts into three categories: unrefined salt, refined salt, and iodized salt.

Sodium chloride – what most folks think of as salt – got its bad name from a 1970s study done at the Brookhaven National Laboratory. Researchers found that rats eating the human equivalent of 500 grams of salt a day experience increased blood pressure. This amount is nearly two cups of salt, and it's next to impossible to imagine any sensible conclusions from that study about salt's effects on humans.

The average American consumes about 3,400 milligrams (mg) daily... less than the 500,000 milligrams used in the Brookhaven study.

Yet people fell for the hype. And subsequent studies with humans have had short durations and with too few participants to provide conclusive evidence...

Eliminating salt from your diet has serious consequences. Too little sodium lowers blood pressure to dangerous levels. Without salts, many of the mechanisms that keep the muscles of the walls of vessels and organs working don't work. This prevents the organs from getting the blood and oxygen they need.

One 2013 study from the Institute of Medicine found that consuming less than 1,500 mg of sodium a day raises a person's heart-attack risk.

Some of the better research shows a U-shaped effect with sodium chloride. The key is consuming the right amount, and making sure you get a couple other salts along with the sodium.

If you're eating a regular American diet, your sodium intake is probably plenty. But the average American diet misses some salts that contain strong health benefits. Two of my favorite sea salts – magnesium and potassium – are packed with benefits.

> ### *DO WHAT I DO*
>
> Instead of worrying about the amount of salt in my food, I focus on getting good natural salts and making sure I'm getting enough magnesium and potassium in my diet. I like to put a little sea salt and pepper on a slice of tomato for a perfect, healthy snack.

Magnesium, which is found in some sea salt, helps muscles relax (counters the effects of calcium). It's critical in most enzymes in the body. There's also evidence that magnesium improves mood, energy, and mental stability. High-magnesium foods include seeds, brans, leafy green vegetables, and cocoa.

One of the other benficial salts is potassium. People consuming more potassium had lower rates of mortality and morbidity (other disease problems). Foods high in potassium include avocados, potatoes, beans, bananas, fish, raisins, apricots, and dates.

If you want to cut out refined salt and switch over to sea salt, make sure you're getting enough iodine. Sea salt contains smaller amounts of iodine. So supplement it with foods that contain high amounts of iodine, like fish.

Do what I do... Instead of worrying about the amount of salt in my food, I focus on getting good natural salts and making sure I'm getting enough magnesium and potassium in my diet. I like to put a little sea salt and pepper on a slice of tomato for a perfect, healthy snack.

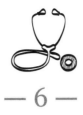

— 6 —

Is Your Doctor Managing Your High Blood Pressure?

Fire Him

If you have high blood pressure, or are worried about developing high blood pressure... *stop relying on your doctor to fix it.*

The medical establishment doesn't care about curing your high blood pressure. It just wants to keep you coming back visit after visit. That's how the doctors and hospitals get paid... for treating you, over and over.

They give you lots of pills and bring you in for an unending stream of doctor's appointments. It's all about feeding the machine – the more you see the doctor and the more pills you take, the more money everybody makes. The pills pay off the pharmaceutical corporations and the doctors on their payroll.

What was the last doctor's office you visited that had the No. 1 best treatment on display? How many doctors keep treadmills in the waiting room for patients to "practice and learn" how to cure themselves?

For those of you diagnosed with high blood pressure... Has your doctor ever written a prescription out for you to "walk 15-30 minutes a day, three times a week?" If he hasn't, fire him today. Here's why...

Blood pressure is created by the pumping of your heart. The blood racing from the heart pushes against the walls of your arteries and vessels.

The squeeze creates the higher pressure – called the systolic number. It should be around 120. When the heart relaxes, the pressure drops to the "resting state" – the diastolic pressure. It should be around 80. This gives us the normal blood pressure of 120/80.

But if your cardiovascular system is working at 140/90 or higher, you have high blood pressure. The problem is, you don't notice blood pressure at those levels – you normally have no symptoms. Your pressure can go higher over time, doing damage to your body, organs, and your brain... that's why it's called "The Silent Killer."

By the time symptoms emerge, it's often too late to avoid dire (even fatal) health consequences. One of the first signs may be a stroke.

I'm against annual doctor visits for healthy people. No scientific evidence shows "annual physicals" help anything other than fill the pockets of doctors. And doctors are much too quick to prescribe pills to fix whatever ails you.

Fortunately, you don't need a physician to monitor your blood pressure. Many stores like Rite Aid and Walgreens (and even some Wal-Mart pharmacies) have blood-pressure monitors in store. I urge you to routinely sit down at one to make sure your blood pressure is OK.

If your first reading shows your blood pressure is high, don't panic... Check its accuracy.

Take the test again in a couple days or at a different store. Ask the pharmacy how often it calibrates the machine (it should be at least once per year). Pay attention to the instructions... and don't drink caffeine or smoke before checking.

If you repeatedly find your pressure is high, you're not alone... The National Heart, Lung and Blood Institute estimates one in three Americans has high blood pressure. *Some estimate 90% of Americans over 55 have high blood pressure.* This is serious.

Over time, the Silent Killer leads to...

- Stroke

- Kidney failure

- Memory loss

- Erectile dysfunction

High blood pressure is the leading cause of stroke in the U.S. Seventy percent of strokes are linked to high blood pressure. People with high blood pressure are four to six times more likely to have a stroke.

It's also the leading cause of kidney failure. High blood pressure can damage the tiny blood vessels in the kidneys, preventing them from properly removing waste and excess fluid from the body. Excess fluid in the blood will raise blood pressure even more.

If you find you have elevated pressure, you need to reverse the ongoing processes as soon as possible. That means not falling for the standard doctor's line about sodium. (I'll talk about this more in Chapter 33.)

This myth first gained fame in the 1940s when a doctor named Walter Kempner found that restricting table salt (sodium) lowered blood pressure. Several studies done around that time showed removing sodium from a diet lowered some people's blood pressure.

But reducing salt intake is helpful only for those who are salt sensitive. More important is to *increase* your uptake of another salt – potassium. Low potassium levels are more likely to increase blood pressure than high levels of sodium are. The average American consumes about 1,500 milligrams less than the recommended 4,700 milligrams of potassium.

To make sure you're getting lots of potassium, focus on eating foods like bananas, tomatoes, and sweet potatoes. Also try to balance the amounts of sodium and potassium you consume.

And I have good news... Four of my favorite foods to lower your blood pressure are delicious treats...

1.   Chocolate

2. Eggs

3. Wine

4. Olive oil

Researchers in Germany found that eating six grams of **dark chocolate** per day (about one and a half Hershey Kisses) lowers blood pressure. This also significantly reduces cardiovascular risks like heart attacks or strokes.

Antioxidant-rich foods (like chocolate) help blood vessels expand and regulate the flow of blood.

But this isn't a license to gorge yourself... Eating too much chocolate can pile on the calories, making you heavier and more likely to develop high blood pressure. If you don't want the 30 or so calories you get from six grams of dark chocolate per day, I have a solution...

Park your car walking distance from work and eat a Kiss each way, every day. A few months of this, and you might not even need blood-pressure medications (or your doctor).

You can also eat **cooked eggs**. Lab research shows chemicals, called ACE inhibitors, are abundant in fried eggs. ACE inhibitors stop the body's production of angiotensin-converting enzymes. These enzymes are known to cause blood vessels to narrow, making the heart work harder.

This is one of the best drugs known by doctors to lower blood pressure. And since cooking eggs releases the chemicals, feel free to eat your eggs fried, boiled, poached, or scrambled.

Wine has been praised for all the health benefits it offers. The regular consumption of wine improves digestion and decreases the risk of diabetes, stroke, arthritis, high blood pressure, and even Alzheimer's disease.

I prefer red wine. It is more powerful than white wine (although whites have plenty of benefit) because dark grape skins provide more antioxidants. The antioxidants help increase levels of high-density lipoprotein (HDL) cholesterol ("good" cholesterol). HDL cholesterol inhibits excess levels of harmful cholesterol (a.k.a. low-density lipoprotein, or LDL) from sticking to arteries. That keeps your blood flowing easily.

I try to drink at least one four-ounce glass of wine each day. The health benefits of drinking wine (and other alcoholic drinks) are unquestioned in medical literature. The key is to drink in moderation. Drinking too much alcohol will actually raise your blood pressure. Men should limit alcohol consumption to two glasses per day. Women, to one glass daily.

Solid scientific evidence shows a Mediterranean diet, which includes tons of **olive oil**, is not only generally healthy, but actually lowers LDL. The mechanism for this is not fully known. It may be simple micronutrients within olive oil that bestow the benefits.

Moreover, due to its chemical structure and function, olive oil also protects other cholesterols in your body from oxidation. Thus, the antioxidants in olive oil discourage diseases of inflammation, including heart disease, arthritis, and high blood pressure.

Once you've added potassium and these four foods to your diet, you're on your way to lowering your blood pressure. These things combined can lower your pressure eight to 10 points.

But the most important things you can do are the simplest and most relaxing...

First, **exercise** regularly. People who exercise regularly are 35% less likely to have high blood pressure than those who are inactive.

All you have to do is walk for 15-30 minutes three times a week for 80% of the benefits of regular exercise. And it doesn't matter if you walk up stairs, around the mall, or inside the gym on a treadmill. The key is to get out there and move the hips and shoulder joints.

Part of the benefit comes from the movement. Part comes from the state of relaxation that follows exercise. Walking (along with most types of exercise) and the cooldown afterward release chemicals that relax blood vessels and promote healthy blood pressure.

After a month or two, most people can throw away their blood pressure pills.

The second thing you should do is **meditation**.

Regular meditation lowers your heart rate and increases both your blood's oxygen saturation and the delivery of oxygen to tissues. As I said in Chapter 10, this is the exact same measured benefit you get from exercise. So you don't need to run three miles every day to get the benefit of exercise.

People who meditate have lower blood pressure, less risk of heart disease, better oxygen uptake, and report feeling less stressed. This is another way meditation helps lower your blood pressure.

I meditate at least three times a week, usually in the morning. And the older I get, the clearer the benefits of meditation become. In addition to the physiologic benefits, I also enjoy the peace and mindfulness it brings.

After a couple months of walking and meditation, you can easily lower your blood pressure by 10 points (and as much as 20 points after a year).

If you want to know more about the science of stress and relaxation on more than your blood pressure, you should read the book *The Relaxation Response* by Herbert Benson.

Be sure to get your blood pressure checked, and try some fun foods like chocolate and red wine after your daily walk or meditation. You'll keep yourself much further away from the doctor.

— 7 —

10 Questions You Must Ask Your Cancer Doctor

Pat felt like vomiting, but couldn't. The pain made her double over several times... She wasn't really sure what to do.

She was just flying back from a cross-country trip, where she'd been attending an award banquet for her husband. Could it be the shrimp? The nausea and bloating were getting worse. The abdominal pain, unbearable.

The ER nurses quickly triaged her and noted "ascites" in the chart. When fluid fills the belly, it gets bigger and painful. When family members mentioned the term to me, I shuddered. Ascites in a woman of her age – mid-60s – is often a death sentence...

But not always...

Pat had the prerequisite radiology scans and blood work. The CT scan showed cancer-like lesions. The blood test, a CA-125 (which should NEVER be used as a cancer-screening test), was showing positive for cancer.

And the doctors did what you do when you have ascites – they tapped her belly to draw off the fluid with a long needle. The fluid and cells were sent to pathology to determine the type of cancer.

But without waiting for the pathology report, doctors decided she had ovarian cancer and stressed she should begin chemotherapy. While waiting a day or two for the pathology report would make no difference in her chances for survival, the doctors and the hospital wanted it *stat*.

The first-line therapy for ovarian cancer is called carbotaxel – a combination of carboplatin and paclitaxel. Both are powerful poisons that have side effects too numerous to list. The death rate just from the drugs ranges from 2%-3%.

But just before they began treatment... the light bulb went off for my friend. What sort of cancer were they planning to treat? Where was the pathology report?

It turned out that the fluid from her belly had *no cancer cells*. But the doctors still recommended treatment. How could this be? Pat jumped ship and checked herself out of the hospital late that Friday night. She left "AMA" (against medical advice)... which may have saved her life.

She went immediately for a second opinion at the cancer center at the University of North Carolina at Chapel Hill. The doctors there performed a similar ascites biopsy, but this time guided with CT scans. This allows you to get right up to the tissue and be certain you've got the offending cells.

Again, they recommended she start in on the poisonous chemotherapy before the results came in... But a mutual doctor friend of ours intervened and demanded to know what cancer they were treating. Until the cells came back from the sampling session, the answer was: We don't know.

Then the biopsy came back "non-diagnostic," which is the technical term for "we still don't know." And she still hadn't started the repeatedly recommended chemotherapy.

Pat was persistent and wanted a definitive tissue diagnosis, which you should too if you ever have cancer. She went under the knife for an exploratory laparoscopy. That's when she was diagnosed with large, benign masses called "chocolate cysts" that are related to a disease called endometriosis.

The surgeons cleaned up several of the larger, painful cysts. After, Pat was both pain- and cancer-free. She's lucky she didn't start the chemotherapy. At best, it would have made her vomit, lose her hair, and feel terrible. At worst, it would have killed her.

After hearing Pat's story... I put together a list of questions you should always ask your doctor if you've been told you have cancer. Doctors are sometimes wrong. They're human and make assumptions about what's most probable and likely.

But you're not a statistic. And you need to make sure you're really getting the care you deserve. I've consulted experts in the field of cancer and spoken with several general doctors as well about the issues...

Here's what you must ask your doctors...

1. "**What is my specific diagnosis?**" Your doctor should be able to openly and freely tell you what you have. There shouldn't be any hemming and hawing.

If they think it may be one of two or three things, they should tell you. After you've been told what the doctor thinks you have, demand proof. Just like Pat above, you need to know.

2. "**Has my diagnosis been confirmed with pathologic tissue?**" This means they'll need to get a biopsy or blood sample to confirm the cancer diagnosis by looking at real cells from your body.

If the answer is yes, ask to have a copy of the signed report from the pathologist. You can share it with your regular doctor or even take it to a second doctor for a confirming opinion. You'd be surprised how often pathology samples get lost, misplaced, or mislabeled.

Be sure and wait for this pathology report before starting any therapy. There's no sense in risking your health and life because your cancer doctor thinks the results will be positive. Be sure.

If the answer is no, ask why not. If you've been told you have cancer, but your doctor refuses to get tissue to confirm it... get right up and leave. Find a second doctor immediately who will confirm your diagnosis. There are a few exceptions, like pancreatic cancer... But your cancer doctors better have a good reason as to why they won't do a biopsy.

3. "**What is my prognosis?**" Ask for the five-year survival (FYS) or 10-year life expectancy. This is one of the hardest things to get from most

doctors because your doctor is worried that whatever he tells you will be interpreted as a death sentence. For example, if he told you the FYS was 80%, would you "hear" that number or would you hear you have a 20% chance of dying?

Once you have this number, it can help you consider your treatment options as well as what life changes, if any, you want to make and how quickly you need to make them.

And when you get the number, ask your cancer doctor and regular doctor to explain what it means. It should become clear that the number is an average and may not even be close to your actual outcome.

There are hundreds of stories of people with very low FYS that went into remission and lived another 20 years. So don't let the numbers shake you... Just take them for what they are.

4. "**What is the recommended treatment?**" Make sure your doctor explains and spells out (preferably in writing) what he recommends for treatment. And more importantly...

5. "**Is it in the National Cancer Center Network (NCCN) guidelines?**" Millions of dollars and hours go into figuring out what the best and most likely outcomes will be for cancer treatments. The NCCN is a compilation of smart folks who spend tons of time thinking about the pros and cons of different treatment plans.

If the doctor recommends a non-NCCN plan, be sure there's science to back it up. And ask for proof and background of the reasons for going off the path.

6. "**What are the top three centers in this field of cancer?**" You may not have the resources to go to these centers for treatment – the costs and travel may be outside your budget – but these centers may have the resources to help you. The world is getting smaller, and you may be able to be a part of cutting-edge and important research from these centers while you stay in your hometown.

Clinical trials often pay for medications. These trials usually come from the top centers... Please ask who's doing the cutting-edge work in your cancer field. If your cancer doctor is offended or bored by the idea or effort needed to get you involved, get another doctor. Or contact the centers yourself.

7. "**How many people have this disease in the U.S.?**" If it's less than 5,000 people in the U.S., get to a major cancer center right away. If you have a rare and deadly cancer, you'll want the best in the field thinking and working on your cancer.

8. "**How many patients like me have you seen in your career? How many have you treated successfully?**" This relates to the question above. Whatever your doctor says, get him to put it in writing. Make him be truthful and honest with you about his success.

When I was training, it would drive me crazy to watch doctor after doctor lie about their level of experience and success. Most doctors, even surgeons, don't keep good records of their procedures or treatments. But ask anyway and see what you get.

If you see squirming and evasiveness... find another doctor who will at least tell you he hasn't kept a perfect track but can offer an approximate level of experience and success.

9. "**Are there clinical trials for my diagnosis?**" It's helpful to know about alternative ideas for treating your cancer. And you may be able to get financial assistance for parts of your cutting-edge treatment. You can read about the possible trials on the government website here: www.nih.gov/health/clinicaltrials/index.htm.

10. "**What's the goal of treatment? Palliative versus cure**." It's important to know whether you're going to get treatment to make you comfortable or to try to cure you. If it's the former, you'll want to get your affairs in order sooner than later.

As you consider asking your doctor these 10 critical questions, I encourage you to do a few things to make the process easier and clearer for you. These tips will go a long way to help you.

It's important that on every visit to your doctor, you do several things...

First, have your doctor give you a written diagnosis on a piece of paper.

Second, always bring a friend or close family member with you. It's so hard to pay attention to everything going on all the time during a visit. And different people hear different things in different ways.

A friend there in the room with you for support can remind and encourage you to keep asking the 10 questions. A friend can also help you recall what the doctor said or meant when you're reflecting on it after the visits.

Third, take written notes at each office visit. Ask for your doctor to write things down for you if it isn't clear. He should be willing to spend time with you and help you get the information you need about your situation.

Finally, it's critical that you consider the issues surrounding death and dying at this point. Please discuss end-of-life issues with your next of kin (and family). This means doing things like executing a living will and health-care power of attorney.

I hope these critical questions and tips will make your path through the issues surrounding a cancer diagnosis a little easier. As you contemplate your mortality and the short time you have on this earth, I also hope these ideas help you communicate more easily with all those around you to face the decisions you'll be making together.

By talking about this stuff openly with your doctor, friends, and family, you'll feel safer and calmer. Find a doctor who'll work honestly with you, and your chances of healing improve.

— 8 —

The Antidepressant Myth

Antidepressants are a big business...

Sales of antidepressants bring in about $10 billion a year. With one in 10 Americans suffering from some form of depression in 2014, it's little wonder that more than 17 million people in the U.S. take some form of antidepressant medication.

Despite its prevalence, the treatments can be misrepresented and – more alarmingly – useless.

Depression is a mental illness that most often involves prolonged feelings of intense sadness. Some of the more common symptoms include loss of interest in previously enjoyable activities (known as anhedonia), fatigue, overeating or loss of appetite, thoughts of suicide, trouble sleeping, or excessive sleeping.

Anyone can suffer from depression. The most susceptible groups are women, people between 45 and 64 years old, the unemployed, uninsured, blacks, and Hispanics.

Some of the more common types of depression include...

Major (or Clinical) Depression: It can prevent normal functionality. Symptoms are severe, present daily, and persist for several weeks.

Chronic Depression (or Dysthymia): This is two years or more of a depressed mood. It's slightly less severe than major depression and doesn't prevent daily functionality.

Atypical Depression: Regular symptoms include increased appetite, oversleeping, and extreme sensitivity to rejection. Unlike major or chronic depression, positive events can lead to mood improvement.

Bipolar (or Manic) Depression: Moods alternate between extreme highs (elation) and extreme lows (depression).

Seasonal Depression (or Seasonal Affective Disorder): This is depression that comes with the seasons. Typically, seasonal depression starts in the fall or winter and ends in the spring or summer. (In rare cases, the opposite can occur and depression can develop in the late spring or early summer and end in fall.)

Psychotic Depression: This includes psychosis or delusional thoughts mixed with symptoms of depression.

Postpartum Depression: New mothers can experience this type of clinical depression within the first month after delivering a baby.

Before a diagnosis, doctors will test for physical ailments with similar symptoms, like a viral infection, thyroid disorder, or a low testosterone level. Once those ailments are ruled out and the type of depression is diagnosed, treatment begins.

One common treatment is psychotherapy... A doctor gives the patient "talk therapy" and helps teach coping skills to minimize symptoms. Doctors will often prescribe a pill to make things better.

The main types of antidepressants are selective serotonin reuptake inhibitors (SSRIs), serotonin and norepinephrine reuptake inhibitors (SNRIs), tricyclic antidepressants (TCAs), and monoamine oxidase inhibitors (MAOIs).

SSRIs are the most common antidepressants and include big sellers Prozac, Zoloft, and Paxil. SSRIs block the reuptake of serotonin in the brain. This allows the brain to better send and receive chemical messages, boosting mood.

But antidepressants aren't as effective as television ads lead you to believe. A 1998 study from the University of Connecticut found that as much as 75% of an antidepressant's power comes from the placebo effect.

In other words, the act of simply taking something they believe will help – even if it has no physiological effect – makes the patient feel better. Many subsequent studies came to the same conclusion.

The placebo effect shows how important belief and attitudes are in final outcomes. Irving Kirsch, the originator of the 1998 study (and several studies thereafter), studied the placebo effect for decades. In an interview on *60 Minutes* in 2012, Kirsch said that in many cases, placebos were just as effective as antidepressants.

But here's the part that upsets me: *The drug companies are well aware of this.* In 2010, two reports – one from the *New England Journal of Medicine* – showed drug companies buried the results of 74 studies conducted between 1987 and 2004 on 12 FDA-approved antidepressants.

All 74 studies showed the drugs did nothing more than a sugar pill. Worse... another 11 studies that showed *negative* results for the medications were published as if they supported the pills' benefits. Trials for Effexor, Paxil, Prozac, and Serzone showed the medications had the same effect as a placebo.

Depression can be a serious problem for people. But the good news is folks who struggle with depression have ways to fight it without resorting to expensive and probably useless pills.

You can try something simple like **spending time in the sun**. Your body naturally converts sunlight to vitamin D, which helps lift your mood. (Just remember not to get overexposure.)

Exercise is another powerful tool... Scientists report that physical activity cuts your risk of depression in half. Just two and a half hours of exercise per week offers the peak benefit. That's less than 22 minutes of activity a day.

And the exercise doesn't have to be extreme or overly vigorous. It can be activities like going for a walk over the lunch hour or working in your garden.

Meditation is another simple way to combat depression. It helps calm and decreases activity in your amygdala – the walnut-shaped tissue in the brain that controls fear. There is also strong evidence that adding **magnesium** to your diet will improve mood, energy, and mental stability.

So before you decide to spend your money and health care energy on antidepressants, try one of the healthier alternatives that do work. If you try these things, I can almost guarantee your mood will improve, you'll worry less, and you'll sleep better at night.

— 9 —

The Antibiotic Myth

For decades, antibiotics have been used as a cure-all.

But this widespread use is putting you at risk. Let me explain...

The use of antibiotics became common after World War II with the manufacturing of penicillin (one of the most widely used antibiotics). They were initially created to fight or destroy deadly infections.

From the common cold to skin infections, doctors prescribe more than 50 million antibiotics per year. Unfortunately, 10 million of those prescriptions are for viral infections that don't benefit much from antibiotics. And this created a health crisis...

Antibiotics treat bacterial infections (like strep throat). Most bacteria are single-celled organisms and survive on their own. Antibiotics destroy the bacteria by attacking the bacterial wall or machinery on the wall.

Viruses (like the common cold) embed themselves into a cell to survive. That makes viruses difficult to treat and antibiotics ineffective against them.

Despite this, doctors misuse antibiotics...

In children, antibiotics are commonly prescribed for ear infections. But a 2010 study published by *The Journal of the American Medical Association* found most ear infections are viruses and are not treatable with antibiotics. (One common exception: otitis externa, or "swimmer's ear.") And for children, the negative side effects of antibiotics are the leading cause of emergency-room visits.

Adults are often prescribed antibiotics for colds and sinus infections, neither of which can be treated with antibiotics.

During cold season, Azithromycin (or the so-called "Z-pak") is one of the most widely used antibiotics. It makes up 20% of all prescription antibiotics. A Z-pak is meant to be used to treat bacterial infections like strep throat and bronchitis. But doctors use this bacterial-infection medicine to treat viral ailments like the flu... even though antibiotics can't treat the flu.

And more alarming, the Z-pak has dangerous side effects (even when used correctly). It can cause liver failure and increase your risk of cardiovascular death. So if you already have heart problems, talk to your doctor about other solutions before taking Zithromax.

In most cases, your immune system handles these types of viral infections and clears them up eventually. One well-known exception is the human immunodeficiency virus (HIV), which requires antiviral medication to survive it.

It gets worse, though... Humans aren't the only ones being over-treated.

About 80% of antibiotics sold in the U.S. are used on animal livestock. More than 30 million pounds per year is used on food (compared with 6 million pounds used as medication for humans).

Antibiotics are used at "concentrated animal feeding operations" (CAFOs). A CAFO is where animals are kept in small spaces to be fed directly rather than allowing the animal to graze. It's generally recognized as a cheaper and more efficient way to raise livestock. But due to the confined spaces, disease runs rampant among the animals. So companies use antibiotics to stop diseases from spreading...

The overuse creates drug-resistant superbugs like methicillin-resistant Staphylococcus aureus (MRSA), which causes more than 18,000 deaths in the U.S. annually. Even salmonella is becoming resistant to antibiotics.

There's no clear evidence that consuming meat exposed to these antibiotics has consequences for your health... But it's wise to limit your intake of unnecessary chemicals like these.

Whole Foods Market only sells antibiotic-free meat. You can also look for meat labeled "Organic," which doesn't contain antibiotics.

You should also wash off your meat and poultry before cooking it to limit your exposure to the hearty bacteria created by the overuse of antibiotics in food. Keep your cooking utensils far away from the sink, and scrub down the surrounding area with soap and water when you're done.

And when you get sick... try to let your immune system do its job. You may feel miserable having a cold or the flu. But if you're not deathly ill, it's best to let the illness run its course.

When you do visit the doctor and he offers you a prescription for antibiotics, ask if your illness is viral or bacterial. If he tells you it's viral, find another treatment option like an antiviral medication... or simply rest and drink fluids.

PART VII

Health Tips and Secrets

— 1 —

Boost Your Health With Flowers

I love fresh flowers. I've grown to appreciate the effort it takes to garden and cultivate flowers. It's not easy, but the results are miraculous. And no shopping list is complete without flowers.

Flowers are nature's way of saying life will go on. Something about looking at flowers (especially in the dead of winter) reminds us that "this too shall pass" and gives us that extra little nudge to look forward to the future. This is perhaps the reason flowers have been shown to improve depression and lift our moods.

A 2005 article published in *Evolutionary Psychology* reported the results of three studies showing the positive effects of flowers.

In the first study, women smiled virtually every time they received flowers. In the second study, women and men were friendlier when given a large Gerber daisy versus a pen. The final study reported older men and women who received one or more bouquets of flowers over a two-week period showed an improvement in mood and memory.

In addition, Chinese researchers have shown extracts from the beautiful hibiscus flower lower blood pressure and even cholesterol. Chemicals in the flower are similar to the antioxidants in red wine... the polyphenols and anthocyanins known to improve heart health in wine drinkers.

Drug companies looking for new chemicals are interested in flowers. The sight of flowers and their extracts have been shown to:

- Improve sleep (Lavender)

- Decrease anxiety (Lavender)

- Decrease depression (Rose)

- Decrease cholesterol (Hibiscus)

- Lower blood pressure (Hawthorn)

- Improve resistance to colds (Echinacea)

- Increase energy (the sight of almost any flower)

The conclusions are clear... **Cultivated flowers bring out positive emotions in humans**. And with positive emotions comes health and longevity.

Want a good workout? Try growing flowers yourself. Research has shown that gardening for 30 minutes is just as beneficial for your health as jogging.

— 2 —

Beware BPA

A chemical in the liner of canned goods is an estrogen mimic. It's the same chemical in some water bottles, too – Bisphenol A (BPA). This chemical is linked to prostate and breast cancers, diabetes, and heart disease.

> ### *DO WHAT I DO*
> Choose fresh foods over canned and look for containers that say they are "BPA-free."

Campbell's soup and Del Monte green beans tend to have some of the highest levels. But most mainstream brands contain the stuff. Do what I do... choose fresh foods over canned and look for containers that say they are "BPA-free."

New research has discovered high levels of BPA in paper receipts – the ones from cash registers and ATMs.

Do what I do... Don't take receipts. I use my credit-card statements as quick confirmation of my spending. I also wash my hands after handling a receipt, especially if I'm eating.

The problem is, you can't tell which receipts contain BPA. It's the same story with newspapers and magazines, which can also contain high levels of BPA. Worse, touching a product with BPA transfers the chemical to whatever you touch, including food. If you ingest it, you increase the risk of the health issues I mentioned.

Wash your hands thoroughly after reading a newspaper or magazine.

And don't touch your mouth while reading.

Even "BPA-free" isn't as safe as we thought...

Unfortunately, many manufacturers have replaced BPA with Bisphenol S (BPS) – which is probably just as dangerous. Studies show it alters proper hormone function in the same way that BPA can. I don't want something near my body that is already known to mess with hormones and kill living cells.

To avoid BPA and BPS, don't buy foods stored in hard plastic containers. When possible, buy products in glass or soft plastics. And switch out your plastic water bottle for a stainless-steel one. Klean Kanteen is a leading manufacturer of stainless-steel bottles.

> **DO WHAT I DO**
>
> **Don't take receipts. I use my credit-card statements as quick confirmation of my spending. I also wash my hands after handling a receipt, especially if I'm eating.**

When you do use plastic, there's a helpful guide you can use to avoid BPA.

The recycling symbol on the bottom of containers indicates which containers have BPA. Inside the symbol, you'll find a number one through seven. No. 1 means the container is BPA-free. Avoid the No. 7 – the container probably has BPA. This is commonly found in water bottles and baby bottles. Two through six aren't as widely used for food containers. But three and six can also be dangerous.

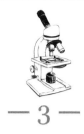

— 3 —

Millions of People Have This Disease and Don't Know It

Two-year-old Porter Lynch was growing well.

His pediatrician measured his growth to be perfect for his age... right in the 50th percentile. His twin sister, Katie, was a different story.

She was falling off the bottom of the doctor's charts. She was in the low single-digit percentile. And she was miserable.

Katie struggled her whole life with generalized weakness in her walking, balance, and constipation. She lived with melancholy every day. It was hard on her parents (my friends) Chris and Brenda. With Katie crying for hours every night until she passed out, Mom and Dad hardly got any rest...

Doctors fed her elemental iron for anemia, along with other drugs and minerals that lab tests showed she lacked. (Iron's most common side effect is constipation. Her parents countered the iron with stool softeners and daily physical manipulations. It was brutal.)

Her doctors remained puzzled, too. Most couldn't explain the lab tests and developmental issues. It wasn't until a physician friend of mine visited and we put our heads together that everyone agreed on the likely diagnosis: the gastrointestinal disorder Celiac disease.

People with Celiac disease essentially have an allergy to gluten, a protein found in grass-like grains such as wheat, rye, and barley.

Celiac disease is common. The medical establishment says one in 133 people suffer from it to some degree. But I'm convinced it's more like two or three in 100 people – that would be 9 million Americans, more than the population of New York City.

Technically, gluten is the combination of two smaller proteins glutenin and gliadin. The combination gluten essentially triggers an allergic reaction in the gut wall. This leads to inflammation of the intestinal surfaces.

Over time, chronic inflammation leads to destruction of parts of the gut-system surfaces, which results in the symptoms of Celiac disease. With the surface broken down, nutrients like iron and fat don't get absorbed properly. This leads to frustrating and painful symptoms like...

- Gas

- Bloating

- Anemia

- Diarrhea

- Weakness

- Bruising

- Infertility

- Osteoporosis

With Katie's diagnosis made, the family shifted her to a gluten-free diet. They found it harder than you might think to find gluten-free foods, even living in northern California. In addition to obvious things (like virtually any sort of bread), many food supplements contain added proteins and flavorings with gluten. Katie's family had to scrutinize every label carefully. (By the way, grocery chain Whole Foods offers an extensive line of gluten-free products.)

Within weeks, Katie's digestion, appetite, growth, and all-around countenance improved dramatically. Within months, her lab values normalized. Her sleeping habits approached the same pattern as her twin brother.

Kids aren't the only ones with Celiac. Older patients with no previous gluten intolerance can suddenly develop Celiac. And not all cases are as severe as Katie's… Many folks suffer with lower levels of discomfort, never realizing a dietary change could make them feel much better.

Remarkably, Katie's father, Chris, also reported life-changing improvement after the family adopted a gluten-free diet. For years, he suffered with GI distress and irregular bowel movements. After the diet change, Chris said he can "set the house clocks" to his morning routine. He also reported improvements in things like his skin and mood.

Finding 100%-gluten-free foods used to be difficult. There was no legal definition of the term "gluten free." But in August 2013, the FDA issued a rule that states foods labeled "gluten free" can have no more than 20 parts per million (ppm) of gluten. This rule applies to dietary supplements as well.

While 20 ppm could still be too much gluten for highly sensitive people, it's likely to make life a little easier for the majority of Americans suffering from Celiac.

Do what I did… Try out a gluten-free diet for a few months to see if you have any benefit from it. I didn't, but I have a half-dozen friends who did feel it improve their quality of life.

One word of caution… Look for labels that say "gluten free," "free of gluten," "without gluten," and "no gluten." These are the only phrases the new rule encompasses.

— 4 —

Relief From Seasonal Allergies

If you suffer from seasonal allergies, you're not alone... More than 30% of the U.S. population has seasonal allergies. But you can do a few things to relieve your symptoms...

Since I live in the city, I keep an air filter in my bedroom, which has helped with seasonal allergies as well as general stuffiness in the mornings. I clean the filter weekly.

One thing to remember when you have allergies is to be careful when blowing your nose. Researchers at the University of Virginia studied the flow of snot and mucous in sick people. They found that blowing your nose with both nostrils clogged creates large pressures in your sinuses. This just pushes the mucous and "bugs" back up into your sinuses and can cause more of an infection.

It's the same story with allergies. Blowing lightly with one nostril at a time restricts airflow less and is the best way to avoid this.

Another trick is to try a Neti pot. The Neti pot is an old Hindu device used to wash the sinuses. (Neti means "nasal" in Sanskrit.) You can purchase plastic ones with balanced salt solutions (in packets you mix with water at home) at your local drug stores for about $10. By using gravity and the solution, you can gently rinse your sinuses.

When I get tickles in my nose or post-nasal drip and sneezing, I know it's time to do a rinse once or twice a day... It feels funny at first... But if you're stuffy from pollen, this is a great way to clean out the areas in your nose that trap the pollens.

Be careful... Overuse of the Neti pot (either more than twice a day or for more than a couple weeks) can worsen things, leading to bacterial sinus infections.

For itchy eyes, purchase eye drops that "stabilize the mast cells" in your mucous membranes. Mast cells maintain chemicals used to protect the body from infections and parasites. When they are stimulated, they release these chemicals, which increase blood flow and direct immune-modulating cells to migrate to that area. Think of them as the fire alarm in a building.

Once released, you start itching, which leads to rubbing, which serves to spread even more of the cells and chemicals around to fight whatever it is that's bothering the body. If you can prevent the alarm from going off, you can avoid the redness and itching. After all, you know you're not suffering from an infection or parasites, so why not block it for a couple of weeks and feel better?

The drugs require a prescription, so you'll have to ask your physician to prescribe them. Ask for Patanol or Zatidor, or the generic versions, alocril and crolom. If used at the first sign of itchy eyes, they can help cut your allergy symptoms in half. I use them for about 3-4 weeks to get me through the worst of the season.

Foods That Can Control Allergies Without Drugs

Roughly 35 million Americans dread "allergy season" each year... And I'm one of them.

Like most people, I start to experience seasonal allergic rhinitis – or "hay fever" – in spring.

Exactly how and when you experience symptoms depends on your trigger allergen. In early spring, tree pollen is the major culprit. By the late spring and summer, grass pollen takes over. And weed pollen comes out in the fall.

Seasonal allergies occur when your immune system treats pollen as an invader. Antibodies called Immunoglobulin E (IgE) are produced to defend your body. This causes stuffiness, sneezing, and other allergic reactions.

There is no "cure" for seasonal allergies yet, but there are treatment options to relieve symptoms...

Claritin is another popular way to treat allergies. The drug is an antihistamine that blocks histamine binding to prevent allergies. But its side effects include drowsiness, headaches, constipation, and dry mouth. It can also raise your blood pressure.

Allergy shots work by regularly injecting small doses of the allergen causing your allergic reaction. However, they can take years to become effective and can have dangerous complications, like anaphylaxis (a life-threatening allergic reaction).

Nasal sprays are a popular over-the-counter medicine to treat congestion. But the relief is only temporary and can actually cause your nasal lining to swell up, leading to even more congestion. Some people have even become addicted to nasal sprays. Overuse can lead to holes in your nasal septum. Worse, the drugs can permanently kill your sense of smell.

Certain eye drops relieve itchy, red eyes. But some drops can't be used when wearing contacts, sting when put into the eye, and can make the eyes appear more red once the drug wears off. My choice for itchy eyes is Zatidor, a histamine-receptor blocker. It helps me with nasal and eye reactions.

And if your allergy symptoms are severe enough... your doctor can prescribe other medications. (One colleague in our office says his airways get so constricted in the spring, his doctor prescribes asthma medications.)

However, if you want to avoid drugs... some alternatives to medicine have been shown to ease symptoms.

To start, here are some "hygiene" steps you can take to reduce symptoms...

- Close windows and doors during higher pollen times.

- Shower and change clothes after being outside.

- Avoid going outside on dry, windy days when the pollen is blowing around or on days when the pollen counts are high.

- Don't exercise in the morning when counts are usually highest.

- Use a HEPA air filter in your bedroom. I keep one in my bedroom and clean the filter once a week.

The Neti Pot is one of my preferred methods. This is an old Hindu device used to wash the sinuses. But if you try it, be careful... and follow the instructions. If you don't use sterilized or distilled water, brain-eating organisms in the water can enter the brain through your sinuses. In late 2011, two deaths in Louisiana were blamed on the improper use of a Neti pot.

Also, you should avoid some foods that can exacerbate symptoms... Some people with seasonal allergies also have "oral allergy syndrome" – also called "food-pollen allergy" syndrome. This occurs when your immune system attacks proteins in certain foods like it would pollen. The food you react to can depend on the type of allergy you have.

People with weed allergies can react to honeydew, cantaloupe, watermelon, tomatoes, zucchini, and sunflower seeds.

Tree allergies are often associated with kiwi, apples, pears, peaches, plums, celery, cherries, carrots, hazelnut, almonds, and parsley.

If you have grass allergies, you might have a reaction to peaches, celery, tomatoes, melons, or oranges.

— 5 —

Meditation Isn't for Kooks

The first time I tried this out, I wasn't completely sure I wasn't joining a cult.

One day early in my freshman year at Carleton College, I came back to my dorm room and found my roommate sitting up stock-still in bed.

When I asked him what he was doing, he motioned in a slow arc with his finger for me to wait a moment. A few moments later, he came out of his "trance" and told me of this amazing practice he claimed would improve my life – I'd get better grades, have fewer colds, contribute to world peace...

I was skeptical, but decided to tag along for the hour-long bus ride to Minneapolis (no cars allowed at Carleton College), where we would sit with his instructor. Bouncing along Interstate 35W, I tried to ignore the vague worry I'd soon be riding shotgun with Patty Hearst and the Symbionese Liberation Army cult.

But the day was fantastic and the start of my learning about meditation and health.

Meditation Holds Up Well Against the Skeptics

Meditation is a nearly effortless way to improve your health and happiness. Paradoxically, the less effort you exert, the more benefit you get.

It turns out that the physiologic process of meditation is similar to the process that occurs in times of deep prayer. But you don't have to practice any specific religion (or any religion at all) to enjoy the health benefits of this process.

A cardiologist named Herbert Benson studied meditation in the 1970s and wrote a great book called *The Relaxation Response.*

The relaxation response is the root of meditation's benefits. Meditation changes our body's physiology. And although it feels like sleep, the brain waves we generate during meditation are different than sleep waves. Importantly, unlike sleep or napping, meditation releases chemicals that literally fight the chemicals released when we're under stress.

Even better, just like exercise, regular meditation improves your body's ability to use oxygen and actually lowers your resting heart rate. Again like exercise, meditation lowers blood pressure and boosts your immune system.

Meditation even increases the serotonin in your brain. This is the chemical that antidepressant drugs try to increase, but meditation works better than any drug.

I encourage you to start today, and meditate every day for 10-15 minutes. After a week, I guarantee you'll feel better. Here's what I do:

I sit upright in bed propped by about four pillows, but none behind my head. I try to keep my head nearly perfectly balanced on my neck – so that if I absolutely relax, my head won't tip over.

Next, I begin saying my mantra – a two-syllable word you repeat silently to yourself throughout the process. It can be a word like "Two-Ray" or "Oom-day." I try to time my breath with each syllable. Inhale with one. Exhale with the other.

Stay focused on relaxing and letting your breath in and out slowly, but also lightly focus on the mantra sound.

I find that suddenly, my mind will wander... all the things I need to do, or things I've forgotten to do, often flood my mind. When those thoughts flood in, I slowly turn my focus back to my breath and the mantra.

After a few attempts, I find my breath and thoughts slowing. Occasionally, I find myself taking a super-deep, slow breath. The breath scares me because it feels as if I don't need to breathe for a long time – which I don't.

Yet again, I'll turn back to my breath and my mantra.

After 15 minutes or so, I quietly and slowly take a few minutes to start to move my fingers and toes and then arms and legs as I come out of the "relaxation state."

That's it... It's that simple.

It's funny... Regardless of the success I've had with meditation, I still retain a bit of superstition from that first day. Transcendental Meditation teaches you how to meditate. The instructor gives you what he claims is your specific, personalized mantra to "get you into" your state of meditation.

Your mantra is supposed to be a secret. Instructors advise you to never reveal the mantra to anyone or it will stop working.

I know it's nonsense. (I often joke everyone gets the *same* personalized mantra.) But you won't pry my mantra out of me. No way. I'm not taking the chance.

— 6 —

Instantly Improve Your Physical and Mental Health

One of my top health tips every year is to **get better sleep**.

We keep discovering more things that sleep helps balance and prevent. Lack of sleep is connected with heart disease, obesity, colds, and even cancers. Research shows losing a half-hour of sleep can impair verbal skills, reaction time, and stamina. Men who don't sleep enough could experience erectile dysfunction.

> ### *DO WHAT I DO*
> **Darken the room as much as you can (or wear eye shades – seriously). Remove your television and radio. Get rid of electronic gear and unplug things near your head and body.**

Great research from Stanford University years ago suggested poor sleep leads to heart disease. It turns out, without sleep, our immune systems don't work well. That leads to more inflammatory molecules in our blood stream, which leads to many diseases like heart disease, diabetes, and cancer. You need sleep to "recharge" and balance the immune system at night.

I try to get at least eight hours of sleep a day (including naps). Almost everyone should sleep a minimum of seven and a half hours a day. Even people who think they're getting enough are probably not.

Here are some simple and easy tips to help sleep better tonight...

Do what I do... Darken the room as much as you can (or wear eye shades – seriously). Remove your television and radio. Get rid of electronic gear and unplug things near your head and body – the chargers and transformers in them emit electromagnetic radiation.

Turn down the thermostat in your bedroom. The optimal temperature for quality sleep is cooler than you'd imagine (and it's been studied extensively) – around 60 degrees.

Maintain a set time of day you either wake up or go to sleep. Importantly, try to make your bed a place of relaxation, sleep, and sex.

And one more thing: Don't fight in the bedroom. Let it be a sanctuary.

A great way to improve your mental health is through smell.

As the days grow shorter in fall and winter, many of us spend increasing amounts of time indoors... which can breed a sense of claustrophobia and gloom.

One of the easiest ways to counteract those feelings is to stimulate your brain with smells. Many odors are uplifting and stimulating to the soul, body, and mind. And they are proven to have powerful effects on your mood and wellbeing.

Sit quietly, close your eyes, and start thinking about roses or baking bread. My guess is you smiled and your breathing slowed... That's because our memories and feelings about life are tightly connected to scents.

Many animals would have a hard time surviving without smell. Animals with poor eyesight (like bears and rhinos) have a heightened sense of smell to compensate. They use smells for various things... to find food, find a female in heat, mark territory, mark trails, and even find lost offspring.

Humans use their sense of smell more than they realize... One study showed that people may convey emotions – like fear and anxiety – through smells.

Some research documents that humans can detect small changes in the way something smells. For example, someone can tell the difference between the smell of a pool versus the smell of a pool with one drop of sweat in it.

Other researchers have documented how a mother can tell the difference between the smell of her baby and the smell of another woman's baby within a few days of birth.

What makes a smell good or bad? Evolution is the only answer scientists have right now. We sniff our food to determine if it has a rotten or sour sort of smell. How many times have you taken a whiff of your milk to see if it smells fresh or not?

> ### DO WHAT I DO
> Go to any health food store (even Whole Foods) and ask for the essential oils. Buy one small bottle. Sprinkle a drop or two on your bed covers, a rug, or a small dish.

Humans have also learned to fear smells like smoke or gas – as these can signal potential dangers. Of course, the perception of whether something smells good or bad varies by culture.

Research shows certain smells can increase a man's arousal. The scents that arouse men most are lavender and pumpkin pie.

Most people can discern between 4,000 and 10,000 different smells. But as you get older, your sense of smell decreases. You can't completely prevent it from happening, but you can take steps to minimize the loss by exercising your sniffer.

Smoking damages your olfactory system – so avoid it. Also pay attention to the side effects of medications you're taking. Certain medicines, like Nasonex and Xanax, can alter or cause you to lose your sense of smell. Talk to your doctor if you think this might be happening.

Do what I do... Go to any health food store (even Whole Foods) and ask for the essential oils. Buy one small bottle. Don't be put off by the seemingly high price for such a small bottle ($5-$6 each) – the stuff lasts for months. Just sprinkle a drop or two on your bed covers, a rug, or a small dish.

Adding enjoyable aromas to your environment is a simple and cheap way to improve your mood. I sprinkle several around my home, and even travel with a bottle of rose oil. I place a few drops or sprays of my favorite scents around the house – lavender in the bedroom, inside of pillow cases... orange on the side of the air cleaner... pine on the bathroom rug... bergamot or patchouli on the papers in the trash can in my study...

My two favorites are rose and patchouli. I love adding the smell of roses to towels in the hotel bathroom. And patchouli around the front door in the winter is a heartwarming smell to walk into from out of the cold.

For more stories about smell, read one of my favorite books of all time, *A Natural History of the Senses* by Diane Ackerman.

— 7 —

What Men Must Know About Prostate Cancer

Ron from Spring Hill, Florida, hadn't been to a doctor in 40 years.

"Why go if there isn't anything wrong with me?" he said. He had never been sick. And at 73, he was still feeling good.

Until he read an article I wrote about prostate cancer. Ron says it saved his life.

Prostate cancer is an odd disease... It's incredibly common and incredibly slow-moving. In medical school, we were taught that if men lived to 120, each one would get prostate cancer... But it's so slow-growing, most men who develop it die of something else – often without any clue their prostate was diseased.

The fact that prostate cancer IS a cancer – and one that involves our "private parts" – makes it all the more frightening... and hard to talk about for many men. But it is a critical aspect of men's health.

The American Cancer Society estimated that in 2014, there would be 233,000 new cases diagnosed and nearly 30,000 men would die from it. The terrible irony of prostate cancer is it is very curable if caught early. But it's hard to catch. Prostate cancer can go on for years before producing some of these classic symptoms...

- Frequent urination

- Hesitancy with urination (hard to get started)

- Erectile dysfunction

- Burning with urination

- Pain in the lower back

- Stiffness in the upper legs

After reading an issue of my *Health Report* – a newsletter I wrote from 2006 to 2009 – on prostate cancer, Ron recognized he had five of these six symptoms. That's when he raced to the doctor.

His regular physician wouldn't see him for *six weeks,* and the first urologist he called laughed at him when he said he had symptoms. That urologist said prostate cancer has no symptoms. (This is the sort of BS doctors say and do that drives me crazy.)

Ron persisted and found a urologist to see him right away. During the exam, the doctor was troubled by the prostate's texture. (By the way, the prostate is only about the size of a walnut, and it can be an uncomfortable couple of minutes while the doctor searches for it.)

Immediately after the exam, Ron's doctor ordered a standard prostate-specific antigen (PSA) test, which looks for prostate-produced material floating around in the blood. Well, his test result was sky-high, and cancer cells were found in four out of eight biopsy sites.

Ron's story ends well. He had 43 radiation treatments. (Many people believe surgery is not necessary in men older than 70. Surgery has risks of impotence and incontinence.) Ron also took the drug Leupron, which stops cancer cells from growing, for a couple years during his radiation treatment. He later stopped all treatments.

His PSA has been at zero for two years (although Leupron may be the reason).

There are a few other things that men can do to lower their risk of prostate cancer:

- Ejaculating more than 12 times a month lowers the risk... 21 times a month is thought to be ideal. (It was assumed that masturbation was better than intercourse, due the risk of STDs, but further research has disproved that notion.)

- Exercise. Even walking 30 minutes a day lowers your cancer risk.

- Diet is critical. (And you can control it!)

- Tomatoes are high in lycopene, which reduces prostate cancer risk.

- Vitamin D is associated with decreased cancer risks.

- Calcium is related intimately to Vitamin D... Make sure you get enough calcium and sunlight.

- Vegetables: cabbage, broccoli, Brussels sprouts, onions, carrots, and parsley all lower cancer risks.

- Green tea and even black teas have known antioxidant and anti-cancer properties.

Finally, if you are diagnosed with prostate cancer, be sure to talk with many people about possible treatments. Robotic surgery may have a faster recovery time than conventional surgeries and has outcomes equal to conventional surgery. It's also less painful.

Also, be sure to find a doctor who understands the benefits of herbs like saw palmetto and its role in prostate health... Many doctors laugh at the notion that benefits shown in studies using herbs are real. Avoid those laughing doctors.

Beware of the PSA test, though. It could cause more harm than good...

Don't Let This Test Send You to Needless Cancer Surgery

Prostate cancer is among most older men's biggest fears... And you can understand why...

One in 14 men in their 60s develops the disease. And the treatment options can come with some discouraging side effects: sterility, urinary incontinence, and even impotence.

The American Cancer Society recommends men over 50 have the digital rectal exam (DRE) and prostate-specific antigen (PSA) test done annually.

Don't do it...

These tests can do more harm than good. Let me explain...

First, remember... despite its ominous reputation, prostate cancer is a slow-moving disease. Most men who've been diagnosed die of something else. And you can live a long and happy life with prostate cancer.

The U.S. Preventive Services Task Force (USPSTF) recommends against getting a PSA done every year. The USPSTF is the agency that advises the U.S. government on preventative medical measures. According to the USPSTF, "There is moderate or high certainty that the [PSA test] has no benefit or that the harms outweigh the benefits."

I tend to follow the recommendation of the USPSTF. Once I found out the truth about the PSA, I stopped getting them. And I don't plan to have one in the future.

Some doctors use the PSA as a baseline... Once you have the basic levels of both your prostate anatomy and the PSA test, a doctor may monitor your levels to watch if they increase. If your symptoms worsen, you can compare with the first test... if the doctor finds a change, it might be time for treatment.

But be careful... don't allow yourself to be overtreated.

Several studies now question the usefulness of a PSA. High PSA levels alone do not necessarily signal cancer. Some benign conditions – like inflammation of the prostate, an infection, or recent ejaculation – can increase PSA levels. *Because of this, PSA tests are known for having a high rate of false positives.* But it's still an often-used exam to test for prostate cancer.

With institutions like The American Cancer Society telling men to get regular and frequent prostate screenings, many men are being overtreated. And treatments for prostate cancer can damage your quality of life more than the disease would.

There are four common options after you've been diagnosed: active surveillance, surgery, radiation therapy, and drugs. And as I said, the side effects of surgery and radiation can be harsh.

As for drugs, there are risks there, too. Some doctors use drugs that lower the levels of dihydrotestosterone (DHT). DHT is a male hormone that's a precursor to testosterone. It binds receptors that trigger cancer growth. Blocking testosterone slows and even stops prostate growth. But it leaves uncomfortable side effects, like impotence and heart problems.

On the other hand, doing nothing – so-called "active surveillance" – can carry its own risks. Active surveillance requires regular testing of PSA levels. But this can narrow the window of opportunity to effectively treat the cancer.

So What Should You Do If You're Worried About Prostate Cancer?

The best option is prevention. Do what I do…

1. Remember the number 21 (the ideal number of times you should ejaculate each month).

2. Reduce your weekly intake of high-fat red meat. I eat red meat high in fat only occasionally. (Rib-eye is my favorite and my nemesis.)

3. Eat tomatoes whenever and however you can. (They're packed with lycopene, which helps reduce your risk of prostate cancer.)

4. Exercise several times during the week in varied ways to lower your risks for all sorts of health problems, including prostate cancer.

If you think you may have prostate cancer, talk to your doctor. He should be knowledgeable about alternatives to taking the PSA.

Several other promising alternatives are currently in the experimental stages. One is the A+PSA. This test looks for six antibodies that are found in the blood of men with prostate cancer. Studies show it reduces the rate of false-positives from the PSA because it's not just searching for the prostate-specific antigen.

Another possible alternative to the PSA is a urine-based test that looks for heat shock protein 27 (Hsp-27). Researchers have found this protein in cancer cells, and it can indicate whether a man has an aggressive form of prostate cancer.

> **66** *If you may have prostate cancer, talk to your doctor. He should be knowledgeable about alternatives to taking the PSA.* **99**

And remember... while we've given you the basics here, you should spend time researching screenings and treatments, especially if your doctor is suggesting anything radical, like surgery.

Don't blindly follow the advice of doctors or medical institutions without fully understanding the risks you're taking.

— 8 —

An Essential Part of Cancer Treatment You Might Be Missing

"He didn't know what he was talking about."

That's what Butch – a 37-year police veteran in Maryland – told me about his first cancer doctor.

Before Butch was diagnosed with cancer in 2007, he thought he was pretty healthy. He exercised regularly and was a competitive runner for decades. He ate a mostly well-balanced diet (one of his weaknesses was a sweet tooth). He knew a good diet was essential to living a long and healthy life.

When he was diagnosed with Chronic Lymphocytic Leukemia, his doctor explained the disease and laid out a basic treatment plan... What you'd expect a doctor to talk to a new cancer patient about.

What the doctor didn't discuss was the importance of healthy eating or exercise in cancer patients. As Butch said, "The doctor didn't seem to know much beyond the diagnosis and treatment options like chemotherapy and radiation. Plus, he had a terrible bedside manner."

So Butch found another doctor who suggested he cut out refined sugars, increase the number of vegetables he was eating, and add green tea to his diet. The doctor also suggested Butch exercise as much as possible to fight muscle weakness and lower the risk of depression.

Two years after his chemotherapy ended, Butch was healthier than he'd been in years. He claimed eating a more "natural," balanced diet and exercising as much as he was able to were essential to maintaining his health during treatment and helping him recover after.

Butch's experience is all too common. People are often told about how healthy eating protects their health... But few doctors talk to clients about how important a healthy diet is in people fighting cancer *after a diagnosis.*

Modern cancer treatments – like radiation and chemotherapy – wreak havoc on the human body. Cancer treatment can weaken immunity, cause eating problems (like nausea), weight problems, and extreme fatigue.

A healthy diet keeps your body in the best condition it can be in during treatment and can even lessen symptoms.

"Cruciferous" vegetables – like broccoli, Brussels sprouts, and cabbage – are packed with beneficial chemicals. They fight inflammation and can reduce your risk of cardiovascular disease and diabetes.

Blueberries, strawberries, and raspberries also have incredible health benefits. From improving memory to boosting your immune system to keeping your eyes healthy, berries are an important food to include in your everyday diet.

Ginger is a natural way for patients to fight nausea and vomiting. According to a 2009 National Cancer Institute study, it can reduce nausea 40%.

Another great food for cancer patients is yogurt. The probiotics in yogurt can reduce diarrhea and weight loss. They also help boost your immune system, reducing the risk of illness during treatment.

And green tea, as Butch's doctor told him, is a great drink for cancer patients. Green tea contains catechins, which are polyphenols, or so-called "flavonoids." One of those catechins is epigallocatechin gallate (EGCG). This powerful antioxidant is known to kill cancer cells in vitro and also leaves healthy tissue unharmed.

Interestingly, the tea chemicals' mechanism of action may be due to the inhibition of a unique class of compounds called matrix metalloproteinases (MMPs). This inhibition can be directly linked to decreased cell and blood-vessel growth in tumors in the lab. Keeping the blood supply away from cancer is one of the best mechanisms of fighting cancer, too.

Also, sipping tea can be a great time to sit quietly and meditate... even if for just 10-15 minutes a day. The relaxation response triggered with meditation is great for longevity. And combining it with sipping green tea could be a potent way to fight stress and disease.

All the foods I've mentioned are great if you've been diagnosed with cancer, and if you want to fight cancer.

So do what I do... make sure you include them in your regular diet.

— 9 —

The Cancer-Causing
Chemical Hiding in Your Bathroom

There's a chemical in nearly every cosmetic in your house that may be giving you cancer (and other health problems)...

I'm talking about "parabens."

These cheap chemicals block the growth of molds, fungi, and bacteria. Companies have used parabens in cosmetics, pharmaceuticals, and even food since the 1920s to give their products longer shelf lives. (The cosmetics industry began using parabens in the 1950s after several cases of blindness occurred from people using spoiled lotion.)

Some common parabens you'll find on the ingredient lists in your bathroom are "methylparaben," "ethylparaben," "propylparaben," and "butylparaben." The first part of the name ("methyl," "ethyl," etc.) derives from the number of carbons in the "functional group" of the molecule.

Methylparaben, for example, has one carbon alkyl group; ethyl has two carbons. (Obviously, you can recognize them because they all end with "-paraben.")

Several studies have found high concentrations of parabens disrupt estrogen function... This can lead to dangerous consequences. Parabens are considered "estrogen mimics." This means they can disrupt the normal functions of hormones in our bodies – especially estrogen.

Estrogen is ubiquitous in humans. In women, it regulates menstrual cycles and plays a key role in fertility. In excess, estrogen in men and women is linked to several kinds of cancers, including breast cancer...

Researchers found parabens throughout the breast tissue of women who'd had breast cancer. The highest levels of parabens were found in the tissue closest to the armpit. This study shows one of the strongest links between parabens and breast cancer yet.

In addition to cancer... parabens applied topically can damage your skin. In 2012, researchers found that skin cells treated with parabens and exposed to sunlight died three times more often. In addition, chemicals known as oxidants were also found on the paraben skin. Oxidants cause wrinkling and old age spots.

For younger men, the big concern is infertility...

Several studies show parabens decrease sperm counts. These studies found propylparaben and butylparaben disrupt male reproductive functions and decrease daily sperm production. Scientists found sperm counts fell almost 30% from 1989 to 2002.

Another study found that men born in the late 1980s have lower sperm counts than men born in the early 1980s. And this trend continues as parabens find their way into more of our goods.

Interestingly, parabens may have some benefits. Methylparaben is found in some fruits – like blueberries. It acts like a natural preservative and antimicrobial. But this is the paraben in its natural form and natural concentrations... not man-made like you find in deodorant.

Today, you can find parabens in 75%-90% of deodorants, moisturizers, shampoos, and makeup. Although the cosmetic concentrations of parabens are often less than 1%, it's unclear at what level the chemicals become dangerous.

The FDA, which is supposed to watch what goes into these products, says parabens are "normally used at levels ranging from 0.01 to 0.3 percent." Predictably, the agency that is supposed to be watching out for us doesn't seem to know what's happening. Its assessment doesn't jive with the real concentrations.

In 1984, the Cosmetic Ingredient Review (CIR) trade association said parabens are safe in cosmetics in concentrations up to 25%. In 2005, CIR reassessed its original study and found no reason to change its original guidelines. And while the FDA doesn't monitor the use of parabens, it accepts the findings of CIR.

So what is safe? 1%? 25%? What's really been studied? Sadly, there is no consensus.

What Can You Do to Avoid Parabens in Your Cosmetics?

Buy cosmetics without parabens... This can be difficult because of how ubiquitous they've become. This is especially true for women, who typically use more cosmetics than men. But you can find paraben-free products...

The brand "Burt's Bees" offers many paraben-free cosmetics – including deodorants, lotions, and shampoos. Tom's of Maine has paraben-free soap and deodorant.

> ### *DO WHAT I DO*
> Avoid using underarm deodorants on days you're able to swim or splash around in water. This cleans away much of the bacteria naturally known to cause smelly underarms and body odors. I'll even splash a little cologne or aftershave on my shirt.

Or you can also do what I do... Avoid using underarm deodorants on days you're able to swim or splash around in water. This cleans away much of the bacteria naturally known to cause smelly underarms and body odors. I'll even splash a little cologne or aftershave on my shirt...

To see if what you have in your house is paraben-free, just read the ingredient label. If you see a manmade paraben on the list, I'd try to avoid it (or at least, cut back).

— 10 —

Alzheimer's: The Mysterious Disease You May Not Even Know You Have

Alzheimer's is a terrifying diagnosis... and with good reason.

There's no cure for the progressive neurological disease that slowly saps people of their memories... their personality... and their independence – most of the fundamental things we use to define who we are.

It's a legitimate concern of people who are aging... and children with aging parents.

Alzheimer's is the irreversible deterioration of brain tissue. It's one form of dementia. And it typically occurs in people over the age of 60. But Alzheimer's can also strike people as young as 20 (referred to as "early onset Alzheimer's").

In 2014, more than 4.5 million Americans suffer from Alzheimer's. And some estimates expect that number to almost quadruple by 2050.

Despite its prevalence, not much is known about Alzheimer's. Scientists aren't sure why people develop it. We can only treat many of the symptoms... But those therapies often come with severe side effects.

It's generally agreed that several factors increase your risk of developing the disease. These include...

- Age

- A family history of Alzheimer's (genetics)

- Inflammation

- Severe head trauma

- High blood pressure or high cholesterol

The genetic link is often debated. Some studies show a family history significantly increases your risk of developing Alzheimer's. Others claim the increase of risk is negligible.

Many diseases – including heart disease, diabetes, and arthritis – are linked to inflammation. Research shows inflammation can damage the proteins in your brain... starting the degeneration of tissue.

The Seven Stages of Alzheimer's

Alzheimer's progresses in seven stages.

At **Stage 1**, the person shows no symptoms of the disease. But the brain is starting to slowly create plaques and protein tangles. At this point, a doctor wouldn't find any evidence of Alzheimer's.

At **Stage 2**, the earliest signs of Alzheimer's can show themselves. Some memory loss can occur. But at this stage, memory loss is slight enough that people attribute it to simple aging and not Alzheimer's.

At **Stage 3**, doctors can sometimes diagnose early-stage Alzheimer's as problems remembering words or names of people increase.

By **Stage 4**, most patients will have been diagnosed with Alzheimer's. At this stage, a person forgets recent events or even his own personal history. The patient could also have great difficulty performing tasks that involve planning or organization (like paying bills or planning a party). Some people also begin to have mood swings.

At **Stage 5**, a person begins to experience cognitive problems, like trouble with math (for example, the inability to count backward) and choosing weather-appropriate clothing. Memory loss worsens, and the patient loses memory of significant details about himself or the lives of his family.

At **Stage 6**, memory deteriorates further... some even forget their own names. During this stage, someone with Alzheimer's may struggle to complete daily tasks – like getting dressed, eating, and going to the bathroom – and often requires supervision. Major personality changes occur at this stage. Aggression can be a concern with many patients by this point.

Once patients enter **Stage 7**, they often lose the ability to have a conversation or respond to their environment... although they can still speak at times. Many also become completely dependent on others to get through the day. And some people even lose the ability to smile or sit up on their own.

Someone experiencing the symptoms of early-stage Alzheimer's may not have the disease. But if you or someone you know has them, visit your doctor.

As I've said... unfortunately, there's no cure for Alzheimer's. Medications are available to treat some of the symptoms (like memory loss and mood swings). But the side effects can be severe... and are known to worsen the older the patient is.

The best thing you can do to stave off Alzheimer's is to live a healthy lifestyle. Eat a healthy diet. A healthy diet can prevent inflammation. And you can start with three foods to instantly improve your health...

Three Foods to Fight Alzheimer's

Olive oil works well to fight inflammation. The chemical structure and function of olive oil protects other cholesterols in your body from oxidation, which leads to inflammation. Do what I do...

> **DO WHAT I DO**
>
> Use olive oil to cook eggs in the morning and sauté foods in the evening.

Use olive oil to cook eggs in the morning and sauté foods in the evening.

Fish is another food to promote good health. As we discussed in Part V, Chapter 14 fish fat is packed with omega-3 fats, which reduce inflammation.

The third food is **ginger**. Two active ingredients in ginger – zingerone and shogaol – act as anti-inflammatories. I like to eat ginger whenever I eat sushi. But you can also find ginger supplements that offer the same benefits.

There's another substance in some foods called "medium-chained fatty acids" that may fight dementia. Research showed amazing preliminary results. It's exciting stuff – with the potential to reverse mind-destroying plaques and show actual improvement (reversal) of dementia in some patients.

Finally, make sure you keep your body and mind active. Some of my favorite ways to get moving are going for walks and doing yoga. I keep my mind active by learning new activities. I also enjoy working on Sudoku puzzles in newspapers and magazines.

Just remember that eating sensibly and exercising your body (and mind) daily will help you live a longer, healthier, fuller life.

Exercise Your Brain

Researchers know working different parts of the brain in new ways will trigger growth of new brain tissue. (This notion was laughed at when first proposed.) No matter your age, stimulate it by doing silly things – most are harder than you'd imagine.

Do what I do...

Brush your teeth with your left hand. Try to listen with your left ear to stimulate the nonverbal right side of your brain. Walk backward on flat surfaces for a few minutes every day (on carpet only, if you're over 60). Get dressed with your eyes closed at least twice a week. Stop and smell flowers when you see them. Try to write daily notes with your left hand.

Research also shows that learning a second language can help delay the onset of Alzheimer's. Learning languages activates your memory and exercises the part of your brain that gives us our ability to think in complex ways. It also helps you to multitask by learning to focus. Scientists believe

DO WHAT I DO

Brush your teeth with your left hand. Try to listen with your left ear to stimulate the nonverbal right side of your brain. Walk backward on flat surfaces for a few minutes every day (on carpet only, if you're over 60). Get dressed with your eyes closed at least twice a week. Stop and smell flowers when you see them. Try to write daily notes with your left hand.

that knowing more than one language forces our brains to lay down new tracts to prevent the two languages from interfering with each other.

You can learn a new language through several sources: One popular method is with a software program like Rosetta Stone. You can also find applications and audio books through online store iTunes that are easy to download to your iPod. And there's always the old-school method – take a class at a local college. Some schools offer discounts for senior citizens.

Reading is great exercise, too. And there's no need to pay for books. For free reading without going to your library, try the University of Pennsylvania's digital library. While many of the books offered are academic, you can find books from classic authors like H.G. Wells and Alexis de Tocqueville. With more than one million different titles, you'll find plenty of choices.

To get access to the books, just visit the University of Pennsylvania's website. You can read the books on your computer (or Internet-enabled device, like the iPad).

You can also get free or discounted ebooks with BookBub. The free online service BookBub finds special, limited-time offers on ebooks and then e-mails you deals on books matching your interests. Publishers create the deals to spur interest in a book. To join, you just enter your e-mail address and pick the types of offers you'd like to receive.

BookBub allows you to choose between genres like historical fiction or nonfiction. You also choose which device you use to read ebooks – like a

Kindle or iPad. Then you receive e-mails whenever a new deal pops up (about once per day). You can also browse current deals on its website. If you ever want to stop receiving the e-mails, it's easy to unsubscribe.

Another tip to exercise your brain: drum roll please... real exercise. Exercise boosts growth factors that stimulate brain-cell growth. And it doesn't take much. Just stretching for one hour three times a week brings improvements in 60-79 year olds – as good as aerobic exercise.

So get moving. You've got no excuse... Just lie on the floor and stretch like I do. It will make you smarter. I recommend you buy the best book on stretching ever written, *Stretching* by Bob Anderson. I like the spiral-bound version.

— 11 —

The Danger Lurking
on Your Stovetop

When in Miami, visiting my friend and Stansberry Research founder Porter Stansberry, I walked into the kitchen to find him cooking eggs and black beans in a nonstick pan... and using a metal fork to stir and flip the food.

I told him how bad it was for the pan... and worse for our health... to improperly cook with nonstick pans. I even showed him the little nicks on the surface that meant we were ingesting the nonstick material (and ruining our breakfast).

Porter – like many people I've spoken to – was skeptical... But I urge everyone to read the manufacturer's label on your cooking equipment. If you do, you'll see a warning to never use metal utensils or cook with high heat.

Our quick-to-sue society has led manufacturers of all kinds of products to inundate us with silly warnings about one-chance-in-a-million dangers. But the warnings on these pans are serious. Let me explain...

Nonstick pots and pans account for more than 90% of aluminum cookware sales in the United States. One of the most popular (and well-known) nonstick coatings is "Teflon."

DuPont Chemical – the only company in the U.S. that manufactures Teflon – first introduced it in 1945 and derived the brand name from its chemical designation, polytetrafluoroethylene (PTFE). PTFE is produced using a chemical with another long name, perfluorooctanoic acid (PFOA).

PFOA contains chains of molecules with deadly fluorine atoms attached. Those molecule chains are what keep food from sticking to your cookware. But it's also what's exposing you to danger...

For most people, the biggest danger arises when the nonstick cookware gets too hot. The coating starts to decompose at 500 degrees Fahrenheit. At this temperature, your pan releases toxic particles and gases (including known carcinogens). These gases soak right into the food you're cooking.

At 660 degrees, the fumes are strong enough to cause polymer-fume fever. Polymer-fume fever has symptoms similar to flu – including muscle pain, fever, chills, and fatigue. At this temperature, the fumes are toxic enough to kill birds.

The hotter it gets, the more gases and toxins get released... a total of 15 toxic gases.

According to the advocacy group Environmental Working Group, it takes less than three minutes for a pan to get hot enough to start releasing toxic gases.

To DuPont's credit... that's why the company warns people to not use Teflon-coated pots and pans over more than medium heat... Not many people take that warning to heart.

I boil water and regularly cook oils and butters using higher heat. So only using low- or medium-heat settings may not work for most people.

Fortunately, there are several alternatives to cooking with pots and pans made with PFOA...

Stainless steel is an inexpensive alternative. All you need to do is add a little bit of oil or nonstick cooking spray – like Pam – to the pan before using it.

Cast iron is another good alternative. But cast iron can be expensive... And without proper care, it can rust. Foods can also stick easily to cast iron if the pan isn't seasoned properly (coating the pan with oil *after* each use).

You can also use cookware with a nonstick enamel or ceramic coating. Companies like GreenPan and Le Creuset manufacture these products. But as with cast iron, they are expensive (GreenPans can run upwards of $300) and require careful handling.

If you don't want to spend the money to buy a new set of pots and pans, do what I do... Use Teflon-coated cookware for foods that only require low or medium heat. I always use silicone or rubber utensils with them. This prevents scratching and chipping, which keeps pieces of the pan out of your food.

However, for hot-oil cooking, use cast iron or stainless steel.

Here are some general and simple safety tips for using non-stick cookware...

- Don't preheat an empty pot or pan. This allows the cookware to heat up too quickly and release toxic fumes.

- Never cook on high heat. If you need to cook higher than the medium setting on your stove, use one of the alternatives I mentioned above.

> **DO WHAT I DO**
>
> Use Teflon-coated cookware for foods that only require low or medium heat. I always use silicone or rubber utensils with them. This prevents scratching and chipping, which keeps pieces of the pan out of your food.

- Always keep your kitchen well ventilated – open a window or turn the fan above your stove on.

- Use heavier pans... they take more time to heat up and are easier to control with medium heat.

- Never use metal utensils. This causes chipping and scratches.

- Replace your pans every few years or when a chip or severe scratch occurs.

— 12 —

The Biggest Threat to Your Eyes

Losing my eyesight from old age is one of the biggest fears I have... Without good vision, I could lose the ability to drive, read, or even recognize the faces of loved ones.

For people over the age of 60... the leading cause of vision loss is called "age-related macular degeneration" (or AMD). About 10 million Americans have some form of macular degeneration – and in many cases, it results in blindness.

AMD is an eye disease that damages the macula – the part of the eye that provides central vision. It's the part of the eye that gives you the ability to read and drive. It's located in the back wall of your eye... in the center of the retina.

There are two types of AMD – "wet" and "dry" macular degeneration. They can damage eyesight in one or both of your eyes.

Wet macular degeneration is the more severe – and thankfully, less common – form. The onset of wet macular degeneration is rapid and often happens in people who already suffer from dry macular degeneration. The cause isn't clear.

In wet macular degeneration, blood and fluid all build up between the retina and the macula... causing the macula to lift from its normally flat position. This is what distorts your vision.

Dry macular degeneration represents about 85% of AMD cases. It gets its name because the macula dries out, causing the loss of vision. Unlike wet macular degeneration, there is no swelling or blood leaking involved. But as I mentioned, dry macular degeneration can become wet macular degeneration.

There are three stages of dry macular degeneration: early, intermediate, and advanced. Early AMD involves getting small deposits in the eye (called drusen). And there may not be any other symptoms or vision loss.

People in the intermediate stage could have medium-sized or a few large drusen in the eye. Some people might experience blurriness in their central vision or need more light to read.

Once people are in the advanced stage of dry macular degeneration, the drusen are large. There will also be a big, dark spot in your central vision that can grow and darken over time.

Like many other diseases, there are several risk factors which make you more likely to develop AMD:

- Age – Most people with AMD are 60 and over

- Smoking

- Race – Caucasians have a higher risk of AMD than other races

- Family history

- Obesity

- High blood pressure

- Gender – Females are more likely to develop AMD

The symptoms for wet and dry are similar. They include:

- Need brighter light to see clearly.

- Blurriness while reading.

- Blind spot in the central field of vision.

- Straight lines appearing wavy.

- Decreased intensity of colors.

Your eye doctor has several ways to test you for AMD.

One is by examining the back of your eye. Your doctor dilates your eye to see the back part, looking for yellow drusen deposits. He can also test your central vision using various techniques and paper grids. You could have AMD if any of the lines on the grid are faded, broken, or distorted.

Another test is an angiogram that uses a colored dye to highlight abnormalities in the blood vessels in your eye. Another option is the optical coherence tomography (OCT). This imaging test can find thinning or thickening of areas around the retina – which can be associated with either wet or dry macular degeneration.

If you have these sorts of symptoms, you should see your doctor. And if they came on rapidly, you may have wet AMD... Make an urgent appointment.

There's no cure for wet or dry AMD. But there are treatments to slow the progression.

Common treatments for wet macular degeneration include medications that are injected into your eye. They shrink the blood vessels, allowing fluid under the retina to re-absorb. This can partially improve your vision as the function of the retinal cells improves.

Another possible treatment is laser light therapy. A laser is used to destroy the blood vessels that are leaking blood and fluid. This often stops any further progression of the disease.

Your doctor could also suggest photodynamic therapy. The light from a laser is used in conjunction with a medication (sensitive to the laser light) to destroy abnormal blood vessels. This therapy helps slow down the rate of vision loss.

Dry macular degeneration has treatment options, as well. The National Eye Institute recommends a combination of nutrients to improve vision for people in the intermediate stage of AMD. Interestingly, the randomized controlled trial using supplements for AMD is one of the few trials that has shown any benefit to using supplements in human diseases.

The nutrients that slow progression are vitamins A and C, beta carotene, zinc, and copper. I'm usually skeptical of taking large doses of any one vitamin... But for AMD, this does work. And the doses are relatively small.

How Can You Prevent AMD?

Have a routine eye exam with an ophthalmologist (an eye doctor) after the age of 55 to check for any signs. Ophthalmologists have M.D. after their names. (Optometrists do not.)

Exercise regularly (three to four times a week), even if it's just walking for 20-30 minutes.

Eat fruits and dark-colored vegetables.

Eat foods with tons of omega-3s (like fish and nuts).

Diabetes Also Poses a Risk to Your Vision

Your vision is in danger, and you don't know it... if you have diabetes.

A study from the Wilmer Eye Institute of Johns Hopkins School of Medicine in Baltimore found that more than half of the diabetics in the study had no idea diabetes was affecting their vision... despite their doctor knowing about the patient's eye problems.

Researchers found doctors weren't telling patients they had a diabetes-related disease.

Diabetes causes a dangerous – but treatable – eye condition called diabetic macular edema (DME). DME is the thickening of the retina, which can lead to permanent vision loss. Doctors can easily detect DME through a test that dilates the pupils. The earlier you catch DME, the more treatable it is. The American Diabetes Association recommends diabetics have their eyes tested annually.

When you do get your eyes tested, don't be afraid to ask your doctor questions. You can even request to see the comments he writes down – take a copy with you when you leave his office.

And don't forget that one of the best ways to fight off diabetes is to walk 20-30 minutes every day.

— 13 —

Focus on Improving Your Health, Not the 'Scare Studies'

As a doctor, I've signed a few death certificates in my life... and never once listed "cola drinking" as the cause of death.

Yet in 2013, Harvard researchers claimed soda kills 25,000 people a year in the U.S. and 180,000 people worldwide.

This study is dubious at best. At worst, it's another example of the "nanny state" trying to control you with fear. Government-sponsored boondoggles like this deserve letters to your congressman and senator.

As a believer in evidence and common sense, I follow the science and research on many health issues. And I debunk them when it's appropriate...

What makes the Coca-Cola health nonsense so dangerous is that it's partly based in truth... I advise against consuming large amounts of sugary drinks, including sodas and fruit juices. So what's wrong with the Harvard study?

Yes... downing a sugary soda or fruit juice causes an immediate spike in blood-sugar levels. And if that happens frequently over a long period of time, it can *increase the risk* of illnesses like diabetes and heart disease. But to extrapolate that and identify a single factor as the cause of death for tens of thousands of people a year is preposterous.

Death – and the development of diseases that precede it – results from many interwoven factors. If you're drinking a six-pack of sodas (or fruit juice) a day, you probably have other harmful habits, like smoking or sitting on the couch every night and watching TV instead of going for a 20-30 minute walk.

> ### *DO WHAT I DO*
>
> **Worry less about the things that might kill you. Instead, focus on doing the things that help you.**

The money wasted on silly studies like this would be much better spent educating doctors on how to teach the healthy habits that can make a huge difference in your well-being. Ask yourself... How many doctors have talked with you about your sleep hygiene and habits? Sleep may be the most important factor in healthy living.

Most important, eating leafy vegetables and foods high in certain fibers – like green beans, oatmeal, or broccoli – could easily override any risk of drinking a soda once a day.

And daily exercise – or at least regular movement – counters many of the harmful effects any food substance could do to your health. So if you're running 5k races on the weekends or walking 30 minutes a day, an occasional soda isn't going to kill you.

Do what I do... worry less about the things that might kill you. Instead, focus on doing the things that help you. If you do these things – improve your sleep habits, increase the high-fiber foods in your diet, and exercise (or move) regularly – I guarantee your health will improve right away. *And* you can treat yourself to a soda now and again.

— 14 —

Half of Americans Are in Danger Thanks to This $27 Billion Industry

"All natural"... "Doctor approved"... "Clinically tested"...

The makers of herbal dietary supplements love to slap these descriptions on their bottles to reassure you that their products are safe and healthy... But don't be lured by these meaningless deceits... These supplements aren't always safe. And they usually don't benefit your health.

The supplement industry in the U.S. is huge. It's worth more than $27 billion. Not surprising, considering more than 50% of Americans use supplements.

But if you take some of these supplements, you might be surprised to learn that no one is making sure these products are safe for humans... let alone whether they do what they claim.

Companies can claim a product is safe and healthy. But there's no oversight to verify these claims.

Don't get me wrong... I'm not a fan of Big Brother government-type regulations. But I do believe in giving people the information they need to make informed decisions. The FDA should gather the studies on these supplements and require more research that's not sponsored by the supplement companies.

The FDA does monitor complaints concerning supplements. The FDA has MedWatch – an adverse-event reporting program. If there are concerns about a supplement or an ingredient in a supplement, the FDA will issue a warning... and maybe do some of its own research.

But researching a supplement after it has already damaged people's health is too late.

In 1994, Congress passed the Dietary Supplement Health and Education Act (DSHEA). The act says, "The manufacturer of a dietary supplement or dietary ingredient is responsible for assuring that the product is safe before it is marketed."

This means the FDA doesn't verify claims made on labels or check the safety of a product. So you're unlikely to see a supplement that's FDA-approved. The FDA only investigates possible problems with a supplement in the event of consumer complaints.

The government does limit what manufacturers can put on a label. The makers can't claim a supplement cures or treats a disease. For example, you may find – as we did – a vitamin K supplement claiming to be "good for bone-building process," but it can't claim to "prevent osteoporosis."

"All natural" is a claim I find particularly harmful because people regularly associate it with being healthy and safe. But plenty of things in nature will kill you: the flowering plant foxglove, certain mushrooms (like the destroying-angel variety), and ricin (derived from castor beans).

I'm not trying to warn people completely off supplements. In the cold months, I regularly take vitamin C to ward off colds. And I occasionally take a multivitamin. But you should educate yourself about the real risks before blindly popping pills.

In addition to the FDA's MedWatch, the consumer watchdog group *Consumer Reports* is another good resource to help you avoid harmful supplements.

Consumer Reports has a list of 12 dangerous supplements and ingredients it calls "The Dirty Dozen." It looked at the effectiveness of the ingredients and their availability to consumers.

The Dirty Dozen are...

1) **Aconite** is used in Aconitum supplements to ease inflammation and fevers. While aconite can help, the difference between a safe amount of aconite and a toxic amount is small. Aconite poisoning leads to muscular paralysis, vomiting, and death. So leave the use of aconite in medicines to companies that are obligated to monitor how much aconite is in each pill.

2) Weight-loss supplements use **bitter orange** to control appetite. Nature's Way sells a bitter orange supplement that claims to "provide thermogenic action" – another way to say "burn fat." Bitter orange contains a chemical called synephrine – a powerful drug that can lead to heart attack or stroke.

3) **Chapparal** supplements claim to reduce inflammation, pain, and skin irritation, and fight cancer. But no evidence supports these claims. The truth is that chaparral can cause permanent, even deadly, liver damage.

4) **Colloidal silver** is silver particles suspended in liquid. You'll find bottles of colloidal silver with claims that it boosts your immune system. Some bottles also say the liquid is nontoxic. However, consuming too much colloidal silver will not only turn your skin blue, it can lead to kidney damage and seizures.

5) People typically use **coltsfoot** to treat respiratory issues like bronchitis and asthma. But studies show chemicals in coltsfoot cause liver damage or cancer.

6) In 2001, the FDA recommended the removal of **comfrey** supplements from the market. Comfrey is safe for external use. Most companies sell comfrey in the form of ointment or oil. Some sell the whole herb or powders to use in teas. Ingestion of comfrey can damage the liver or lungs.

7) **Country mallow** is used as a weight-loss supplement. It contains ephedrine – an ingredient known to cause high blood pressure, heart attacks, or numerous other health difficulties. Country mallow is banned in the U.S. because it contains ephedrine, but it's still in use around the globe.

8) Some "health professionals" say **germanium** prevents cancer (although you're unlikely to see this exact claim on a germanium product). The American Cancer Society refutes this. Some of the side effects of germanium include kidney damage, nerve damage, and heart problems.

9) **Greater celandine** is sold in bottles with handy eyedroppers to put drops of it in water for easy consumption. Greater celandine supposedly treats gastrointestinal issues or lung problems like asthma. Despite these "benefits," greater celandine can also damage the liver or cause a skin rash.

10) Supplement manufacturers of **kava** claim it reduces anxiety. According to the National Institutes of Health (NIH) – a government medical research center – it does. But both the NIH and the FDA say the risk of liver damage or death is too great to make it a worthwhile treatment.

11) **Lobelia** is another supplement that supports the health of your respiratory and nervous systems. Despite those possible benefits, lobelia can dangerously increase heart rate, lower blood pressure, cause a coma, or even lead to death.

12) **Yohimbe** is marketed as a "natural" alternative to Viagra. The danger with yohimbe (and most supplements) is the difficulty in monitoring the dosage. The potency depends on what part of the yohimbe tree is used. Too much yohimbe dangerously increases heart rate and blood pressure.

Often, marketers of natural products don't measure and report on the dosages accurately. The potency and purity of something thought to be perfectly safe – like vitamin D – varies. Some supplements had 80% more of the compound than the label indicated. So you could easily be taking twice the amount the marketing company recommends... or taking next to nothing.

Even worse, all of these "natural herbs" have potentially lethal interactions with other over-the-counter or prescription medications. The FDA has issued warnings on chaparral, colloidal silver, comfrey, germanium, kava, and yohimbe. Currently, none of them are banned.

Despite the mounting evidence showing the dangers of supplements, the FDA has only banned two: ephedra and DMAA.

The FDA banned the use of ephedra in supplements in 2004. Before the ban, ephedra was used as a weight loss supplement. Supplements containing ephedra also claimed to boost energy and athletic performance. More than 30 deaths were linked to ephedra use.

In July 2013, the FDA banned a second ingredient – 1,3-dimethylamylamine, methylhexanamine or geranium extract (DMAA). Many bodybuilding supplements included DMAA, until five deaths were linked to it.

More bans don't occur because it's difficult to monitor supplements and their dubious efficacy. The FDA has to take many steps to prove an ingredient or supplement is dangerous through scientific and legal routes. The FDA claims it doesn't have the resources to undertake these steps. This is largely the reason the FDA just issues warnings.

So before you decide to start taking a supplement, do your research. First, use the FDA's MedWatch site to check for current alerts on ingredients. Then, check your supplement against *Consumer Report*'s "Dirty Dozen" list. WebMD is a trusted resource. The website gives an overview of supplements and potential side effects.

If you suspect you have suffered an adverse reaction to a supplement, please report it to the FDA. And depending on the severity, visit your doctor or hospital for treatment.

The supplement business is filled with claims that prey on laziness and the belief that all it takes to restore health is a potion or pill. Whether it's fluoride, X-rays, statin drugs, or vitamin D... at *Retirement Millionaire*, we look out for your health, wealth, and happiness. By looking at the evidence and reporting the facts, we believe most of it is under your control.

Avoid spending your money on the biggest drug market in health care and instead get a pair of walking shoes, a gym membership, or a new pillow to help you sleep. Much of the pills and potions you buy over the counter are unproven at best. At worst, they can kill you.

— 15 —

Alcohol and Your Health: Some Amazing Facts

Moderate consumption of red wine has great health benefits. So does drinking beer. Consuming one to two beers per day lowers insulin levels, which lowers your risk of getting Type 2 diabetes.

The grains and yeast in beer are packed with vitamin B, which helps maintain healthy insulin levels. Some of the nutritional benefits are lost in the winemaking process. But the grains used in beer – typically barley and wheat – hold their vitamins during fermentation.

Here's another reason to drink beer. Beer contains a lot of vitamin B, which helps maintain healthy insulin levels and that lowers your Type 2 diabetes risk. But beer also aids bone health. Beers with high levels of barley and hops are rich in dietery silicon, which is a key ingredient for increasing bone-mineral density. A higher bone density prevents diseases like osteoporosis.

Drinking wine helps maintain bone strength for women better than milk does.

Researchers from the University of Oregon found postmenopausal women (ages 50 to 65) who drank two small glasses of alcohol a day had lower rates of "bone resorption" – a natural process that slowly erodes your bones – than women who didn't drink alcohol at all.

Resorption is a process of shedding old bone cells and recycling calcium. When the women in the study weren't drinking, their resorption rates

> ### *DO WHAT I DO*
>
> Stick to Pinot Noir when having seafood. Pinot Noir has very little iron. When I grill a nice piece of salmon, I like to pair it with a glass of Pinot Noir.

outpaced the production of new bone cells... weakening bone strength. This leads to an increased risk of osteoporosis and bone fractures.

I've previously reported that women who drink red wine have a significantly higher bone density in their spine than women who don't drink red wine. This new research points to the actual mechanism of action and benefit of drinking red wine for overall bone health.

Recall that red wine has many other benefits for women and men... It decreases the risks of diabetes, stroke, arthritis, and Alzheimer's disease. I try to drink four ounces of wine a night to get the maximum benefits.

Science backs the traditional "white wine with fish" pairing. Japanese scientists found the iron in red wine creates the strong, fishy aftertaste (white wines have little to no iron). The subjects had no fishy aftertaste when the iron was "bound to" a special chemical added to red wine.

If you're a committed red-wine drinker, do what I do... Stick to Pinot Noir when having seafood. Pinot Noir has very little iron. When I grill a nice piece of salmon, I like to pair it with a glass of Pinot Noir.

By the way, if you're ever hungover, try drinking pickle juice if you want an alternative to sugary sports drinks. The salt and water act much like sports drinks, adding back electrolytes and fluid to a dehydrated brain.

— 16 —

13 Tips for Weight Loss and Exercise

1. Cutting calories and losing weight may be as simple as changing your plate...

According to a 2006 study from the Cornell University Food and Brand Lab, people who used plates with large borders ate less than those who ate off plates with small or no borders. The researchers believed people instinctively keep their food from overlapping the borders, making their portions smaller.

This can also work with plates that are small... The key is to choose a plate with a central white space of nine inches or less in diameter. This tip helps cut your caloric intake 20% or more because it tricks your brain into thinking the portion size is bigger.

2. Another simple way to fight pounds is to add black pepper to your food.

The peppercorns used in standard pepper grinders contain an ingredient called "piperine." That's the irritant that makes you sneeze when you sniff the spice (a great trivia fact for a holiday dinner).

More important, the piperine blocks the formation of fat cells, according to a 2012 study from Sejong University in Seoul and published in the *Journal of Agricultural and Food Chemistry*. Researchers aren't sure why this occurs... But the pepper inhibits the genes responsible for forming new fat cells.

347

Black pepper has other health benefits as well... For centuries, it was used to treat cholera and diarrhea. In modern times, studies have found black pepper has chemicals with cancer-fighting properties, like d-limonene. I use pepper daily... I try to put a pinch on any food I can.

3. Enjoy your food and lose weight.

People who take large bites of food and only chew for three seconds consume 52% more food than people who take smaller bites and chew longer. Dutch researchers found that chewing small bites of food for nine seconds sends a signal to your brain to feel full sooner. So chew more, enjoy your food, and you'll lose weight.

4. You can burn fat by eating fat.

An Italian study showed men who increased their fat intake to 55% of their daily calories burned more fat during exercise. The muscles adapt and become better at converting fat into energy. Just remember to lower your carbohydrate calories (things like white breads and chips) to counter the increased fat calories.

5. Hot peppers are a delicious weight-loss aid.

Capsaicin, the compound that gives peppers their heat, also heats your body temperature when eaten. This causes you to burn more calories (like when your core temperature heats up during physical activity). The spicier the pepper, the more calories are burned.

Bell peppers don't contain capsaicin, so they don't heat your body's temperature. Stick with peppers that have spice, like habañero peppers. If you're really brave, you can try the Bhut Jolokia – also called the ghost chili – which is widely recognized as the world's hottest pepper.

A great hot sauce is Texas Pete hot sauce. You can get Texas Pete in just about any supermarket.

6. When you run for exercise, be sure to use your whole foot.

It's a myth that you should run on your toes. All the world-class long-distance runners use their heel and midfoot to run. The human foot has a dozen built-in levers with its 26 bones (one-fourth of all the bones in the body), 33 joints, and 100-plus muscles. This machinery is designed for heel-to-toe use. Use your full foot by running with a rocking motion. And after a workout, be sure and stretch your foot or find someone to exchange foot rubs.

7. Become healthier and stronger just by changing the shoes you wear.

The human foot was made to support and balance your weight when walking or running, but the cushioning in traditional shoes might be weakening your foot and leg muscles.

Vibram FiveFingers has a shoe that simulates bare feet. My friend and Stansberry Research Editor in Chief Brian Hunt loves his FiveFingers. The shoes look like gloves for your feet. Brian runs in them and swears by them.

But don't go completely caveman yet and throw away your conventional shoes... These shoes are as cold as bare feet and too casual for formal occasions.

8. The next time you exercise... have some whey protein afterward.

When exercising strenuously – like weightlifting – muscles get microscopic tears. These tears are often why you feel sore after a workout. But they're also the reason your muscles can become stronger and grow.

When your muscle tears, your body works to not only repair the muscle, but to make it stronger to prevent the tears from happening again. If you want to increase your body's efficiency at repairing these tears, have some whey protein after you work out.

Whey protein releases amino acids into your bloodstream to help your body repair the muscle quicker. You've probably seen whey protein touted by bodybuilders. But anyone who exercises strenuously can benefit. Research shows that 20-25 grams of whey protein immediately after a workout helps speed up your body's repairs.

> **DO WHAT I DO**
>
> Mix the whey protein with frozen blueberries in a blender.

The pure version of whey protein comes in a powder, usually in a large container. You can find it in many flavors – including plain, vanilla, and chocolate. Many people are a little put off by the taste. But my assistant Laura likes to put hers in a smoothie so she hardly notices the taste. Or do what I do... Mix it with frozen blueberries in a blender.

If you don't want to buy protein whey powders, you can supplement your diet with similar protein in yogurt. In particular, Greek yogurt has about twice the amount of protein as regular yogurt and half the carbohydrates... almost 20-25 grams of protein in an eight-ounce serving.

9. **Many studies have found regular marathon runners and professional cyclists have a higher risk of heart attack due to the hardening of large vessels near the heart**.

Even people who exercise more than one hour per day, run a total of 20 miles or more per week, or run more than seven miles per hour have a higher risk of premature death than people who exercise less.

Let me be clear... This is not an excuse to skip exercise and lead a sedentary lifestyle... Movement and moderate exercise are extremely important to your overall health. You just don't need to be a masochist about it... That's counterproductive.

> **DO WHAT I DO**
>
> Make sure to walk for about 30 minutes a day. It's an easy way to get moving without being too strenuous. If the weather is bad and you can't get outside, yoga is another favorite of mine.

Do what I do... Make sure to walk for about 30 minutes a day. It's an easy way to get moving without being too strenuous. If the weather is bad and you can't get outside, yoga is another favorite of mine. You get all the benefits of exercise (like cardiovascular health and stress relief) without the extreme strain on your heart.

10. **Jogging regularly can add years to your life**.

A Copenhagen City Heart study found that women who run regularly have a life expectancy 5.6 years longer than nonrunners. Male runners have 6.2 more years of life expectancy than nonrunners.

This study focused on moderate exertion. The runners in the study kept a slow to average pace and ran from one to two-and-a-half hours per week. Participants were also long-term runners... They had been running for 10 years on average.

Moderate, regular exercise is one of the keys to living a healthy life.

11. **Walking is just as good for your heart as running**.

Scientists at the Lawrence Berkeley National Laboratory found that walking and running similarly reduce blood pressure, cholesterol, and diabetes risk. The key, according to researchers, is not how long you walk or run, but how far.

People who walked the same distance as runners experienced similar health benefits. One example... walkers lowered their risk of diabetes 12.1%. Runners lowered their risk 12.3%.

Walking is one of my favorite ways to get up and get moving. Walk just six miles each week, and you are 50% less likely to develop memory problems.

As you age, your brain begins to shrink, which is associated with memory problems like dementia. People with age-related dementia consistently show a loss of white brain matter. Walking builds brain volume, which helps fight off the disease.

I take daily walks outside when the weather is comfortable. If I don't want to walk outside, I'll hop on the treadmill with a few magazines to read.

12. Research has long shown that exercise can help lessen the symptoms of Parkinson's disease.

A 2012 study showed that cycling three times a week for eight weeks improved patient mobility for up to four weeks. But this was only true if the cycling pace was fast enough to raise the heart rate and sweat. Other studies have shown strenuous exercise can slightly counter or delay the effects of Parkinson's.

The belief is that exercise increases dopamine-producing cells. These cells can slow the loss of mobility – one of the major issues Parkinson's patients experience.

This is just another reason why I list movement as one of the most important things you can do to better your health. I typically recommend people take walks or do yoga. But if you want to start a rigorous exercise regime, talk to your doctor first to make sure you don't harm yourself.

13. Could your antibiotics be making you fat?

In an August 2012 study, New York University researchers exposed mice to small doses of antibiotics. After just seven weeks, the mice had 10%-15% more fat mass than mice in the control group. The researchers believe antibiotics increase the ability of the microbiota in your gut (bugs that break down food) to convert carbs into body fat.

Antibiotics are already used to help fatten animals (in addition to being used for preventing disease among livestock). While this link hasn't been proven in humans, it's just another reason to avoid antibiotics, especially for regular viruses that cause colds.

— 17 —

47 More Ways to Protect and Improve Your Health

1. I always travel with a tennis ball in my suitcase.

It's the quickest headache and back-pain reliever I know. I lie down with the ball under my upper back and roll around on it until I find the pressure points that are painful. By moving my hips up or down I can adjust how much weight is on the ball and the pressure points. In minutes, the tension melts away.

2. Want to prevent vision loss?

Here are a couple ways I maintain my vision... Two separate studies from the U.S. Department of Energy's Lawrence Berkeley National Laboratory showed that exercise, like running, can preserve your eyesight. And don't forget the other benefits of lower blood pressure and cholesterol.

The second thing I do is wear sunglasses whenever I'm outside. This slows down the sun damage to the lens in the eye and thus slows cataract formation.

3. Doctors occasionally (7%-8% of the time) forget to inform patients of abnormal test results, according to research from Cornell Medical College.

The next time you go to the doctor, record what tests were done, why your doctor ordered them, and when the results will be available. Also ask what makes the test abnormal and what's normal.

Follow up with the office on the date the test results are due. And save yourself the worry by asking the doctor to write the list of tests down for you... it's the least they can do.

4. The World Health Organization elevated tanning beds to the highest cancer-risk category.

This is the same level given to dangerous chemicals like mustard gas and arsenic. As of 2014, several states are trying to put age limits on tanning... and a health care bill is taxing tanning salons 10%.

Moderate exposure to ultraviolet rays is good for your health. Sunlight (the broadest form of UV radiation) allows your body to produce vitamin D, which prevents diseases like depression and multiple sclerosis. Natural sunlight is best, but a tanning bed is a good substitute in the winter... you just need to *limit your use* to five minutes or less.

Tanning beds provide mostly UV-A and a little bit of UV-B radiation. The A goes deeper and B is what leads to burning. Because of this, your body can't really tell you when it's had too much "sun" in a bed.

5. Don't keep your toothbrush near your toilet.

When you flush a toilet, it sprays germs all over the bathroom – even if the lid is closed. Do what I do... Rinse your toothbrush before using it. You can also do what my assistant Laura does and keep your toothbrush in a plastic case, which you can get for $2 at your local drugstore.

6. Three easy ways to avoid colds in the winter: sleep eight hours or more, take Vitamin C, and get exercise.

A lack of sleep weakens your immune system, which makes you more vulnerable to illness. A study from Carnegie Mellon University found that people who get less than seven hours of sleep are three

---

DO WHAT I DO

Rinse your toothbrush before using it. You can also do what my assistant Laura does and keep your toothbrush in a plastic case, which you can get for $2 at your local drugstore.

times more likely to develop a cold than those who sleep eight hours or more. You can include naps in your total if you have a hard time sleeping eight-straight hours.

Walking stimulates your bone marrow to produce immune fighting cells. As for the "C," if I feel a tickle in my throat, I go on a Vitamin C blitz. I take 2,000-3,000 milligrams a day for a couple days to knock out the viruses. Of course, that requires taking a supplement... Your typical glass of O.J. has about 50 milligrams.

Other good ways to help stave off colds... Don't share drinking glasses or eating utensils. Exercise regularly... Exercise gives your immune system a boost, helping your body keep illnesses at bay.

7. Your meat is not safe... despite what the government tells you.

Two out of three chickens in the grocery store harbor bacteria like salmonella and campylobacter (the leading causes of food-borne illness). These bacteria sicken millions a year and kill around 500. These bacteria are quickly becoming resistant to antibiotics as animals get the same drugs to keep them "healthy."

> ### *DO WHAT I DO*
> Rinse any meat well before cooking it. I cook chicken to 165 degrees (with a $10 meat thermometer). And keep the raw chicken and juices away from other foods.

According to *Consumer Reports*, the worst offenders are chicken-processing companies Tyson and Foster Farms (80% of chicken infected). The most reliable is Perdue with a 56% infection rate (still more than half).

Do what I do... Rinse any meat well before cooking it. I cook chicken to 165 degrees (with a $10 meat thermometer). And keep the raw chicken and juices away from other foods.

8. Cool your tea before you drink it... unless you want to develop cancer.

Researchers have found people who drink tea or coffee (or any other beverage) hotter than 158 degrees (water boils at 212 degrees) are five times more likely to develop esophageal cancer than those who drink tea cooler than 140 degrees. It's believed that hot liquids damage esophageal cells, leading to cancer.

It's best to wait five to 10 minutes before drinking a cup of tea. But if you can't wait that long for your tea to cool, do what my assistant Laura does... She drops an ice cube into her tea so it's safe to drink in about one minute.

Our Editor in Chief, Brian Hunt, prefers to buy bottles of green tea. You avoid drinking hot tea while getting all the health benefits of green tea. He likes the Wegman's brand.

9. **Gardening is a great way to improve health, and I've found the perfect starter kit for growing tomatoes**.

The easiest way to grow tomatoes is with the Topsy Turvy tomato planter. It's the bright green planter you've probably seen on TV and in home-improvement stores. I tested some planters with regular, in ground, tomato planting. The Topsy Turvy planter was, by far, the better choice. I was able to grow about 70%-100% more tomatoes than traditional plantings.

And harvesting the tomatoes is easy... There's no digging or walking through mud. I can just walk right onto my porch and pick a few tomatoes. You can find these planters at Home Depot for only $9.99.

10. For years, government health scolds have peddled the idea that egg yolks are cholesterol-laden and bad for you.

That's nonsense. **Egg yolks are healthy for you**. A whole egg contains about a full day's worth of cholesterol and six grams of protein. The truth is your body manufactures cholesterol all day long. It does this because every cell in your body needs cholesterol. Without it, you would die within days.

We use cholesterol to produce hormones, vitamin D, and digestive fluids. Moreover, chemicals in the egg yolk help your body transport cholesterol properly. Just remember not to cook them too much... and never scramble them.

> **DO WHAT I DO**
>
> Eat eggs "over easy" to keep all the health benefits of the yolk.

Cooking the eggs until they are solid oxidizes the cholesterol and degrades the other antioxidants and vitamins found in the yolk. I prefer to eat my eggs over easy to keep all the health benefits of the yolk.

11. **The next time you feel like going for a walk, avoid downtown and head to a park.**

A 2010 study showed people who walk in a park perform tasks that require memory and attention better than those who walk through downtown streets. Walking in a park promotes mental restoration and relaxation versus the distracting hustle and bustle of the city.

But don't stop walking outside even if you don't have a park nearby. Walking outside is a favorite exercise of mine and gives your body a chance to absorb vitamin D – critical in preventing diseases like depression, cancer, and multiple sclerosis. Doing stress-releasing activities like walking is also among the best ways to lower your blood pressure without pills.

12. **The next time you buy berries, choose frozen berries.**

Frozen berries contain more antioxidants because they are picked and then frozen at the peak of ripeness. Antioxidants have several health benefits, including improving heart health, lowering cancer risk, and helping your metabolism. I eat blueberries year-round and always keep a bag of frozen ones in my freezer for yogurt or a healthy fruit smoothie.

13. **The more colorful your diet, the more likely you are to be eating healthy food.**

Remove colorless foods like gray meats, white bread, and potatoes from your diet. You can start by eating foods like blueberries, romaine lettuce, broccoli, and tomatoes.

The colors come from antioxidants (like beta-carotene and lutein), which remove waste products (free radicals) from tissues throughout the body.

My assistant Laura eats berries (blues and blacks), cauliflower, carrots, mangos, and kiwi. She told me it increases her energy levels, especially around 3 p.m. when most of us get drowsy.

14. The next time you buy orange juice, make sure it has pulp.

The pulp adds a boost of fiber, which helps block the recycling of cholesterol into your blood from your gut. Orange juice with pulp also contains 30% more cancer-fighting agents than pulp-free OJ. If you don't like OJ packed with pulp, you can start with a brand that offers low pulp. You'll still get many of the benefits without the stringy pieces of orange.

When it comes to OJ, buy whatever brand has pulp and is on sale. From November through April – prime cold season – you can drink a small glass of fresh-squeezed juice several times a week for extra Vitamin C and fiber.

15. The next time you buy potatoes for dinner, try purple potatoes.

Purple potatoes contain an antioxidant, known as anthocyanin, that can lower inflammation, reducing your risk of heart disease and cancer.

Many big chain stores don't carry purple potatoes. But you can find them at Whole Foods or gourmet food stores. I like to grill mine sliced (like a chip), brushed with a little olive oil, and sprinkled with fresh rosemary. You can use them in recipes calling for russets. I've also mashed them with garlic and the skins... They're fantastic.

16. The old saying "an apple a day keeps the doctor away" is true.

One 2011 study showed women who ate one cup of apples (roughly a fist-sized apple) per day for six months lowered their LDL ("bad" cholesterol) 26%. They also raised their HDL "good" cholesterol and even lost weight. Apples were also shown to reduce plaque and inflammation in the heart's artery walls.

Do what my assistant Laura does... Eat an apple every day. She pairs them with organic peanut butter, which balances the carbohydrates with the protein in peanuts.

17. Researchers have found that household plants decrease volatile organic compounds (VOCs) by 75%-90%.

VOCs are the toxic fumes from paint, carpets, and cleaning supplies emitted into the air. How plants do this is still unknown. And some plants are better than others at removing VOCs from the air – including the peace lily, Boston fern, and umbrella plant. These plants also increase the humidity in the air, which helps decrease dust.

18. In 1980, X-ray computed tomography (CT) scans represented 15% of the radiation Americans absorbed. Today, CT scans account for 50%.

CT scans are a high-speed version of X-rays. More and more people get these scans unnecessarily. A 2011 survey showed even doctors think patients are overtreated.

Radiation is known to cause many types of cancer. And the danger increases incrementally... The more you get, the higher your odds of getting sick.

> ### DO WHAT I DO
>
> "Opt out" of TSA security scans. That requires them to frisk you and adds a few more minutes on the screening time. But it's worth keeping the unknown radiation effects down as much as you can.

What can you do to cut down your exposure to radiation? If you're a perfectly healthy adult, don't consent to unnecessary medical procedures. If your doctor suggests an X-ray or CT scan, be sure the results will make a difference in your treatment decision...

Also, refuse to get irradiated at the airport security screening area. (You know, those machines where you have to put your arms up and then get "quickly" scanned.) The scanners emit radiation. And the idiots employed by the Transportation Security Administration have no idea about safe dosing levels or how to administer radiation...

Do what I do... "Opt out." That requires them to frisk you and adds a few more minutes on the screening time. But it's worth keeping the unknown radiation effects down as much as you can.

Maybe if enough of us opt out, they'll realize that most of us can get expedited screening – I mean really, folks, where's the common sense? Do they really need to pat me down? Am I really a risk to society? Are you? But unless we tell them, "Hell no, I won't be irradiated by morons," nothing will change.

19. **A 2012 study shows fasting once a month improves long-term heart health**.

Researchers found fasting just one day a month can cut your risk of heart disease 58%. The belief is fasting shrinks fat cells and prevents insulin resistance. This helps lower your risk of heart disease and even diabetes.

Sip water and hot herbal teas. Do less vigorous activity that day. Read, walk, and meditate quietly.

20. **Practicing good oral health is another way to lower your risk of heart attack**.

> ### *DO WHAT I DO*
>
> **Alternate between nonalcoholic and regular mouthwash, 50% diluted with water and hydrogen peroxide (1.5%)... in conjunction with a good, long tooth-brushing before flossing.**

Bacteria in your mouth enter the bloodstream and can travel to other areas of the body. This includes the heart, where plaque can build up.

If you're using an alcohol-based mouthwash to sterilize your mouth, you could be doing more harm than good. Several studies have shown that the alcohol in mouthwash increases the risk of oral cancers. The proof isn't absolute, but the link is strong. The alcohol used in mouthwash breaks down into a known carcinogen, acetaldehyde.

What can you do to protect yourself? Try a nonalcoholic mouthwash. Listerine makes one. Just check the label for alcohol. Many brands advertise that the mouthwash is alcohol-free on the front label.

Do what I do... Alternate between nonalcoholic and regular mouthwash, 50% diluted with water and hydrogen peroxide (1.5%)... in conjunction with a good, long tooth-brushing before flossing.

21. **I've told you about the benefits of drinking coffee, wine, beer, and green tea. But what about water?**

The standard in the medical world is to tell people to drink up to 64 ounces of water per day. However, the history of the 64-ounces-a-day recommendation stemmed from research on people lost at sea – not the reality of a normal day.

The marketing machinery of the water-cooler industry twisted the research, claiming the human body needed extra water to function.

A 2012 water study shows that drinking just 34 ounces of water a day lowers the risk of developing high blood sugar.

The study found that people who drank 34 ounces of water per day were 21% less likely to develop high blood sugar than people who drank 16 ounces or less per day. Researchers think dehydration causes an increase in a hormone called vasopressin. It triggers blood sugar production in your liver, raising your blood sugar levels.

What's the ideal? No one is certain, but this new research will lead me to drink a little bit more. New bottles make it easy to keep track of how much you're drinking, too. Retailers like Target and Wal-Mart carry bottles that measure the ounces of water you're drinking.

22. According to a 2010 study, people who only have sex once a month are 2.7 times more likely to suffer a heart attack than those who have more regular sex.

People who have sex two times a week are 45% less likely to have a heart attack.

The key here is getting regular exercise, whether it's sex, jogging, or bike riding. It's especially important to have good heart health when you're engaging in any activity that causes your heart to pound, which could lead to a heart attack if you're not healthy.

23. Bacteria in your gut may influence your mood and behavior.

Your digestive tract hosts hundreds of different types of bacteria, most of which are beneficial. They help with digestion and keep your intestines working properly. According to new research... a lack of these beneficial bacteria might increase your anxiety.

A study done on mice found that rodents fed a diet of Lactobacillus rhamnosus – commonly found in dairy products like yogurt – were less anxious and had more "confidence" than mice without the bacteria in their system.

While the study hasn't been done on humans yet, it gives me another reason to eat yogurt. In addition to adding beneficial bacteria to your stomach, yogurt moderates the immune system, reduces allergies, and lowers your risk of certain cancers.

24. A midlife crisis can increase your risk of developing dementia later in life.

A 2012 study showed people who suffered depression in their 40s and 50s developed dementia in their 70s and 80s at a rate 20% higher than average... A high number of depression recurrences tripled the risk.

> **DO WHAT I DO**
>
> Get outside during the daytime. Just make sure you don't get burned by going out when the sun is at its highest point in the sky.

Dementia involves loss of brain functions. It can impair memory, judgment, and behavior. And its prevalence is growing. As of 2014, more than one in eight seniors has some form of dementia. But that number may quadruple by the mid-21st century.

Remember... there are time-tested ways to lessen your risk of depression. Regular readers know that simple exercises like yoga and walking can prevent depression. Sunlight is another easy way to stave off depression. Just a few minutes a day lowers your risk of depression.

Do what I do... Get outside during the daytime. Just make sure you don't get burned by going out when the sun is at its highest point in the sky.

25. Skip the emergency room.

If you're having a non-life-threatening health issue, go to an urgent-care center or convenience-care center. You'll wait less and pay less. Urgent clinics can perform basic exams, dispense shots and prescriptions, do lab work, and perform X-rays. You can easily save up to one-third of the cost of medical issues (like sore throat or an upper respiratory infection).

The downside is these private clinics don't have to be open 24 hours per day (unlike emergency rooms). But if you can wait, look for a clinic near you. CVS' Minute Clinic is one of the larger national chains. And it's easy to find one near you. Just search for "urgent care clinic."

26. If you've had a stroke or have a family history of stroke... please get tested and (if necessary) treated for anemia.

A 2012 study found men with severe anemia are 3.5 times more likely to die in the hospital after having an ischemic stroke (a lack of oxygen) than men without anemia.

Anemia is a lack of healthy red blood cells or hemoglobin. It results most often from an iron deficiency. But vitamin deficiency, bone-marrow problems, or other health conditions can also cause it. Because anemia reduces the amount of oxygen your brain gets, it hinders recovery from a stroke.

Your doctor has several ways to test you for anemia with physical exams and simple blood tests. Depending on the reason you have anemia, treatment ranges from supplements to blood transfusions. But you can also help prevent anemia...

Do what I do... Strive for a nutrient-rich diet. I make sure the foods I eat contain iron, folate, vitamin B-12, and vitamin C. You get these from dark green leafy vegetables – like spinach and kale – berries, or citrus fruits.

> **DO WHAT I DO**
>
> Strive for a nutrient-rich diet. I make sure the foods I eat contain iron, folate, vitamin B-12, and vitamin C. You get these from dark green leafy vegetables – like spinach and kale – berries, or citrus fruits.

27. Many athletes (mostly football players) face long-term damage resulting from concussions.

The individuals most at risk from suffering concussions are men aged 15 to 24 – mostly because of their involvement in sports. But another group that's highly vulnerable to concussions and brain trauma is people over the age of 65.

The U.K. National Health Service describes being over the age of 65 as a major risk factor for having a concussion. Falls cause most of the concussions in that age group. About one-third of people over 65 fall every year, and 30% of those falls lead to head trauma.

Compounding the problem… less than 50% of seniors seek medical attention after a fall, according to data from the Centers for Disease Control (CDC). This is incredibly dangerous. Also, the older a person is, the longer it takes to recover from a concussion and the more severe the symptoms.

One of the best ways to prevent falls is to exercise regularly. Walking, yoga, and working in your garden are all low-impact ways to maintain balance and muscle and bone strength. You can also get rid of tripping hazards and add grab bars to your shower or bath.

28. Don't let stress kill you.

The holiday season is one of the most stressful times of year. Not only do we deal with our everyday stresses like work and home life, but we pile on stress about buying gifts, traveling, visiting family, and getting sick. These stresses shorten your lifespan.

Several studies show stress actually alters the structure of your cells, shortening the things called "telomeres," which are like "caps" on chromosomes. These caps protect the chromosome from damage and keep it from sticking to neighboring chromosomes.

Telomere length also predicts lifespan. As we age, telomeres naturally shorten. Although the exact mechanism is unknown… the medical community generally accepts that the longer the telomeres, the longer a person will live.

Studies found stress accelerates the shortening of telomeres ... thus raising the risk of chronic diseases and shortening lifespan. Reducing stress (or more likely your reaction to it) helps reverse the effects.

A 2013 study published in British medical journal *The Lancet* found men adhering to healthy lifestyles (stress-reduction education, diets higher in whole foods, and adequate exercise) had longer telomeres than men with unhealthy lifestyles.

29. The U.S. Office of the Surgeon General created "My Family Health Portrait" – a website that allows you to share family health history with health care providers and family members.

My Family Health Portrait provides you with a form to fill out a detailed record of the health of your immediate family. Depending on how large your family is, the form should only take about 20 minutes to complete. And you can save the information on the website and never worry about remembering your health history details ever again.

Once you've filled out the form, you can give copies to your doctors and family. Just visit www.familyhistory.hhs.gov to get started.

30. Try to schedule any surgery in the morning.

According to researchers at Duke University, surgical problems are most common from 3 p.m. to 4 p.m. Surgeons made the fewest mistakes in the hours between 9 a.m. and 12 p.m. Some of the common problems the researchers found were prolonged sedation, infection, and problems with operating-room equipment.

Several factors could increase the late-day errors. Patient stress can be a factor... someone who hasn't eaten all day or spent the day worrying about surgery can suffer adverse effects.

The late afternoon hours are also a time when our bodies experience a dip in circadian rhythms... which is why many people experience the "three-o'clock slump" (when you become tired in the middle of the day). Surgeons and anesthesiologists are not immune to this slump. I try not to do anything that requires a lot of attention between 3 p.m. and 4 p.m. for the same reason.

31. A 2013 study published in *Optometry and Vision Science* shows wearing contacts is harming your vision... if you don't keep them clean.

In 2014, more than 36 million people wear contacts in the U.S. Researchers found 98% of them are breaking hygiene rules and setting themselves up for infections.

Some of the most common mistakes are wearing contacts for too long (like wearing two-week lenses for longer than two weeks)... having dirty hands when handling contacts... and just topping off cleaning solution instead of using fresh solution each day. These mistakes can lead to bacterial infections... causing corneal ulcers and even blindness.

The American Optometric Association has a full list of steps to take to properly take care of your lenses. These include replacing your storage case every three months and removing your contacts before swimming.

32. Be careful with your medications and grapefruit.

In 2010, only 17 known drugs interacted dangerously with grapefruit... In 2014, that number jumped to 43 (plus more than 40 other drugs with less severe interactions).

> ### *DO WHAT I DO*
> Skip any pills on the days you decide to have grapefruit.

Cholesterol-lowering statins, cancer drugs, some antibiotics, and certain pain medications are among the problematic drugs. Eating a grapefruit with these drugs can increase their potency, causing an overdose. It can increase the blood concentrations of some drugs hundreds of percent.

One study showed that the concentration of simvastatin – used for lowering cholesterol – can increase 330% when taken with grapefruit juice once a day for just three days.

So check with your doctor to see if any of your medications interact with grapefruit juice and avoid it if need be. Or do what I do... Skip any pills on the days you decide to have grapefruit.

33. **A 2012 study from Stony Brook University in New York found CFL bulbs can cause skin cancer.**

CFLs have a phosphor coating on the inside that uses UV light to produce the bright white light the bulbs emit... without letting any UV rays out. But researchers found that this coating wears out over time. And in some cases, the coating gets cracked early in the life of the bulb, allowing ultraviolet radiation to escape.

Healthy skin cells experienced damage from the ultraviolet radiation emitted from these government-required CFL bulbs. On the other hand, the old incandescent bulbs caused no adverse effects on healthy cells.

Keeping the bulb behind a glass cover helps lessen the risk from CFLs. But there are safer ways to help save money on your energy bills, like using a "smart" surge protector.

The U.S. Department of Energy says replacing incandescent bulbs with CFLs (or other energy-efficient light bulbs) can save you $50 per year because CFLs use less energy and last longer. But the cancer risks of replacing all your old-fashioned light bulbs with CFLs may not be worth the savings.

34. **Not only are your dollar bills full of germs... But your credit card and cell phone may be dirtier than your toilet.**

A small study out of London found 8% of credit cards contain contamination found on a toilet (like fecal matter). And 10% of credit cards in the study were contaminated with the E. coli bacteria.

Credit cards and money aren't the only contaminated items you're carrying around, either. Another study in 2011 found almost one in six cellphones have fecal bacteria other germs and viruses that transmit diseases on them. And the warm battery in phones makes for an ideal breeding ground.

Most people know it's important to wash their hands after touching a toilet. It's unlikely many of us think about washing our hands after using a phone. But just a small touch of your eyes or mouth might mean a few days with a cold.

Getting rid of most of the germs is simple...

Washing your hands before and after using your phone keeps germs at bay. Avoid letting others use your phone. Some doctors recommend using either alcohol or antibacterial wipes to clean your phone. However, alcohol can damage the protective coating on the phone.

> ### *DO WHAT I DO*
>
> **Use a dampened cotton cloth to wipe your phone down at the end of the day, and avoid taking it into the bathroom with you. It's also important to wash your hands before eating.**

Do what I do... Use a dampened cotton cloth to wipe it down at the end of the day, and avoid taking it into the bathroom with you. It's also important to wash your hands before eating. Otherwise, you could transfer those germs on your credit card to your food.

35. A 2012 study from the University of Aberdeen found a high-fat diet not only causes weight gain, but also damages your brain.

> ### *DO WHAT I DO*
>
> **Limit your intake of saturated fat, but don't cut out fat entirely. I like to get healthy fatty acids through fish and eggs.**

In the study, mice fed a diet high in saturated fat over 16 weeks experienced damage to the hypothalamus – the area of the brain that controls appetite and energy usage. Scientists determined that a high-fat diet "perpetuates the development of obesity" as it hinders the body's ability to limit the amount of food you eat and the energy you expend.

Saturated fats also increase your risk of inflammation and blood clotting in your arteries. But it's important to realize not all fats are bad for you. Essential fatty acids – like omega-3s – decrease musculoskeletal pain and can improve mental and eye health.

So do what I do... Limit your intake of saturated fat, but don't cut out fat entirely. I like to get healthy fatty acids through fish and eggs.

36. **Just having two bad nights of sleep in a row can harm your health**... according to a 2013 study from the University of Birmingham.

Researchers found that sleep deprivation for two consecutive nights showed a decrease in breathing control (irregular breathing) and reduced vascular function (stiff blood vessels). After five nights of 10 hours of sleep, the negative effects were reversed. But if you regularly lack a good night's sleep, these dangerous effects could be more permanent – raising your risk of cardiovascular disease and sleep apnea.

Regular readers know that getting seven to eight hours of sleep each night is one of the most important things to do to maintain a healthy lifestyle. To get the best night's sleep, keep your room cool and dark... and free of electronics. If you can't get at least seven straight hours of sleep a night, take a nap during the day.

37. **Statins are some of the bestselling drugs in the U.S. But they have dangerous side effects**...

Drugmakers rake in billions of dollars from the more than 100 million prescriptions written each year. Statins are believed to lower cholesterol and reduce inflammation. But a study published in *JAMA Internal Medicine* tied statin use to muscle weakness, muscle cramps, and tendon problems. People who used statins had a 13% higher risk of dislocations or sprains and a 19% higher risk of musculoskeletal problems.

> ### *DO WHAT I DO*
> Get moving. Losing just a few pounds lowers your cholesterol while avoiding the risks and expense from costly or dangerous pills.

Statins also raise blood sugar, increasing the risk for diabetes. And in 2012, the FDA added a new warning to statins concerning memory loss.

Instead, eating foods like fish and broccoli lower your cholesterol and reduce inflammation without drugs. Get rid of white, processed foods like white bread and refined sugar.

And do what I do... get moving. Losing just a few pounds lowers your cholesterol while avoiding the risks and expense from costly or dangerous pills.

38. **Fighting cholesterol is costing people their eyesight**.

New research confirms that statins also increase your risk of cataracts. Millions of people in the U.S. currently use statins like Lipitor. But studies continue to show statins are dangerous.

A 2013 study from the University of Texas Southwestern Medical Center and the Dallas VA Medical Center found people using statins have a 27% greater risk of developing cataracts. The longer you use statins, the more likely you are to develop cataracts.

A 2012 study from Canada's University of Waterloo found statins increase the risk of developing cataracts 50%. People with Type 2 diabetes have an even greater risk. Yet, doctors practically demand their diabetic patients take the drug.

The government is catching on to the danger. At the same time the FDA added a warning label saying statins may lead to memory loss, it also warned that statins may raise blood-sugar levels (increasing your risk of diabetes).

If your doctor says you have high cholesterol, try to lower it naturally before resorting to statins. Wine, white onions, and blueberries all lower cholesterol. Exercising – and losing weight if you're overweight – also helps. Above all, make sure you avoid the "white killers," like sugar, white bread, and white rice.

39. **How good is "good cholesterol"?**

Healthy levels of high-density lipoprotein (HDL) – often called the "good cholesterol" – are believed to decrease your risk of heart disease. But a 2012 study published in the *Journal of the American Heart Association* found that a protein in HDL – apolipoprotein C-III (apoC-III) – may increase your risk of heart disease. In the study, people with high levels of both HDL and apoC-III had a 60% increased risk of developing heart disease.

But the research is controversial, and only a small group of people have the variant in their genetics that caused them to have this riskier form of HDL.

To keep your risk of heart disease low while still increasing your HDL, make sure you eat a healthy diet, do mild to moderate exercise, and get plenty of sleep. And don't forget that regular and moderate amounts of alcohol is one of the best ways to increase your HDLs.

However, if you have a family history of heart disease, in spite of good habits, you may be interested in checking your own cholesterol pattern for this variant protein. Simply get blood drawn and request the Vertical Auto Profile (VAP) cholesterol test.

40. **People with a low-risk form of thyroid cancer are being dangerously overtreated.**

In a 2013 report published in the *British Medical Journal*, researchers from the prestigious Mayo Clinic say use of diagnostic technologies results in overtreatment.

Ultrasound, magnetic resonance imaging (MRI), and computed tomography (CT) scans detect small amounts of the most common type of thyroid cancer in its early stages. However, this cancer is unlikely to cause symptoms, let alone death, for a long time.

Much like prostate cancer in men... papillary thyroid cancer is so slow-growing, many patients die of something else long before any symptoms develop. (Many people never even learn they have it.) Of patients diagnosed, 95% are still alive 30-40 years later.

The standard treatment of papillary thyroid cancer can be costly and harmful. One such treatment – thyroidectomy – is the surgical removal of part or all of the thyroid gland. The costs and complications of this procedure are numerous. One ominous complication: Many patients permanently lose the ability to speak due to nerve damage to their vocal cords and larynx.

If you get diagnosed with thyroid cancer, explore the real risks of your particular form with the doctor before allowing treatment. And get a second opinion. Otherwise, you may be putting yourself through unnecessary emotional stress and possible financial strain.

41. **Don't let your doctor examine you with dirty hands**.

The next time you're at the doctor's office or hospital, ask the medical staff treating you if they washed their hands first. Doctors and nurses should always wash their hands before and after treating patients. But don't assume they have.

The World Health Organization found up to 40% of doctors don't wash their hands properly. This lack of hygiene is a quick way to spread bacteria and infection. So take your safety into your own hands and ask...

My assistant Laura did this at a doctor's office. Both the doctor and the nurse washed their hands in front of her. She was able to see them properly washing their hands before – and after – her treatment. When I was practicing medicine, I always washed my hands in front of the patient. It's shameful this isn't standard procedure everywhere.

42. **Your dishwasher may be cultivating a deadly fungus**.

A dishwasher is the perfect breeding ground for fungi. The science journal *Fungal Biology* published findings that 62% of dishwashers tested (in more than 100 cities) contained fungi... 55% of those had two types of black yeast – Exophiala dermatitidis and Exophiala phaeomuriformis. These fungi cause potentially fatal lung infections. They're especially dangerous to people with weakened immune systems.

Scientists had previously thought the high temperatures, detergents, and salts found in dishwashers would kill fungi. But certain types of black yeast thrive in these conditions.

Keeping your dishwasher free of fungi is simple... Leave your dishwasher open for at least 30 minutes after you've washed dishes. This gives the rubber seal around the door – the place most of the fungi live – time to dry.

To clean your dishwasher, use equal parts baking soda and vinegar to clean the seal. To get the inside clean, pour a cup of baking soda on the dishwasher floor. Then, put vinegar where you would put detergent. Run your dishwasher on its hottest setting to kill the fungi.

43. **Stop eating microwaved popcorn, and reduce your risk of developing Alzheimer's.**

According to a study from the University of Minnesota, the flavoring that gives popcorn its buttery taste and smell – known as diacetyl – could trigger Alzheimer's plaques.

> ### *DO WHAT I DO*
> Enjoy air-popped popcorn, with a little melted butter (the real stuff) and olive oil tossed in.

A common sign of Alzheimer's is too much clumping of a brain protein called beta-amyloid, commonly referred to as "plaques." Researchers found diacetyl increases the clumping of this protein and hinders the brain's ability to clear it.

But don't let this stop you from eating popcorn in general. Popcorn can provide twice the antioxidants of a serving of many fruits and vegetables.

So do what I do... Enjoy air-popped popcorn, with a little melted butter (the real stuff) and olive oil tossed in. You'll have great buttered popcorn with even more antioxidants benefits from the olive oil's monounsaturated fats. And you'll avoid those harmful additives of microwave popcorn.

44. As we said in Part V, Chapter 12, **20% of the U.S. water supply has dangerously high levels of arsenic.**

Arsenic is a chemical naturally found in rocks, soil, and water. But exposure to high levels of arsenic causes cancer, high blood pressure, Type 2 diabetes, and even strokes.

Unfortunately, arsenic isn't the only unsafe chemical in your water. Most drinking water contains high levels of hexavalent chromium – a known carcinogen. A study found that 31 cities (out of 35 tested) had hex-chromium in the tap water. (The four that didn't were Indianapolis, Indiana; Reno, Nevada; Plano, Texas; and San Antonio, Texas.)

Water filters with activated carbon remove up to 90% of the hexavalent chromium in drinking water. Brita – the global leader for manufacturing household water filters – sells filters with activated carbon for less than $30. You can also purchase a reverse-osmosis filter. They cost up to $500 if professionally installed, and more effectively remove the toxic chemicals in your water.

45. Living near a busy international airport raises the risk of heart disease and stroke, according to two separate studies.

The U.S. study from researchers at the Harvard School of Public Health and Boston University School of Public Health studied people 65 years of age and older living in areas with ambient aircraft noise. They found that every 10-decibel increase in noise corresponded with a 3.5% increase in their likelihood of being admitted to a hospital due to cardiovascular disease.

London-based researchers discovered similar results. Residents of London who lived closest to Heathrow Airport had increased risks of stroke, coronary heart disease, and cardiovascular disease. The exact causes are unknown. Several studies show that regular, loud noise can increase blood pressure and disrupt sleep.

So does this mean you should move if you live near an airport? Probably not. Until more research is done, I wouldn't recommend putting your house up for sale. But make sure you're getting seven to eight hours of uninterrupted sleep.

If you can hear planes flying overhead, try soundproofing your bedroom or – if you don't want to spend time and money on that – wear earplugs to bed. This will soften the noise and improve the quality of sleep.

46. Vitamin E appears to slow the progress of Alzheimer's disease.

In the *Journal of the American Medical Association* – a peer-reviewed general medical journal – researchers who studied military veterans diagnosed with Alzheimer's disease reported those who took high doses of vitamin E were better able to handle daily tasks such as getting dressed and preparing food for six months longer than veterans not taking vitamin E.

The veterans were taking up to 2,000 international units of vitamin E, 50 times higher than recommended doses.

People taking vitamin E also needed caregiver assistance for two hours less per day. The vitamin showed no effect on memory or cognitive ability. But this knowledge could give Alzheimer's patients more independence for longer.

A 2005 study claimed vitamin E supplementation increases the risk of death. But no other studies found those results. Vitamin E is a fat-soluble vitamin, so long-term dosing could lead to build-up in the body.

47. **Eating a diet high in antioxidants can lower your risk of cataracts**.

More than 50% of Americans 80 years old and older will develop cataracts. If we lived long enough, it's likely nearly everyone would develop cataracts. But there's a simple way to lower your risk: Increase the antioxidants in your diet.

A 2013 study out of Sweden found women who ate a diet high in antioxidants lowered their cataract risk 13%. People with adequate levels of vitamin C were 39% less likely to develop cataracts.

Vitamin C is just one type of antioxidant. Other antioxidants include vitamin E, beta-carotene, and selenium. Some foods with the highest amounts of antioxidants are blueberries, red wine, broccoli, and tomatoes.

— 18 —

Always Check the Pills You're Given, It Could Save Your Life

The pill the nurse was trying to get my mother to take could have killed her.

My sister didn't realize how dangerous things were and her less-than-frantic call implied Mom was just being a little ornery in the hospital. But after talking to my mother, I soon discovered where I got some of that *Retirement Millionaire* attitude...

My mom was fighting the nurses.

Mom was post-surgery and waking up in her hospital room. The nurses were bringing her medication to take that night, and my mom didn't recognize the pills' colors or shapes. The nurse had a blue round one, an oblong white one with numbers on the side, and only one that looked familiar to my mom.

When she questioned the nurse about the pills, the nurse got annoyed and refused to bring the packaging so my mother could see what the medication was – the maker, the name, and the milligrams.

It turns out, they were the wrong drugs. Neither the blue nor the white pills were medications she'd ever had, and they weren't meds to try right after surgery. Those medications were potent by themselves. Mixed together, they can kill some post-surgical patients.

When I called the nurses' station and spoke with the staff, it was immediately clear why thousands of people die every year from medication errors. And why hundreds of thousands are injured...

In 2002, an Institute of Medicine study uncovered nearly 7,000 people die every year in the U.S. from medication errors. The causes range from physician handwriting to nurses not distinguishing among look-alike packaging.

Please scrutinize the pills you're given.

My mom did the right thing, and you should too. When you go to the hospital or even a doctor visit, bring your own list of meds. List the colors of the pills, shapes, milligrams, and schedule you've been taking them. If you sense any deviation from the plan, ask for clarification. Get a copy of the medications the staff claims you're supposed to get.

And under no circumstances should you back down if you think the staff is wrong. Ask for the head nurse or even the doctor to come and explain what medications you're taking and why. The *why* is the most important piece – you need to understand the purpose for each and every medication. Otherwise, you're dependent on the staff to get it right. And as I've told you, the systems aren't in place to prevent these errors.

My mom was in pain, which compounded the frustration. But it didn't change the fact that the hospital was making mistakes. My mom was about to get the wrong medications. After surgery (or anytime, actually) that could be deadly.

The nurse who fought with my mom (and me) was suspended for a couple days. Although the nurse was wrong in her approach, the hospital's system was truly at fault. What really happened? Did someone fill the order incorrectly in the pharmacy? Did the doctor write the wrong drug and dosage? Or did the nurse simply grab the wrong medication?

There's no way to know. It's just part of a "systems" breakdown. And in this day and age, these errors are unacceptable.

Hospitals Can Prevent Infections, They Just Have to Try

Medical systems can be made to work well. In 2001, Johns Hopkins hospital showed how dramatically systems can improve.

An intensive care doctor named Peter Pronovost examined intravenous-line infections in the Intensive Care Unit (ICU) at Hopkins. In the ICU, doctors and nurses insert intravenous lines inside patients' veins to deliver drugs and monitor the blood. The lines often remain in a patient's body for days.

The problem is bacteria crawl down the line and infect the patient 10%-15% of the time – which often leads to death.

Pronovost created a simple checklist of the things doctors are supposed to do, including washing hands and using clean gloves and gowns. After he convinced the hospital to mandate use of the checklist for a year, the rates of infection went from 11% to 0%.

Simply reminding doctors and nurses of basic steps to ensure a sterile environment eliminated IV-line infections.

It turns out doctors and nurses were skipping one or more of these critical steps with nearly a third of all patients. Nurses played a large part of the success because the hospital authorized them to stop the procedure and tell the doctors to comply.

Interested in evidence-based medicine, Michigan mandated a five-step checklist protocol in 2003. The infection rate at its 108 hospitals dropped to... 0%. The checklists saved about 4,000 lives that year alone.

Literally eliminating IV-line infections in the ICU was unheard of as recently as the 20th century. Taking a systems approach instantly fixed the problem. Yet a 2006 *New England Journal of Medicine* article reported most ICU doctors still were not using the checklist.

I've been on the inside. I've seen the errors that are made, sometimes with the blessings of supervisors.

What do I do? I ask the hospital treating one of my friends or relatives if it uses the Pronovost five-point checklist. Call the ICU directly if you can't get a straight answer from your doctor. If you discover it doesn't use it and you have the luxury of going to a hospital that does, change hospitals.

> ## DO WHAT I DO
>
> Ask the hospital treating one of your friends or relatives if it uses the Pronovost five-point checklist. Call the ICU directly if you can't get a straight answer from your doctor. If you discover it doesn't use it and you have the luxury of going to a hospital that does, change hospitals.

It's easy to look on the Medicare website for lists of the best hospitals in your area... If you have the choice, go there and don't give the others your business.

Otherwise, be extra vigilant in monitoring the care you receive. I'd also write the president or CEO of the hospital and ask why he doesn't require it. Send a copy of your letter to the local newspaper. Local journalists love stories like this.

We need to demand a change and act on it. The government isn't going to change it for us.

PART VIII

Beat the Health Care System

— 1 —

The Six End-of-Life Questions You Must Discuss With Your Family

My dad and stepmother always thought they were prepared.

Many years ago, doctors diagnosed my father with dementia as a result of football concussions he suffered as a young man. My stepmother labored as hard as any person could to care for him in their home.

She and I both believed that was the best care he could receive. But a couple years later, she reached her breaking point coping with his physical and mental incapacity... So we called the transport to take my dad to an assisted living center we had picked out.

I cried for nearly 30 minutes as I followed the ambulance carrying my dad. Even then, we had no idea how little we knew about what was to come.

But the experience taught me important lessons about life, health care, and ways most people should (but don't) take control of their lives. It's vital you talk with your family and friends about how you want your last days to play out... And not just in generalities. I've included six specific issues you must address.

I know this conversation can be difficult. (I avoided it myself.) But I urge you to make time to talk it over.

That's why I want to tell you about what I went through when we made this choice. Until it's your dad or mom dying, it's easy to think you're prepared for the process. But I wasn't...

Like most of the things in the world that are institutionalized, the residences, hospitals, insurance companies, and bureaucracies you and your family must deal with at that time don't give a damn about your situation. And unless you've spelled it out clearly and completely, someone else will make end-of-life decisions for you.

Your family will, of course, try to make the best decisions. But it's an emotional time. Things happen fast. And usually, there's someone sitting across a desk trying to make money off you or save money by getting rid of you.

Please don't let the medical system tell you how your last few months will be.

Now, let me tell you what happened with my father...

The Deposit for Nothing

We knew about my dad's condition for years. It was progressive. And in his case, it was slow moving. So we put down a deposit on an assisted living center with a good "memory center," as they call the dementia holding cells.

My stepmother had carefully checked the place out, spoken with management and the finance department, and was expecting a graceful transition when the time came to take him there. But it was not to be.

My dad's physical health took a sharp downturn. He was repeatedly admitted to the local hospital as doctors searched for some "acute" illness to treat. But they found nothing (other than low potassium), and he was discharged back to my stepmother's care each time.

Then one night, my stepmother called telling me she was stuck with dad on a landing halfway up the stairs in their home. She had been struggling to help him up the stairs, and they couldn't make it any farther. Turns out she slept the night with him on the landing, holding him in her arms.

I raced down the next day to help. As painful as I knew this trip would be, I thought at least the process would be quick. Call for transport, sign dad in, and start adjusting to our new lives... Little did I know how little I knew.

When I arrived at their home, I could tell my father was close to dying. Part of me wanted to take him to the family's lake cabin he loved and just sit there with him until he passed. But we decided we could at least move him from home to the assisted living center. And so we arranged for the transport because he couldn't walk or sit easily.

Yet when we arrived at the center, they seemed strangely uncomfortable with him. "If he can't sit up and pivot, he can't be here." My stepmother looked puzzled. And frankly, I was too emotionally drained to care. My dad was dying. Who cared about their silly rules?

The young guys who transported him had already left with a tip (although I truly don't know if that's a time to take tips from anyone). Earlier at home, I actually did most of the heavy lifting when we moved him – from the blow-up mattress on the floor to the stretcher. The whole time, Dad grabbed at my arms, crying and yelling, "No, no, no." He somehow knew he had spent his last day in his home with his wife and companion of so many years.

So there we were, in his new home at the assisted living center, but not wanted. After a couple hours, it was clear my stepmother had kept him at home (out of love and kindness) too long. He no longer qualified for this assisted living center... He needed more vigilant care than it would provide.

"Assisted living" is a misnomer. To stay, my dad had to be able to sit up in bed on his own and pivot on his feet on the floor to get in and out of a wheelchair. Sure, they would help cut food or tie a shoelace. But that's the extent of their "assistance." They wouldn't lift and carry anyone to and from bed. This was not the time or place to discover this.

As this reality dawned on us, the center's staff pitched the false hope that he might still have an acute illness. They sent him off to the hospital to have tests and a few drugs, hoping that like replacing spark plugs on a car, he'd be back to his room at the assisted living center in a few days. And with new hope for dad, we agreed.

Sadly, the story goes on like this. He was sent back to the center only to get worse and sent back to the hospital again. Each time, the health care system thought he could be tuned up.

Eventually, my stepmother and I got fed up with the back and forth and agreed to find a new home for dad.

Please Raise These Questions with Your Loved Ones

The facts about the end of life are shocking.

Medicare spends 30% of its dollars on people in their last 12 months of life. And worse, people aren't dying peacefully or in dignity. About 41% of people in their last three months of life receive a "burdensome intervention." These are things like tube feedings, emergency room visits, and heart shocks. Over and over, people are dying without dignity and apparently without much common sense.

People don't need to be admitted repeatedly to the hospital when they're dying or gripped by advanced dementia. It creates a sense of false hope for everyone and discomfort for the patient. But most importantly, it's just feeding the hospital's coffers with money it doesn't deserve. I understand that in the heat of the moment it seems like the right thing to do, but it doesn't change the outcome. All it does is waste money at the end of life.

So read these six questions with your friends and family. Talk about the issues and plan for the future. Don't let some cold, faceless hospital dictate how you or your loved ones spend those last months on the Earth.

Urge your family members to create living wills, health care proxies, and powers of attorney. And do it for yourself, too.

1. **Do you and your family (parents, siblings, etc.) have a living will?** This document spells out what your wishes are regarding ventilators, heart shocks, and other interventions if you're sick. It's hard to know. But imagine you had dementia, didn't know your husband's

name, and couldn't feed yourself. Would you want extraordinary measures done to keep you alive? Would you want to be treated for pneumonia? Or just left to die?

2. **Do you have a <u>health care proxy</u>?** This is a document that says who you want making decisions for you if you're incapacitated. Talk about it. I've known of families where two kids thought dad wanted everything done to keep him alive and two thought the exact opposite. You can't have both. Someone will make the decision, and relationships can fracture over it.

Be sure and sit down with your designees and make your wishes clear. I recommend doing it with at least two family members and have them write out your wishes so you're sure they understand.

3. **Have you thought about <u>where you want to die</u>?** At home? The nursing home? Don't forget about "hospice care," which provides pain medication but nothing else. No treatments, no tests, no interventions in your last months of life... This is how I'd like to go: At home with little pain. But everyone's decision is personal. If you expect to care for a loved one through this last stage of life, please ask him or her now.

4. **Have you considered <u>nursing homes and assisted living centers?</u>** If so, be sure and look at the fine print.

In my dad's case, no one ever explained the sit-and-pivot rule to us. We thought a place with a dementia center would naturally be prepared for someone like him. As a result, we kept him home too long to qualify for the sort of care of an assisted living center... It's a rough way to find out on the day you bring your loved one for admission.

And be sure to look online at the federal government's website on nursing homes: www.medicare.gov/NHCompare. The site allows you to compare ratings and locations among thousands of nursing homes. For a U.S. government site, it's surprisingly useful and chockfull of information to help you decide what's best for your situation. My stepmother was able to find a place half the distance from home but higher-rated than the other choices farther away.

5. **<u>What's covered by insurance</u> when someone is dying?** Once you or your family member are in a nursing home, who pays for a hospitalization? What will be your out-of-pocket expenses for each major decision? If you had $250,000 to leave to your daughter but you were in your final year of life, would you want to be treated out of pocket or forgo it and let your child get the money?

It doesn't seem like a big deal now, but you and your daughter should talk about it. Imagine if you discovered she felt the exact opposite... you should know these things before you're in the midst of it and don't have any control to take your time and consider what is best for you.

6. **Have you addressed your <u>spirituality</u>?** Whatever your beliefs, make them known to your family and loved ones. Do you want your priest coming by? Do you want music? Do you want to give or get forgiveness from anyone? These issues should be discussed if not explicitly planned for. Is there anyone you want to talk to about love... to say the words I love you? Again, all things to talk about.

I hope these six topics open up a dialogue with at least yourself... and that this chapter has added a little something to your life. I truly hope that as you contemplate yours or another's mortality, you can talk about it safely with friends and loved ones.

— 2 —

Don't Fall for AARP

AARP is one big lie.

I used to assume the American Association of Retired Persons (AARP) was looking out for the interests of... well... retired people. But it's not.

According to its own financial statements, in 2008, the organization took in $773 million in ads and royalties from private insurance companies. AARP and its foundation are as left-leaning liberal as you can get without falling out of a tree. Essentially, <u>it is one big advertising billboard for insurance businesses</u>.

You're a fool if you think AARP is going to protect you when it comes to health care issues. Ask for your membership money back, and tip your garbage collector instead. I guarantee you'll get more personal benefit from it.

— 3 —

High-Quality Dentistry for 75% Off in Mexico

You can pick up a lot of things cheap in Tijuana, Mexico... including a new set of dental filings and some good bridgework.

Tijuana has one of the highest numbers of dentists and pharmacists per capita in the world, many of whom trained in the U.S. and Europe. But the fees in Mexico are much less than for similar work in the U.S. And increasingly, Americans are venturing across the border, taking advantage of the unbeatable values.

Look, folks. America doesn't have a monopoly on science and medicine or even common sense. Plenty of doctors around the world are perfectly capable of performing knee replacements, heart bypasses, and cataract surgery.

"Medical tourism" is a great answer for retirees. It's not that difficult to do either.

Jack Vincent – a subscriber of my *Retirement Millionaire* newsletter – had been traveling to Mexico for dental surgery for nearly a decade.

It all started after a dentist in his hometown of San Diego told him his painful teeth needed $2,200 of work. (That bill included a preposterous 5% "senior discount.")

His insurance was little help. Jack had Medicare and looked up its dental coverage. "I checked into the prices... and I checked into a dental insurance policy," he said. "Basically, it's a discount policy. There's no such thing as dental insurance anymore."

At about that same time, Jack read a story in the *San Diego Reader* and found several valuable reviews of dentists in Mexico. He had a referral from a friend for a particular dentist in Tijuana.

Jack was stunned when the Mexican dentist told him he would do the work for $465. And so he went.

Jack got the root canal done in Tijuana and went back three more times for other procedures. He never had any problems and always saw great results.

This is how Jack described the practice...

> It's a husband and wife team. They are on a little side street off the main tourist drag there, in the heart of the tourist downtown. He speaks excellent English. I'm guessing he's in his 50s or 60s. They have a grown daughter and a grown son.
>
> Apparently, they're doing quite well because the daughter's a lawyer and the son is also a dentist.

I joined Jack on a dental trip to Tijuana in 2010.

The actual trip was easy. We parked at the border on the U.S. side and walked into Tijuana. The streets were dirty with spit, just like much of Times Square in NYC. And poverty was everywhere. I felt uncomfortable most of the time walking around. I was glad to be buddied up with 6-foot-6-inch Jack, who, even at 68 years old, was an imposing figure.

The dentist saw Jack right away, but I waited nearly three hours. It was never clear why. Jack simply said... This is Mexico, be prepared to wait.

Aside from that, the dental experience was superb. The office was clean, and the dentists (father and son) were knowledgeable. The wife (and mother) is the hygienist. She was kind and careful. My gums were no sorer than any other cleanings I've had. She repeatedly checked on my comfort level, more than I've ever received in the States.

As for cost... the first visit was a mere $46. They told me it would be $30 if I came regularly.

If you need major dental work and live near Mexico, at least get an estimate over the phone from these guys... but I wouldn't go just to save on routine teeth cleaning.

But first, here are some tips for anyone interested in getting dental work in Mexico...

- Make sure your dentist speaks English.

- Call and get him to give you an estimate based on what your U.S. dentist proposes.

- Get a few personal referrals from the dentist, call those references, and check their results.

- Take a friend along – Tijuana, just like New York City, can be a rough place. And thieves could prey on Americans (especially older ones).

Doing your homework is vital. Never act rashly when it comes to your health. I've seen news articles about botched surgeries – like Miss Argentina dying in 2009 from a butt lift gone badly. So please be diligent about your research, and count on references from close friends.

This holds true in the U.S. as well. The U.S. health care complex is not the only answer to your questions. Mistakes and bad doctors happen everywhere – and they happen all the time in America.

— 4 —

The 13 Most Important Things You Can Do For Your Health

Deciding on the best ways to improve your health is tough.

One day, you hear a self-appointed expert tell you one thing. The next day, a different talking head claims something that sounds like the exact opposite. Often, the advice is contradictory and confusing. Much of it also lacks scientific evidence.

That's why in 2006, I started publishing a list of my top ways to improve your health. I wanted to give patients and readers a simple, straightforward way to start on the path to a healthier life.

I originally created this list for myself in 1997. I kept the list on my refrigerator to remind myself of the importance of these tips. I have continued to update it for my *Retirement Millionaire* subscribers every winter...

Below are 13 ways to improve your health. Please don't let the number of tips overwhelm you. Read the list and then pick out a couple each month to focus on as the year rolls on.

One of These Ideas Will Change Your Life

1. **Movement**: Movement offers dozens of benefits, more than just keeping you at a healthy weight. Regular exercise reduces stress, releases endorphins, improves brain function, and improves cardiovascular

health. A 2014 study published in *Frontiers in Human Nature* showed exercise even boosts creativity.

Here's the GREAT news... you don't have to engage in strenuous exercise... *Light exercise* (walking is my favorite) for about 20 to 30 minutes a day gives you nearly all the benefits, while avoiding injuries like muscle strains and joint pain.

And it's never too late to get started. Even people who start exercising later in life lower the rate of senior dangers, such as falling and osteoporosis.

So don't make excuses about exercising this year. One of the most popular excuses is being too tired. If you're tired, go for a walk. You'll see an improvement in your energy. And you'll do this better...

2. **Sleep**: More than a third of Americans are chronically sleep deprived. Chronic sleep deprivation impairs memory, alertness, and concentration. It leads to serious injury... Driving while tired causes more than 100,000 accidents a year, according to the National Highway Traffic Safety Administration.

Getting around eight hours of sleep a night helps reduce stress, makes you three times less likely to catch a cold, helps you maintain a healthy weight, and reduces your risk of diseases like cancer and diabetes.

The key is setting yourself up for a good night's sleep. Keep your room dark, quiet, and cool. Get rid of electronics by your head and bed. And make sleep a routine. Go to bed at the same time each night. This helps your body know when to wind itself down.

When possible, avoid using an alarm clock to wake you up. Our bodies naturally wake us up when we've had enough sleep. This will leave you feeling better rested and more awake throughout the day.

3. **Meditation**: I paradoxically consider this the "No. 1 exercise in the world." For thousands of years, various cultures have used meditation as a way to focus the mind and heal the body. Scientific research continues to prove the health benefits of regular meditation. Like exercise,

meditation reduces stress, improves brain function, and lowers the risk of depression.

A 2013 study from a group of researchers in the U.S., Spain, and France found meditation suppresses genes that trigger inflammation. (Inflammation is linked to diabetes, cardiovascular disease, and cancer.) The type of meditation used in the study – called "mindfulness meditation" – involves focusing on something in the present while you meditate.

Meditating is simple. And it only takes 10-12 minutes a day. You can sit in a chair or lie in bed, relaxing your body while you concentrate on taking deep breaths. That's it. You can let your mind wander as it chooses, as long as you keep breathing steadily and deeply. I make sure to meditate when I'm feeling stressed or tired.

4. **Sunlight**: You can stave off the "winter blues" by spending time in the sun. The reason people feel depressed in the winter – known as seasonal affective disorder – is mostly due to a lack of sunlight. Many of us leave for work in the morning when it's dark and come home in the evening after sundown. This wreaks havoc on mental health.

Sunlight benefits our health by triggering our bodies to produce vitamin D isomers (different versions of the basic chemical). Studies show having adequate amounts of vitamin D reduces the risk of Alzheimer's, lessens symptoms of mild depression, and helps our bodies regulate calcium absorption, which keeps our bones strong.

Simply exposing your skin to sunlight for 20 minutes or so a day can be enough to fight winter depression. I try to take a walk or two during the day when I'm at my office in Baltimore... even if it's just to go get lunch. I also keep the shutters on my windows open to let in as much light as possible while I sit at my desk.

5. **Massage**: It's an ancient way to reduce stress and relieve pain. Several studies have proved massage relieves depression and anxiety, improving mental health. One study published in the journal *Applied Nursing Research* found back massages help chemotherapy patients combat anxiety and fatigue.

There are several different types of massage, each with their own benefits. A Swedish massage is great for relaxation and reenergizing yourself. This is when a masseuse uses long, flowing strokes to improve blood and lymph flow. (The lymph system is the thick infection-fighting fluids that travel in their own "tubes" alongside the blood vessels.) I get several Swedish massages a year.

I've also done regular Thai yoga massage. During a Thai yoga massage, the masseuse will move you into several different yoga positions to help stretch you while you receive massage strokes. This is a great massage if your muscles are sore or tight. It's also a great stress reliever.

If you can afford it, I recommend getting a professional massage as often as once per month. A masseuse can suggest the right massage for what ails you. If you can't afford a massage, even something as simple as trading hand or foot rubs with your partner has similar benefits.

6. **Eating green vegetables**: The health importance of eating plenty of leafy green vegetables is well-documented. But many people still don't eat enough. Americans eat less than two servings of vegetables per day. In several states, including North Dakota and Mississippi, the average person eats less than 1.5 servings. The Centers for Disease Control and Prevention recommends eating at least two and a half cups of vegetables per day (or about three servings).

As far as health benefits go, leafy green vegetables – the scientific term is "cruciferous" – are king. Vegetables like spinach and kale contain nutrients like omega-3 fatty acids, vitamin C, vitamin B-12, folate, and iron.

Dark leafy vegetables are also a good source of the antioxidant lutein. Lutein helps protect your eyes from sunlight damage, maintaining your vision. A 2013 study from Harvard found lutein reduces the risk of developing amyotrophic lateral sclerosis (ALS) – also known as Lou Gehrig's disease.

In addition to eating other vegetables, I like to eat at least one serving of cruciferous vegetables per day (about two cups). I try to eat a salad during the day – either at lunch with some soup or as a side with dinner.

My assistant Laura adds two cups of spinach to her breakfast smoothie. She can't taste the spinach when she combines it with strong-tasting fruits, like pineapple.

7. **Don't share utensils and glasses**: Eating and drinking from other people's utensils and glasses is one of the quickest ways to get a cold. And not just colds... it can result in cold sores.

Known as the "herpes simplex virus type 1," cold sores are the painful blisters you get around your mouth and nose. They last for about a week and can lead to cold or flu-like symptoms.

That's why I tell people every year to stop sharing utensils. As a young man, I was a regular offender of this rule. Sharing a meal with friends or family would always lead to food sampling... whether we passed plates around or just took food from one another.

I'd also share glasses of wine with friends, to let them sample whatever wine I happened to be enjoying. During the winters I shared utensils, I'd suffer multiple colds. Once I stopped, I had only a handful of colds during the winter.

If you feel the need to let someone try food or drink, use clean utensils and glasses.

8. **Alcohol**: Booze has suffered a bad reputation for decades. From 1920 to 1933, the U.S. outlawed the sale, production, import, and transportation of alcoholic beverages.

"Prohibition" was part of a religious movement whose followers believed alcohol was one of the evils of society – leading to an increase in divorce, accidents at work due to drunkenness, and alcoholism.

They were partially right. Drinking too much alcohol comes with severe consequences. But in moderation, alcohol is good for you. Drinks like beer and wine raise high-density lipoprotein (HDL), or "good" cholesterol.

Moderate alcohol intake also decreases the risk of dementia 23%. Having a drink or two, three to four times per week also lowers the risk of blood clotting. A 2009 study even found moderate drinking cuts the risk of developing gallstones by a third.

And there's little difference between beer and wine. Both provide similar benefits. What matters is the amount you drink. About a glass of wine or one beer per day for women and two for men gives you the benefits without the risks of overconsumption.

9. **Clean air**: We breathe about 3,000 gallons of air per day. Much of it contains pollutants like car exhaust, dust, and ozone. And it's not just the air outside. The air in your office or home likely contains pollutants as well. So making sure we have a chance to breathe clean air is vital.

You may think that wood-burning fireplace in your home just offers warmth and charm. But it gives off particulates that make it harder to breathe. Other pollutants lead to cancer, neurological problems, and even death. In an effort to make people aware of the dangers of indoor pollutants, the Lung Institute started an initiative to help people "lung-proof their homes."

One of the institute's top tips is to stop smoking inside. To get rid of pollutants already in your home, use a vacuum with a HEPA (high-efficiency particulate air) filter. A HEPA filter can remove lead, pet dander, and other pollutants. You should also fill your home with plants. Plants are natural air filters.

10. **Music**: A 2013 study presented at the European Society of Cardiology's meeting in Amsterdam found listening to music bolsters the recovery of people with heart disease.

People who listened to music for 30 minutes per day in addition to exercising improved their heart function more than people who just exercised. The researchers said the type of music wasn't important. They believe listening to music releases endorphins (mood-lifting and healing chemicals), helping to improve heart function.

> **DO WHAT I DO**
>
> Listen to music during the day. As most people in my office could tell you, I listen to a mix of classical and jazz during the workday. It keeps me calm and helps me to concentrate.

Do what I do... listen to music during the day. As most people in my office could tell you, I listen to a mix of classical and jazz during the workday. It keeps me calm and helps me to concentrate. Toward the end of the day, when people typically get tired, I'll switch to music with more of a beat to keep me energized.

And you don't just benefit from listening to music. Playing music gives your brain a workout, keeping your mind sharper as you age. Playing an instrument also boosts your immune system. Just the act of playing is similar to light exercise, giving you a small workout.

11. **Pleasant aromas**: Surrounding yourself with pleasant aromas is a simple way to reduce stress, improve your mood, increase brain function, and more.

An assisted-living center in Minnesota found patients with dementia slept 42.5 minutes more at night after exposure to the smell of lavender. People

> **DO WHAT I DO**
>
> **Pick whatever scents you like best and buy essential oils and not fragrances. Essential oils are stronger and natural. Avoid synthetic fragrances that contain harmful manmade mimics.**

with Alzheimer's often get agitated and have trouble sleeping at night, a problem known as "sundowning." This makes essential oils a natural alternative to giving patients medications with potential side effects. Lavender can help anyone sleep. I've often put a drop or two of lavender on my pillow for this reason. I also travel with a bottle of rose oil.

Certain essential oils are alleged to have specific health properties. But most of these claims are unsupported by science and are false. Do what I do... pick whatever scents you like best and buy essential oils and not fragrances. Essential oils are stronger and natural. Avoid synthetic fragrances that contain harmful manmade mimics.

12. **Aspirin**: More than one-third of Americans take it regularly to prevent heart disease. Aspirin prevents blood clots, reducing the risk of heart attack or stroke. If you suspect you're having a heart attack, chewing an aspirin can prevent clots from getting larger.

The best time to take aspirin may be at night. Researchers from the Leiden University Medical Center discovered that taking aspirin at night bolsters the effects of the drug. Blood thinned better with a nighttime dose, and people taking their pill at night suffered no increase in side effects.

I started taking it once a week in the early 2000s. I sometimes vary my routine by taking one tablet (about 81 milligrams, or a quarter of a regular sized aspirin) each day. A daily baby aspirin or one 325 mg aspirin per week is enough for most people.

Taking aspirin does involve some risk, like bleeding in your nose or stomach. But for most people, these are minor compared with the benefits.

13. **Blueberries**: Blueberries are a true superfood. They are packed with antioxidants (like vitamin C, vitamin E, beta-carotene, fiber, and manganese), flavonoids, anthocyanins (this gives them the blue color), and other chemicals. They lower cholesterol, improve eyesight, and reduce inflammation.

A team of researchers from the U.S., U.K., and Singapore showed eating blueberries reduces the risk of Type 2 diabetes 26%.

I eat them year-round in yogurt, oatmeal, and by themselves. I always keep packages of blueberries in my freezer so I can eat them even when they're not in season. I eat at least a cup per day to get the maximum health benefits.

These tips are the best ways to get started living a healthier life. As I said before, please start using these tips immediately. But just try one (or two) at a time. After a few months, you'll have built them into your life as regular habits.

— 5 —

Grow Your Money and Get Insurance for Long-Term Care. It's as Easy as 'ABC'

In 2010, I found the most fascinating financial product I had ever seen. It addressed the biggest fear most every American has: That late in life, our health will fail, and we'll run out of money, ending up sick and destitute.

Just consider: In 2014, 401(k) behemoth Fidelity Investments reported 65 year olds will need $326,000 for health care before they die. The Employee Benefit Research Institute pegged the figure at $151,000.

Please don't count on the president or Washington DC to pay your bills and hold your hand while you die. Medicare doesn't cover everything you'll need (long-term care, for instance).

And worse, it lowers your chances to die with dignity.

Bureaucrats are worried about budgets, not your quality of life... That focus means payouts and benefits rarely match patient needs. Most of us are going to need a pile of cash or the ability to easily tap assets to make ends meet. How much probably depends on your health and family history.

But if you already have a little cash for emergencies – and you should – you can at least quadruple the value of your cash overnight.

This product will allow you to safely move rainy-day money from one type of savings to another and guarantee the care and comfort you want should your health turn sour. If you remain healthy until you die, you still keep your savings (and can pass them on to your children).

Annuities and Long-Term Care

The investment I'm talking about is called Asset-Based Care (ABC). It didn't exist before November 1, 2009. ABCs are safe, liquid, and yield more than most certificates of deposit (CDs) at your local bank.

Essentially, an ABC is an annuity on steroids.

You can find all kinds of annuities on the market. But in essence, they are insurance products that guarantee income for a holder's lifetime (or periods like five or 10 years).

For example, you could pay $10,000 at age 50 in exchange for a payment of $50 a month until you die. If you live to 80, you'd receive $18,000 (30 years x 12 months/year x $50) from that initial $10,000.

However, the details vary. You can buy annuities with a single, lump-sum payment or extend your principal across multiple payments. Annuities can pay at fixed or variable rates, and you can opt for deferred or immediate payouts.

Again, Medicare doesn't pay for long-term care like nursing homes. You have to use up your personal assets and declare yourself broke before Medicaid will cover it... Even then, not all costs are covered.

Worse, statistics say about 50% of us will need nursing-home care at some point in our lives. And it's not cheap. A nursing home can cost about $78,000 a year. Even in-home care can run $35,000 a year.

Insurance companies offer policies designed to cover these costs. But conventional policies are expensive, and the application process is burdensome. For example, a 70-year-old male might pay close to $3,000 a year for $4,000-a-month of benefits. And the benefits last for only three years, which adds up to only $144,000 of benefits. And that's if you can actually get insured at age 70. Most policies require full underwriting, including physicals, blood tests, etc...

And remember, it's only a 50%-50% chance you'll even use that policy. It's a coin flip. You could easily spend $60,000 of your money for nothing except a little peace of mind. If you don't go to a nursing home (or similar facility), the insurance company keeps your premium. It's a "use it or lose it" proposition.

But ABCs are different. You keep everything. Let me explain...

How to Leverage Your Cash Safely

The ABCs combine annuities with long-term-care insurance. Here's what you get:

- Long-term tax-deferred growth of savings

- Long-term care benefits

- A meteoric increase in the value of your benefits

- Retain all money if you don't use the long-term care (LTC) benefit

- The ability to pass on the money to your heirs

Here's how ABCs work: Imagine you're 74 years old and have $100,000 in four different certificates of deposit (CDs) with credit unions all earning 1.5% to 2.5%. The CDs are simply contracts that pay a fixed amount of interest over an agreed upon term. You pay taxes on the interest, and your heirs get the money on your passing.

If you needed to go to a nursing home, your money would dry up in 18 months (three years if you could use in-home care). Then, you'd have to tap the rest of your assets. If you outlived those assets, your family would pay for the rest of your care (and decide your fate since they control the purse strings).

Instead, if you bought an ABC plan with that $100,000, the insurance company places it in an account with a guaranteed fixed rate of 3%. Your money grows tax-deferred... but you also get long-term care insurance. A small percentage of your account balance pays the insurance.

Your Cash Explodes in Value

At the end of one year, your long-term care accumulated value becomes $101,070. But should you actually need to tap that value for a nursing home, the total care benefit explodes to $404,280.

You can tap into that total care benefit the moment you are unable to perform your daily living – formally called "activities of daily living." I'll tell you exactly what that means in a moment.

In this case, you'd get $4,211 a month for up to eight years (total payments: $404,256). Again, that's from an initial deposit of only $100,000. This is a true quadrupling of your savings or assets into protection for long-term care. It's as if you earned 50% a year on your initial investment for eight years.

If you don't ever use long-term care, your initial deposit is still earning 3% interest. It's not a use-it-or-lose-it deal. You're free to use the $100,000 at any time.

To top it all off: **The money you receive from these policies is tax-free**. Yep, not just *tax-deferred*... but actually 100% *tax-free* at the federal and state level. This is a true win-win deal.

Here's a way to shift money from one form of savings (money markets and CDs), put it into another (an ABC plan), and make your net worth explode in value and grow tax-deferred and tax-free.

Use the Money Any Way You Want

To tap the funds for long-term care, a physician must declare the annuitant (that's you) unable to perform two of the six "activities of daily living" <u>OR</u> has cognitive impairment. These are the six critical activities:

- Eating

- Bathing

- Dressing

- Toileting

- Transferring (moving from bed to chair)

- Maintaining continence (able to hold your urine or stool)

Cognitive impairment essentially means you have medical documentation of a dementia, including Alzheimer's.

The beauty of these policies is you can buy them on what's called an "indemnity" basis. This means once a doctor signs off on two of the six or the cognitive impairment, the money is sent to you monthly, no questions asked. The money is yours to pay for home nursing care, flowers, babysitters, or anything else.

This is different from policies that use a "reimbursement basis," like most long-term care policies. You should never consider one of those because you'll spend the rest of your life or your spouse's bickering with the insurance company over which bills are covered and which aren't. Don't waste your time. Make sure you get a policy with an indemnity feature.

The Risks Are Covered

Of course, with any investment, ABCs come with some risk. But it's the same risk you take any time you buy insurance... Does the company have the ability to pay the claims?

First, in the case of ABC plans, companies are required by state law to keep cash and securities liquid to pay benefits on their policies. Thus, the risk with companies in this business is low. Second, you can check out the claims-paying abilities of any insurance company by looking at ratings provided by either Standard & Poor's or A.M. Best.

What to Do Next...

If this sort of policy makes sense to you and you have a pile of savings for a rainy day, I urge you to look into setting up an ABC. Especially if you sense you'll eventually need long-term care.

Qualifying is easy if you're healthy. The application can be done and approved over the phone, unlike the regular LTC plans that require a full underwriting process.

Only a handful of national insurance companies offer them – Genworth and Nationwide among them, but their terms vary. Some states don't even have these products.

One option to investigate is Indiana-based insurance company State Life. In 2014, it garnered S&P's fourth-highest (out of 21 possible) rating and A.M. Best's second-highest (out of 16). State Life offers one of the better "explosions" of your asset value out there. Your money is safe with companies rated so highly.

— 6 —

How to Get Free Medical Care

It's no secret that medical care in this country is outrageously expensive.

According to financial analysts, a couple that retires at age 60 will need over $200,000 in savings to cover their medical bills during retirement.

Well, get this... one woman in North Carolina was able to get more than $200,000 worth of medical care simply by using the techniques I'm about to describe... Another man, in Virginia, was able to get Lasik eye surgery by bartering.

Sure, not every story about free medical care fits your situation. For example, the lady with the huge bill didn't want to declare bankruptcy but she wanted to pay back what she owed the hospital. She worked out a deal with the hospital administrators to write off some of what she owed in exchange for thousands of hours of volunteer work. It took her several years, but she felt good about it.

My doctor friend, Peter Kline, exchanges free medical care for things like trees and wood (he's a woodworker on the side), plumbing, and general lawn maintenance on his home and office buildings. He has even done minor procedures and given medication out numerous times in exchange for fruits and vegetables from farmers without health care.

As Pete says, "It's win-win. I come home with groceries, and I don't have to mow the lawn."

Many dentists will barter for dentistry, so don't be shy about asking your medical provider if he'll barter with you. Many health care professionals are on an exchange called IMS (International Monetary Systems), which keeps track of the bartering they do and builds up credits.

IMS has been in business since 1985 and is "the largest full-service, membership-based trading network in the U.S." IMS is a for-profit business. It's more useful to businesses than individuals interested in bartering.

To get health care, it's much easier to simply ask your doctor or your dentist if they'd be willing to barter. If you're not willing to do this in person, call up the receptionist, and ask them to ask the doctor. Also ask them if they're a member of a barter organization. If so, ask them which one(s) and sign up for the same one. Some of the exchanges like IMS have lists of which doctors or dentists are members.

Many doctors (less so dentists) don't really want to barter directly with you. There's debate within the American Medical Association about bartering violating the medical ethics of doctor-patient relationships. It's utter nonsense but they didn't call me to ask.

If you do bring up the topic, be sure and clarify exactly what you are exchanging for your "health care coverage." Is it something like "Doc, can I mow your lawn twice a month in exchange for health care"? Or is it, "Can I mow it just two times for my antibiotics"?

Only you and your doctor can decide. But you can easily have the discussion. And if your doctor prefers the indirect method of a barter exchange, try and join the exchange and build up credit, so you can visit that doctor as needed.

There's an old saying in sales that's appropriate here: "if you don't ask, you won't get the order."

If you don't ask your medical care provider if they barter, they probably won't ask you.

— 7 —

Save Hundreds a Year on Medical Expenses

In this chapter, we'll focus on saving money on prescription drugs... as well as two special savings accounts you can use to pay for your health care.

Cost Cutter No. 1:

Shop for the Best Price

Tired of being ripped off by U.S. pharmaceutical companies? If you can't cut costs with generics, you should try buying foreign.

Until Wal-Mart and Walgreens launched their dirt-cheap plans, many smart Americans were buying from companies outside the U.S. Canada is a great place to buy brand-name drugs.

Don't worry, buying prescription drugs from Canada via the mail is perfectly legal. It's also safe and a great way to pick up the brand-name drugs you need. Be sure and deal with a reputable company like one of these three well-known and respected Canadian mail-order pharmacies...

- TCDS.com (888-372-2252)

- TheCanadianPharmacy.com (866-335-8064)

- CanadaPharmacy.com (800-891-0844)

Even among the online mail-order companies, prices can vary drastically. So if you pay out of pocket for your drugs, and you and your doctor agree you must have a brand name, shop around for the best price.

Naturally, if you need the drugs to treat an immediate problem or you've run out of a critical medication, this option may not be appropriate. But if you're able to plan ahead, mail-order services can save a bundle.

But beware... not all pharmacies are reputable. Some of these so-called "pharmacies" make money selling fake medications. If you ever receive pills that smell unusual or are falling apart, throw them away and alert your doctor for reporting and a new prescription.

Cost Cutter No. 2:

Free Drugs

The best-kept secret of the drug business is that you can get almost any prescription drug in the world, free.

Don't expect to hear this secret from your pharmacist... or even your doctor. But these programs are perfectly legal... and are used by thousands of Americans across the country.

Most people don't take advantage of these freebie programs, simply because they – and their doctors – don't know the programs exist. Drug companies don't disclose the exact criteria it takes to qualify, but it's easier to receive free drugs from a private company than it is to get assistance from the federal government.

There is a great website to help you discover whether you can get free drugs. The first step is to go to the website www.pparx.org and click on the button for patients. There, you can enter the drugs you take and fill out a simple form. The website will tell you which drugs are available for financial assistance and from what company.

I highly recommend this site for determining where to find free medication. But if you already know who makes your drug, call that drug company directly and see if you qualify.

When you call, ask the operator for the "patient-assistance program." They can help determine your qualifications. And don't forget the complete list of free drug programs on the Pharmaceutical Research and Manufacturers of America (PhRMA) website.

Keep in mind, companies initiated these programs as assistance for low-income folks who struggle to afford their medications. Each has different criteria for giving free medications. In general, to apply, you'll have to verify your income and medical expenses. And not everyone qualifies.

Cost Cutter No. 3:

Find the Best Place to Buy in Your Town

Want to know the nearest place to buy the cheapest medications? Be sure to visit the website www.goodrx.com. This site tells you where to buy medications nearest to your home. The best part is that it also identifies the cheapest place near your home.

Not all pharmacies charge the same amount. One recent investigation on AOL's financial site Daily Finance found that CVS charged $133 more for the generic of Lipitor than Costco did. Costco charged $17 for a month's supply versus CVS' $150.

One elderly friend of mine saved almost $140 the first time she used this tip.

Get an FSA Now

In 2003, the U.S. government created a program that allows people to pay for many over-the-counter (OTC) medications and even nutritional supplements with tax-free money. The only catch is that you need to have what's called a **Health Flexible Spending Arrangement (FSA)** with your employer.

These special accounts allow you to save 30% and more on your medical costs. The way they work is simple...

Essentially, you have money deducted from your paycheck and placed in a special account. It can be as much money as you'd like. (The IRS sets no limits, but your employer may.) And the money comes out pre-tax. Because it's pre-tax money, you're saving whatever percent is your tax rate.

You can spend your money on anything that alleviates or treats personal injuries or sickness. For example, this includes:

- Reading glasses

- Insulin

- Birth control

- Diagnostic tests

- First Aid supplies

- Band-Aids

- Hearing aids

- All prescription medications

The IRS publishes a list (IRS Pub. 502) specifying the many medical and dental expenses you can cover with an FSA. Go to www.irs.gov and type "502" in the search box to see the list.

The best part is, you can use pre-tax dollars for:

- Health insurance premiums

- Amounts paid for long-term care

- Amounts not covered under another health plan

This means almost all of your medical expenses can be paid with pre-tax dollars through your employer's FSA plan. And by not paying taxes on the money, it's like getting a great return on your investments without any risk. Here's how it works:

Medical Expenses – No FSA Account:

- Income of $60,000

- Tax @ 21% on income

- Gross Income of $47,000

- Medical Expenses of $3,000

- Net Income = $44,400

Medical Expenses with an FSA Account:

- Income of $60,000

- Medical Expenses of $3,000

- Gross Income of $57,000 ($60,000-$3,000)

- Tax @ 21% on gross income

- Net Income = $45,030

This is an immediate income increase of $630. The benefit increases as your income or medical expenses go higher.

There is one catch to these plans: **You must use all the money you've set aside by year-end**. It's the so-called "use it or lose it" rule. But since you can buy many OTC medications, you can easily use up any money that may be expiring at year-end by stocking up on things like aspirin, Tylenol, and cold medication.

The FSA plans are easy to use. Most plans provide a debit card (just like your bank ATM card) for expenditures. That makes your record-keeping requirements virtually nil. And by federal law, the card also allows you to get an advance on amounts earmarked for the account in the coming year.

Say in January, you agreed to put $4,000 into the account over the coming year. By law, your plan sponsor puts up $4,000 immediately. This allows you to take that money out and use it immediately, even though it hasn't been deducted from your pay yet. And another insider health secret: *If you quit or are fired before year-end, you don't have to pay it back. It's the law.*

If you're not retired and don't yet have an FSA, you should call your human resources department immediately and open one.

Discover the HSA

President George W. Bush signed into law the Tax Relief and Health Care Act of 2006. Initially meant to help Americans pay for their health care, it's also a loophole for amassing wealth for retirement.

More than six million Americans are covered by this plan, but almost none of them know about the lucrative loophole. Best of all, it's legal. And the IRS spells it out in Publication 969. Let me explain...

The government wants you to have health care coverage. It has long believed health care to be a tax-free benefit. What would our American way of life be without the belief in health care for everyone? The problem is, insurance that pays for 100% coverage with no deductibles is pricy. Many of us can't (or won't) pay for that kind of coverage.

If you are one of the many people (like myself) who thinks paying for health care that covers every possible test, medication, and visit is absurd, you'll love insurance plans known as "high-deductible health plans," or HDHPs. Here's how the IRS defines HDHPs:

- A higher annual deductible than typical health plans.

- A maximum limit on the sum of the annual deductible and out-of-pocket medical expenses that you must pay for covered expenses. Out-of-pocket expenses include co-payments and other amounts, but do not include premiums.

HDHPs also involve minimum and maximum annual deductibles plus out-of-pocket expenses. Specifically, to qualify as an HDHP plan, the deductible limits are:

- $1,250 minimum and $6,250 maximum for individuals

- $2,500 minimum and $12,500 maximum for families

The beauty of the plans is the government allows us to pay for your care today using tax-free dollars, and the money can also fund your retirement if your health needs don't use it up before then.

When you open an HDHP with your employer or even through private parties (for years, I did one directly with Blue Cross Blue Shield), you simultaneously open a **Health Savings Account (HSA)** with a financial services firm you trust.

Typically, this will be a brokerage... if you set one up with an employer, you may not have a choice. HSAs act a lot like FSAs, allowing you to bank pre-tax dollars and pay for health expenses. *But there's one key difference – you don't face use-it-or-lose-it deadlines!*

There are some limits: You can put in up to $3,250 a year as an individual and $6,450 for a family. If you are 55 or older, you can add $1,000 to the maximum contribution. This money is kept in an account that you control and any earnings or interest accumulates tax-free.

Again, the amount you put in is immediately deductible from your gross income. Thus, you get the full benefit of $3,250 to spend on qualified medical expenses, not $3,250 minus taxes. And just like the FSAs, you can withdraw the money whenever you need to pay any medical expenses, including OTC medications and supplies.

Here's the kicker... Because you don't have the "use it or lose it" issue, HSAs are a great way to save money for future health care, too. *Unlike the FSAs, this money can stay in the account and build up until you die.* Your spouse can inherit it without paying taxes (other beneficiaries must pay taxes on the inheritance).

And here's the big loophole... **Saving extra money in the HSA creates another tax-free account you can tap in retirement**. The IRS allows you to use your health care plan like a garden-variety IRA. You just keep putting money in it until age 65. Once you hit 65, you can withdraw the money without penalty for any expense, not just health care.

Imagine starting at 45 years old and putting $3,250 per year away until age 55. After age 55, you can put away $4,050 per year until 65 years old. It's all tax-free. And by age 65, if you earned a conservative 6% per year, you'll have more than $140,000 sitting in this account for your retirement.

The beauty of it is, you can take it out for health care expenses tax-free. Of course, if you end up using it for everyday living expenses in retirement, you will pay income taxes (just like you do in a regular IRA).

So consider an HSA along with an HDHP to maximize your retirement nest egg. The savings from the lower insurance costs plus the tax-free deduction and build-up of capital in the HSA can provide you hundreds of thousands of dollars in your retirement.

Give this loophole a good look and see if it's for you.

PART IX

How to Create a Richer Retirement

— 1 —

A Rich, Low-Cost Way to See the World

Imagine signing up for an all-inclusive, five-star tour of China... for easily half the going price for airfare and lodging.

Many local chambers of commerce arrange high-quality group vacations at dirt-cheap prices... And they're open to anyone, not just members.

"We stayed in all four- and five-star hotels. And all of the dining was top quality," said Ed Baker.

For less than $2,000 per person, Ed and his wife spent nine days – minus two days of travel – touring areas of China, including Beijing, Suzhou, Hangzhou, and Shanghai. And all he had to do was make a phone call.

Ed retired in 2000 from his job as a project manager. A Navy veteran, Ed had spent most of his life living outside Akron, Ohio with his wife and three children. He had always wanted to visit China. So when he read a newspaper ad for a trip to China offered by the Greater Akron Chamber of Commerce, he called without a second thought.

The chamber took care of all travel arrangements and even gave Ed a booklet on what to expect on the trip, right down to what he should wear.

Ed's trip included a charter bus to New York's John F. Kennedy International Airport from Ohio (and from JFK to Ohio after the trip), round-trip airfare from JFK to Beijing, three full meals a day, an English-speaking tour guide, hotel stays, and all attractions included. Just the flight alone would have been more than $1,000 per person.

Ed traveled with a group of more than 150 people, which was divided up into smaller groups. "It was probably the best-coordinated trip that my wife and I have ever been on," he said.

The chamber sets up trips like this to create connections that could lead to some business exchange. So the only catch is you have to attend a few events arranged by the chamber – factory or warehouse tours. But most of the trip is open for typical sightseeing.

Check out your local Chamber of Commerce to find these all-inclusive trips.

Another Great Way to Vacation on the Cheap

Feel like having a vacation, but can't afford a week at a hotel? Try swapping your home.

How it works... choose where you want to go, find a listing that looks interesting, and setup the exchange. Most sites (like www.homeexchange. com) require an annual fee, which can range from around $35 to $100.

While home exchange is an inexpensive alternative to paying for a hotel, remember to take some precautions.

Before the exchange, always lock any valuables away and check with your insurance company to make sure any possible, however unlikely, damages that might occur are covered. Also make sure the agreement states that your house will be "broom clean" when they leave, meaning tenants must wipe down flat surfaces and sweep before leaving.

— 2 —

Never Stop Learning

Some states encourage seniors to return to school by offering breaks on tuition and fees. For example, Vermont offers non-degree-seeking senior citizens free classes...

Better yet, seniors can apply for special grants to pay for classes. You can check out your local colleges for any financial assistance they offer to seniors or go to studentaid.ed.gov.

I read about a 100-year-old teacher in New Hampshire who received her bachelor's degree a day before she died. Spending 70 years working on a degree (like she did) may not be for everyone... but picking up a few college courses is a great way to keep your mind sharp.

— 3 —

Save 50%-80% on Almost Everything You Buy

I recommend you join the major "warehouse" retailer Costco today.

If you're already a member, you're probably familiar with the discounts it offers on myriad household items. But Costco runs a little-known program that lets shoppers buy high-end merchandise at up to 80% off. Costco calls its secret program the "Treasure Hunt," and it's like nothing I've ever seen.

Costco regularly stocks about 4,000 items. Of that, 3,000 items are priced with Costco's standard 14% mark up (a lot smaller than most retailers). But Costco designates the other 1,000 items for its Treasure Hunt.

It offers them at eye-popping discounts and then "plants" them throughout the stores like parents hiding Easter eggs for their kids. This is where you find great bargains of 50%-80% off.

These items aren't advertised and can't be found at every store. But if you know what you're looking at when you see it, you'll find deals like:

- Car insurance at 50% off

- Calvin Klein Jeans at 55% off

- Ralph Lauren sweaters at 70% off

- Samsung TVs at 65% off

- Pellegrino water at 50% off

- Dried chicken strips for dogs at 90% off

The list goes on and on. The Treasure Hunt items vary from store to store and state to state. And occasionally, truly fantastic items find their way into the stores. Some lucky shoppers have stumbled across fine art, luxury watches, and diamonds... and purchased them at ridiculous discounts.

Some consumers swear the shopping for high-end merchandise is the best in the world. And no one pesters you while you shop. What a great feeling, too... knowing you're not paying for the bricks and mortar and salespeople of some name brand.

You might think these deals aren't for you. (How many people shopping at Costco are in the market for rare art?) But Costco uses all kinds of items for its Treasure Hunt and rotates the stock all the time. That's the fun of the Treasure Hunt.

I once noticed a stack of Garmin GPS navigation systems I'd been considering buying for my car. They were on sale for 30% lower than anything I had seen.

The everyday prices and the Treasure Hunt are what keep people coming back over and over. Customers can walk in intending to buy a couple bundles of diapers and walk out with a GPS, a Tommy Hilfiger shirt, or a Fila warm-up jacket at a fraction of the cost you'd find elsewhere.

How Does It Provide the Deals?

Everything at Costco is 14% above cost. That's why *Consumer Reports* rates the company No. 1 in prices compared with other warehouses – Sam's Club, BJ's, and Wal-Mart Supercenters. And it's the main reason Fortune ranked Costco the No. 1 "Specialty Retailer" for three consecutive years.

To keep prices down, Costco is fanatical about holding the line on its costs. Heck, CEO Jim Sinegal's pay is only $350,000 a year (low for a position like that) with $100,000 in bonus if he meets company goals. One year, he refused the bonus because he felt he didn't earn it. Where on Wall Street would you ever see that from the CEO?

But the main value it creates comes from its bulk buying and selling. Costco "turns" its inventory 11.9 times a year, which means it has already sold all the purchases by the time it has to pay its suppliers. Thus, it has no financing costs for inventory, which means savings for you the customer.

So be prepared to buy 48 rolls of toilet paper or 20 pounds of rib-eye steaks or 20 pounds of cheese and 10 quarts of berries. But trust me, you won't be disappointed in the quality. The toilet paper – Kirkland brand – is truly the best I've ever used.

As I walked through the warehouse, I was impressed with the quality, particularly its food. It had gorgeous whole-wheat pastas, plump and dark berries and cherries. The colors were bright on the fresh foods, and the obvious lack of chemicals in many of the packaged products was encouraging to me.

And little did I know Costco is the No. 1 wine retailer in the U.S. (by dollar amount).

For instance, when I visited the store with my friends in Calistoga, California, we spent $450 on groceries. But I added things up and quickly realized a family of four could easily save 8%-10% a month.

If you currently spend $1,000 or more a month on "stuff" for your home, you'll save nearly $1,000 a year. And that's including your $50 fee to join.

— 4 —

How to Get Up to 50% Off Three Major Expenses

Half-Off College Tuition

Are you bothered by the expense of college? You can cut the cost almost in half.

Dozens of colleges, like George Washington University in Washington, D.C., have the gall to charge more than $47,000 year. That's more than 80% of the average family's annual income. According to *The Chronicle of Higher Education*, 151 colleges charge more than $50,000 (including room and board) as of 2014.

Private colleges charge an average $40,000 per year. Public colleges, of course, charge a lot less, especially for state residents – $18,391 in-state versus $31,701 out-of-state, according to College Board (includes room and board).

But what about local community colleges? If we look at the numbers for the 2013-2014 school year, the average cost for a full year of tuition and fees at a community college was only $3,154, compared with $8,893 at a public, four-year university and $28,500 at a private, four-year university.

So here's the secret way to get college at almost 50% off. Start at your local community college and transfer into the bigger college after two years. Hold off attending the university for two years while taking courses that transfer from your local community college instead. Save a ton of money but graduate in the same amount of time.

For example, Maryland law *requires* the University of Maryland to accept junior college transfers with a GPA of 2.5 and Cs in their major. Say you live in Baltimore County, Maryland. You could attend the Community College of Baltimore County for two years and then transfer to University of Maryland for your third and fourth years. The two-plus-two strategy would cost only about $61,440 (including room and board) for four years versus $109,680. You'd save almost $48,240 in tuition and fees over two years. Nearly 50% off.

If you're a parent looking for ways to save for your retirement and make sure your children get a great education, this is the trick. You save a lot of money, and your kids still get diplomas from a big-name school.

Half-Off Cable Bill

Nothing is worse than dealing with the hassle of a cable company.

Whether it's poor customer service, mismanagement, or the technician promising to show up sometime between 8 a.m. and 2 p.m., I wish Americans could collectively punish cable companies and go on strike. That won't happen. But there is a way to shave 50% a month off your cable bill.

Just call and ask for the best deal they have.

That's it. Just ask. If they refuse, threaten to move your service to another company (almost all cities in the U.S. have a competitor in town). Then ask to speak to the retention department. I once called Comcast and got my bill lowered from $170 a month to $89.

I've heard stories of some phone operators refusing to do anything. If that happens, just call back another day at a different time. Chances are slim the cable company will cancel your service entirely. After all, the company wants your money.

So whether it's Comcast, Time Warner, or Verizon, call your cable company and request a better rate. I can almost guarantee they'll lower your monthly bill. It may not be as drastic as a 50% reduction, but it's worth trying.

Worst case, you do have to shift over to the competitor. But after the initial hassle of setting up the service, you'll save hundreds of dollars a year.

40% Off Your Restaurant Bill

Dining out can get expensive. Thankfully, there's a way to save 40% off your restaurant bills.

When I first discovered this opportunity, I figured there was a catch. I didn't think it was possible to save this much money on restaurant tabs.

But if you go to www.restaurant.com, put your zip code in, and search for restaurants nearby, you can find at least 60%-off coupons for dozens of local restaurants. The first time I put in my Baltimore zip code, I found 65 restaurants within five miles and an amazing 230 places within 30 miles.

Each listed restaurant offers online gift certificates – or what I call their "Black Cards" – that allow you to purchase $25 of value for only $10. You can buy a $50 gift certificate for $20. You can buy a $100 gift certificate for only $40. If you and a group of friends go out and spend $100 on dinner, it would only cost the table $40 (plus the cost of the certificate). This can save you more than 40% on the total cost.

When I first found this website, I was a bit skeptical... So I decided to try it out on a little Thai place a few blocks from my office. Two friends and I bought a $50 certificate, ordered summer rolls with shrimp, Panang chicken, Pad Thai, and sautéed broccoli. We ended up paying $20 for a $48.76 tab.

The restaurant took the certificate no problem. After that, I used hundreds of dollars' worth of certificates at other restaurants... saving $1,000 or more.

Restaurant.com guarantees its certificates. The company lists its phone number and e-mail, and it is quick and helpful. If you're still not convinced, call the restaurant before you purchase a certificate to make sure it still accepts them.

You should also keep these two things in mind...

1) Each restaurant has a minimum purchase requirement that ranges between $35 and $50. This often excludes alcohol. If you're out with a couple friends, you'll surely hit the minimums.

2) Also, some restaurants automatically add 18% gratuity. This is only fair... You've found a special loophole, but those waiters and waitresses shouldn't be hit with lower tips.

The founders of Restaurant.com wanted to create a way for people to find new restaurants where they work and live. As they put it, "We wanted to encourage the celebration of dining, but make it more affordable."

— 5 —

Unusual Vacations Across America for Next to Nothing

Hundreds of Dollars Off an RV Rental

Traveling for almost nothing, getting 10 times the value it would normally cost, makes the adventure all the more exciting.

It's like the first blindfolded wine tasting I conducted in 1978 when we discovered that wine for $15 can taste as good as stuff the French wine snobs charged $65 for. What a joy.

There's a way to take an RV trip for just $24 a day... rather than the typical $200 per day.

How does this it work?

The company that rents these RVs is called Cruise America – you may have seen its vehicles with brightly painted landscapes on the sides. The company constantly needs to move its vehicles around the country. Rather than hire expensive drivers or moving companies, it seeks out "volunteers" to make the trip. In my case, I got a 90% discount on what it normally charges. You can do the same thing.

Here's how I did it. I flew one-way on Southwest into Las Vegas ($189) and took a cab ride ($30) to a lot run by Cruise America.

From Las Vegas, I drove to the Grand Canyon... Sedona, Arizona... and through the desert of northern Arizona on my way to the drop-off in

Phoenix. I had nearly unlimited miles and up to six days to make the trek. Best of all... I got to use a $95,000 RV for just $24 a day.

After my drive, I flew home from Phoenix – only $179 on Southwest.

Total cost – airfare, gas, and RV rental... everything for five nights and six days – was only $700.

Keep in mind, you don't need any special license. Your regular driver's license works fine. Driving an RV is simple. And most campgrounds are designed to make it easy.

Cruise America has hundreds of rental locations in the U.S. and Canada.

Camping World offers other great RV rental deals. Camping World has dozens of rental locations across the U.S. Much like Cruise America, Camping World rents RVs that need to be moved between locations.

Camping World's deals often range from $9.95 to $29.95 per day.

A Working Wine Vacation that Feels Free

Consider a "crush" vacation. Working the crush means helping a winery pick, destem, press, and move juice, barrels, and waste during the harvest. It is one of the most unique cultural experiences you can imagine.

This is a physically demanding vacation. But in the end, you get a vacation and a few bottles of good wine to take home.

For the 2007, 2008, and 2009 harvest, I traveled to Calistoga, California, and stayed with my friends, owners of the Mutt Lynch Winery. Their Sonoma winery produces some of the best unwooded (fermented in steel tanks rather than traditional oak ones) chardonnays I've ever tasted. The description on their website says it all...

"Fresh, juicy fruit aromas and flavors of peaches, pears, and apples, with a creamy and zingy finish. The fruit 'jumps out of the glass'..."

For more than a week, I worked for the Lynch family. I did everything from helping the grape pickers pluck dead leaves under a warm September sun, to dumping the pomace (the solids left over after juicing) at the end of the day.

I didn't get paid a thing, and the work conditions were sometimes a bit difficult. But the benefits included room, board, and a great experience. Most importantly, I learned about winemaking – from world experts.

One of the experts I learned from, Phyllis, is half owner of a winery called Deux Amis that shares space with Mutt Lynch.

I watched (and helped) Phyllis and her colleague Brenda measure levels of sugar and pH in the fermenting juice and "punch down" grape skins floating in the nascent wine to ensure a uniform fermentation.

Seeing them monitor and adjust the winemaking process to tease the flavor they want from every unique batch of grapes taught me how much of an artist's touch great winemakers bring to their work. It's not the sort of perspective you get from reading the Wine Spectator.

Phyllis and her partner Jim have been in the wine business of northern California for more than 70 years combined. It was an honor to learn from them.

It turns out there are dozens of small local wineries like Mutt Lynch and Deux Amis around the world that desperately need help during the harvest season. These tiny wineries simply can't afford to pay for full-time help. Instead, they offer free room and board to ordinary folks who are looking for a memorable experience.

In most of America's wine-producing regions – including Napa and Sonoma in California, Willamette Valley in Oregon, and the Finger Lakes region in New York – you can work a crush. If you're interested in a wine-country vacation, I recommend you contact your favorite vineyard directly.

For example, some small and less-known vineyards in Ohio love having volunteers help them with the harvest. Simply register your interest prior to the season by contacting the individual winery, or just visit the winery on public picking days that get advertised in local newspapers. In Ohio, you can try these vineyards:

- Debonné Vineyards in Madison, Ohio

- Troutman Vineyards in Wooster, Ohio

- Rainbow Hills Vineyards in Newcomerstown, Ohio

- Slate Run Vineyard in Canal Winchester, Ohio

By the way, my friends at Mutt Lynch specialize in dog-themed wines. Their wines include names like Merlot Over and Unleashed Chardonnay. Give them a call or check out their website.

And it goes without saying, by mentioning their info, I get nothing from my friends... other than a thanks.

Mutt Lynch Winery
www.muttlynchwinery.com

Deux Amis Winery
www.deuxamiswines.com

— 6 —

How to Get Almost Anything For Free

In 2003, an Arizona man named Deron Beal put together a network of 30 or so friends and some Tucson-based nonprofits to help those less fortunate.

The plan was to collect stuff people no longer wanted and give it to those in need. They envisioned it as a way to reduce landfill waste and encourage people to recycle their belongings.

They expanded the network nationwide and to 85 different countries. They opened it to anyone worldwide, not just the needy. The network is called Freecycle. You can find it online at www.freecycle.org, and it's a great way save hundreds of dollars (even thousands if you have the time) on household items.

Here's how it works...

You can sign up for free. It only takes a few minutes, and you'll be connected with people in your area who are looking to both give and receive things. There's no obligation to do anything. You can get things, and you're not required to give anything in exchange...

It's simple to participate. You'll receive daily e-mails informing you what's being "freecycled" in your town. (But don't worry, the company won't sell your e-mail address to any third party.)

If you see something you like, send an e-mail to the person offering the item. Make sure to be enthusiastic in your e-mail. Some items may be popular, and the person offering it decides who gets it.

Also realize, it's your responsibility to go and pick up your item, although most of the places will be located within 10 miles of your house. Some people will just leave the item on their front porch. You just pick it up – no cash exchanged.

If you're looking for an item that's not being offered, you can post a "wanted" message. If anyone has that item and is willing to give it up, they can send you an e-mail. Doing this is completely free!

Freecycle is a great way to pick up items you need around the house.

There are many ways to get experiences for free as well...

Free Cruises for a 'Gentleman Host'

If you can dance, socialize, and are a man between the ages of 40 and 68, I have the dream getaway for you.

On many ocean cruises, women outnumber men by a wide margin, especially among senior passengers. To balance things out, cruise lines recruit male social hosts to dance and socialize with female passengers. The only requirement for these hosts is to be able to carry a conversation with a stranger and know formal dance styles like swing, fox trot, and waltz.

The biggest benefit to becoming a "gentleman host" is the nearly FREE cruise you get in return. By signing up to become a gentleman host, you get to spend several weeks a year at sea where you can wine and dine on luxury ships for next to nothing.

Depending upon the cruise line, you may pay a small daily fee of $25. But compared to the thousands of dollars you'd otherwise spend for the same accommodations, this is a great bargain.

Benefits vary from cruise to cruise. However, gentleman hosts typically receive:

- Dining-room privileges

- Regular cabin accommodations

- Beverage and laundry allowances

- Round-trip airfare for some cruises

- Inclusion in shore excursions

- A gratuities allowance

- A 20% discount from Jos. A. Bank men's clothier

- A chance to travel the world and meet new friends

Cruise lines offering "gentleman host" programs include some of the biggest names in the industry: the Delta Queen Steamboat Company, Regent Seas Cruises, Holland America Line, Crystal Cruises, Silversea Cruises, Fred Olsen Cruises, and NYK Cruises.

Chicago-based company The Working Vacation, owned by Lauretta Blake, is a recruitment agency for gentleman hosts on cruise ships. Contact Lauretta Blake's agency at www.compassspeakers.com to see if you qualify to be a gentleman host.

And of course, you can contact the cruise lines directly.

Another Way to Cruise for Nearly Free

For anyone who doesn't fit the criteria to be a gentleman host, there is another way to travel for free. Sixth Star Entertainment is looking for a variety of people to provide entertainment.

Whether you're an art history expert, a computer expert, or a caricature artist, you can have your passage (and a guest's) on a luxury cruise ship paid for. You just have to be an expert at your craft and be able to pay a small daily fee of up to $65.

You can be an expert in fields ranging from geography, to art history, to health. You'll need to be prepared to give a presentation (preferably visual) every sailing day.

Daily lectures range from 45 to 60 minutes. Caricature artists spend about two hours during each day at sea drawing for passengers. After that, you can spend the day like any other passenger.

Free Golf and Golf Lessons

If you love to play golf, there's a way you can play for free and even generate a little income. (You don't have to be any good… you just have to love the game.)

I learned this secret from my friend Hank. And to be honest, at first I thought Hank had fallen on hard times.

Hank was one of my internal medicine instructors at the University of North Carolina… and a highly respected liver specialist. That's why I was surprised to see him standing at the first tee with a clipboard in hand. He was the starter that morning at UNC-Chapel Hill's Finley Golf Course.

A starter maintains the starting times and order of groups playing each day. They ensure golfers get off the first tee promptly and keep track of the number of golfers on the course. That's it. This is not a full-time job. In fact, calling it a job is blasphemy. Anyone can do this.

"Hank… what are you doing here?" I asked him.

"Getting free golf," he replied.

Hank was semiretired. He loved to be outside… And he loved to play golf. Green fees at Finley (the price for a round of golf) can run up to $100 during peak time. So Hank worked a couple days a week as a starter during its busy times. In return, his golf games were free the rest of the week.

The money wasn't a big deal to Hank. He was still a part-time doctor… He just loved to be around a golf course.

So if you love golf, are able to pair off players, assign starting numbers, and greet the public on weekend mornings, I suggest you contact your local country club or visit a nearby golf course and ask them to hire you as a starter.

Another way you can play golf for free is through the Professional Golf Association's (PGA) Play Golf America marketing effort.

Among the freebies, the PGA offers...

- Free club fittings with fair market trade-in value offered for your old clubs

- Free Lessons with a PGA professional

- Two-for-one golf lessons with a PGA pro if you have an American Express Card

- Free range balls for your children

- A free round of golf for young ladies accompanied by a paying adult

By the way, the lessons are from real PGA instructors who donate their time.

Each year, more than 7,500 PGA professionals nationwide give nearly 150,000 free lessons for those in need of a tune-up. Give it a try.

To take advantage of these offers, go to www.playgolfamerica.com. Click on one of the choices in the left column under "Featured Programs." Then enter your zip code and a list of programs in your area will appear. There you'll find several things you can do for free. Make sure to take a look... Some of these events are only offered in certain months.

See Movies for Free

If you like movies, as I do, you'll like these deals...

Free Movies: Many theaters offer free showings of family movies, especially during the summer. Regal Entertainment Group, for example, hosts a Free Family Film Festival every Tuesday and Wednesday morning from June to August.

Movies from AAA: Check the American Automobile Association (AAA) online. Through its site, you can get tickets to Regal, United Artists, and

Edwards Theatres for $87.50 for a 10 pack of tickets in many areas of the U.S. (you have to be a member to get the deals).

Costco Warehouse: At retailer Costco, you can get discount movie tickets online to Regal Theaters for $8.50 per ticket when you purchase four.

Free Online Trading

Unless you're a daytrader, there's a way you can trade online for free. If you don't need a trading account with a lot of bells and whistles or hand-holding, Bank of America has an account service for you.

As of 2014, Bank of America offers 30 free trades per month for account holders with at least $25,000 total in their deposit accounts (such as CDs, savings, and checking accounts).

The trading service, Bank of America Investment Services, is powered by Merrill Lynch and allows clients to trade stocks, bonds, mutual funds, and ETFs up to 30 times per month online without having to pay commission fees. You will need to have a self-directed trading account.

Free Phone Calls

If there's one thing that irritates me, it's paying the phone company.

I'll admit it, I use my cell phone a lot. And whether it's texting or sharing pictures with friends and family, my cell phone is always on. So when that $100 phone bill rolls around each month, I only have myself to blame.

But in 2014 – in the midst of a poor economy – less than a third of cell-phone users in the U.S. had cut back on their cell-phone spending, as reported by *Forbes*. The average cell-phone user spent about $600 a year on wireless phone service. And that estimate doesn't include the many extras and add-ons cell-phone companies charge, which easily swell a bill into the hundreds monthly.

What if instead of handing over thousands of dollars a year to the phone company, you could pump that money into a savings account or investment vehicle? Well, I discovered a way to never pay a phone bill again. Here's how it works...

If you live in North America, you can call any landline or cell phone in the U.S. or Canada for FREE by using an online phone service called Skype. You may have heard about Skype if you have children. That's how I heard about it.

Signing up is simple. As of 2014, there's no prepayment, no minimum use, no subscription, no monthly fee, no nothing. With Skype, you can call other Skype users around the world for FREE.

It's easy to use, too...

First, you download the software from Skype's website that enables you to make these FREE phone calls.

Once you download the Skype software onto your cell phone or computer, install it onto your hard drive. Then you're all set to call.

If you have Skype and want to call a non-Skype user, you can pay $2.99 per month for unlimited calling within the U.S. and Canada. This is much less than the $50 a month the phone company would charge. And you can take your phone with you and use it wherever there's Internet service. If you're willing to pay a little more, you can make unlimited calls to more than 40 different countries.

I suggest you tell your closest friends and family members about Skype right away so you can start saving and investing for your retirement dreams.

By the way, Skype is great for overseas calls. If you're in the U.S. or Canada and calling any other country, OR if you're in any other country and calling landline or mobile numbers in the U.S. or Canada, the standard SkypeOut rates apply.

Skype even allows you to hold a conference call with up to nine other people.

Still, the best part for me is the video feature. I hate talking on the phone, but when I can see the other person as I talk, I actually enjoy the call.

All you need is a webcam on both computers (or cell phones) and you can talk AND see each other simultaneously. It's as close as you can get to real life without being together. And the video calls are also FREE...

If you're looking to cut back your phone bill to zero, Skype is something I highly recommend.

After canceling my landline service and slashing my cell-phone minutes nearly in half, I saved $564 per year.

Even More Phone Deals

For those of you who aren't interested in calling people on your computer, I have a couple other great money savers.

Vonage

Vonage works much like Skype. As of 2014, you get 400 minutes of outbound calling across the U.S. and Canada and unlimited calling to other Vonage customers for as little as $12.99 a month.

The best part is, you use Vonage anywhere. All you need to do is travel with a small adapter that you can use with any high-speed Internet connection. And your existing phone number might be eligible to be transferred to Vonage.

With Vonage, you don't even need to have your computer turned on to make phone calls. All you need is to connect the Vonage adapter to your Internet, and connect your phone to the adapter. Then you can start calling.

Google Voice

Google has its own Skype-like calling product called Google Voice. As of 2014, it offers UNLIMITED FREE calling within the U.S. and absolutely rock-bottom international call prices.

With Google Voice, you can make and receive calls to or from any other Google users for free through your computer or cell phone. Sprint customers can use their cell-phone number as their Google Voice number.

Save 75% on Home Improvement

The next time you start a project, skipping the home improvement store could save you more than 75%.

Habitat for Humanity runs ReStore. These are home improvement outlets that sell new and used goods such as appliances, building materials, and furniture. The goods are donated from individuals and businesses. You can purchase the items at a fraction of the retail price. A portion of your purchase goes to fund the construction of Habitat for Humanity homes.

I was making some improvements on my home in Augusta, Georgia and found a brand-new basement door originally priced at $180. I only paid $40.

Most of the items are priced under $100. You can save hundreds on home improvement projects. The stores are like a permanent garage sale, but with many new things, like my door.

Not all Habitat for Humanity ReStores carry the same items, since everything is donated. If your local store doesn't have what you're looking for, check back every week or so. Their inventory constantly changes.

— 7 —

Learn to Barter

Another way I've discovered to get the things you need without spending your cash is bartering.

This isn't technically "free" because you'll be exchanging things of value. And the IRS expects you to pay taxes on the exchange. But it's a great way to get value out of assets that are otherwise wasting away.

Let me explain…

I'm sure you're familiar with the basic concept of bartering: swapping goods or services without using money. Bartering is the world's oldest form of commerce. American colonists used to barter beaver pelts and tobacco for corn and ammunition. (Using the term "buck" to mean money comes from the trading of deerskins back in the early days.)

Bartering came back into vogue during the Great Depression, when people had little money but lots of time to exchange things they each wanted and needed.

Bartering is enjoying a renaissance again in the 21st century. People use the concept creatively to get things like vacation homes and health care.

But before you read on, there are a few things you need to understand about bartering…

1. **Determine the value of what you're swapping**.

The key to bartering is to understand the value of the item or talent you can offer. You'll have to agree that the value of the things you're swapping is identical. Otherwise, one party will have to add cash or another item to the swap.

Depending on the item you have, there are a number of resources that can help. If you need to value a house, Zillow.com is a good place to start. Just remember that Zillow uses data from recent sales and listings in your area along with actual inputs from the owner of the property. You can also look on real estate sites in your area to get an idea of how properties are priced.

For cars, you can use the websites Kellybluebook.com or Cars.com to give yourself a good idea of your vehicle's local value.

For more specialized items, auction websites like eBay or personal-ad sites like Craigslist can give you an idea of what people will pay for items like yours.

2. Decide if you want to use a formal barter exchange.

One problem with bartering is finding someone who wants what you have. Over the years, people have tried to expand the network of potential trading partners by creating barter exchanges.

Often, these networks are designed for people in specific professions to swap like services. For example, it's common to find exchanges set up for retailers, dentists, doctors, or operators of small hotels or inns.

The IRS formally recognized these exchanges in U.S. Tax Code 1.6045-1. The tax code says:

> The term barter exchange means any person with members or clients that contract either with each other or with such person to trade or barter property or services either directly or through such person. The term does not include arrangements that provide solely for the informal exchange of similar services on a noncommercial basis.

This means that if you join a formal group organized as a "barter exchange," the exchange is obligated to report to you and the IRS the fair market value of things exchanged. Annually, you'll get a 1099-B form – the same form you might already get from your stockbroker.

Personally, I prefer dealing with people directly and deciding the value between us. Unless you plan to do a lot of exchanging, you should stick with local organizations like Craigslist and Freecycle.

For those of you who like the protection and organization of formal exchanges, they do offer a few benefits. They get rid of the hassle of calculating and reporting the barter taxes that the IRS expects of us. The exchanges do the work for you. As a member, you get a statement at yearend that tells you how much you've earned from bartering.

And, yes, when you barter...

3. **You must pay taxes**.

People don't like to hear this. But yes, bartering is taxable. The IRS expects you to report the fair market value of things exchanged. Exchanges do make this easier by tracking your trades and providing you a 1099-B at yearend.

Swapping Homes

One of the most creative assets to barter is your home. It's a great way to get a short vacation cheap...

There are several exchanges that do this, but the most popular is HomeExchange.com.

As of 2014, it costs only $9.95 a month. If you don't complete an exchange in one year, you get a second year for free. You can click on listings that take you to a map of worldwide listings. There are tens of thousands of listings across more than 100 countries. It's hard to imagine you can't find a place to swap.

Craigslist is a great way to find vacation swaps. The best thing about Craigslist is it's totally free. It's so easy, I frequently used Craigslist over the years to list my home in Augusta, Georgia for rent during the annual Masters golf tournament. (We talked about that in Part II Chapter 4.)

I once found a real estate listing for a Beverly Hills, CA home with "17 bedrooms, 30 baths, swimming pool, and hot tub." The place was a villa-style mansion with wood burning or gas fireplaces in almost every room, hardwoods floors, a great view of the city, tile roofing, security system, and separate parking garage.

It also had a built in dishwasher, intercom, range and oven, refrigerator, marble floors, bar, and wine cellar. Living here would be like spending your life in a five star hotel, without all the annoying guests.

Note that the vacation swaps are usually one-to-one swaps. That means you deal directly with the other party.

One advantage of one-to-one is you'll get a chance to talk and build trust with the other party before finally swapping homes. Also, since many people are swapping second and third homes, there's not much pressure to do it at exactly the same time, either.

But be sure to agree on some basic things when bartering your home. Decide upfront who will do the cleaning. For example, I always use the phrase "broom clean." And I clarify it so people know it means wipe down flat surfaces, vacuum, and sweep. There's nothing as frustrating as coming home to a mess.

As you've seen, there are plenty of ways to barter for either a home or a vacation. Since you've worked hard your entire life to take time off, bartering is a great way to do it cheaply...

If you're particularly ambitious, **you can try bartering as a way to sell your home**...

Once you've agreed on value, it's just a matter of working out the details of swapping or assuming loans, or if needed, creating new mortgages for each party on their new home.

And check with your tax advisor on home swaps because you are allowed $250,000 in capital gain exemptions from the sale of a house ($500,000 if married), and this may affect your situation.

Selling homes is another case where formal exchanges are useful...

Tradeaway.com, for instance, charges nothing for a regular listing and only $3 for a more detailed property listing. This site currently has several hundred real estate listings and almost all of them are willing to trade for even more than just another property. I found one ranch in New Mexico where the listing was willing to swap for beachfront, heavy equipment, or classic trucks.

Simple Things to Barter

I can picture some of you saying, "Doc I'll never swap for a vacation or home. It's too big and risky." If that's true, this next section is for you... and it's fun, too.

There are several sites that allow you to swap for books or music.

On many sites, books are mailed to you for free from other members (although you have to pay postage to return them). You can even buy new books at huge discounts of 50% or more.

If you still use textbooks, you can find websites where the prices are about 50% of a new book and most of the books are described as nearly new condition. This is a simple way to cut costs for college students. Before signing up, spend a few minutes searching the site to see if any of the books you need are available. If you are finishing school, list your books for sale.

There's little risk in bartering anything. Even the president of the United States barters – he gets a free home and garden in exchange for working. I'll bet they didn't know they could swap for food, too...

My No. 1 Food Exchange

Bartering for food is much easier than you might think. In many early societies, food was used as a form of money. Staples like salt, tea, and fine spices were so valuable, they were under lock and key in some societies.

In modern times, it's much easier to barter for foods. My favorite time to do it is on Saturday mornings.

On Saturdays, take vegetables and fruit from your garden and go to your local "farmer's market." You may be able to exchange your goods for things like eggs, honey, and breads. The best thing about it is that you don't have to stand at a table and try to sell your blackberries or tomatoes. Instead you get to wander the area and trade for things you run across and want.

A good friend of mine, Lisa, in Minnesota took deer meat and apples by the bushel to her local Saturday market to trade for fish, rice, other fruits, potatoes, and pies. Again, all at no cost.

By the way, one of the oldest ways of bartering for food is sharecropping. This is where the landowner gives up some land ("the back 40 acres") in exchange for the sharecropper's labor on the other 120 acres.

In California wine country, vineyard owners often allow farm supervisors (and a handful of pickers) to plant gardens on the ends of vineyard rows in exchange for their labor.

Bartering is one of the best-kept secrets there is. In a recession, it's a great way to save on cash and cash expenses. Bartering is one of the great and easy ways to get things for next to nothing. And not only to get food, but also to get medical care.

— 8 —

You Need to Know Your Credit Score

Before you apply for a credit card, a car loan, or a home loan, you need to know one essential piece of information – your credit score.

When you apply for a loan or line of credit, the company offering the loan looks up your credit score to judge your creditworthiness. Knowing your score helps you bargain for a better deal. But a credit score isn't easy to obtain...

Many different companies and organizations offer credit scores: FICO Score, Equifax, and VantageScore are just a few examples. The scores from the credit-ratings agency FICO are the most commonly used.

In 2013, FICO announced its new program – FICO Score Open Access. This program allows lenders to share credit scores with their customers. This service is still in limited use... The two credit-card companies using it are Barclaycard and First Bankcard. FICO is pushing to roll this program out to more financial service providers throughout the U.S. So call your lender and ask if it has implemented FICO Score Open Access.

Also commonly used are the credit reports from TransUnion, Experian, and Equifax. These companies offer *free credit scores*. However, you have to sign up for a membership, which you'll have to pay for after a free trial period (usually about 14 days).

Beware... Canceling within the trial period can be next to impossible. We tested this and couldn't cancel the membership before a $14.95 charge showed up on our card (even though we tried to cancel several times).

> ### DO WHAT I DO
>
> **Request one annual report about every nine months or so.**

Federal law entitles each of us to free annual credit reports from the three major providers. The government website for this is annualcreditreport.com. Do what I do... Request one about every nine months or so.

Rotate which company you get one from so you get new and sometimes slightly different information. Sometimes a mark will show up on the report that can easily be taken off with a letter to the correct company.

— 9 —

Seven 'Don't Waste Your Money' Tips

1. Change your oil every 3,000 miles… only if you want to spend a lot more than you need to.

Most modern cars are able to run efficiently up to 7,500 miles between oil changes. Unless you have severe driving conditions that wear on your car – like mountainous terrain or constant stop-and-go driving – save yourself the cash. Just make sure you check your car's warranty, in case something does go wrong.

> ### DO WHAT I DO
>
> **Take one multivitamin a week in case you don't get all the micronutrients you need from your diet.**

2. Stop taking multivitamins! Research shows that not only are they a waste of money but now it looks like they may be harmful.

Studies show people who take multivitamins every day have an increased risk of diabetes, lung cancer, and prostate cancer. One study even showed a slight increase in death… although this might be because of people on their last leg who are trying anything to stay alive.

Do what I do… Take one multivitamin a week in case you don't get all the micronutrients you need from your diet.

3. **Cut your laundry detergent costs by 75%.** Many detergent makers market "concentrated" versions of their soap. These are the versions with "2X" on the bottle. In theory, this means you can use less of the stuff with each load. The manufacturers lowered the measurement line in the cup and raised the price on the same volume.

But guess what? Most people dump into the washer the same amount they used before, wasting lots of money over the course of a year... You don't need all that detergent to clean your clothes. I use only about a fourth of the cup they provide (probably a third of what the manufacturer recommends). My clothes are just as clean as before, but I save $40-$50 a year.

4. **Don't waste your money on products that claim you need a 100 SPF to protect your skin from sun damage.**

One easy way to think about SPF (Sun Protection Factor) is to multiply it by how long you plan to be outside. For example, if you plan to use 100 SPF, and you're of a normal complexion... multiply 100 by 10 minutes, you get 1,000 minutes.

> ### *DO WHAT I DO*
> Try to stay indoors between 11 a.m. and 3 p.m. And don't use sunscreen with an SPF higher than 8.

That's 16 hours of protection you don't need. Worse, the sunscreen chemicals themselves are toxic to the skin. Instead, do what I do... Try to stay indoors between 11 a.m. and 3 p.m. And don't use sunscreen with an SPF higher than 8.

5. **The "Energy Star" labels are worthless.** Appliance makers slap these government-issued stickers on their products to signify they are energy-efficient. I used to imagine it was a valuable rating when I was younger and hugged more trees. But an investigation by the U.S. Government Accountability Office (GAO) proved me wrong.

The GAO submitted a bunch of phony products for the Environmental Protection Agency (EPA) rating. Several of them got approved. One of them was an 18-inch-tall gas-powered alarm clock. The EPA also approved a "room cleaner" that consisted of a space heater, fly traps, and a feather duster. The stickers clearly mean nothing.

The next time you're comparison-shopping for a new appliance, ignore the little star sticker. Instead, read the actual energy usage numbers given on the appliances (usually on a bright yellow sticker).

6. **Be careful which printer you buy**. Certain companies put computer chips in their ink cartridges that stop the printer from printing when it reaches a certain age... even if there is still plenty of ink left.

These chips also prevent you refilling the ink. For instance, Epson uses ink cartridges with smart chips. The company claims the ink is no good after a certain period of time. Hogwash, I've had a cartridge in my Lexmark printer for three years that still works fine.

My co-worker took her Hewlett-Packard ink cartridge to Walgreens and paid just $10 for a refill (which typically cost $25 new).

7. **Throw out your heart pills**. A review published in the *British Medical Journal* found that for patients recovering from a stroke, exercise was just as effective as medication. People with heart disease or prediabetes had similar results... *Drugs were no more effective than exercise.*

This is more proof you don't need to waste your money on medications that can come with a dozen or more harmful side effects. Even better, you don't need to do intense exercise, like marathon training. Regular moderate exercise is enough to get the benefits. Just 20 to 30 minutes a day, four or five days a week helps. I go on short walks during the day or walk on the treadmill while I read.

— 10 —

Month by Month: The Best Time to Buy Nearly Everything

Loopholes in industries' annual sales cycles, consumer trends, and sales all create windows of opportunity to buy everything – from big-ticket items to groceries – at bargain prices.

This chapter compiles those loopholes month by month.

Some of the tips repeat on consecutive months, because these loopholes don't follow a strict monthly calendar. But they should give you the information you need to save hundreds (or thousands) on the purchases you need to make.

January

January is the best time of year to buy **carpeting** and **new flooring**. Demand hits its high point in November and December when people prepare their homes for the holidays. Demand drops in January and prices plummet. For example, some flooring companies, like Empire Today, offer 60% or more off hardwood and carpet.

January is the best time of the year to buy **bedding** and **linens**. In 1878, John Wanamaker, founder of the landmark Philadelphia department store Wanamaker's, declared January to be the time for a sale on bed linens. He termed it a "white sale" because at the time, linens only came in white.

In January every year, Wanamaker put on the white sale and sold bed linens at steep discounts. Retailers have carried on the tradition ever since. Look for sales at retailers like Bed Bath & Beyond and J.C. Penney.

January is the best time to buy **outdoor gear**. Sales for summer outdoor gear slow in the dead of winter... So look for retailers like REI and Dick's Sporting Goods to offer great deals on summer gear (like bicycles). Although if you live in a warm climate, you may not find as good "off season" deals as you would in snowy winter areas like Maine...

February

February is the best time to buy **a house and furnish it**. Stores are getting rid of indoor furniture, making way for the spring line. As for homes, statistics show that people just don't buy homes in the winter. Who wants to house hunt in the snow or move when it's cold?

February is a great month to save on **produce like broccoli, cauliflower, and winter squash**. Farmers harvest these vegetables during winter, and the vegetables are at their peak, so they're not shipped unripe from warmer climates.

February is the best month to buy **a boat**. Boat sales are slow in the winter months, especially February. And dealers are trying to clear their floors for the next year's models. You can find price cuts at dealerships or through merchants at boat shows.

February is the best month to purchase **a new camera**. Manufacturers release new camera models in January and February right after the Christmas sales. So if you don't mind buying the previous year's model, you can save more than $100 on some of the higher-end cameras. In early 2014, Best Buy offered up to $300 off on select models.

March

March is the best time to save on **winter coats** and **sports gear** as stores switch inventories to spring apparel. Major retailers like Sports Authority and Target offer up to 65% off some items ranging from gloves to jackets to snowboards. Clearance racks of last season's stuff are even better (up to 80% off). I once bought a $100 Nike jacket (2009 season) for $20.

March is the best time to buy **a snow blower** if you're looking to prepare for next winter. Major retailers, like Home Depot, start to fill their stores with spring and summer essentials this time of year. And bulky items like snow blowers take up space for new items. You can find discounts of up to 40% in many stores.

March is the best time of year to save on **frozen foods**. The National Frozen and Refrigerated Foods Association dubbed March "National Frozen Foods" month. The association will send a special insert in your local newspaper in March with coupons from participating brands (including Dole and Tyson)... Just look for the insert in your Sunday paper and stock up on frozen foods.

March is a great time of year to get your **gardening tools**. Stores offer sales on items like garden shovels, racks, and hoes right before the gardening season gets into full swing. (Don't forget... gardening is one of the easiest ways to follow my No. 1 best guideline to improve your health – movement. So get up and get moving in the garden.)

April

April is the best time to buy **cookware** and **digital cameras**. Camera companies know spring and summer are peak seasons for camera buyers... people are taking pictures of vacations, proms, and graduations. New models are sent to stores in March. So if you don't need the latest version, you can find a great deal on the previous year's models.

If you're starting to get into shape for the summer, April is the best time to buy **sneakers**. Spring is when people start going to the gym and outdoors to work out... many of these people need new shoes. Manufacturers make and stockpile shoes all winter and retailers – like Foot Locker – take advantage of the spring wave of customers by offering great deals on sneakers. So look for coupons or sales on your favorite brand.

May

May is one of the best times of the year to buy **a new vacuum cleaner**.

In June, companies introduce new vacuum cleaner models... as people get into spring-cleaning mode. Retailers typically lower prices in April and May to make room for the newer models. Some retailers offer up to 25% off select models. Manufacturers, like Bissell, also offer special discounts and free shipping when you order directly from them online.

May is the best time of year to buy **a new mattress** or **box spring**. Retailers make room for new models meant to entice spring-time cleaners looking to spruce up the bedroom and the kitchen. You can find greatly reduced prices on older models. You can also find great deals on a **fridge** this month for the same reason.

June

The best time to buy **a gym membership** is June. Gyms get a lot of signups around the first of the year when people are making weight loss their New Year's resolution. But gyms don't usually see many new members in the spring and early summer.

Check out local gyms for special offers or haggle your way into getting the membership fee waived. Just be sure to pay your balance in full each month.

If you're in the market for **furniture**, June is one of the two months to buy. Stores are clearing out old inventory to make way for the manufacturers' new releases. You can get great deals at retailers like Crate and Barrel as they prepare to stock new furniture in August.

If you're thinking of sprucing up your house, June is the best time of year to buy **paint**. Paint sales typically fall as the temperature rises – people spend less time indoors and play more outside. So to help boost summer sales, retailers offer great deals on interior and exterior paint. Just visit your local home improvement store or paint retailer to save.

You can also find great deals on **champagne** and **sparkling wines**. June is wedding season, and liquor stores lower prices to entice couples to purchase the beverage. One of my favorite values year in and year out is Mumm's non-vintage Brut.

June is typically the best production month for **butter**. Grasses and pastures are growing, and cows are grazing more. Rising inventories means prices are low. And since butter freezes for six months, you can stock up for the fall and your holiday baking.

July

July is another great month to stock up on **paint**... The summer is one of the slowest times of year for paint sales. In most parts of the U.S., it's too hot to paint outside... or inside, since you can't leave the windows open for fresh air. Take advantage of sales on both interior and exterior paint... and do the work for the cooler months.

July is also a great month to buy **furniture**. Twice a year – in February and August – new furniture (styles for the seasons) hit showrooms. Stores need to clear out older styles to make room for the new, so many have sales around this time July. Retailers like Value City Furniture can offer up to 60% off inventory. Higher-end retailers like Pottery Barn often have savings worth $1,000 or more on furniture costing $4,000.

July is one of the best times of year to buy **a new men's suit**... In the summer, retailers need to begin making room for new fall suits, so you can find great deals on spring suits. Look for discounts at retailers like J.C. Penney, Men's Wearhouse, and Joseph A. Bank.

August

August is a great month to save on **computers**. Students are preparing to go back to school, and retailers offer sales on computers – including laptops and desktops.

August is the best month to start stocking up on **back-to-school supplies**. Many states offer sales-tax holidays for back-to-school necessities like computers, clothing, and school supplies. The holidays typically last for a couple days and can save you hundreds of dollars. Connecticut and Maryland both give a full week. North Carolina even extends the offer to sports equipment.

August is the best time to buy **a new lawnmower**. In August, retailers like Lowe's and Home Depot start making room for fall products. Lawnmowers take up a lot of store space, and grass has been growing for months. People who needed mowers urgently bought in the spring. So retailers try to move out the machines with big sales this time of year.

Late August is also the time to save on **patio furniture**. Sales for patio furniture tend to spike in the spring and summer as people get ready to spend time outside. But in late August, major retailers need to get rid of patio furniture to make room for holiday decorations.

September

September is the best time to buy **china** and **flatware**. The summer wedding season is ending and sales tend to be highest as newlywed couples buy or are given flatware. You can find great deals at retailers like Bed Bath & Beyond. Target occasionally offers sets of china for as much as 50% off.

September is one of the best times to buy **small electronics**. Retailers like Amazon and Best Buy need to move out older electronic models to prepare for the coming holiday season.

September is the best time of year to buy **local produce**. It's when fruits and vegetables come to market... from broccoli to apples to pumpkins. I love to hit local farmers markets on the weekends to pick up fresh produce, especially things I don't grow at home. But if you can't get to a farmers market... many grocery stores now offer locally grown produce.

Buying locally helps support your local economy and means you're getting fresher produce since it's not traveling from hundreds – even thousands – of miles away.

Like August, September is another great time to buy **new patio furniture**. As the summer season ends and the weather cools, sales of outdoor furniture dip. Retailers are trying to make room for holiday decorations. So you'll see big discounts on patio furniture. Some retailers – like Home Depot – may even throw in free shipping when you order online.

October

October is the best time to buy **air conditioners** and **other large appliances**. Once temperatures cool, people stop buying air conditioners and prices fall to move old inventory. Prices of most other large appliances, like **washers** and **dryers**, also drop. Companies are rolling out new models, so retailers will cut prices to get older stock out of the store.

October is the best month to buy **a new car**... Manufacturers introduce new model-year cars toward the end of the summer. By fall, dealers try to move "leftover" cars from the previous model year before the next year's models show up at their lots and devalue the "old" cars.

October is one of the best times of year to stock up on **wine**. In September and October, grape harvests come in – called the "crush." These new grapes are soon turned into wine. And in a few weeks or months, they'll be put in barrels. To make room, wineries must release the old vintages from these barrels before the new harvest is in.

That means bottling old wine and selling it quickly. To make room for new inventory, retailers mark down overstocked wines. You'll find great deals in almost every price range and quality.

November

November is also the perfect time to stock up on your favorite **wines**... for the same reasons as in October. You can usually find a great selection at low prices.

November is one of the best times to buy **frozen turkeys**... But wait until after Thanksgiving. Demand for frozen turkeys drops sharply after Thanksgiving. So you can find great deals from grocery stores trying to clear out their surplus. In 2013, I bought a frozen turkey for $0.25 per pound.

And you can use the turkey for Thanksgiving the next year... According to the USDA, you can keep a frozen turkey for up to a year. But don't just stick the turkey in the freezer in its original packaging. (Most packaging tends to be permeable to moisture.) You can use special "freezer" bags or aluminum foil to ward off freezer burn.

November is a great time to buy **small kitchen appliances**. The summer wedding season has ended, and the holiday season isn't in full swing yet. These are the two times of year people traditionally buy small appliances. So you can find great deals on products like blenders and mixers.

Also this month, don't forget to take advantage of **Black Friday** and **Cyber Monday**. These two business days immediately following Thanksgiving are when retailers offer the best deals on electronics you'll find all year.

November is the best time to buy a **recreational vehicle (RV)**. RVs are popular purchase items in the spring and summer as families plan vacations. But as winter approaches, sales slow down. Dealers try to offload inventory and keep the cash coming in... thus the great deals on new RVs.

December

December is a fantastic time to buy **items for outdoor activities** like **bicycling** and **swimming**. Peak seasons are naturally late spring and early summer, when people plan to use these items. Slow sales mean good deals. Check out your local bike shop or pool store for deals.

But avoid the week before Christmas. Some retailers will temporarily raise the price because of the holiday. You can get big discounts at retailers nationwide.

Just avoid buying a bike the week before Christmas. Some retailers temporarily raise the price because many parents buy their children bikes as Christmas gifts.

December is one of the best months to save big on **hardware** and **tools**. This is the time of year hardware retailers push sales of tools for the "man in your life."

Ace Hardware and Home Depot advertise that you can do all your shopping for dad at their stores alone. You can easily save 15% or more on items like drills and reciprocating saws if you're looking for equipment for upcoming projects the next year.

December is one of the best months to save on **electronics**, like **computers** and **televisions**. Many companies release new models of their electronics at the beginning of the year, so December is the time to find good deals.

— 11 —

Stop Giving Your Money to Wall Street, Join a Credit Union

One of the joys of holding cash is sleeping well at night, knowing you won't lose money. But what about in times of runaway inflation?

There's a safe way to earn more on your cash, lower your risks, help local communities, and turn your nose up at the big money-center banks.

Here's what I want you to do: Join a credit union.

You've probably heard of a credit union. But if you're like most folks I've talked with, you figure there's no real practical difference between them and a big, name-brand bank... at least not to you, the small, private account holder. But they are different. And the benefits of joining a credit union are important.

Very simply, credit unions are nonprofit companies that act as local community banks. And guess what? The rates credit unions offer are spectacular.

Even better, Wall Street doesn't have access to your money anymore. You see, the credit union turns around and loans your money to other members. Rather than investing in insider shell games, like mortgage-backed securities, the credit union's bread and butter is car, boat, and housing loans that charge 5%-8%.

That's how they make money to pay their employees and rent. They borrow from depositors at 2% and get 5%-8% from their lending.

Unlike Wall Street, the board members of credit unions meet locally in a conference room... not on some island resort, spending the shareholders money. Even better, the board members are usually volunteers. Is this sounding good or what?

I can't stand loaning my money to Fidelity or TD Ameritrade for 0.01% in my brokerage accounts.

The way I see it, by banking with a local credit union, I'm giving my capital to local people and businesses, instead of the huge Wall Street firms that steal my taxes and pay their cronies big, fat bonuses.

Putting your money with local credit unions will help stimulate your local economy. These institutions don't keep plush offices or send their board members on luxury island trips. They exist solely to turn deposits into small business loans, home mortgages, and car loans.

Keeping your money local, you'll support small and local business ventures near you. I don't know about you, but I don't want to pay for any more golf trips, big bonuses, or million-dollar office decorations. **Together, let's stop the fraud of Wall Street and support our local community banks and credit unions**.

Are there any risks? Not really. Your money is as safe, if not safer, than at the larger commercial banks. Just like the Federal Deposit Insurance Corporation (FDIC), which is supposed to insure your deposits in a commercial bank... credit unions have the National Credit Union Share Insurance Fund (NCUSIF). This fund is backed by the "full faith and credit of the United States government." Just like at commercial banks, the standard share owner is insured up to $250,000.

The only catch is, to join a credit union, you're legally required to have some sort of affiliation with the group that sponsors it. For some credit unions, you have to work for particular employers. But in other cases, you need only be a resident of a particular state. For example, if you live in Florida or California, you can join any number of credit unions. As of 2014, several pay more than 2% for your checking and savings business.

In my case, my dad was a state employee in North Carolina, which qualified me to join its state credit union.

— 12 —

Avoid These 13 Common Hassles and Scams

1. Are marketers harassing you? Just sign up for the National Do Not Call Registry. Signing up is easy...

Once you type "National Do Not Call Registry" into your Google search engine, the only information you need to provide is your phone number and e-mail address to be put on the registry. You'll be sent an e-mail that you simply click on to complete the process. You can also stop spam by contacting the Direct Marketing Association at thedma.org.

Now, let's say you've done all this, and you're still receiving annoying phone calls and e-mails. When a telemarketer calls, explain to him if you receive another call you'll never use the service they provide again. I've done this with my cable company, and it worked immediately.

2. CBS News investigated a warehouse of used copiers and found more than 300 pages of data (including Social Security numbers and birth certificates). It turns out that most copiers made after 2002 store pages that have been copied. If you have a printer/copier/scanner/fax combination, you're even more vulnerable.

Many copiers work similarly to computers... They contain hard drives that store information, just like saving a file on a computer.

You can protect yourself in several ways. Use copy machines that only make photocopies – they only hold data long enough to print something once. Multifunction devices – ones that double as scanners, faxes, or printers – store the files for longer. Also, don't copy sensitive information on machines in public places like libraries or Kinko's.

You also can physically destroy the hard drive, and then recycle it. Or you can contact the manufacturer and ask a representative to explain how to erase the hard drive. (Many companies' websites and user manuals also provide information on how to do this.)

3. **The next time you pay for a purchase with a credit card and the cashier demands your ID, refuse**. It's against the credit-card companies' agreement with the vendor. The information can give a dishonest employee what he needs to make purchases on your credit card. A store can also use the information on your ID to add you to a mailing list – not as dangerous but still annoying.

I refused to show my card at the Las Vegas airport when I was trying to buy lunch once. I called American Express immediately and put them in touch with the manager.

4. **Those pre-approved credit-card offers you receive in the mail are not just annoying... they can be dangerous**. If you're not taking the time to shred them, an identity thief could easily open the card in your name. And even if you diligently destroy sensitive information before throwing it out, a thief can steal the mail from your mailbox before you get there.

But you have an easy way to protect yourself... Opt out of junk mail. Optoutprescreen.com is a joint venture of the credit-reporting agencies. You can opt out from receiving these offers for five years or permanently. (Opting out permanently requires you to mail in a form.)

You will have to provide personal information, like your date of birth and social security number. But all the information is secure and only used to verify who you are.

It can take up to six weeks for you to stop receiving the card offers.

5. You could be paying more for online purchases if retailers think you're willing to... Many retailers charge different prices to different groups of people. This is known as "dynamic pricing." Retailers gather information on your past purchasing history to determine the highest price you're willing to pay for an item.

How can you prevent this from happening to you? Use different Internet browsers when you shop for goods online. Make sure one is a browser you don't often use to make purchases online. Or you can do what I do... Regularly clear your Internet history and cookies.

So-called "cookies" are digital identifiers attached to your browser by the websites you visit. The site operators (including legitimate, mainstream sites) use them to track visitor activity.

> **DO WHAT I DO**
>
> **Regularly clear your Internet history and cookies.**

Erasing them is fairly simple... Just go to your "history" page, and select the option that reads something like "Delete Browsing History and Cookies."

6. Fastcustomer.com allows you to talk directly to a customer service representative and skip the long hold times. It's easy to use... and it's free.

Here's how it works... Using your cell phone, send a text message with a company's name to (936) 225-5757. Within minutes, you'll receive a phone call from a customer service representative with that company.

If you have a smartphone, you can download FastCustomer's app to easily access more than 3,000 companies. Just select a company from the list and choose the "Have someone call me" option.

We tested this service and found the response incredibly fast. We asked for a representative from cable company Comcast to call. Comcast is notorious for its slow service. It was actually fined in 2013 for making customers wait too long. But using FastCustomer, we got a call back from a Comcast representative in just four minutes.

Even if you don't have a cell phone, you can use FastCustomer's service through your Internet browser. This program will save you time and stress.

7. Unlike with FastCustomer, the website Gethuman.com lists shortcuts to getting the help you want when dealing with a company's customer service department... For example, if you want to get a person at Verizon Wireless – one of the companies with a difficult-to-figure-out trick – enter your mobile number and then press the pound key.

The site also allows you to request a call back from some customer service lines... You don't have to wait on hold. Just enter your phone number with Gethuman (which doesn't store it), and you'll receive a call within minutes. No waiting.

8. The next time you travel out of the country, call your credit-card company first to tell them where you're traveling. Most banks have antifraud systems that flag transactions from unusual locations far from your normal patterns. When the bank identifies these transactions, it may block them and call you to authorize the purchase.

That's great for security, but it can be inconvenient when you're trying to enjoy your vacation. A simple call to your credit-card company lets it know to approve these unusual transactions without any added scrutiny.

9. The business-rating website "Yelp" may not be as unbiased and informative a resource on local businesses as it's made out to be.

Thumbs down for Yelp.

The site allows users to post online reviews of restaurants, auto shops, doctors, etc. But the website has been controversial since its launch in 2004. Several lawsuits have claimed Yelp unfairly favors businesses that pay to advertise on the site. Also, many businesses claimed Yelp's review filter is too harsh... and removes legitimate reviews.

We tested the review filter and found Yelp removed our accurate reviews of different businesses. And it provided no exact reasons for removing the reviews. After we tested it, it started including a way to see all of a business' reviews.

If you use the site, make sure you see all of the reviews by checking the "filtered reviews." Once you find a business you're interested in, scroll down to the last review. Below it, in light grey text, you'll see an option to view "Unfiltered Reviews." This will give you a better view of what people really think.

10. **Having a secure password is essential in our modern, computerized world**... From paying bills to shopping and sending e-mails, we need passwords to do just about everything online. But weak passwords make it easier for hackers to steal your personal data, like bank account numbers.

SplashData (a software company) released the top 25 most popular passwords used in 2012. No. 1 on the list? "Password."

Keep your passwords "long and strong." A strong password has a combination of numbers, letters, and symbols (the characters above the numbers on your keyboard) that are nearly random. And avoid using the same password repeatedly. For example... you can remember a long and strong password like "C4S3Y12*s" as "Casey Twelve Stars."

It's a good tip... But using these guidelines makes it difficult – even impossible – to remember all your passwords. A couple online services can help safely store and track your passwords.

LastPass is a password manager that logs into sites for you after you add websites and login data to the LastPass data vault. All you need is your LastPass master password, and you can use it from any computer. You can also access it on your smartphone. Although if you want to use the mobile feature, the service costs $12 a year.

Norton – the online security software – features a similar service. If you use Norton on your computer, it will save your login information for different sites. It works much like LastPass and comes free with a subscription to Norton software.

There is a chance these services could be hacked. But it's less likely because they're more dedicated to security than retailers.

To keep your password secure, remember my tip to make it "long and strong." And use services (like LastPass and Norton) that required two-step verification.

11. When you visit Starbucks, you could be putting your personal information at risk. Cafes, hotels, and airports often offer free Wi-Fi (wireless Internet). Most people in airports use free Internet access to pass the time. However, a hacker could also be monitoring your public access.

Using free Wi-Fi puts your computer at serious risk. First, you're logging onto a connection that isn't secure... allowing hackers to retrieve whatever information they want from your computer.

Second, the connection you're using could be a fake. Hackers can make their Wi-Fi connections look identical to a legitimate connection. If you log on to one of these, the hacker gets access to your passwords, credit-card information, and other personal information.

The easiest way to protect yourself is to never use a public Wi-Fi connection. If you don't want to give up the convenience of sitting in a Starbucks while you work, make sure you use a virtual private network (VPN).

VPNs secure your Internet connection and encrypt your data. One of the top providers is WiTopia. All you have to do is download software to surf the web securely.

12. Never give retailers your zip code... unless you enjoy junk mail clogging your mailbox. You've probably had a cashier ask for your zip code... Decline. Sometimes retailers use zip codes just to figure out the best place to open new locations. But often, companies use your zip code (when paired with information from your credit card) to market to you... meaning you'll likely receive more junk mail and telemarketer calls.

> ### *DO WHAT I DO*
>
> **Just say no. If a merchant claims to need your zip code, give it a phony number.**

There are only a few times when giving a merchant your zip code won't result in more mail... American Express may require you to enter your zip code for security reasons. Gas stations often require a zip code when paying at the pump to prevent fraud.

But in most cases, do what I do... Just say no. If they claim to need it, give them a phony number.

13. Tell your bank to keep its "convenience" checks... They're dangerous. Credit-card companies often send them with monthly statements or just on their own. These checks can be used to make purchases or as a cash advance – with the charge going to your credit card.

But you're probably charged a fee (and paying a higher interest rate) every time you use one of these checks. You may get them with a special offer waiving the fee or lowering the interest rate... but not always. Convenience checks sitting in your mailbox or trash can also open you up to theft.

To protect yourself, do what I do...

Call your credit-card company and ask it to stop sending convenience checks. My assistant Laura did this. The phone call took less than five minutes. It can take a month or two for the checks

> ### *DO WHAT I DO*
>
> **Call your credit-card company and ask it to stop sending convenience checks.**

to completely stop coming. And in the meantime, be sure to shred them before you throw them away.

— 13 —

20 Everyday Money Savers, And Where Not to Die

1. Save \$250-\$300 a year for a family of four's water bill.

Change to a low-flow showerhead (from five gallons per minute to two gallons per minute).

With a simple wrench and a roll of inexpensive "plumber's tape," anyone can change out a shower head in two minutes or less.

Check for home energy leaks with Black and Decker's infrared Thermal Leak Detector. Use it around windows, doors, electrical outlets, and recessed lights to find leaks. Once you find them, caulk or weather-strip will seal the leak and save hundreds of dollars on AC and heating bills.

2. Slash those high-energy costs.

I always welcome the fall season, a time when you can turn off your air conditioner and open your windows. But what can you do to save money during the summer and winter months?

Many utility companies offer programmable thermostats that allow the company to change the temperature settings during peak hours, but only for a few minutes at a time. For BGE, a utility in Maryland, summer peak hours typically fall between 10 a.m. and 8 p.m. BGE offers credit of up to a \$100 a year for those enrolled.

You might worry about the energy company controlling your thermostat, but most customers report never noticing a thing... except the savings.

3. Save hundreds of dollars a year by keeping food fresh longer instead of throwing it away.

There are produce bags that release ethylene gases, preventing food from ripening too quickly. Put your fruits and veggies in these bags after a shopping trip, and double their shelf life.

4. Some dietary supplements can be helpful, but they are also expensive.

Consumer Reports profiled some popular vitamins and rated them on affordability and nutritional value. The generic Costco brand Kirkland beat all the name-brand vitamins. Kirkland items are as good, if not better, than name brands.

5. Get free shipping when you shop online.

Online shopping is convenient, and many stores offer special discounts you only get online. But some sites rarely advertise free shipping. Freeshipping.org finds all the useable codes. In 2014, the site had more than 2,000 free shipping codes for vendors like Amazon and Home Depot.

Best of all, you don't need to enter any personal information to get the free shipping codes. Some of the offers are conditional and require a minimum purchase. Some offer shipping around $1.

6. Lower your thermostat by 10% at night while you sleep and save hundreds of dollars per year.

This will also help you sleep better at night. The optimal temperature for quality sleep is cool – around sixty degrees. This tip will save you money and improve your health.

And don't forget about the thermostat on your water heater. Water heaters contribute to about 20% of your energy costs. So turn down the temperature on your water heater. The U.S. Department of Energy suggests you set your heater to 120 degrees. (Many manufacturers automatically set the temperature to 140 degrees.)

If your heater is in a cool area of your house, wrap it with an insulating jacket. You can find one at a hardware store. This simple step could save you up to 5% on your energy bill, or about $110 a year.

7. **Replacing old appliances could save you hundreds of dollars a year**.

If your appliance is more than 15 years old, it may be time to get a new one. For example, if you replaced your old dishwasher, refrigerator, and washing machine, you could save $202 a year on energy and water bills. Just replacing an old washing machine saves around $122 a year.

8. **Unplugging appliances is a quick way to save on your energy bills**.

Some people plug their appliances into a power strip to help them save. (Instead of turning off several appliances, you can just turn the power strip off.) But many of these people admit they forget to turn the power strip off before leaving home. There's a way to prevent that.

The Smart Strip automatically turns itself off when it senses appliances aren't in use... saving you the need to remember to turn it off. The company behind the Smart Strip – SmartHomeUSA – claims you can save up to $20 per month on your energy bill. It pays for itself in less than two months.

9. **Ordering your prescriptions through the mail is an easy way to save money on drugs**.

Most health care plans allow people to use a mail-order company instead of having to visit a pharmacy. Most plans lower the cost of your prescription if you order your drugs through the mail... And you'll receive a full three-month supply (instead of the usual 30-day supply you might get at a pharmacy).

Prescriptions are cheaper through mail-order services because of the lower overhead costs and high volumes dispensed. It's also more convenient than going to your pharmacy. You can refill your prescription over the phone, via the companies' websites, or by filling out a paper form and mailing it to the companies. Then you simply wait while your medications are delivered straight to your door.

The drugstore chain Walgreens allows you to sign up for mail-order delivery. CVS offers a similar service.

My assistant Laura switched to mail-order and saved 20% off her prescriptions. To get started, call your health plan to find out if it allows you to buy your medicines through the mail.

10. **Stop using the mail to pay your bills, and save more than $82 a year.**

The average U.S. household pays 15 bills a month. And you could be paying more than $82 a year just on postage.

Many companies make it easy for customers to pay bills without using the mail. Utilities, credit cards, and service providers (like your cable or phone company)

> ### *DO WHAT I DO*
>
> Set up automatic debits from your bank account or automatic charges on your credit card. Do this for bills that are a consistent amount each month.

allow users to make payments online. You can either visit the company's website or call them to learn the procedures for paying your bill online. With most companies, you just need to create an online account and enter your billing information.

If you don't want to (or can't) use a computer, do what I do... Set up automatic debits from your bank account or automatic charges on your credit card. Do this for bills that are a consistent amount each month.

For payments that fluctuate from month to month... just log onto your bank account website and set up a one-time payment every month. (I prefer the credit card because I collect frequent flyer miles. But some bills charge a fee for credit, so I use my bank account for those.)

11. Save money on your daily cup of coffee by bringing your own mug to the coffee shop.

Starbucks will give you a $0.10 discount if you bring a mug instead of using one of its cardboard cups. Ten cents a day adds up to $36.50 a year. Many local shops will offer a similar discount... you just have to ask for it.

Another way to save money on your daily coffee is to use a Starbucks card. The Starbucks Gold card gets you a free cup of coffee every day.

12. Dealnews.com is a great way to find the best deals on items from laptops to shoes.

Each day, Dealnews scours more than 2,000 retailers and finds the best 200 (or more) deals. Every deal is verified, and Dealnews checks that the retailer is reputable. You can also find great travel deals from airlines and resorts.

13. The next time you're shopping for a new cell phone plan, use Myrateplan.com.

MyRatePlan compares your cell-phone plan with others that may offer you a better deal. If you need a new cell phone, you can use filters to search the dozens of cell phones on the site to find one that suits you. The site also shows you coverage maps for the major wireless providers, so you can choose the one that has the best service in your area.

14. There's a simple way to read articles online from the *Wall Street Journal* or the *New York Times* that are for subscribers only... Google them.

Both services participate in a "First Free Click" program with Google. This allows you to see a handful of articles – that are only meant for subscribers – for free.

It's simple to do... You can copy and paste or retype the headline of the article into Google's search box. Mostly likely, the article you want will be the first in the search results. Simply click on the link and enjoy. (We found the program limits you to five articles a day.)

15. To save on prescriptions, go to PharmacyChecker.com and put in the name of the drug you want to shop.

The site will not only give you the generic name that is also available, but the cost from all the approved pharmacies.

You can use this site to purchase some medications not covered by your insurance.

Do what I do... Explain to your doctors that you shop for your medications. And ask them to write the prescription for 90 days, to include any refill times, and to give the script to you rather than send it directly to the pharmacy where you lose control of it. When you tell them of the vast difference in cost, they'll be happy to do it.

> ### *DO WHAT I DO*
>
> Explain to your doctors that you shop for your medications. And ask them to write the prescription for 90 days, to include any refill times, and to give the script to you rather than send it directly to the pharmacy where you lose control of it.

16. A 2013 study from Johns Hopkins University found that doctors order fewer lab tests during a patient's hospital stay if they realize the costs of the tests.

As we have discussed many times in this book already, doctors are notorious for overprescribing treatment. One survey found $226 billion was wasted on unnecessary lab tests in 2011.

These tests weren't just wasting money. They were harming patients with overtreatment – exposing patients to unnecessary radiation from CT scans and X-rays and potential side effects of needless medications. Even doctors think patients are over treated (about 28% of the time, according to the *Journal of the American Medical Association*).

The next time your doctor orders a test... make sure he explains exactly why the test is needed and ask him for the price. This may make him think twice before subjecting you to a test you don't need.

17. States hold more than $30 billion in unclaimed property that you can profit from...

This money comes from stocks, bonds, payroll checks, checking accounts, utility deposits, pension payments, and more.

If the money is left untouched for a certain number of years (past the statute of limitations), by law, it is often turned over to the state. Over the years, I've helped *Retirement Millionaire* subscribers find thousands of dollars in unclaimed property using sites like www.missingmoney.com and www.unclaimed.org.

You can find unclaimed pensions through the Pension Benefit Guaranty Corp. Search for the pension participant's name, the company that provided the pension, or the state the company is or was located in. This is a great way to profit from unclaimed funds.

18. There's a simple way to organize all your finances... and avoid overspending.

Mint.com is one free online program that automatically categorizes spending, creates budgets, and helps you set goals.

To get started, enter your bank accounts, trading accounts, credit cards, and loans onto Mint's secure website. You'll need the username and password you use to access your different accounts. But once you've done that, Mint automatically keeps track of transactions and balances.

Mint also categorizes your spending. You can see how much you spend on groceries, utilities, clothes, etc.

Some people worry about having all their financial information in one place. But Mint has the same level of security used by major banks. And it sends an alert if there is suspicious spending on any of your accounts.

My assistant Laura used Mint for years. One of her favorite features was the bill alert. She received an e-mail seven days before a bill was due. She also liked the convenience of using one website to see how all her finances were doing... even tracking how positions in her stock trading accounts were working out.

19. The next time you want to hear a symphony orchestra play... save money by visiting your local university's orchestra performance.

In Maryland, two tickets to the professional Baltimore Symphony Orchestra could cost $140. Or you could drive a few miles to hear the University of Maryland Symphony Orchestra for just $50.

20. Don't die in Maryland or New Jersey if you want to avoid paying heavy estate and inheritance taxes.

In 2013, financial news source *Forbes* said Maryland and New Jersey are the two states that levy both an inheritance tax and an estate tax. This can quickly eat away at the money you plan to leave your heirs.

So where can you go to make the most of your estate?

Colorado, Delaware, Missouri, and Oklahoma have some of the best (lowest) inheritance and estate tax regimes.

As for retiring: In 2014, New York was the most expensive place in the U.S. to retire... followed by West Virginia, Alaska, Arkansas, and Hawaii. A survey from Bankrate found taxes on retirement were high thanks to the high cost of upkeep in the state (like the subways and parks in New York City). Also, New York had the fourth-highest cost of living in the U.S.

— 14 —

Six Money-Saving Car Tips (and One for Safety)

1. The best time to buy a new car is at the end of the month.

This is when salespeople are under the most pressure to meet sales goals. But if you want to get an even better deal, buy your car during the week or in the evening.

According to the United States Automobile Association – the insurance and financial-services provider for military families – shopping during the week means you avoid the crowds, giving you the salesman's undivided attention. And if you shop in the evening, the salesman is less likely to try dragging out the negotiation... since he's probably ready to go home after a long day.

My research assistant Laura reported one of her family members tried this tactic. He knew exactly what he wanted to buy and which dealership had the car he wanted. So he went to the dealership about an hour before closing on a Thursday. As he told me, "The salesman was obviously anxious to get home for the evening, so he got the deal done fast with almost no haggling."

He saved nearly $3,000 on a brand-new car and paid nearly $1,000 less than he was offered by other dealers he visited over a weekend.

2. Walk more, and cut your auto insurance bill by 10%.

By walking, you'll cut the miles put on your car and improve your health.

Give your insurer a call, and tell them you're driving less. This will cut your rates.

3. Stop overpaying for car insurance.

The average person drives about 12,000 miles per year. But people 65 years old and over drive less than 8,000 miles per year on average. This means auto-insurance firm MetroMile could save you up to 40% on your car insurance.

MetroMile is one company that offers pay-per-mile insurance policies, so you only pay for the miles you put on your car. The company gives drivers a "metronome" to track your travels and measure mileage.

> **66** *The average person drives about 12,000 miles per year. But people 65 years old and over drive less than 8,000 miles per year on average. This means auto-insurance firm MetroMile could save you up to 40% on your car insurance.* **99**

The metronome hooks up to your car's diagnostic system. MetroMile's software tracks what you spend on gas, mileage, time driving, and several other statistics. Then it uses this information to determine your auto insurance rate.

Progressive also does this with its "Snapshot" tool. Just plug the Snapshot device into your car, and it tracks your driving habits. This helps Progressive determine if you deserve lower rates.

4. Earn an extra $2,150 a year renting out your car.

If your car sits in a parking lot all day while you're working – or you live in an area where you don't drive much – you can rent it out for a little extra cash.

Car-sharing networks match you up with people looking to rent a car for a few hours. And many, like Spride Share in San Francisco, offer insurance in case of an accident. How much you earn depends on how often you make your car available and the type of car you have. Premium cars cost more to rent than a modest sedan like a Honda Civic.

5. Slow down on the road, and save money on gas.

Driving at 75 miles per hour (mph) gets four miles per gallon less than driving at 65 mph. Some studies show that slowing down saves you 6% a year or more on gas. And if you have a bulkier vehicle like a van or SUV, you could save even more. An average family could save $80 a year.

6. A good credit score could get you a better deal on car insurance.

Insurance agencies check your credit report when you apply for a policy. Agencies believe people with low credit scores are more likely to file an insurance claim.

Studies show people with stable finances (the same people likely to have a higher credit score) have fewer car accidents and traffic violations than less financially stable people.

So if you're shopping for a new policy or your credit score has gone up since you first began your policy, use that as a negotiating tool to get a better deal.

7. Your airbag should change the way you drive.

When most of us learned to drive, our instructors told us to keep our hands at the "10 o'clock" and "2 o'clock" positions on the steering wheel.

This technique worked well before power steering became standard. On older cars, you needed more leverage to turn the wheel. Not so today... Modern steering wheels turn much more easily. And driving with your hands at "10 and 2" could cause your forearm to smash into your face and eyes or even fracture if your airbag deploys.

Both the American Driver and Traffic Safety Education Association and AAA driving club state that keeping your hands at 9 o'clock and 3 o'clock is best. This keeps your arms out of the way of airbags and pushes them to the side instead of backwards into your face. And you'll still have plenty of control of the steering wheel.

— 15 —

Six Great Travel Tips

1. If you want an unbiased, informative view of a hotel before you book a room, check out Tvtrip.com.

TVtrip shows videos of hotels around the world that allow you to see what the hotel actually looks like inside and out, including the surrounding area. The videos on the site are straightforward and aren't used to promote the hotel.

A friend had been considering staying at a hotel in Orlando. The hotel's website showed beautiful rooms and a huge breakfast setup included. But after watching the videos on TVtrip, she could see the rooms were outdated and the breakfast was little more than toast and coffee.

2. For the best deals on rental cars... visit the website Autoslash.com.

AutoSlash searches for the best car-rental rates.

All you need to do is enter where you want to pick up the car, the date, and any car preferences you have. AutoSlash will show you the best car deals available in the area. Better still... if a cheaper rate comes along, AutoSlash will rebook you automatically at the lower rate.

My coworker Fawn registered for this service on a cross-state trip. She needed a compact car from major rental-car company Avis for nine days. With no effort on her part, AutoSlash lowered her rental cost from $313 to just $180... and upgraded her to a mid-size sedan.

AutoSlash is a simple way to find great car deals so you don't have to spend your time searching for coupons.

3. Many rental-car companies will pressure you to accept their insurance when you pick up one of their cars... Resist the hard sell.

The premium can add $10-$20 extra a day.

Instead, just pay with a credit card (which most people do anyway). Many cards offer auto-rental collision damage on domestic (and even foreign) car rentals. Visa, for example, will reimburse your auto-insurance deductible, towing charges, administrative fees, and loss-of-use charges imposed by the rental company.

You just need to do a few things to make sure you're covered. Most credit-card companies require you use the card that offers the coverage to pay the rental in full. You also have to decline any coverage the rental car company provides.

Visa, MasterCard, American Express, and Discover all have slightly different policies. And not every card offered by the company has this coverage. You can call your credit-card company's customer-service line to determine if you have this coverage.

4. The next time you travel overseas... make sure you have a credit card that doesn't have a foreign-transaction fee.

Years ago, most credit-card companies and banks charged a fee (typically 3%) for all foreign transactions. In 2014, more than 80% of cards still charged a foreign-transaction fee.

Banks like Capital One as well as Discover and certain MasterCards are exceptions. These companies charge no foreign credit-card purchase fees.

5. The next time you're ready to book a vacation rental, make sure to use a trustworthy website.

Renting someone's home can be risky... The property may not look like or offer what was promised. Or you may find it was double-booked.

If you want to be protected the next time you rent, use HomeAway.com or one of its sister sites. HomeAway offers a "Carefree Rental Guarantee." This guarantee protects you (the renter) up to $10,000 if the property is double-booked or misrepresented. This helps give you a worry-free vacation.

6. The next time you book a hotel for your vacation, try the travel website Booking.com.

The global research firm J.D. Power and Associates gave Booking.com a score of 816 (out of a thousand) based on overall consumer satisfaction. The travel site beat well-known sites Hotwire and Priceline. Some of the lowest scores went to Expedia and Travelocity.

One catch with Booking.com: You can't use it to plan your whole trip – airfare, rental cars, etc. You can only book your hotel room. But Booking.com doesn't charge any additional fees. And it provides information on property rankings, how many people are looking at staying there, and user reviews.

I love the detailed information on how many rooms are left. That way you can still wait to solidify plans that require input from friends or family who are traveling with you.

— 16 —

Seven 'No Work' Retirement Jobs

Don't ever retire.

Never retiring is one of the best things you can do for your health and financial stability.

Too many people work and save all their lives only to retire and discover they are bored... literally to death. People who retire at age 55 die twice as fast as those who keep working. Many succumb to depression and disease (even terminal illnesses) because they are unprepared for the mental shift into retirement.

And people who stop working worry they will go broke in retirement. A 2014 poll showed 55% of Americans aged 44 to 75 feared running out of money in retirement more than death.

The facts are only a third of Americans will have enough money to survive retirement. Planning a nest egg for retirement can be daunting at any time... But if you retire early, you're going to have to sock away even more money than someone retiring later in life.

Too many people nowadays rely on tools that supposedly tell you how much you'll need for retirement. That's bunk. There are just too many variables involved to know how much money you'll need. How long will you live? How high will inflation be? What will happen to the stock market and the economy? All these things affect your retirement income... and it's impossible to know the answers.

But that doesn't mean you should spend your life chained to a desk and a computer. I'm not suggesting you get a part-time job at Wal-Mart or Home Depot or some work-at-home scheme, which barely pays you more than minimum wage.

There are moneymaking opportunities that are a heck of a lot more fun than watching TV or playing bingo. You'll learn a lot... and you could make great money at the same time.

I'm an example of this. In 1995, I retired from Wall Street. In 2007, I retired from practicing medicine to start writing financial newsletters for Stansberry Research. As of 2014, I spend my days traveling, searching for great money-making opportunities for my subscribers, and just doing the things I love. I'm in great health, and I don't fear I won't have enough money.

I'm not the only one... Most retirees think they want to stop working altogether. They think they have more than enough money to retire.

My good friend Brenda of Mutt Lynch Winery slowly left her corporate job and turned her love of wine and winemaking into a viable business to do in "retirement." She was able to spend time with her twins, her husband, and her dog. And she could spend half the amount of time "working" as she used to... while making the same amount of money.

You can do the same...

'No Work' Job No. 1:
Take a Nearly Free Vacation

With the cost of gas, plane tickets, and hotel rooms, taking regular vacations seems out of reach for many people.

But there's a way you can take a vacation every month if you want to... without having to pay for a hotel (and often without paying for a rental car).

Sound too good to be true?

It's not. There's a way for you to take a nearly free vacation. All you have to agree to do is take some time out of your day to take care of someone's house.

I'm talking about **housesitting**.

Housesitting is exactly what it sounds like... You spend a certain amount of time taking care of someone's home. This could include looking after pets or watering plants. It's that simple.

You could travel around the world for weeks or months at a time and stay in someone else's home. Feel like spending two months in Provence, France in a beautiful, 200-year-old home? All you have to do is watch the homeowner's cat.

There are networks that connect homeowners and housesitters from all over the world. All you have to do is choose a location. And these networks will show you listings for people who need a housesitter. The amount of time you housesit for could range anywhere from a week to a year or more.

Many homeowners allow a housesitter the full use of the home (including the car)... all for free. You just agree to complete certain tasks (like feeding and walking a dog) during your stay. For longer time frames, the homeowner might even pay for utilities during your stay.

'No Work' Job No. 2:
Live in Your Dream Home for Nearly Free

Become a **caretaker** or **estate manager**.

Keep in mind, the details of caretaking vary widely depending on the needs of the homeowner. These are things you want to clarify (and negotiate) upfront before taking the job.

For example, some caretakers are unpaid, although they get to live in the home without paying living expenses. Others can earn up to $60,000 a year managing estates across the U.S. I know of a couple retired engineers who got paid $120,000 a year to live on an estate in Connecticut and manage the place.

As long as you're physically able to do manual labor, caretaking is a good option for a job after retirement. Caretaking usually involves looking after any animals on the property, lawn work, cleaning, and an array of typical odd jobs around the home.

My caretaker Kristen mows the lawn, takes care of the garden, and basically anything else that needs to be done when I'm not around. In my case, I'm flexible about what's required beyond the basic "taking care of it as if it was your own" philosophy. And she still has some expenses – like cable, electricity, and water.

One drawback is that you might be on call 24 hours a day, depending on the job requirements. If you take care of a home that isn't often occupied, it's a great opportunity to live in a beautiful home.

If you find yourself (or you and your partner) willing and able to manage someone else's home while they're away, you should consider caretaking. Of course, it's not for everyone. Different owners might not let you stay in the home when they're around or have animals to keep you company when they're gone.

If you want to learn more about caretaking, or don't have caretaking experience, you can check out *The Caretaker Gazette.* It's a bimonthly newsletter that explains the ins and outs of being a caretaker and also lists new opportunities – both temporary and permanent.

'No Work' Job No. 3:
Earn $40,000 a Year in Your Pajamas

Imagine a job with no deadlines... no fear of getting fired... and no meetings with people sucking up to the boss. Even better, you can work anywhere – at your local coffee shop, for example.

This is a job where you work as your own boss. You make your own schedule. And most importantly, you never have to leave home. I always wanted a job I could do in my pajamas.

Walking around the house in PJs and a robe, sitting in front of a sunny window in early spring with a cup of warm Panamanian coffee... mmm... What could be much better than getting paid to do it?

This is the life of a **copywriter** – a job that offers benefits most people only dream about.

What exactly is a copywriter?

Copywriters write the words used to market a specific product or service. They write ads. Typically, copywriters work within the realm of direct marketing. This means their ads go directly to people and ask for a specific action. Think of infomercials or direct-mail catalogs.

Unlike typical advertising campaigns, copywriters aren't asked to build brands. A copywriter's job is to write an ad or sales letter with the sole purpose of getting a sale. This gives copywriters the flexibility to write about almost anything. For example, a copywriter can write an ad for an alternative health product as easily as he can for a travel book.

Copywriting requires no formal training. And you don't need prior experience in any particular field. As long as you learn about the product or service being sold and put together reasonable sentences, you can be a copywriter.

What's so good about copywriting?

Unlike other jobs, you get paid repeatedly for the work you did just once. Let's say you write a sales letter for a vitamin-supplement kit that cost $100. As a copywriter, you get a small percentage – technically known as a "royalty" – of whatever profit your letter generates.

If you were commissioned for 5% of total sales and your letter generated $50,000, you'd collect a $2,500 royalty check. If it generated $100,000, you'd collect $5,000.

But here's the best part... Let's say the business likes the results of your letter and sends it out to more people the following month. This time, your letter generates $200,000 for the company. For you, it means a $17,500 royalty check over two months for a sales letter that may have taken you only a few weeks to write.

The reason you get paid so much as a copywriter in direct marketing is because you can easily measure the results of an ad. If you created a new TV commercial for a company like Toyota, you would have no accurate way of measuring how your ad boosted company sales over any period of time. But with direct marketing, a company can determine exactly how well your copy performs and pay you based on these results.

Also you can negotiate advances of $1,000, $2,500, or $5,000. This is in addition to the royalties you collect.

If it sounds too good to be true... it's not. Just take 38-year-old Sean McCool of Knoxville, Tennessee. For several years, Sean worked in a variety of fields from construction to financial sales. All the while, he generated an extra $30,000 a year, on average, by writing copy for various businesses... including a local home-improvement company, a construction company, a discount magazine (coupon book), a water-treatment system company, and an ink-and-toner franchise.

Sean said: "Not one of these projects took more than a day to write, yet I made an average of $1,000 on each one. The best part is, I see my kids leave for school in the morning and am always at home when they get back."

Or look at Dennis Rome of New Orleans, Louisiana. Dennis ran a successful computer consulting business for more than 15 years. But as the 1990s wore down and the market began to change, Dennis wanted something more. He wasn't a writer, and the only thing he'd ever designed was a family newsletter every Christmas. He decided to learn about copywriting. Just two years later, 100% of his income came from copywriting.

If becoming a copywriter intrigues you, here's what to do:

Step 1: Find out more about the copywriter's life. A few free e-mail blogs cover the topic exclusively.

Step 2: Take a look at the following books. They will teach you what copywriting is all about...

Scientific Advertising by Claude Hopkins: This business classic covers everything from headlines and mail-order marketing, to advanced subjects like negative advertising and how to test an ad campaign.

Tested Advertising Methods by John Caples: This great read explains what direct marketing is... how it works... and how it can make you rich.

Ogilvy on Advertising by David Ogilvy: Written by the "father of advertising," this book offers great commentary on the business.

Copywriters Handbook by Robert Blys: This step-by-step guide will help you understand what copy is and the basics of how it works.

Step 3: If you're still interested, look into the American Writers and Artists Association's (AWAI) Accelerated Program for Six-Figure Copywriting. This program teaches you some of the best techniques to writing successful copy. We actually use this program in our own publishing business at Stansberry Research.

Don't misunderstand me, it's hard work and takes a lot of practice. But you can learn the skills no matter what previous experience you have and no matter your age. Most importantly, it is a job you can do from home that requires little start-up capital. If someone you know has just lost his job, pass this idea along. It could be a huge help.

Again, you'll need to dedicate at least a few hours a day, and you'll need a computer and e-mail access. If you're retired, this might be a great way to earn some income in your free time. If you're still working, don't quit your day job until you actually earn enough money to make it worth your while.

Either way, I hope these three steps help you decide whether copywriting is for you.

'No Work' Job No. 4:
Make Up to $125 an Hour From Home

If you've ever read a magazine or turned on a television, you've probably seen advertisements claiming you can make $100,000 a year working from home.

As you've probably guessed, those are outrageous come-ons. When someone claims that you can make $4,000 or more a month stuffing envelopes, more than likely, they're trying to cheat you.

These offers result in hundreds of complaints each year to the Better Business Bureau. (You can page through them on the bureau's website.)

But there this is a legitimate way to make up to $125 an hour working from home.

You can work part time matching companies with potential employees.

The people who do this are called recruiters, or more commonly **"headhunters."**

A headhunter finds candidates who match a company's need for an employee. It can also work in the reverse – finding a company that matches what a jobseeker is looking for.

Most headhunters work on a commission basis. They make a certain percentage of the new employee's salary. But charging per-hour helps to ensure what you'll actually make each time.

There are two ways to become a headhunter... You can join a recruiting company or work freelance. (Many choose to become freelance once they've established a list of clients.) Most recruiting companies look for people experienced in a certain industry to recruit within that industry.

For example, if you were a pharmacist, your skills could be used to recruit employees for pharmaceutical companies.

Sherry, a headhunter from Chicago began her recruiting career when a company she had previously worked for asked if she could help them find an employee. She originally charged $75 an hour for her services. After a few years, once word spread of her success, she was able to charge $125 an hour to recruit new employees.

Headhunters working for an agency can make anywhere between $27,000 and $85,000 a year. Again, the pay is typically based on commission.

If you're interested, you can start your search with Monster.com or Careerbuilder.com. Just type in "recruiter" or "headhunter" into the search bar, and you'll find agencies to work for.

You can also ask a previous employer, like Sherry did. The best part is, as a self-employed headhunter, you make your own hours and accept any job you want.

'No Work' Job No. 5:
Get Paid for Answering the Phone

Another easy way to work from home is **customer service**.

Companies try to cut costs by allowing employees to work from home. Some companies even look specifically for people who will work entirely from home (without ever having to go into an office building).

The customer-service departments of companies like J. Crew, 1-800-Flowers, and AAA work from home. When you call one of these companies, the person on the other line is likely sitting at his kitchen table.

This helps both the employer and employee. It cuts down on energy costs for office buildings (fewer people there to use lights and computers). And for companies that compensate for travel, it can cut down this expense as well. Many corporations are also trying to rely less on customer service in countries like India, where finding cheap labor isn't as easy as it was years ago.

But employees also see huge benefits. Working as a customer-service agent at home allows for flexibility and can save money on transportation.

There are a few general requirements for being hired. You'll likely need at least one year of customer-service experience, a work-dedicated corded phone line, and a fast Internet connection (no dial-up). Companies also require you to have a phone headset and a quiet environment to work in. In some cases, you will have to travel to do some basic training.

Because you're working at home, you can usually set your own hours. Some companies just require that you work a specific number of hours during the day or during the week.

'No Work' Job No. 6:
The Perfect Retirement Job for Teachers

If you're a teacher, or have expertise in any field, **tutoring** is a simple way to earn extra money.

And now, you can tutor from the comfort of your couch...

Tutor.com is one of the most well-known online-tutoring websites... The site provides services to children in fourth grade up to the first year of college. So tutors are expected to be at least sophomores in college.

The service is like a classroom that's open 24 hours a day, seven days a week. This makes it the perfect job to fit into any schedule. If you're an expert in just about any academic field – English, chemistry, physics, etc. – and you live in the U.S. or Canada... you may be eligible to work with Tutor.com.

The process to become a tutor is somewhat extensive...

After filling out a tutoring application, you take exams in the subjects you're interested in tutoring. If you pass, you'll have a mock tutoring session, a background check, and a final exam.

People who pass exams to tutor in several subjects are given preference over people who can only tutor one subject. And if no tutors are currently needed for that subject, you'll be placed on a waiting list. Although, if you can tutor one of the many high-demand subjects – such as calculus and economics – you're more likely to start tutoring right away.

How much you make depends on the hours you tutor and subjects you tutor. Tutoring high-demand subjects means you make more money. Tutor.com also has performance-based incentives and bonuses.

Once you start tutoring, you'll work with students one-on-one in an online classroom. The site has a whiteboard that allows tutors and students to draw diagrams or equations. Through the online classroom, tutors and students can also share documents. And you don't need to keep records of your sessions or plan out any lessons.

You can learn more at www.tutor.com/apply/what-our-tutors-do.

'No Work' Job No. 7:
Donate… And Get Paid $500

This last opportunity doesn't necessarily qualify as a job… as it is not something you can do everyday.

I'm talking about **getting your blood drawn**.

In 1975, the World Health Assembly passed resolution 28.72, which urged countries to only accept blood that has been donated voluntarily and without compensation.

Due to this resolution, you can no longer be paid to donate *blood*… BUT there is a little-known loophole that allows you to be paid $200-$500 (or more) for something else when you donate.

If you've been recently diagnosed with an autoimmune disorder or viral infection, there are companies willing to pay for the plasma in your blood.

Plasma is the liquid portion of your blood that holds proteins like antibodies. Antibodies are your immune system's primary defense against disease. They are a key component in finding treatments for diseases like cancer, arthritis, and human immunodeficiency virus (HIV).

Research companies are trying to find cures for these illnesses and use the plasma of someone who has been recently diagnosed to find out how the diseases work. This helps researchers develop treatments.

And if you've been diagnosed with an autoimmune disorder or viral infection, these companies may pay hundreds of dollars for your plasma.

Donating is easy and mostly painless... you just need to meet the criteria before you are selected as a donor. Donors must be at least 18 years old, weigh at least 110 pounds, and be recently diagnosed or be actively treated for a disease.

After you've been accepted, you'll have to travel to a donation center approved by the FDA. (Your travel expenses might be compensated.) The first donation can take two to three hours to complete. You'll give a small amount of blood first to make sure you're not anemic and that the fat content in your blood isn't too high.

Then you'll give amounts much similar to a regular blood donation. The big difference is much of your blood will be put back into your system. This process is called plasmapheresis, which is the process of removing plasma from your blood. Essentially, your red blood cells and platelets are returned to your body.

Because this process only takes plasma, it can be done up to two times in a seven day period.

After a donation, the donor is given a check as compensation. Depending on the donation, it can range from $200-$500. And this donation can be done twice a week as long as there are at least two days between each donation.

Two of the most well-known plasma donation researchers are Access Biologicals and SeraCare Life Sciences. Access Biologicals will not accept people who test positive for HIV or Hepatitis C. SeraCare will accept these donors (although it's only used for research purposes).

PART X

Protect Your Privacy:
Essentials of Digital and Everyday Privacy in America

— 1 —

Privacy Is a Thing of the Past

Americans have enjoyed stunning technological improvements to their lives just since the 1990s...

E-mail, social networks, satellite radio, Internet, and smartphones have reshaped our society.

Most people can't go a day without coming into contact with these technologies... and we're all aware of their benefits.

But what most Americans aren't aware of is how **these technologies have left us stunningly vulnerable to government overreach, unethical corporate monitoring, and worse, thieves**. Technology today has made it easier than ever to track you and steal your personal information.

Without realizing it, you're disseminating almost every detail of your life to entities that *can and will use this information against you.*

Fortunately, every American can employ a few simple techniques to reduce his exposure to these serious privacy threats. In this chapter, I'll identify these threats and show you simple countermeasures you can use right now. They'll help you keep your personal information as safe as possible.

A good buddy of mine and some of his friends were fishing in the Florida Keys. They were on two boats a mile or so apart. It was early in the morning, and there was not another boat for miles.

The guys on one of the boats had forgotten to pick up ice for the day. As they drew closer together, they signaled to their friends on the other boat about the predicament. The two boats backed themselves stern to stern so the men on the boat with the ice could toss over a few large bags to their buddies.

They thought nothing of it... But within minutes, an armed Coast Guard cutter appeared on the scene. The officers asked them all kinds of questions and shadowed them for the rest of the day.

Why?

Because a group of guys tossing large bags from one boat to another, sitting stern to stern, looks an awful lot like a drug meet, right?

The real question is, how did the Coast Guard see these guys?

The fishing buddies never made radio contact. They never made a phone call. The only way the Coast Guard officers could have seen what was going on was if they were monitoring the boats with drones or satellites. That's frightening... And this type of surveillance will only increase...

As of 2014, the Federal Aviation Administration had authorized 20 states and 24 universities to fly remotely piloted "drones" in U.S. skies to spy, take photos, etc. And according to a source quoted in Bloomberg News, "The federal government has already allocated billions [of dollars] for these, and state and local governments will follow."

Yes, the military uses the same type of miniature flying machines to spy on enemy movements in Iraq and Afghanistan. Not long ago, using this technology on U.S. citizens was unthinkable.

We expect the National Security Agency and the government to spy on foreign countries... sure... but not on us.

Of course, corporate America is doing its part to essentially end privacy in America, too...

Did you know that Apple was granted a patent in 2012 that allows it to disable the camera in iPhones with the simple flip of a switch?

The story went mostly unreported in the mainstream press, but a little blurb did appear in the September 17, 2012 issue of the *International Business Times*.

> 66 *Everything you eat, watch, buy, and do is tracked, cataloged, and used by the government to spy on you and by big companies to market to you more effectively.* 99

Imagine if the government or the company itself didn't want something filmed... It could simply flip a switch and disable all cameras in all iPhones located in a certain area.

And that's not all...

There was a report about secret tests at a Wal-Mart store where "radio-frequency identification" (RFID) tags were inserted in packages of lipstick, so they could track customers' movements.

CVS Pharmacy sold private information about what kinds of prescriptions its customers were taking... just so drug companies could improve their marketing.

Everything you eat, watch, buy, and do is tracked, cataloged, and used by the government to spy on you and by big companies to market to you more effectively.

As one former tire company executive stated: "If you show us what you buy, we can tell you who you are, maybe even better than you know yourself."

The government and corporate America are in this together. And of course, it's all being done to keep us "safe"...

Well, we are not safe. With our aggregated privacy data easily accessible, we are more vulnerable than ever before. And trust me, the criminals know it.

Thieves are getting much cleverer and bolder. In 2014, the FBI issued a warning about how thieves steal identities and use the personal information to take out mortgages in other people's names – even filing fake papers to steal people's homes.

In Los Angeles, a man defrauded more than 100 homeowners. The amount of money missing was more than $12 million.

You actually have more to worry about with identity theft than the money and the hundreds of hours it will take you to get the situation properly resolved... *Some completely innocent people who have had their identities stolen are getting locked up in jail.*

You're probably wondering how that is possible.

Basically, it's easy for a criminal to use someone else's identity when they get arrested. And once police book a criminal under a fake name, it can be a problem for the identity theft victim for life. That's because so many agencies now share databases... and these agencies are reluctant to take a name out once it's been added.

In 2013, I read an article about a Wisconsin man who was arrested several times because a criminal stole his identity and gave it to police when he was arrested.

As a result, the innocent man spent several nights in jail... was handcuffed face down on the side of the highway... lost his job... was denied government benefits... had his driver's license taken away... and nearly had his children taken away by Child Protective Services.

Again... *entities can and will use every detail of your life against you...*

— 2 —

Where Your Main Vulnerabilities Lie

Three powerful forces have collided to create the ideal conditions for privacy violations...

First, **government programs and regulations have formed the foundation of a massive tracking grid for all individuals**. Identification tags like Social Security numbers, passports, and drivers' licenses are almost inescapable in today's society.

Beyond this, the government has sweeping "snooping" authority... It can legally peer deep into our daily lives.

Second, **corporations want to know as much as possible about their customers**. They use this data for research and development of new products and services, as well as for marketing these goods. The government also forces them to hand over certain records of their customers' transactions.

Banks, Internet service providers, airlines, car-rental agencies, cell-phone companies, and more have all become proxy agents of the government's domestic intelligence apparatus.

Third, **we live in a hyper-connected technological age... and criminals know it**. Smartphones, "cloud" computing, and credit cards have made it easier than ever to rob someone's resources... even his or her identity. This provides unprecedented opportunity for crooks to use your data against you in cases of fraud, blackmail, and even wrongful arrest.

One of Stansberry Research's analysts worked within the United States intelligence community for years. He personally vetted all the solutions you're about to read.

In modern day, it's impossible to build an impenetrable wall around your privacy. The good news is, a few simple steps can reduce your vulnerability. By following the suggestions below, you will have protected your privacy better than about 98% of the population. That should help you sleep better at night.

Government:
Big Sister Is Watching You

From 2009 to 2013, Janet Napolitano headed the Department of Homeland Security (DHS), the organization created in the wake of the 9/11 terrorist attacks to consolidate most federal police forces.

DHS uses the powers granted to the government via the Patriot Act to inspect your banking transactions, restrict your ease of travel, and even monitor your routine actions out on the street. The undertones of Napolitano's media blitz – the one that had her face plastered everywhere – were hard to miss...

Big Sister is watching you.

Perhaps you may trust what your "public servants" in government are doing with your private data... But a mountain of data on every citizen presents an enticing target for all who would harm you. In the points that follow, I'll show you where the five major government-caused vulnerabilities in your privacy exist, and the best ways to "plug" these holes...

1. **Passports**.

In 2007, the U.S. State Department started issuing passports with "radio-frequency identification" (RFID) chips inside them. The government added these chips to make the passports "more secure."

This may have provided an added level of security for Immigrations and Customs Enforcement (ICE), but it blew a gaping hole in your individual privacy and security...

Anyone with an RFID reader device could access your passport information. This includes all of your biometric data and even your digital picture. And get this... RFID scanners can communicate with chips up to 100 feet away. It is an identity thief's dream.

> ### *DO WHAT I DO*
>
> **Wrap your passport in aluminum foil. It prevents communication between the RFID chip in your passport and an identity thief's scanner.**

But there is a solution...

You can block the RFID chip from connecting with any scanner device by cloaking the passport in a "secure sleeve." These sleeves shield the passport inside a metallic composite material. This prevents communication between the RFID chip and the scanner.

You can find "secure sleeves" for passports (as well as credit cards with internal RFID chips) for $5 to $20. And if you don't want to buy the sleeves, you can do what I do... Wrap your passport in aluminum foil. The result is the same.

The problem with using the sleeves is that you are still vulnerable to theft during the moment you give the passport to a customs agent. An identity thief loitering in the vicinity could steal your data. I'm not too worried about people and scammers loitering near border agents. But you should at least be aware of it.

2. **A way around TSA's "unfriendly skies."**

The federal Transportation Security Administration (TSA) changed passenger-screening policies in 2010. Travelers were forced to submit to irradiating "full-body scanners" that amount to a virtual strip search.

These machines are so invasive, they were even held up for a time in the United Kingdom... The graphic images they provided violated the U.K.'s child pornography laws. And this doesn't even count the machines' harmful health effects.

If you're traveling through an airport and want to avoid the radiation exposure and the dehumanizing search, you can "opt out." In this case, you must endure an invasive "pat down" search, where a TSA screener lays hands all over your body.

> **66** *The TSA initiated a 'trusted traveler' program in 2013. It's called 'TSA Pre-check.' Travelers who enroll in the program must undergo a background check and pay a $100 fee. The background check lasts for five years.* **99**

It's hard to believe these degradations now happen in "the land of the free."

But there is a solution...

The TSA initiated a "trusted traveler" program in 2013. It's called "TSA Pre-check." Travelers who enroll in the program must undergo a background check and pay a $100 fee. The background check lasts for five years.

After approval, Pre-check travelers can go through expedited screening lines about 80% of the time. These lines somewhat mimic the bygone days of air travel, including:

- Keeping shoes, belts, and light jackets on.

- Leaving laptops and toiletry bags in carryon items.

- Greatly reduced time in line (a Minneapolis screening took about 30 seconds)

Not every airport or airline is a part of the program, but the number is growing. By the end of 2014, 11 airlines and 120 airports participated in the program.

Pre-check is not open to all passengers... but there is a "back door" way into the program. Travelers enrolled in the Customs and Border Patrol (CBP) program called "Global Entry" are eligible for Pre-check.

Participating in the Pre-check program is not a perfect solution. The TSA can still subject you to random screening and/or pat downs. But your odds of having a simple travel experience are improved. For some, this is well worth the background check and application fee.

3. **Register your car in another name**.

"It's one of the most rapidly diffusing technologies I've ever seen." That's what a former police officer said about the automatic license-plate scanners sweeping through police departments across America.

The scanners sit atop police cruisers and log the license plate number and location of every vehicle within the scanners' line of sight. This means logging the name and location of the vehicle's registered owner, too.

According to a *Wall Street Journal* article, in 2010, more than one-third of all large police departments were using the technology. Private repossession firms and insurance companies also use the scanners. Suffice it to say if you live and drive in a major metropolitan area, the government is tracking your movements... without you even knowing it.

But there is a solution...

You can title the car in the name of a limited liability company (LLC). Here's how:

1. A New-Mexico-chartered LLC is the best choice due to the state's privacy protections. (You don't have to be a resident.)

2. Make sure the LLC is managed by a single member.

3. List a ghost address as the principal place of business (doesn't have to be in NM).

4. It costs about $100 to form the LLC and $100 for annual maintenance fees.

5. The LLC name is not required to appear on a state or federal tax return.

6. When you buy a vehicle, buy it with cash, normally from a private party.

The hardest part in this process may be establishing a "ghost address." In essence, a ghost address entails renting a mailbox from someone else. Examples might be a vacant commercial or office suite. Instead of getting zero cash flow from the vacancy, the property manager or owner might appreciate a small fee to let you use the address for the LLC's correspondence.

None of the processes listed above are illegal. Sure, they require a little more time and effort than a conventional vehicle purchase. So the question becomes... how much is your privacy worth to you?

4. Get a new Social Security number.

The government's programs form the foundation for a universal tracking grid. Inside this grid, the tracking program *par excellence* is Social Security.

If your Social Security number falls into the wrong hands, you are in for a world of pain. Identity theft, credit destruction, and lingering trouble with law enforcement are just a few of the pitfalls.

But there is a solution...

The government does not want to issue replacement Social Security numbers. It undermines the tracking grid. However, the rule has three main exceptions. If you can prove...

1. You have religious objections to certain numbers or digits

2. You're a victim of domestic violence or harassment

3. You're a victim of identity theft

... you can get a new Social Security number.

If any of these applies to you, contact the Social Security Administration to arrange for a new number.

If you've been the victim of identity theft, getting a new Social Security number won't necessarily solve all your problems. Instead of having ruined credit, you will have no credit to speak of... and it will take time to build it up again.

If you do get a new number, do whatever you can to keep it under tight wraps from the beginning. Many organizations and people (from banks to landlords) will ask for your full Social Security number... but most do not have a legal right to demand it.

Always try to establish another identification number with the party. For example, if a landlord requests your Social Security number to run a credit check, offer three months of rent up front as a "bond" against credit risk. Be creative... suggest alternative solutions.

Always keep this in mind: *Only supply your Social Security number when you have no other alternative.*

5. **Beat facial recognition technology**.

I've already shown you how the government uses your Social Security number as the core element of a massive tracking grid. It's the underlying basis to monitor your financial transactions, your business relationships, your medical history, your vehicles and property, and so much more.

But the Social Security number only provides a "paper trail." For more advanced, real-time surveillance, the government employs state-of-the-art technology. One of the most alarming is facial-recognition software.

Facial-recognition technology measures the distance between features like the eyes, nose, and mouth. And we're not talking about just a few key points... most programs compare around 45,000 unique points on the face. The average system then crosschecks this biometric data with the profiles of 13 million other faces... all in the blink of an eye.

Most people make the task of facial recognition even easier... They flood the web with their pictures. Social media websites like (the aptly named) Facebook and LinkedIn are chock full of "mug shots."

If you want more privacy, there is a solution...

The technology is not foolproof. Here are some ways to thwart facial recognition...

- Wear a low-lying hat

- Grow out facial hair

- Wear big, dark glasses

- Wear a clear plastic mask

- Put on dark eyeliner or "eye black" used by some athletes

- Comb hair strands down into your face

- Tilt your head more than 15 degrees to the side

- Smile

- Attach LED *infrared* lights to eyeglasses or headwear

Now, some of these techniques will attract attention. They may even single you out for closer scrutiny. But on second glance, many of these techniques are more innocuous than they appear...

Some of these techniques try to cover up facial features. Beards and dark glasses do this without garnering extra attention. Other techniques attempt to distort the distances between measured facial points. A smiling face is markedly different from a deadpan facial structure. This is why we're told not to smile when taking ID photos.

The most ingenious technique of all is to utilize infrared lights. One nine-volt battery can power these for days on end. The bulbs are pea sized and emit no visual light... but to a facial recognition camera, bright streams of infrared light will cloud out a person's face.

Corporations and Commerce:
The Privacy 'Threat Matrix' Expands

Government is the core of the privacy-threat matrix. It "sets the table" for rampant privacy violations. Unfortunately, private companies and corporations are almost as bad as the government...

The cozy relationship between government snooping agencies and dominant corporations like Verizon and Google is bad enough in its own right. But where government snooping tends to interfere with your civil liberties the most, corporate privacy violations may be an immediate threat to your wallet.

The widespread use of credit cards, online banking, and smartphones created several holes in your personal privacy "firewall." If this information falls into the wrong hands, your credit, even your savings, can get erased in a blink.

The good news is protecting yourself from these risks is simple. Follow the suggestions below to keep your business, credit, and personal activities as secure as possible.

1. **Slow, even freeze, your credit**.

In "the old days," credit was a two-part relationship between business and customer. Mutual trust grew with time... and with it, the issuance of credit to the customer.

The 1950s saw a new idea enter the credit market. Banks became a third-party middleman to the traditional two-party credit relationship. Businesses could outsource the responsibility of determining the customer's creditworthiness to the banks. Now, these businesses only had to assess the credit of the middleman. This reduced the businesses' risk and streamlined their efficiency.

The customers benefited, too. They found great convenience. They no longer needed to allow credit relationships to grow over time, on a case-by-case basis.

And of course, the banks made money coming and going, through transaction fees and by charging interest on unpaid balances.

> **❝ You can limit, even freeze, the issuance of new credit under your name. ❞**

The irony of this system is that its greatest strength (extreme efficiency) is at the same time its greatest weakness.

The mass centralization of credit scores into just a few hands (there are only three credit rating bureaus) is dangerous. A blemish in one area of a person's credit sphere has the potential to cause a catastrophic loss of his creditworthiness to *all* businesses across the board.

The blemish could have been accidental (a reporting error by one firm). It could have been intentional (credit cards or whole identities stolen by thieves). It really doesn't matter how it occurs... the results are the same: You may be locked out of the credit markets for years. Even when you do regain some access to credit, your interest rates may remain sky high.

The average American does not realize how vulnerable his creditworthiness is... until it's too late.

But there is a solution...

You can limit, even freeze, the issuance of new credit under your name.

Limiting the issuance of new credit just means establishing an extra layer of credit security, across the board. You can do this by issuing a "fraud alert" for your credit. (You don't have to suspect your credit has already been hacked to do this.) It's free and takes less than two minutes to do. You'll even get a free update of your credit report in the process.

Once the fraud alert is active, lenders are to double check with you whenever new credit is requested and verify you did the asking. Here's how to set this up...

- Go to the website of any of the three credit-rating bureaus (Equifax, Transunion, or Experian).

- Search for "Fraud Alert."

- Submit the appropriate information.

- Once the alert is active, it lasts for 90 days. You can renew the alert every 90 days, indefinitely. For active-duty military, the alert lasts one year, and can be renewed indefinitely.

It's important to note that this measure does not stop the issuance of new credit... but it does make the process more accountable to you. It's a great, free way to establish an additional layer of credit security.

If a fraud alert doesn't give you enough peace of mind, you can take things a step further. **You can place a freeze on any new credit issuance**. This method is typically not free, but it does ensure that no lender will issue new credit in your name. It locks your credit profile and prevents any lender from accessing it.

The fee to freeze your credit profile is minimal and varies depending on the state in which you reside. It ranges from free to $10. The credit bureaus may charge to both "freeze" and "unfreeze" your profile. It takes a few business days for the changes to apply.

If you are in the market for a home or business loan, you may want to avoid doing this. But if you have no new credit needs, this technique brings great safety and peace of mind.

Search for "freeze" on any of the three credit bureaus' websites and follow their instructions.

2. **Monitor your credit for free**.

Once again, in the old days, monitoring your credit was an annoying ordeal. You could pay someone to alert you to any changes for around $10 per month (some services charge more). And even then, you still had to pay extra to receive your "FICO" scores – the numbers lenders use to judge creditworthiness.

By law, you're entitled to receive your credit report for free, but only once per year from each of the credit agencies. If you used an aggregated website to do this, you'd get all three bureaus' reports at the same time... and then not see them again for another 12 months. You'd have to cough up some money to peek again before the 12 months passed.

Twelve months is a long time not to know what is happening in your credit profile. One work around was to request a report from each bureau, every four months. But this still means 120 days passed without seeing what transpired. In a world of one-click identity theft, 120 days might as well be a lifetime.

There is a free service called CreditKarma. This service monitors your credit every day, and sends you an e-mail if it detects any significant change. It also creates a CreditKarma score similar to the FICO credit score.

The website also helps you do debt analysis and suggests how to improve your scores. It even extrapolates what type of interest rates to expect for various purchases like houses and vehicles. And again, this is all free.

With this tool, there's no excuse for anyone not to have a firm grip on his credit.

A similar service is called LifeLock, but don't waste your money. This company charges for many of the same things that CreditKarma offers for free. The company has also been investigated for making promises it can't fulfill. Don't waste your money.

3. **Get a temporary credit-card number**.

Since paying with "plastic" is so commonplace, people can forget how vulnerable they are to credit-card number (and identity) theft.

Think about how easy it is to order a pizza with plastic. You need to give them the name on the card, the card number, the security code on the back, and the expiration date. Did the pizza parlor have any way of verifying this was really you?

Each time you use your card, you expose these critical details. Even if you did order the pizza, who says the clerk won't later use that data for himself?

But there is a solution...

You can get a temporary credit-card number. Most major cards offer this service. Log onto your card's website and search for "temporary card number" or call them directly. They should be able to give you an alternative number to use for your next transaction.

Depending on the company and your own preferences, this number may be good for one transaction or for unlimited transactions up to a certain pre-determined date. You may also be able to set maximum credit amounts for this "virtual card."

One of my favorite ways to use a temporary card number is for limited, free trials. Let's say I get the first month free, but then must pay monthly after that. I can establish a temporary number that's good for one month only. Then, if I really want the service and trust the company, I can supply my regular payment details later.

Internet transaction king PayPal also offers this option. You can establish your own temporary PayPal numbers by looking under the "Profile" section of your account. Click the "secure cards" link and then select "generate new card." You can then specify rules for how you want to use your temporary "virtual" card.

4. Use your credit card to *enhance* your privacy.

It's almost impossible to fly on a plane, stay in a hotel, or rent a car without a credit card anymore. Of course, this just provides more opportunities for malicious entities to decimate your privacy and steal your identity.

But there is a solution...

There's a trick that will allow you to stay in a hotel using a credit card and no one will know you're there...

Credit-card companies give you the ability to request multiple cards for one account. Parents add their children onto their own account in this way. But you can also add a "stage name" or "professional name" to your account... and use this when booking a hotel room.

When providing ID to the desk clerk, use your passport (for added security – it doesn't show your home address). If questioned why the card differs from your picture ID, just explain it is your business or professional name. There shouldn't be an issue.

I first learned of this trick when I read the great privacy masterpiece, *How to be Invisible* by J.J. Luna. I recommend it to all those looking to "plug the holes" in their privacy firewalls.

5. Credit cards and bank wires are not the only way to transfer money.

Credit cards form a perfect paper trail for every person and every transaction. No wonder governments, banks, and corporations love them so much.

I enjoy the anonymity of cash purchases, but those are becoming more and more difficult, as in our hotel example.

Many people believe electronic transfers of funds are the only alternative in today's environment.

But there is a solution...

You can send large sums of cash anywhere in the United States via the U.S. postal service. It's legal, it's safe, and it's inconspicuous... if you follow these easy steps:

- Go out and buy 50 business-size envelopes, 50 first-class stamps, and a magazine (one with lots of pictures is best).

- Wrap five $100 bills in one page of the magazine and seal them in an envelope.

- Repeat 49 more times.

- Do NOT place extra tape along the flap or do anything to make the envelope stand out.

- Mail these from different post offices, over a few days, if possible.

Total Cost: around $25

Total Cash Sent: $25,000

Privacy expert J.J. Luna has used this technique for more than 25 years and has never lost one dollar in the process.

6. **Global, anonymous "cash" transfers also exist**.

In the post 9/11 world, any transaction that happens outside the banking system has been under attack. Heck, the government has even cracked down on little kids' lemonade stands.

Of course, it's all being done in the name of "fighting terrorism." We can't have terrorists laundering money through little Suzy's lemonade stand, can we?

Those with any degree of understanding know the real reason. Every exchange of goods or services is a "taxable event"... even barter. And our government wants every last cent. That's why most people think credit cards, wire transfers, and tax ID numbers are the only way to transfer money abroad.

But there is a solution...

Hawala banking is a tried and true means of transferring money... anonymously. It began in the Middle East in the eighth century. It's still thriving in the modern world... for those who know where to find it. It works like this...

- You go to a "hawaladar" (hawala banker/broker).

- You give him, say, $25,000 in U.S. dollars and tell him you want to transfer it to your friend in Australia.

- He accepts your money and gives you a password.

- He also tells the password to his hawaladar counterpart in Australia.

- You then give the password to your friend in Australia.

- Your friend goes to the Australian hawaladar and tells him the password.

- The passwords match, and that hawaladar gives your friend the equivalent of $25,000 in Australian dollars.

- Both hawaladars take a small commission. They promise to settle up with each other at some point in the future.

This private money transfer system is still 100% legal in the U.S. and around the world. The problem is, it can be difficult to find your local hawaladar. But if you are patient and resourceful, you can do it.

The websites Howtovanish.com and Runtogold.com can offer you a good starting point.

Communication Breakdown: We're Our Own Worst Privacy Threat

A government tracking grid doesn't belong in a free society. And corporate complicity across this structure is perhaps more disappointing. These are serious threats to our privacy rights. Yet, the greatest threat of all remains ourselves.

Criminals of every sort are out to steal your data. Some sophisticated hackers are dead set on hacking into a government Social Security database or getting behind Apple's firewall. There's not much any one of us can do to prevent such a breach.

But most crooks are not so sophisticated. They're happy to go after the easy, low-hanging fruit... *And our personal communications are an easy target.*

Think about it... Let's say you own a rare, jeweled necklace. Would you leave this out on a table in your front yard, just so others could admire its beauty? How long would it be before someone steals it?

In the modern age, *your personal information is more valuable than exquisite jewelry*. Yet we flaunt this information and broadcast it for all to see...

Patching the holes in your communication security is one of the best precautions you can take. The simple steps below will show you how to eliminate all the "low-hanging fruit" from your digital existence.

Let the crooks focus on somebody else.

1. **Block the restaurant "entry point."**

In the last section, I showed you how crucial it is to keep your credit-card number under tight control. It's not just about protecting your credit rating... or avoiding identity theft. It's about every facet of your digital life.

In a 2012 *Wired* article, one of the magazine's senior writers described how a hacker "dissolved" his entire digital life in about 60 minutes...

> In the space of one hour, my entire digital life was destroyed. First my Google account was taken over, then deleted. Next my Twitter account was compromised, and used as a platform to broadcast racist and homophobic messages. And worst of all, my AppleID account was broken into, and my hackers used it to remotely erase all of the data on my iPhone, iPad, and MacBook.

Among the casualties in this "digital massacre" was every digital photo he had of his newborn daughter's first year of life.

The article details the key weak spots the hacker exploited. It turns out one of the easiest points of entry comes through something most people do every day... signing credit card receipts.

You may notice that credit card receipts "X-out" all but the last four digits of your credit card number. You may think this provides a strong degree of security. Think again.

Any company that uses passwords also uses "recovery tools" in case their customers forget these passwords.

In mobile-device maker Apple's case, the recovery tools require the last four digits of the credit card linked to the account, and the account holder's billing address. Addresses are easily attainable via public records searches. Combine this with the last four digits of a credit card and *voila,* you have taken over access to someone's AppleID.

It's not just Apple that works like this. Any number of corporations have similar programs.

But there is a solution...

Whenever you use your credit card, *always black out the last four digits on your receipt.* Do this on the business copy as well as your own. If anyone hassles you, explain you have a legal right to do so. The digital transaction has already occurred... you are just keeping your personal data private.

2. **Understand the No. 1 way people get hacked**.

The *Wired* writer I referenced admitted he made a lot of mistakes. Had he taken some simple online security precautions, his digital life would still be intact.

But he didn't. And chances are, you haven't either. Your passwords may be "long and strong" with 50 lower-case and upper-case letters and numbers... and you may still be as vulnerable as ever.

But there is a solution...

The No. 1 way people's accounts are hacked has nothing to do with the actual password. It has everything to do with the password recovery tools.

Most websites allow you to select what your password recovery "security questions" will be. These are often mundane questions like...

- What town were you born in?

- What is your mother's maiden name?

- What was your high school mascot?

- What was the name of your first pet?

It is vital you do NOT supply answers to these easily identifiable questions.

A simple search of public records and social networking sites (like Facebook) should yield these answers. At the very least, it will give a hacker a short list from which to deduce the correct answers.

If you're given the option to choose your own recovery question, make it a tough one. Make it nonsensical. Make it something that *only you* would know. And if you have no choice but to use the stock questions provided, provide false answers.

For example, if the question asks for your mother's maiden name, make up a name like "MacSmithowitz." Keep the answers written down *on paper* (never in digital form) in a secure location that only you can access!

3. **Provide the most strenuous defense to your "inner sanctum."**

A hacker can use the tactics above on any of your online accounts... but the greatest "prize" is your primary e-mail account. That's because on the Internet, all "roads" lead to your e-mail address. It's the nexus of your online environment.

A hacker with access to your e-mail can immediately:

- Change the password and shut you out from it.

- Gain access to your other accounts by resetting their passwords. (The confirmation e-mails for these are sent to your primary account, which he now has control over.)

- Peruse financial data and gain partial account numbers, like the last four digits of your credit card and Social Security numbers.

- Rummage through all your private data, including photos, videos, and more.

- Gain access to your cloud-based files and devices.

- Delete things of value to you.

This is exactly what happened to the *Wired* writer.

But there is a solution...

You can make hacking your e-mail account difficult. For most hackers, it's not worth the effort. There are a million easier targets out there. Follow these simple guidelines...

NEVER "daisy-chain" your passwords. This means do NOT use the same password for every account you own. A compromise of one means a compromise of all.

NEVER provide an easy/logical password recovery answer.

NEVER select "remember me" or "keep me signed in" on your e-mail website. (This allows others who use the same computer to access your e-mail without needing a password at all.)

NEVER keep a list of any passwords or recovery questions online. (Unless you store your passwords using secure sites like LastPass and Norton, which we discussed in Chapter 12 of Part IX.)

ALWAYS use "two-factor" authentication <u>whenever it is offered</u>. (For example, you need your password plus a code sent to an alternate e-mail or mobile device that is associated with your account.) Bank of America does this.

4. **Use this easy method to remember highly complex passwords**.

Most websites encourage you to use complicated character sets for your password. But who can remember all those random numbers, letters, and special symbols? This is hard enough for one account, let alone several. It's just too much work for most people.

But there is a solution...

You can use a standardized "random" password that only has minor changes in it. These changes are associated with the individual domain you are accessing. As you'll see, it's easy.

Start with your "core code." It will be a mix of letters, numbers, case sizes, and symbols. Memorize this core code. It will never change.

Example core code: APB@c3p

Next, select your "variable code." This will be, for example, the first and third characters of the website you're on.

Example: You are on gmail.com. So in this case, your variable code will be "ga."

Finally, combine the core and variable codes in a regular manner. For example, you may attach the variable code at the beginning, the end, or the beginning and end of your core code.

Example: gAPB@c3pa

This is a great way to remember different, complicated passwords while still appearing 100% random to an outside observer. If one password does get hacked, the hacker will not be able to use it anywhere else.

5. **Encrypt your e-mail messages**.

If you follow my suggestions to this point, you'll establish a strong "defense perimeter" for your e-mail and other accounts. This is a good thing.

Unfortunately, it's also just the first part of a comprehensive e-mail privacy strategy.

Securing the content of your messages is important, too. That's why you should encrypt every message you send out.

Think of it this way... if you were going to send your bank account number via conventional mail, would you put it on a post card or inside a first-class envelope? Without an extra layer of security, everyone can see the content of your message.

But there is a solution...

Make sure you have selected SSL (secure socket layers) as the default encryption in your e-mail service. If you are using a webmail service, you'll know SSL is active as long the webpage you are on starts with "https://" (The extra "s" stands for "secure" and is not the same as http://.)

Using SSL encrypts the routing information (to:, from:, etc.), but not the actual message content.

The steps to full e-mail encryption differ depending on which e-mail client you use. Both you and the recipient must have full e-mail encryption enabled. This is easiest to accomplish when you both use the identical e-mail program.

If you are using an e-mail program like Outlook or Thunderbird, you can encrypt e-mail contents by selecting this option under the settings menu. If you need help, simply type "how to encrypt Outlook messages" into Google's search engine.

6. Give your web browsing as much privacy as your e-mail.

The techniques above will go a long way toward ensuring your e-mail traffic is safe and secure. But what about your general web browsing? This is another matter altogether...

Every website you visit attaches tracking files that show your browsing history. Companies use these to tailor their marketing around you. Other malware programs may also track your movements through the web for any number of reasons.

But there is a solution...

You can take proactive steps to ensure your privacy remains intact as you browse the Internet. It may require a little extra effort, but it's worth it. Until we return to a society where privacy is the default condition (and not the exception to the rule), I'm going to do whatever it takes to protect my personal data.

A simple Google search for "how to stop people tracking what I do on the web" will teach you how to configure your computer to browse with much greater privacy... as well as safely browse the web faster, with fewer advertisements.

After you've optimized your web-browser configuration, you can also add *another* layer of security. Every computer connects to the Internet via an IP (Internet protocol) address. IP addresses can pinpoint your physical location, as well as which Internet service provider you use.

If you want to eliminate others' ability to know this information, you can use a "proxy" IP address, a VPN (virtual private network), or a P2P (peer-to-peer) decentralized network. Each has its own strengths and weaknesses. For example, a proxy may be faster, but a VPN may ensure a greater degree of anonymity.

One last note: Startpage.com is known as "the world's most private search engine."

Startpage is a proxy server that routes your search terms to Google via its own IP address. It collects zero personal information on any of its users. This means your IP address, browser type, computer platform, and search terms remain 100% anonymous.

After your search results appear, the website even lets you open the pages through its own proxy link – so you never make a direct connection with the results page, unless you want to. It's a great, free online privacy resource.

7. Encrypt your audio communications.

Governments, corporations, and identity thieves love to focus on the "paper trails" that e-mails and browsing histories leave. But don't forget about voice communications. There are programs and devices designed to listen in on your conversations in more ways than you can imagine.

But there is a solution...

You can encrypt your voice communications just as you encrypt your text communications. The easiest way I have found to do this is through "Zfone."

Zfone works for VoIP (Voice over Internet Protocol) telephony. That is a fancy way of saying you can use it to encrypt most voice and video call programs. This includes popular programs such as Google Talk, Yahoo Messenger, and Apple iChat.

8. **Make your cell phone anonymous**.

The advent of the smartphone has been a tremendous technological achievement.

These tools have revolutionized the way we live our lives, often for the better. They've also unleashed a scourge of privacy abuses once believed impossible. Sadly, many are willing to give up every last shred of privacy to enjoy the convenience smartphones provide.

But there is a solution...

You can "rent" a phone from a trusted confidant. This is similar to renting a ghost address. The phone is listed under the other person's name and credit-card account. You may sweeten the deal by offering up a bond of, say, $1,000, as added assurance of your good faith.

Now, if you can live without a smartphone, your options expand. You can buy a used phone from a private party and activate it through a service like Page Plus Cellular. Page Plus offers prepaid cellular phone and texting service, without requiring a contract. If you don't use your cell phone much, it may be more economical than your current plan.

Some companies even offer prepaid phones. They may even be disposable. Once the predetermined number of minutes is up, you can discard it and buy a new one. The benefit is these phones require no deposits, contracts, monthly fees, credit checks, or other identifications. Search Amazon for "prepaid cell" to explore this option.

If you're really serious about keeping your cell communications private, you may also want to look into buying a pager. Yes, that's right, pagers still exist. And pagers cannot provide precise geolocation data (the way a cell phone does).

Keep your cell phone off until you need to use it. In the meantime, use your pager to monitor who is trying to get in contact with you. One added bonus is that you can give your pager number out to strangers, not your cell phone.

When a stranger calls the pager, he'll be able to leave a voice message. You can then determine if you want to call this person with your phone or not. The pager can act as a convenient "gate keeper" for all your cell communications.

9. Regain phone anonymity while "unmasking" others.

Using a pager to "reinsert" another layer of privacy into your cell phone communications can be a smart idea. That's because absolute telephone anonymity is a thing of the past... *even if you pay to have your phone number "blocked."*

You see, when anyone calls an 800 number, the phone number is "unmasked" to the 800 number owner – even if it's "blocked." A company called TelTech uses its TrapCall program to reroute a person's incoming calls through an 800 number. So now, even if you have a "blocked" number, if you call a person using TrapCall, they will still know it's you on the other end.

But there is a solution...

You might not be able to mask your phone number. But you can change the way it appears via a service called SpoofCard (also offered by TelTech). Choose any number you want (e.g., 555-555-5555, 123-456-7890). That's the way it will appear on the other person's caller ID.

SpoofCard and TrapCall offer rates based on usage.

10. Retake control of your own phone.

SpoofCard and TrapCall are two tools you can use to retake control of your cell phone number. But there are larger attacks aimed at the phone itself. In this case, the largest danger may come not from a hacker, but from the device manufacturer...

In 2012, Apple applied for a new technology patent. The stated use of this technology for its iPhone is disturbing...

> ... for preventing wireless devices from communicating with other wireless devices... and for forcing certain electronic devices to enter "sleep mode" when entering a sensitive area. (U.S. Patent No. 8,254,902)

The patent application later gives a hint as to who will determine what is and is not a "sensitive area."

Covert police or government operations may require complete "blackout" conditions.

In other words, government and/or corporations will determine when and where you can use your phone to communicate, take pictures, or record video. They can use cameras, drones, and warrantless searches to snoop into every corner of your life... but you cannot record their own misdeeds.

But there is a solution...

If you can disconnect the phone from its network, you should still be able to use your phone to record video and take pictures. You just won't be able to share them while the phone is offline. Most phones come equipped with an "airplane mode" which keeps them from sending/ receiving external signals.

If a remote source ever hijacks your phone, putting your phone into "airplane mode" should put you back in control.

BONUS: Retake control of your physical privacy.

I've focused on how to protect your "virtual existence" – your credit, your identity, and your lines of communication. But let's not forget all this is meaningless if your physical security is compromised.

Cyber theft may be many thieves' favorite crime. But "old fashioned" burglary is still a major threat to you and your family's safety. As of 2014, more than 47 million Americans need taxpayer assistance (food stamps) just to eat. People become desperate. They may target your home for invasion and burglary... even with you inside it.

But there is a solution...

Jack MacLean is a former burglar. He stole more than $133 million in jewels. After his arrest and conviction, he decided to reform. While in prison, he interviewed some 300 other burglars about their preferred tricks and tactics. He compiled what he learned in his book, *Secrets of a Superthief.*

It turns out there is one technique that 100% of the convicted burglars he interviewed admitted would scare them away from a property in an instant...

One blast from an extremely loud air horn.

Search online or go to your local marine supply store. You can buy one for around $20. Be sure to buy the $20 model... $10 horns are not loud enough.

— 3 —

Privacy Restored

Maintaining your privacy in our hyper-connected age requires more work than ever before. But it can be done.

In Part X of this book, I've shown you the threats governments, corporations, and thieves pose to your privacy. **Please do not underestimate them**.

Together, they form an insidious web that touches almost every aspect of our lives. Given the chance, *they will all use this information against you.*

I've also shown you the steps you can take to neutralize these threats. As you've seen, it's easier than it may first appear. And while 100% anonymity remains a near impossibility, you can rest well knowing your privacy is now stronger than about 98% of the population's.

Unless you join the witness-relocation program or move to a powerless shack in the mountains, your privacy can't get much better. Plus, you still get to enjoy the pleasures and conveniences of our modern way of life.

Convenience. Security. Privacy.

That is the *Retirement Millionaire* way.

More From Dr. Eifrig

High Income Retirement: How to Safely Earn 12% to 20% Income Streams on Your Savings

- $39 -

For the first time ever, Dr. Eifrig reveals his proven options strategy in one easy-to-read manual. This book gives the step-by-step details of the investing strategy he used to close 136 consecutive winning positions... a track record of profitable trading recommendations unmatched in the financial publishing industry.

High Income Retirement contains everything you need to know to begin using this strategy. Doc outlines how stock options work and how to use them to reduce risk. He also debunks the most common misperceptions of stock options and explains why most people misuse them. Finally, he walks readers through exactly how to make his safe, profitable trades.

If you want to trade like the professionals, this book is a must-read.

To order your own copy for $39, call **888-261-2693** and use **reference code BOOKS100**.

The Doctor's Protocol Field Manual

- $29 -

The Doctor's Protocol Field Manual is one of the most valuable books in America today... packed with dozens of secrets, ideas, and strategies that can save you and your family in a time of crisis.

You won't hear these easy ways to guard against threats to your well-being from the media... because an entire

539

industry has emerged to encourage dread and pray on these fears. So Dr. Eifrig constructed a scientific protocol for surviving just about any crisis that may befall you...

In the manual, you'll learn surprisingly simple strategies and tactics for survival, like...

- Four antibiotics you must have in your home.

- What to do if someone starts shooting in a public place.

- The most important thing to do when a loved one is injured.

- How to legally hide money and assets from the government.

Dr. Eifrig moves beyond hype and fear to real, actionable steps for survival and prosperity in the midst of any crisis.

To order your own copy for $29, call **888-261-2693** and use **reference code BOOKS100**.

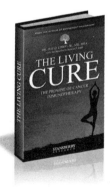

The Living Cure: The Promise of Cancer Immunotherapy

It's one of the most chilling things a person can hear... "You have cancer." Two in five Americans will receive a cancer diagnosis at some point in their lives.

For the first time in decades, you have a treatment option that doesn't involve removing your cancer by surgery or "blowing it up" with radiation and chemotherapy. You have an option to get better in weeks, rather than years (or worse.)

In *The Living Cure*, Dr. Eifrig discusses...

- A science-backed alternative to chemo and radiation.

- Where to go if you're faced with this horrible disease.

- How to access treatments unavailable to the general public.

- One decision that could double your chance of survival.

- And much more...

Dr. Eifrig is certain this research could save your life or the life of a loved one.

To order your own copy, call **888-261-2693** and use **reference code BOOKS100**.

How to Follow Dr. Eifrig's Latest Research and Ideas

Dr. Eifrig writes three newsletters for Stansberry Research: *Retirement Millionaire, Retirement Trader,* and *Income Intelligence*. These are some of the best and most popular advisories in America...

- Doc gives more than investment advice in **Retirement Millionaire**. He shows subscribers how to invest and collect "free cash" without ever worrying about money again. But each month, he also gives invaluable tips for travel, health, and living a happy life.

For example, Doc has shown *Retirement Millionaire* subscribers how to collect "rent" from investments... two foods that prevent cancer... how to receive a free wine vacation... a simple secret to save up to 90% on local attractions... how to get free golf... and much more.

If you want to know more ways to live a wealthier, healthier retirement, try a risk-free trial subscription to *Retirement Millionaire* for just $39. **Call 888-261-2693**

Or you can go directly to our *Retirement Millionaire* order form by typing this unique, safe, and secure website address into your Internet browser: www.sbry.co/0k5cnn.

- In *Retirement Trader*, Dr. Eifrig teaches subscribers a trading secret that can produce quick gains in a matter of minutes. It's one of the safest – yet misunderstood – strategies in the markets. Yet 99% of investors have never heard about it.

Doc used this strategy to close 136 consecutive winning positions for his subscribers... a track record unparalleled in the financial newsletter industry. Once you see how simple this strategy is, you'll never look at trading the same way again.

Retirement Trader is Dr. Eifrig's most elite service, selling for $3,000 per year. To join this exclusive advisory and learn how to trade like the professionals... **call 888-261-2693**.

- ***Income Intelligence*** has a simple goal: Help readers find the safest, most profitable ways to earn income on their savings. It's a full-service approach to income investing that covers dividend stocks, municipal bonds, MLPs, REITs, and other alternative investments.

Dr. Eifrig uses several proprietary indicators, which help him spot little-known investments that can achieve near double-digit returns with unbelievably low risk.

This service is designed for investors of every level, with simple explanations and investments that are easy to make in any brokerage account.

If you want the opportunity to earn high yields on safe investments and understand all the financial forces affecting your income, try a risk-free trial subscription to *Income Intelligence* for $149, **call 888-261-2693**.

Or you can go directly to our *Income Intelligence* order form by typing this unique, safe, and secure website address into your Internet browser: www.sbry.co/dQl7XC.

More from Stansberry Research

The World's Greatest Investment Ideas

The Stansberry Research Trader's Manual

World Dominating Dividend Growers:
Income Streams That Never Go Down

Secrets of the Natural Resource Market:
How to Set Yourself up for Huge Returns in
Mining, Energy, and Agriculture

The Stansberry Research Guide to Investment Basics

The Stansberry Research Starter's Guide for New Investors

America 2020:
The Survival Blueprint

Dividend Millionaire:
How You Can Earn Inflation-Proof,
Crisis-Proof Income Streams in the Stock Market

Index